The **Rough Guide** to

Bruss

D1099193

written and researched by

Martin Dunford and Phil Lee

With additional contributions by

Suzy Sumner and Loïk Dal Molin

ROUGH GUIDES

NEW YORK • LONDON • DELHI

www.roughguides.com

Contents

◄◄ Brussels street entertainer ◄ Rue des Bouchers market

Introduction to

Brussels

Brussels gets a bad press among European cities. It's known as the home of the European Union, and has a reputation as a dull centre of business, bureaucracy and men in grey suits. Yet the EU neither defines nor dominates Brussels, merely forming one layer of a city that since the middle of the last century has become a cosmopolitan, thriving metropolis. It's a surprising – and surprisingly dynamic – place, with a rich ethnic mix, architecture and museums that rank among the best in Europe, and a superb restaurant scene and energetic nightlife. Moreover, most of the key attractions are crowded into a centre that's small enough to be absorbed over a few days.

The **centre** of Brussels is roughly the shape of a diamond with the top cut off, defined by a ring of inner-city boulevards know as the "petit ring". Its layout embodies historic class divisions. For centuries the ruling class lived in the **Upper Town**, an area of wide boulevards and grand mansions which looks down imperiously on the tangled streets of the Lower Town, traditionally the home of shopkeepers and workers. This rarified atmosphere persists to this day: the streets are wider and less congested in the Upper Town, and its air is sweeter, given its height above the maelstrom. This divide in landscape and class is further complicated by the **language divide** between Belgium's French-speaking Walloons and Dutch-speaking Flemish. Rather cumbersomely, the city is Belgium's only officially bilingual region, in which all road signs, street names and all published information must by law be in both languages. French-speakers make up the majority of Brussels' population, but many of the surrounding suburbs are Flemish-speaking, and the ancient Brussels dialect (known as

Brusselse Sproek or Marollien) is a strange mixture of the two languages. As if this wasn't complex enough, the city is as ethnically diverse as any European capital, with immigrants from North Africa, Turkey, Greece and other parts of the Mediterranean, as well as from Belgium's former African colonies (not to mention a host of ex-pats working for the EU, NATO and other multinational organizations based hereabouts) comprising a quarter of the population. There is perhaps no more international, or more linguistically complex, city in the world.

Brussels has been messed about by the planners over the past hundred years or so, particularly in the 1960s when misguided development left parts of the city destroyed by roads and traffic and disfigured by some hideous modern architecture. The centre is still something of a hotchpotch, but that's part of Brussels' charm – and in the last decade or so the city has picked itself up and is looking better than it has done for some time. There's more of a sense of pride in the place these days; some of the most run-down parts of the city centre have been spruced up, and the shabbier buildings renovated; and beyond the centre Brussels' fast-gentrifying inner-city districts have been lent vitality by the city's patchwork of ethnic groups.

What to see

Visitors to Brussels are often surprised by the raw vigour of the city centre. It's not neat and tidy, and many of the old tenement houses are shabby, but there's a buzz about the place that's hard to resist, and it's here you'll find the majority of the city's sights and attractions, restaurants and bars. The centre is also surprisingly compact, sitting neatly within the rough pentagon of boulevards that enclose it – the petit ring – which follows the course of the fourteenth-century city walls, running from place Rogier in the north, close by the Gare du Nord, to Porte de Hal in the south, close to the Gare du Midi. The larger, westerly portion of the city centre comprises the Lower Town, fanning out from the

Art Nouveau Brussels

Brussels is the birthplace of the Art Nouveau movement in architecture, which originated here in the late nineteenth century. As a style it embraced modern materials and building methods, making use of stone, wrought iron and glass, but moulded these into organic forms that were almost deliberately anachronistic. Its chief exponent, in Belgium at least, was Victor Horta. The house that Horta built for himself is now open as a museum (see p.99), and it is as complete and undisturbed an example of Art Nouveau architecture as you're ever likely to see, exuding the complete stylistic vision of the movement. This is just as well, as it's also one of the disappointingly few Art Nouveau buildings you can routinely visit in Brussels, with others either in use as offices or private residences and never open to the public, or only open on certain days of the year, or to specialist tours (if you'd like to get inside those buildings normally closed to the public, consider taking a tour with the heritage group, Arau – for details see p.30). We've detailed the best and most accessible Art Nouveau buildings throughout the Guide.

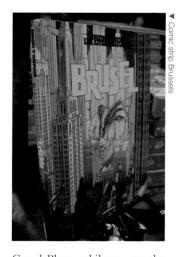

▼ Comic strip Brussels

Grand-Place, while up on the hill to the east lies the much smaller Upper Town, the traditional home of the Francophile upper classes. Broadly speaking, the boundary between the two zones follows the busy boulevard that swings through the centre under several names – Berlaimont, L'Impératrice and L'Empereur.

The magnificent **Grand-Place**, with its exquisite guildhouses and town hall, is the unquestionable centre of Brussels, a focus for tourists and locals alike. It's surrounded by the **Lower Town**, whose cramped and populous quarters are bisected by a major north–south boulevard, variously named Adolphe Max, Anspach and Lemonnier. The Lower Town is at its most beguiling to the northwest of the Grand-Place – a cobweb of quaint, narrow lanes and tiny squares, on one of which stands the sturdy church of **Ste-Catherine**, while on another sits the beautiful St-Jean-Baptiste-au-Béguinage. The Ste-Catherine neighbourhood is one of the city centre's most pleasant, and most recently gentrified, quarters. By comparison, the streets to the north of the Grand-Place are of less immediate appeal, with dreary rue Neuve, a pedestrianized street of mainstream shops and department stores, leading up to the clumping skyscrapers that surround **place Rogier** and the **Gare du Nord**. This is an uninviting part of the city, but relief is at hand in the precise if bedraggled Habsburg symmetries of the **place des Martyrs** and at the Belgian Comic Strip Centre, the **Centre Belge de la Bande Dessinée**. To the south of the Grand-Place lie the old working-class streets of the **Marolles district**, a locale of antique shops and an excellent weekly flea market, and the depressed and predominantly immigrant area in the vicinity of the **Gare du Midi**.

Quite different in feel from the rest of the city centre, the **Upper Town** is a self-consciously planned, more monumental quarter, with statuesque buildings lining wide boulevards and squares. Appropriately, it's the home of the Belgian parliament and government departments, formal parks and the **Palais Royal**. More promisingly, it also accommodates Brussels' **Cathedral**, a fine Gothic edifice with wonderful stained-glass windows, the superb **Musées Royaux des Beaux Arts**, arguably Belgium's best collection of fine art, and some of the city's swishest shops clustered around picturesque **place du Grand Sablon**. There's also the excellent **Musée des Instruments de Musiques**, housed in the wonderful Art Nouveau Old England building, and the preposterous bulk of the **Palais de Justice**,

▲ Le Cinquantenaire

which lords it over the rest of the city, commanding views that on clear days reach way across the suburbs.

Brussels by no means ends with the petit ring. During the nineteenth century Léopold II pushed the city limits out beyond the course of the old walls, grabbing land from the surrounding *communes* to create the irregular boundaries that survive today. To the east, he sequestered a rough rectangle of land where he laid out **Parc Léopold** and across which he ploughed two wide boulevards – Belliard and La Loi. These were designed to provide an imperial approach to the **Parc du Cinquantenaire**, whose self-glorifying and over-sized monuments were erected to celebrate Belgium's golden jubilee and now house three large if rather turgid museums – the **Musées Royaux d'Art et d'Histoire**, and others devoted to cars and the military. The boulevards were soon colonized by the city's bourgeoisie, but in the last few years they have been displaced by the brash modern blocks of the **EU Quarter**, whose flashy new **European Parliament** is probably the best example of the area's largely undistinguished building boom.

Outside the city centre proper, to the south, is the animated and cosmopolitan district of **St Gilles**, and neighbouring **Ixelles**, which has become the favoured hangout of the arty and the cool, its streets nurturing a handful of designer stores and a growing number of chic bars and restaurants. These two *communes* also boast much of the best of the city's **Art Nouveau architecture**. Ixelles is bisected by **avenue Louise**, a prosperous corridor that's home to much of the city's most upscale shopping territory, and to the enjoyable **Musée Constantin Meunier** – as well as the **Abbaye de la Cambre** beyond. On the other side of the city centre, the gritty suburb of **Anderlecht** is famous for its soccer team and is also worth a visit for its Gueuze brewery and the fascinating Erasmus house, one-time residence of Desiderius Erasmus, who lodged here in 1521. Adjacent to this area, **Koekelberg** is the site of the Basilique du Sacré Coeur, another whopping pile built by Léopold II, and the *commune* of **Jette**, just north, was for many years home to the surrealist painter René Magritte, whose house is now a museum. To the north of the city centre, beyond the partly

▶ Belgian chocolate

Food and drink

Food is as good a reason as any for visiting Brussels. Whether you want to eat traditional Belgian food – which some say rivals that of France – or sample the cuisine of some of the immigrant communities that live here, there are few better European capitals in which to eat. The variety of restaurants is huge. There are plenty of places to sample classic Belgian staples – *waterzooi, stoemp, carbonnades à la flamande,* and of course *moules-frites* – at all prices. Wherever you choose to eat, food in Belgium is always well-cooked and served with pride, and it's rare you'll be served a poor meal, no matter how little you're spending (except, perhaps, in some of the restaurants along touristy rue des Bouchers). There are plenty of places serving basic Belgian grub on and within walking distance of the Grand-Place; nearby Ste-Catherine is the place to go for fish; while St Gilles and Ixelles are home to an ever-increasing number of restaurants serving Belgian food with a modern twist. In addition, you'll find great Turkish food in St-Josse, not to mention the usual array of French and Italian restaurants, plus Chinese and Vietnamese, Moroccan and Tunisian, reflecting burgeoning immigrant communities, and the odd Congolese place. Bon appétit!

Turkish districts of St Josse and Schaerbeek, is **Laeken**, city residence of the Belgian royal family, and **Heysel**, with its notorious soccer stadium and the Atomium, a leftover from the 1958 World Fair. And finally there's leafy **Tervuren**, to the southeast, whose giant Africa museum, one of the larger relics of Belgium's shameful colonial past, is busily trying to reinvent itself.

And then of course there's the **rest of Belgium**, none of which, given the size of the country, is more than a few hours away. We've included the pick of the many excursions you could make from the capital, including, of course, **Bruges** – one of the most beautiful towns anywhere, and only an hour away by train, and **Ghent**, its under-rated larger neighbour. Belgium's second city, **Antwerp**, is also only an hour away by train, and is a much trendier place than Brussels could ever be. The ancient student city of **Leueven** and the famous battlefield of **Waterloo** complete what is a varied and intriguing picture.

When to go

B russels – like all of Belgium – enjoys a standard temperate **climate**, with warm, if mild, summers and cold winters without much snow. The warmest months are usually June, July and August, the coldest December and January, when the short daylight hours and weak sunlight can make the weather seem colder (and wetter) than it really is.

▼ Ghent

▲ A Brussels bar

Rain is always a possibility, even in summer, which actually sees a greater degree of rainfall than either autumn or winter. Warm days in April and May, when the light has the clarity of springtime, are especially appealing, and this is a nice time to come as the city isn't swarming with tourists. Similarly September, when the weather is usually still comfortably warm and the crowds that much smaller, can be an appealing time to visit.

Brussels climate

	Jan	Feb	Mar	Apr	May	Jun	Jul	Aug	Sep	Oct	Nov	Dec
Average daily temperature												
°C	1	4	7	11	13	18	19	18	17	12	7	3
Average rainfall												
mm	66	61	53	60	55	76	95	80	63	83	75	88

things not to miss

It's not possible to see everything Brussels has to offer on a short trip – and we don't suggest you try. What follows is a subjective selection of the city's highlights, ranging from our favourite things to eat to the best museums, all arranged in colour-coded categories to help you find the very best things to see, do and experience. All entries have a page reference to take you straight into the Guide, where you can find out more.

01 Grand-Place Page **43** • Quite simply one of the most uniformly beautiful enclosed city squares in the world.

02 Musée des Beaux-Arts
Page **80** • A great museum, combining a wealth of old masters with a fine modern art collection.

04 Musée Gueuze
Page **124** • A traditional brewery specializing in a beer that is only brewed in Brussels.

06 Art Nouveau
Page **98** • Brussels is the birthplace of Art Nouveau architecture, best represented by some great private houses, a couple of which – the Horta house and Cauchie house – are open to the public.

03 Fondation Jacques Brel
Page **68** • Brel died overseas but this is his home town's homage to him.

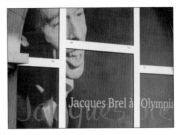

05 Antwerp
Page **148** • Belgium's trendy second city, capital of the country's fashion industry and its club scene.

07 Place du Jeu de Balle
Page **70** • Not as cheap as it once was, but still what a flea market should be, full of delectable old junk.

08 Forêt de Soignes Page **130** • Brussels' largest and most bucolic open space.

09 Cathedral Page **71** • Brussels' cathedral is a fine Gothic building but its stained-glass windows are the real draw.

10 Centre Belge de Bande Desinée Page **65** • This Art Nouveau ex-department store is a homage to one of Belgium's national obsessions – and it's not just Tin Tin.

11 Frites Page **197** • No better place to eat them than on the street here, smothered in mayonnaise, out of a paper cone.

12 Waterloo Page **134** • This sleepy Brussels suburb was at the heart of European history in 1815.

13 Place du Grand Sablon
Page **92** • The Upper Town's most elegant square, perfect for hanging out on a summer's afternoon.

14 Beer
Pages **200–201** • One of the city's greatest pleasures. Belgium has more brewers per head than any other country in the world, and Brussels has a fantastic array of bars to sample them in.

15 Théâtre de la Monnaie
Page **64** • It's not much to look at from the outside, but this is one of the best opera houses in Europe.

16 Musée René Magritte
Page **126** • The former home of the surrealist painter is familiar from some of his paintings.

17 Adoration of the Mystic Lamb, Ghent
Page **162** • It's worth the half-hour train journey to see this incredible painting by Jan van Eyck in the setting it was painted for.

18 Musée des Instruments de Musique Page 78 •

Housed in the renovated Art Nouveau Old England building, this great museum has a fine collection, as well as wonderful views over the city centre from its top-floor restaurant.

21 Ommegang Page 239 •

This religious procession is the city's biggest annual event, culminating on the Grand-Place on the first Tuesday and Thursday of July.

19 Ste-Catherine Page 61 •

The now-gentrified inner-city quarter of Ste-Catherine is the only part of the city that has a whiff of the river about it – and is a good place to come to eat fish and seafood.

20 Groeninge Museum, Bruges Page 170 •

Bruges is worth a trip on many counts – not least to see this first-rate collection of the works of van Eyck, Bosch, van der Weyden, Gerard David and other Flemish primitive painters.

22 Mussels Page 184 •

As long as they're in season, you can't leave without having mussels and chips.

Basics

Basics

Getting there

Brussels has direct connections with airports all over the world. If you're travel-ling from southeast England you should also consider the Eurostar rail link, which makes the journey from London to Brussels in two hours and fifteen minutes.

Air fares usually depend on the season, with the highest being around early June to the end of August; the lowest prices are avail-able from November to March (excluding Christmas and New Year).

Online booking agents and general travel sites

Many airlines and discount travel websites offer you the opportunity to book your tick-ets **online**, cutting out the costs of agents. Good deals can often be found through discount or auction sites.

Ⓦ **www.cheapflights.com** (bookings from the UK and Ireland only; for the US, visit Ⓦ www .cheapflight.com; for Canada, Ⓦ www.cheapflights .ca; for Australia, Ⓦ www.cheapflights.com.au). All the sites offer flight deals, details of travel agents, and links to other travel sites.

Ⓦ **www.counciltravel.com** If your journey originates in the US and you've some flexibility, this site can come up with competitive deals.

Ⓦ **www.ebookers.com** Efficient, easy to use flight finder, with competitive fares.

Ⓦ **www.expedia.co.uk** (for the US Ⓦ www .expedia.com; for Canada Ⓦ www.expedia.ca) Discount airfares, all-airline search engine and daily deals.

Ⓦ **www.hotwire.com** Last-minute savings of up to forty percent on regular published fares. If you're looking for the cheapest possible scheduled flight from the US, this is probably your best bet.

Ⓦ **www.kelkoo.co.uk** Useful UK-only price-comparison site, checking several sources of low-cost flights (and other goods & services) according to specific criteria.

Ⓦ **www.lastminute.com** Offers good last-minute holiday package and flight-only deals from the UK. In Australia, try Ⓦ www.lastminute.com.au.

Ⓦ **www.opodo.co.uk** Popular and reliable source of low UK airfares. Owned by, and run in conjunction with, nine major European airlines.

Ⓦ **www.orbitz.com** Comprehensive web travel source, with good flight, car hire and hotel deals.

Ⓦ **www.priceline.co.uk** (for the US, Ⓦ www .priceline.com). Name-your-own-price website that has deals at around forty percent off standard fares.

Ⓦ **www.travelocity.co.uk** (for the US, Ⓦ www .travelocity.com). Destination guides and a usually great selection of hot web fares.

Ⓦ **www.travelshop.com.au** Australian website offering discounted flights, packages, insurance, and online bookings.

Ⓦ **www.zuji.com.au** Destination guides, good air fares and great deals for accommodation from this Australian site.

Ⓦ **www.travelzoo.com** US site that is a great resource for news on current airline sales, discounts and hotel deals. It links you directly to the carrier's site.

From the UK and Ireland

The quickest way to reach Brussels from the UK is **by plane**, with flights taking just under an hour from London – though, if you live in London or southeast England, the **Eurostar** train service makes an appealing alterna-tive, taking you from London Waterloo to the centre of Brussels in two hours fifteen minutes. If you're looking to get there as cheaply as possible, check out the regular **bus** services operated by Eurolines (part of National Express) – though at eight hours this is also the longest journey time by far.

By plane

You can **fly** direct to Brussels from over a dozen airports in mainland Britain, and from Dublin and Belfast. Competition is fierce, which keeps fares reasonably low, although oddly EasyJet don't fly to Brussels at all and Ryanair only fly to the city of Charleroi, about 50km south of Brussels – which, given the existence of Eurostar and the reasonably central location of Brussels' airport, is only worth considering if the prices they're offer-ing are especially low. Indeed, bearing in mind the length of the journey – just under an hour from London – the choice you make will largely depend on price and the airport you wish to fly from rather than any kind of comfort factor or brand loyalty.

From London, British Airways, bmi and the ex-Belgian national carrier SN Brussels Airlines all fly regularly from London Heathrow; SN Brussels also fly from Gatwick; VLM fly from London City airport, and may be worth considering both for this flight and the flights they operate to Antwerp. As for **regional airports**, British Airways also fly from Bristol, Southampton, Birmingham, Newcastle, Manchester, Aberdeen, Edinburgh, Glasgow and Belfast, as do the Dutch airline, KLM, who also fly from Cardiff and Norwich; Air France fly from Southampton, VLM from Southampton and Liverpool; SN Brussels from Birmingham, Newcastle and Glasgow, bmi from East Midlands, Leeds Bradford, Edinburgh, Belfast and Dublin; and Ryanair from Glasgow, Dublin and Shannon.

From **other parts of Europe**, look out for the budget carrier, Virgin Express, now owned by SN Brussels Airlines and based in Brussels, flying between there and Athens, Milan, Rome, Geneva, Nice, Barcelona, Malaga, Madrid, Lisbon and Faro, among other destinations.

Fares can vary enormously: during the off-peak months it's not difficult to find a return flight for under £50 return from most British destinations; from April onwards you can expect to pay £80–100 return, and usually over £100 during July and August. The way to get the best fare is as ever to shop around online, where you'll find a huge number of alternative deals.

Airlines in the UK and Ireland

Air France UK ☎0845/359 1000, Republic of Ireland ☎01/605 0383, ⓦwww.airfrance.com.
bmi UK ☎0870/607 0555, ⓦwww.flybmi.com.
British Airways UK ☎0870/850 9850, Republic of Ireland ☎1800/626 747, ⓦwww.ba.com.
KLM (Royal Dutch Airlines) UK ☎0870/507 4074, ⓦwww.klm.com.
Ryanair UK ☎0871/246 0000, Republic of Ireland ☎0818/30 30 30, ⓦwww.ryanair.com.
SN Brussels Airlines UK ☎0870/735 2345, ⓦwww.flysn.com.
Virgin Express UK ☎020/7744 0004, ⓦwww.virgin-express.com.

VLM Airlines UK ☎020/7476 6677, ⓦwww.vlm-airlines.com.

Specialist flight agents

ebookers UK ☎0870/010 7000, ⓦwww.ebookers.com; Republic of Ireland ☎01/241 5689, ⓦwww.ebookers.ie. Package deals.
Flightcentre UK ☎0870/890 8099, ⓦwww.flightcentre.co.uk.
Flights4Less UK ☎0871/222 3423, ⓦwww.flights4less.co.uk.
Joe Walsh Tours Republic of Ireland ☎01/676 0991, ⓦwww.joewalshtours.ie.
North South Travel UK ☎01245/608 291, ⓦwww.northsouthtravel.co.uk.
Premier Travel UK ☎028/7126 3333, ⓦwww.premiertravel.uk.com. Discount flight specialists.
Rosetta Travel UK ☎028/9064 4996, ⓦwww.rosettatravel.com.
STA Travel UK ☎0870/1600 599, ⓦwww.statravel.co.uk.
usit NOW Republic of Ireland ☎01/602 1600, Northern Ireland ☎028/9032 7111, ⓦwww.usitnow.ie.

By train

Travelling **by train**, Eurostar operate around ten services a day from London Waterloo to Brussels Midi, via Ashford and Lille, and the journey time is two hours fifteen minutes. Just the fact that you're travelling direct from the centre of London to the centre of Brussels makes it a far more relaxing option than flying – if, that is, you live in London. However, bear in mind that the journey in from Brussels Zaventem airport is really not that long, and that Eurostar's fares are no cheaper than flying, and there are fewer deals to be had. If you can book 21 days in advance then you can do the journey for just under £60 return, but otherwise the cost of a regular second-class return ticket is around £120.

Rail operators

Eurostar ☎0870/160 6600, ⓦwww.eurostar.com.
International Rail ☎0870/751 5000, ⓦwww.international-rail.com. Offers a wide variety of rail options, including Eurostar, all European passes and tickets.
Rail Europe ☎0870/584 8848, ⓦwww.raileurope.co.uk. Broad range of mainstream rail options, including Eurostar and Eurail tickets.

By bus

The cheapest way of getting to Brussels from the UK is, of course, **by bus**. **Euro-lines**, part of National Express, has four daily departures from London's Victoria coach station to Brussels, with a journey-time of around eight hours. Return tickets cost about £50, and there are discounts of roughly ten percent for travellers under 25 and over 60. A company called Anglia Lines also have one departure a day from London to Brussels and are very slightly cheaper – around £45 return.

Bus operators

Anglia Lines ☎ 0870 608 8806, ⊛ www .anglia-lines.co.uk.
Eurolines ☎ 08705 808080, ⊛ www.national express.com/eurolines.

From the US and Canada

From the US, you can fly direct to Brussels **from New York City** (American, Delta, or Continental from Newark) and Chicago (American), but you'll find cheaper deals if you're prepared to stop once, either in the US or mainland Europe. Fares to Brussels can be found for as little as around $800 if you're prepared to change; otherwise reckon on spending around $1200–1500 return. **From Chicago**, non-stop fares cost around $2000, but you can cut this to around $1200 with one stopover. There are no direct flights **from the West Coast**, but plenty of carriers will get you to Brussels with one stop, for as little as $1200 return.

From Canada, the best deals are offered by Air Canada, who fly non-stop to London Heathrow, with onward connections to Brussels. **From Toronto** to Brussels, expect to pay around CDN$1800 in high season and CDN$1300 in low season, while typical fares **from Vancouver** are around CDN$2050 in high season and CDN$1350 in low season.

Airlines in North America

Air Canada ☎ 1-888/247-2262, ⊛ www .aircanada.ca.
American Airlines ☎ 1-800/433-7300, ⊛ www .aa.com.

British Airways ☎ 1-800/AIRWAYS, ⊛ www .ba.com.
Continental Airlines ☎ 1-800/231-0856, ⊛ www.continental.com.
Delta Airlines ☎ 1-800/241-4141, ⊛ www.delta .com.

Specialist flight agents in North America

Airtech ☎ 212/219-7000, ⊛ www.airtech.com. Standby seat broker; also deals in consolidator fares.
Educational Travel Center ☎ 1-800/747-5551 or 608/256-5551, ⊛ www.edtrav.com. Low-cost fares worldwide, student/youth discount offers, and Eurail passes, car rental and tours.
Flightcentre US ☎ 1-866/WORLD-51, ⊛ www .flightcentre.us; Canada ☎ 1-888/WORLD-55, ⊛ www.flightcentre.ca.
New Frontiers US ☎ 1-800/677-0720, ⊛ www .newfrontiers.com.
STA Travel US ☎ 1-800/329-9537, Canada ☎ 1-888/427-5639, ⊛ www.statravel.com.
Student Flights ☎ 1-800/255-8000 or 480/951-1177, ⊛ www.isecard.com/studentflights.
TFI Tours ☎ 1-800/745-8000 or 212/736-1140, ⊛ www.lowestairprice.com.
Travel Cuts US ☎ 1-800/592-CUTS, Canada ☎ 1-888/246-9762, ⊛ www.travelcuts.com.

From Australia and New Zealand

There are no direct flights from Australia or New Zealand to Brussels. Most itineraries will involve two changes, one in the Far East – Singapore, Bangkok or Kuala Lumpur – and then another in the gateway city of the airline you're flying with: most commonly Paris, Amsterdam or London. You can get tickets to Brussels **from Sydney** or **Melbourne** for AUS$1500–2000 if you shop around, and **from Auckland** for slightly more.

Airlines in Australia and New Zealand

Air France Australia ☎ 02/9244 2100, New Zealand ☎ 09/308 3352, ⊛ www.airfrance.com.au.
Alitalia Australia ☎ 02/9244 2445, New Zealand ☎ 09/308 3357, ⊛ www.alitalia.com.
British Airways Australia ☎ 1300/767 177, New Zealand ☎ 09/966 9777, ⊛ www.ba.com.
KLM Royal Dutch Australia ☎ 1300/303 747, New Zealand ☎ 09/302 1792, ⊛ www.klm.com.

Specialist flight agents

Flight Centre Australia ☏13 31 33 or 02/9235 3522, ⓦwww.flightcentre.com.au; New Zealand ☏0800 243 544 or 09/358 4310, ⓦwww .flightcentre.co.nz.
OTC Australia ☏1300/855 118, ⓦwww.otctravel .com.au. Deals on flights, hotels and holidays.
STA Travel Australia ☏1300/733 035 or 02/9212 1255, ⓦwww.statravel.com.au; New Zealand ☏0508/782 872 or 09/309 9273, ⓦwww .statravel.co.nz.
Student Uni Travel Australia ☏02/9232 8444, ⓦwww.sut.com.au; New Zealand ☏09/379 4224, ⓦwww.sut.co.nz.
Trailfinders Australia ☏9247 7666 or 1300/780 212, ⓦwww.trailfinders.com.au.
travel.com.au and **travel.co.nz** Australia ☏1300/130 482 or 02/9249 5444, ⓦwww.travel .com.au; New Zealand ☏0800/468 332, ⓦwww .travel.co.nz.

Red tape and visas

EU citizens, Americans, Canadians, Australians and New Zealanders can enter Belgium for up to ninety days without a visa. EU citizens need a valid passport or identity card; everyone else needs a valid passport. All other nationalities should consult their embassy or the Belgian authorities for details of specific entry requirements.

For stays of over ninety days, EU nationals can apply for a renewable three-month residence permit from the local police; after six months it's possible to apply for an identity card, which enables you to stay for up to five years – and of course work. Non-EU nationals likewise need to apply for a residence permit for stays of over ninety days, though not surprisingly these are much harder to get. Applications must be made from your country of residence, and permits are issued for various lengths of time, but usually one year, depending on your personal financial circumstances. It's even more difficult to get a work permit; your prospective employer must apply locally, and you must do so simultaneously at home; both parties must await its issuance – by no means a foregone conclusion – before proceeding. *L'Office des Etrangers*, 59B Chaussée d'Anvers, 1000 Brussels (☏02.501.81.81; ⓦwww.dofi.fgov.be) may be able to help with any questions you have, as might the *Brussels Capital Region Economy & Employment Administration*, 80 rue du Progrés, 1030 Brussels (☏02.204.21.11; ⓦwww.bruxelles.irisnet.be), for work matters.

Belgian embassies abroad

Australia 19, Arkana St, Yarralumla, ACT 2600, Canberra ☏02.62.73.25.01, ⓦwww.diplomatie .be/canberra.
Canada Constitution Square, 360 rue Albert suite 820, Ottawa, ON K1R 7X7 ☏613/236.72.67, ⓦwww.diplomatie.be/ottawa.
Ireland 2 Shrewsbury Rd, Ballsbridge, Dublin 4, ☏01.205.71.00, ⓦwww.diplomatie.be/dublin.
New Zealand – honorary consulate 15A Rarangi Rd, St. Heliers, Auckland ☏09/575 6202.
UK 103-105 Eaton Square, London SW1W 9AB, ☏020 7470 3700, ⓦwww.diplobel.org/uk.
USA 330, Garfield St, N.W. Washington D.C. 20008 ☏202/333 6900, ⓦwww.diplobel.us.

Insurance

Prior to travelling, you'd do well to take out an insurance policy to cover against theft, loss and illness or injury. Before paying for a new policy, however, it's worth checking whether you already have some degree of cover: EU health care privileges apply in Brussels, some all-risks home insurance policies may cover your possessions when overseas, and many private medical schemes include cover when abroad. In Canada, provincial health plans usually provide partial cover for medical mishaps overseas, while holders of official student/teacher/youth cards in Canada and the US are entitled to meagre accident coverage and hospital in-patient benefits. Students will often find that their student health coverage extends during the vacations and for one term beyond the date of last enrolment.

After exhausting the possibilities above, you might want to contact a specialist travel insurance company. A typical travel insurance policy usually provides cover for the loss of baggage, tickets and – up to a certain limit – cash or cheques, as well as cancellation or curtailment of your journey. Most of them exclude so-called dangerous sports – climbing, rafting and windsurfing and so forth – unless an extra premium is paid. Many policies can be chopped and changed to exclude coverage you don't need – for example, sickness and accident benefits can often be excluded or included at will. If you do take medical coverage, ascertain whether benefits will be paid as treatment proceeds or only after your return home, and whether there is a 24-hour medical emergency number. When securing baggage cover, make sure that the per-article limit – typically under £500 – will cover your most valuable possession. If you need to make a claim, you should keep receipts for medicines and medical treatment, and should you have anything stolen, you must obtain a crime report statement or number.

Rough Guides travel insurance

Rough Guides has teamed up with Columbus Direct to offer you **travel insurance** that can be tailored to suit your needs. Readers can choose from many different travel insurance products, including a low-cost **backpacker** option for long stays; a **short break** option for city getaways; a typical **holiday package** option; and many others. There are also annual **multi-trip** policies for those who travel regularly, with variable levels of cover available. Different sports and activities (trekking, skiing, etc) can be covered if required on most policies. Rough Guides travel insurance is available to the residents of 36 different countries and with different language options to choose – all via our website ⊛www.roughguidesinsurance.com, where you can also purchase the insurance. Alternatively, UK residents should call ☎0800/083 9507; US citizens ☎1-800/749-4922; Australians ☎1-300/669 999. All other nationalities should call ☎+44 870/890 2843.

Health

Under reciprocal health arrangements involving members of the European Union (EU), nationals of all EU countries are entitled to free or discounted medical treatment within the respective public health care systems. For British citizens, this used to mean filling out an E111 form, but in late 2005 this was phased out and replaced with the new European Health Insurance Card. As with the E111, this can be applied for, free of charge, at UK post offices. Non-EU nationals have to pay for most medical attention and should take out their own medical insurance to travel to Brussels.

Indeed this can be handy for EU citizens as well, as it will cover the cost of items not within the EU's scheme, such as dental treatment and repatriation on medical grounds. That said, most private insurance policies don't cover prescription charges – their "excesses" are usually greater than the cost of the medicines. The more worthwhile policies promise to sort matters out before you pay (rather than after) in the case of major expense; if you do, however, have to pay upfront, get and keep the receipts. For more on insurance, see p.23.

Pharmacies

Minor ailments can be remedied at **pharmacies** (French *pharmacie*, Flemish *apotheek*), which supply non-prescription drugs as well as toiletries, tampons, condoms and the like. Most are open Monday to Friday 9am to 6pm or 7pm, some on Saturdays too, and in Brussels a rota system keeps at least one open 24 hours a day. The rota should be displayed in the window of every pharmacy, and the tourist office has details, too, as do some of the better hotels.

Seeking medical treatment

Your local pharmacy, tourist office or hotel should be able to provide the address of an **English-speaking doctor** or **dentist** if you need one. If you're seeking treatment under EU health agreements, double-check that the doctor is working within (and seeing you as) a patient of the Belgian public health care system. This being the case, you'll need to pay upfront for treatment and medicines; you'll then be able to reclaim a proportion of the cost (around 75 percent) by applying to the local Sickness Fund Office (ask the doctor for details) with your European Health Insurance Card (EHIC). There are lots of these sickness fund offices and they have different names – Securex for example – but the generic word you want is "Mutuelle". As a final point, note that Brussels has both private and public hospitals and the latter are, predictably enough, much less expensive. Public hospitals include St Pierre (☏02 535 31 11) and Erasme (☏02 555 32 02), whereas Edith Cavell hospital (☏02 340 40 40) is private.

You can anticipate that some **hospital** staff will speak English in Brussels, though a rudimentary grasp of French is much, much better. If you know you're going to be admitted to hospital and you're an EU national, try to contact the local Sickness Office in advance, producing your EHIC and asking them where to obtain the cheapest treatment. They will give you a certificate confirming they will pay part of the cost of treatment. In medical **emergencies**, you can reach the ambulance service by calling ☏100, and you should – if at all possible – produce your EHIC when you're admitted to hospital.

Information, websites and maps

Information on Brussels is easy to get hold of, either from the Internet, or, after arrival, from the city's main tourist office.

Information

Aside from the branch at Brussels airport (see p.27), there are two **Brussels tourist information offices** in the city, both in the centre. The main one is the **BIT** (Bruxelles International – Tourisme), in the Hôtel de Ville on the Grand-Place (Jan till Easter Mon–Sat 9am–6pm; May–Sept daily 9am–6pm; Oct–Dec & Easter to end April Mon–Sat 9am–6pm, Sun 10am–2pm; ☎02 513 89 40 ℻02 513 83 20, 🖮www.brusselsinternational.be), which handles information on the city only. It stocks a wide range of handouts, including free city maps, has details of forthcoming events and concerts, makes reservations on guided tours (for more on these, see p.29), and sells a variety of general- and specialist-interest guides, the most useful of which is the detailed *Brussels Guide and Map* (e2). In addition, BIT publishes a free booklet listing all the city's (recognized) hotels, and also makes **hotel reservations** for free – the deposit is subtracted from your final hotel bill. This is especially attractive as BIT can often offer substantial discounts on published rates; for more on booking accommodation, see p.177. BIT can help with public transport too: it sells the 24-hour *carte d'un jour* pass (see p.28) and issues free public transport maps. Finally, BIT sells – and promotes – the **Brussels Card**, which combines free and unlimited use of the public transport network with free admission to around thirty museums and a miscellany of modest discounts at shops, bars and restaurants. It costs €30 for three days, which means you have to work fairly hard to make it worthwhile. The second and much smaller **BIT office** (May–Sept Mon–Thurs, Sat & Sun 8am–8pm, Fri 8am–9pm; Oct–April Mon–Thurs 8am–5pm, Fri 8am–8pm, Sat 9am–6pm & Sun 9am–2pm) is in the main concourse of the Gare du Midi, one of the capital's three main train stations and the Eurostar terminus; it's geared up to cater for new arrivals and does not operate the range of services of the main office.

The city centre's third tourist office, the **Belgian tourist information centre**, footsteps from the Grand-Place at rue du Marché aux Herbes 63 (July & Aug Mon–Fri 9am–7pm, Sat & Sun 9am–1pm & 2–7pm; May, June, Sept & Oct Mon–Fri 9am–6pm, Sat & Sun 9am–1pm & 2–6pm; Nov–April Mon–Fri 9am–6pm, Sat 9am–1pm & 2–6pm, Sun 9am–1pm; ☎02 504 03 90, ℻02 513 04 75), provides information on the whole of Belgium. They do stock a few brochures on Brussels, but this is not their main concern – they leave the city largely to BIT. They operate a hotel room reservation service, but again it's for the rest of Belgium, not Brussels.

Brussels on the internet

Art guide to Belgium 🖮www.artsite.be. A comprehensive list of the country's main art galleries and art museums with links to their often impressive websites. Also provides links to private galleries and antique dealers.

The Bulletin

As well as providing good coverage of current affairs, **The Bulletin** (€2.70), the city's main English-language weekly, contains an **entertainment listings** section, detailing what's on and where. The magazine is on sale at most downtown newsagents. BIT also provides *The Bulletin*'s listings section – "What's On" – for free. For more details on entertainment, see Chapters 10 and 11.

Beer ⓦ www.belgianstyle.com. Listings and reviews/tastings of dozens of Belgian brews, along with details of the various brewing techniques used. Also has sections on how to pronounce the names of many beers, a guide to home brewing and even advice on the appropriate glass to use for many beers.

Commonwealth War Graves Commission ⓦ www.cwgc.org. Commonwealth soldiers are buried all over Belgium, the consequence of two World Wars partly fought on Belgian territory. The vast majority lie interned in Flanders, killed in the trenches of World War I. This website provides information on the history of the War Graves Commission and its current workings and also has the ability to locate an individual soldier's grave from surprisingly little specific information.

Belgian brewers and breweries ⓦ www .beerparadise.be. Confederation of Belgian Brewers' website extolling the virtues of Belgian beer, providing details of brewers, brewery tours and beer generally.

Belgium Travel Network ⓦ www.trabel.com. General advice and information, plus useful links to the country's regional tourist offices.

Chocolates ⓦ www.neuhauschocolate.com. Neuhaus is one of the country's larger chocolatiers with outlets in every major Belgian town and city. Their website details the company's history, explains how their chocolates are made and carries pictures of their products – a real palate-whetter. Also has details of their shops along with opening times.

Famous Belgians ⓦ www.famousbelgians.net. Irritated by all the dreary jokes about Belgium, an expatriate Belgian has compiled a list of over 250 famous Belgians along with potted biographies, including the Singing Nun of "Dominique" fame.

Football: Anderlecht ⓦ www.rsca.be. 'Ere we go, the thrilling fields of Brussels' premier football club, Anderlecht.

Lace ⓦ www.belgian-lace.com. Website of one of the few authentic lace manufacturers left in Belgium, Louise Verschueren (see p.221).

René Magritte ⓦ www.virtuo.be. A private company called Virtuo operates this website, which is devoted to Magritte. Carries biographical details and a virtual library featuring over 300 of the artist's works.

Tintin ⓦ www.tintin.be. Blistering barnacles! Anything you've ever wanted to know about Tintin, Captain Haddock, Snowy and all their chums.

Tourist-office websites

Belgian Tourist Office in the Americas ⓦ www .visitbelgium.com. Reliable website providing standard tourist information with an American slant.

Bruxelles International – Tourisme (BIT) ⓦ www.brusselsinternational.be or ⓦ www .brusselsdiscovery.com. Official city tourist board website. Well presented and organized, and full of practical information from museums through to hotels, restaurants and bars.

Tourism Flanders–Brussels ⓦ www .visitflanders.com. Detailed and competent multilingual guide to the capital and the northern, Flemish–speaking half of Belgium. Attractively laid out, the site covers accommodation and sights through to events and practicalities.

Wallonie/Bruxelles ⓦ www.belgiumtheplaceto .be. Portal site with lots of useful links plus details of everything from golfing holidays to festivals. Operated by the official Wallonie/Bruxelles tourist board, covering the capital and the southern, French–speaking half of the country. Try also the OPT's ⓦ www.belgique-tourisme.net.

Maps

The **maps** in this Guide are more than adequate for most purposes, but if you need one on a larger scale, or with a street index, then pick up either the free city map with index issued by the BIT tourist offices (see p.25) or, even better, *Brussels: The Rough Guide Map* (1:10000 to 1:6000), which has the added advantage of being rip-proof and waterproof. The latter also marks all the key sights as well as many of the best hotels, restaurants, bars and clubs, and what's more it's only in French, whereas most of its competitors (including the tourist office map) carry both French and Flemish signage, which makes them very cluttered. The only problem is that the *Brussels: Rough Guide Map* is very hard to get hold of in Brussels, so try to buy one before you set out – either in any good local bookshop or via ⓦ www .roughguides.com. The *Brussels: Rough Guide Map* does not, however, extend to the outer suburbs. For these districts, the best map currently on the market is the widely available *Michelin Bruxelles* map (1:17,500), which comes complete with an index.

Arrival

Brussels is easy to reach by plane, with flights arriving at its airport from every corner of the globe. In addition, the city is on the main routes heading inland from the Channel ports and is well connected by train to major cities across Europe, including direct from London via the Channel Tunnel. Brussels itself has a good public transport system, which puts the main points of arrival – its airport, train and bus stations – within easy reach of the city centre.

By air

Most flights land at Brussels' international airport (Brussels Zaventem), 13km northeast of the city, but some – principally Ryanair (see p.20) – arrive at Charleroi airport, some 50km south of the centre.

Brussels International Airport

Brussels International Airport is in the satellite town of Zaventem, 13km northeast of the city centre. There's a **BIT tourist information desk** (daily 8am–9pm) in the arrivals hall with a reasonable range of information on

---

In Brussels, the languages of the French- and Flemish-speaking communities have parity. This means that every instance of the written word, from road signs to the yellow pages, has to appear in both languages. Visitors soon adjust, but **on arrival** this can be very confusing, especially with regard to the **names of the city's three main train stations**: Bruxelles-Nord (in Flemish it's Brussel-Noord), Bruxelles-Centrale (Brussel-Centraal), and, most bewildering of the lot, Bruxelles-Midi (Brussel-Zuid). To add to the puzzle, each of these three train stations adjoins a métro station – respectively the Gare du Nord (Noordstation), Gare Centrale (Centraal Station) and Gare du Midi (Zuidstation). Note that for simplicity's sake we've stuck to using the French version only in this Guide.

---

the city and its surroundings. It also shares its space with Espace Wallonie, representing the Wallonian tourist board, which covers southern, French-speaking Belgium (daily 6am–10pm). In addition, the arrivals hall has all the usual **facilities** you'd expect of a major airport, notably *bureaux de change*, a bank, a post office and ATMs.

From the airport, **trains** run every fifteen minutes or so to the city's three main stations – Bruxelles-Nord, Bruxelles-Centrale and lastly Bruxelles-Midi. The journey time to Bruxelles-Centrale (the nearest station to the Grand-Place) is between twenty and thirty minutes depending on which train you catch; the cost is €2.60 one-way, and tickets can be bought from the ticket office in the airport-complex train station. If the ticket office is closed, you can pay the ticket inspector on the train at no extra charge, but there is a small surcharge if the office is open and you still choose to pay the inspector. Trains run from 5.30am until midnight; after that you'll need to take a **taxi** – reckon on paying around €40 for the trip to the city centre. The airport also has its own **bus station** with a number of services to the capital, including hourly bus #12 (6am–11pm) running to Métro Schuman in the EU Quarter, as well as several other destinations.

Charleroi airport

Some airlines – principally Ryanair (see p.20) – fly to **Brussels (Charleroi) airport**, some 50km south of the city centre. It's a small airport, though there are plans to expand it, and it has a reasonable range of facilities including car hire and ATMs. From here there are twenty buses daily to Brussels departing from outside the terminal building and these drop passengers just outside Bruxelles-Midi train station; double check pick–up arrangements, as several of our readers have missed the bus back to the airport. Depending on traffic, the journey takes about an hour and costs €10.50 each way.

By train

Brussels has three main **train stations** – Bruxelles-Nord, Bruxelles-Centrale and Bruxelles-Midi, all of them connected to each other by frequent mainline trains which run every ten minutes or so. Almost all **domestic** trains stop at all three stations, but the majority of **international** services only stop at **Bruxelles-Midi**, including Eurostar trains from London and Thalys express trains from Amsterdam, Paris, Cologne and Aachen. Bruxelles-Midi station is located in a depressed area to the south of the city centre, so if you arrive late at night, it's best to take a **taxi** to your hotel or hostel. During the daytime, taxis apart, you can either catch one of the regular connecting trains to **Bruxelles-Centrale**, a five-minute walk from the Grand-Place, or take an underground tram (the **prémétro**) to the Bourse station,

from where it's a brief walk to the Grand-Place. The prémétro also links Bruxelles-Midi and Bourse station with **Bruxelles-Nord**, located in the business area just north of the main ring road.

Note that on bus timetables and on maps of the city transit system, Bruxelles-Nord appears as "Gare du Nord", Bruxelles-Centrale as "Gare Centrale" and Bruxelles-Midi as "Gare du Midi". The former name stands for the mainline train station while the latter signifies the métro or prémétro stop.

By bus

Most **international bus** services to Brussels, including those from Britain, are operated by Eurolines, whose terminal is in the **Bruxelles-Nord** station complex. From here, you can either catch a connecting mainline train to Bruxelles-Centrale or take the prémétro to Bourse station, both a short walk from the Grand-Place. Alternatively, a taxi into the centre from Bruxelles-Nord will cost around €15. Belgium's comprehensive rail network means that it's unlikely that you'll arrive in the city by **long-distance domestic bus**, but if you do, Bruxelles-Nord is the main terminal for these services too.

City transport

The easiest way to get around the city centre – the rough oval contained within the boulevards of the so–called "petit ring" – is to walk, but, to get from one side of the centre to the other, or to reach some of the outlying attractions, you'll need to use public transport. Operated by STIB (information on premium line ☎0900 10 310 at €0.45 per minute; ⓦwww.stib.be), the urban system runs on an integrated mixture of bus, tram, underground tram (prémétro) and métro lines that cover the city comprehensively. It's a user-friendly network, with every métro station carrying métro-system diagrams and with timetables posted at most bus and tram stops.

Tickets

Tickets, which can be used on any part of the STIB system, are fairly cheap: a single–trip ticket costs €1.50, a five–trip

ticket €6.50, and ten €10. Alternatively, a go-as-you-please day–pass (*carte d'un jour*) costs €3.80 for 24 hours, €9 for three days of unlimited travel out of five, and €12 for five out of ten. The day and multi-day passes are sold at métro stations and STIB kiosks, whereas the ordinary tickets are more widely available – from tram and bus drivers, métro stations, and from newsagents displaying the STIB sign. At the beginning of each journey, you're trusted to **stamp your ticket** yourself, either in the machines provided on every métro station concourse or in the machines located inside every tram and bus. After that, the ticket is valid for an hour, during which you can get on and off as many trams, métros and buses as you like. The system can seem open to abuse, as ticket controls at the métro stations are almost non-existent and you can get on at the back of any tram without ever showing a ticket, but there are roving inspectors who impose heavy on-the-spot fines for anyone caught without a valid ticket.

Métro, prémétro, trams and trains

The **métro** system consists of two underground train lines – lines #1 and #2. Line #1 runs east-west through the centre, and splits into two branches (#1A and #1B) at either end to serve the city's suburbs. Line #2 circles the centre, its route roughly following that of the petit ring boulevards up above. Currently, the two métro lines only intersect twice – at Métro Arts–Loi and Métro Simonis – but an extension is currently under construction to link Clemenceau on Line #2 with Gare de l'Ouest on Line 1B. Supplementing the métro is a substantial **tram** network that serves much of the city centre and many a suburb. These trams are at their speediest when they go underground to form what is often called the **prémétro**, that part of the system which runs underneath the heart of the city from Bruxelles-Nord, through De Brouckère and Bourse, to Bruxelles-Midi, Porte de Hal and on underneath St Gilles.

STIB **route maps** are available free from the BIT tourist office on the Grande–Place and from major métro stations. The STIB has information kiosks at Porte de Namur, Rogier and Midi métro stations. Amongst the multitude of routes, times of operation and frequency vary considerably, but key parts of the system operate from 6am until midnight. Finally, note that in most cases **doors** on métros, trams and buses have to be opened manually.

In addition to the STIB network there are **local trains**, run by Belgian Railways (SNCB), which connect different parts of the inner city and the outskirts, though unless you're living and working here, you're unlikely to need to use them. These trains use the city's three main stations, as well as four smaller ones – Bruxelles-Chapelle, Bruxelles-Quartier Léopold, Bruxelles-Schuman and Bruxelles-Congrès.

Buses

STIB **buses** supplement the trams and the métro. In the particular, they provide a limited and sporadic **night bus** service on major routes – often just one bus operating on a route between midnight and around 4am. In addition, **De Lijn** (☎016 31 37 11, ⊛www .delijn.be) runs buses from the city to the Flemish-speaking communities that surround the capital, whilst **TEC** (☎010 230 53 53, ⊛www.tec-wl.be) operates services to the French-speaking areas to the south. Many of these buses run from – or at least call in at – the Gare du Nord complex. Both De Lijn and TEC also run services to other Belgian cities, but they can take up to four times longer than the train.

Taxis

Taxis can be picked up at taxi stands around the city – notably on Bourse, place de Brouckère, Porte de Namur, outside the smarter hotels and at all the city's train stations. There is a fixed **tariff** consisting of two main elements – a set charge of €2.35 (€4.20 at night) and the price per km (€1.15 inside the city, €1.98 outside). If you can't find a taxi, phone Taxis Verts (☎02 349 49 49), Taxis Orange (☎02 349 43 43), or Autolux (☎02 411 12 21).

Guided tours

Guided tours are big business in Brussels and the BIT has details of – and takes bookings for – about twenty operators. On offer is everything from a quick stroll or bus ride round the city centre to themed visits – following, for example, in the footsteps of René Magritte or visiting the pick of the city's Art Nouveau buildings. As a general rule, the more predictable tours can be booked on the day, while the more exotic ones need to be booked ahead of time – BIT normally requires at least two weeks' advance notice. Among the many more straightforward options, **Brussels City Tours**, just off the Grand–Place at rue de la Colline 8 (☏02 513 77 44, ⊛www.brussels -city-tours.com), operates a hop-on, hop-off bus service which loops round the city visiting many of its principal sights daily between 10am and 6pm. Tickets, valid for 24 hours, cost €16 (students & 65+ €14.50).

More promising still, **Chatterbus**, rue des Thuyas 12 (☏02 673 18 35, ⊛www .busbavard.be), runs well-regarded, French–language walking tours throughout the summer, with their first-rate "Brussels through the Ages" tour lasting about three

hours and costing €8. Other choices include Baroque Brussels, Musical Brussels and Belgian beers. Another recommendation is **ARAU** (Atelier de Recherche et d'Action Urbaines), boulevard Adolphe Max 55 (☏02 219 33 45, ⊛www.arau.org), a heritage action group that provides tours exploring the city's architecture, with particular emphasis on Art Nouveau. Their English-language, three-hour-long **Art Nouveau bus tour** runs once weekly from March through to December, and costs €15. Most of their other tours – including a fascinating excursion into the Marolles district – are in French.

Cyclists are catered for by Pro Vélo, rue de Londres 15 (☏02 502 73 55, ⊛www .provelo.org). This company operates several half-day cycle tours round the city and its environs at a cost of just €8 per person per tour, with bike rental costing an extra €6.

Costs, money and banks

By west European standards, Brussels is moderately expensive when it comes to accommodation and food, though this is partly offset by the low cost of public transport. More precise costs for places to stay and eat are given in the Guide, and you should consult p.177 for general guidelines on accommodation. ATMs are routine across the city and are the easiest way to get cash, though currency exchange facilities are widespread too.

Average costs

If you're prepared to buy your own picnic lunch, stay in hostels, and stick to the less expensive bars and restaurants, you could get by on around **£25/US$47 a day**. Staying in two-star hotels, eating out in medium-range restaurants most nights and drinking in bars, you'll get through at least **£65/$120 a day** with the main variable being the cost of your room. On **£100/$190 a day** and upwards, you'll be limited only by your energy reserves – though if you're planning to stay in a five-star hotel and to have a big night out, this still won't be enough. As always, if you're travelling alone you'll spend much more on accommodation than you

would in a group of two or more: most hotels do have single rooms, but they're fixed at about 75 percent of the price of a double.

Restaurants don't come cheap, but costs remain manageable if you avoid the extras and concentrate on the main courses, for which around £10/$19 will normally suffice – twice that with a drink, starter and dessert. You can, of course, pay a lot more – a top restaurant in Brussels can be twice as expensive again, and then some.

Currency

The **currency** of Belgium – like most of the rest of the EU – is the **euro** (€) with each euro comprising 100 cents. There are seven euro **notes** – in denominations of €500, €200, €100, €50, €20, €10, and €5, each a different colour and size – and eight different **coins**, including €2 and e1, then 50, 20, 10, 5, 2, and 1 cents. Euro coins feature a common EU design on one face, but different country-specific designs on the other. All euro notes and coins can be used in any of the twelve euro-zone – or, more playfully, "euroland" – states.

At the time of writing the **rate of exchange for €1** is £0.67; US$1.28; CDN$1.60; AUS$1.67; NZ$1.80. For the most up–to-date rates, check the currency converter website ⓦ www.oanda.com.

Travellers' cheques

The main advantage of buying **travellers' cheques** is that they are a safe way of carrying funds. All well–known brands of travellers' cheque in all major currencies are widely accepted in Brussels, with euro and US dollar cheques being the most common. The usual fee for their purchase is one or two percent of face value, though this fee is often waived if you buy the cheques through a bank where you have an account. You'll find it useful to purchase a selection of denominations. When you **cash your cheques**, you'll find that almost all banks make a percentage charge per transaction on top of a basic minimum charge.

In the event that cheques are **lost or stolen**, the issuing company will expect you to report the loss immediately. Make sure to keep the purchase agreement, a record of cheque serial numbers and the issuing company's emergency contact numbers safe and separate from the cheques themselves. Most companies claim to replace lost or stolen cheques within 24 hours.

ATMS and credit cards

Brussels has lots of **ATMs** with a particular concentration on and around the Grand–Place, including a CBC ATM at Grand–Place 7, though note that they are notorious for running out of money late on Saturday night. Most ATMs give instructions in a variety of languages, and accept a host of **debit cards**, including all those carrying the Cirrus/ Maestro logo. If in doubt, check with your bank before you go to find out if the card

you wish to use will be accepted – and if you need a new (international) PIN. You'll rarely be charged a transaction fee as the banks make their profits from applying different exchange rates. **Credit cards** can be used in ATMs too, but in this case transactions are treated as loans, with interest accruing daily from the date of withdrawal. All major credit cards, including American Express, Visa and Mastercard, are widely accepted in Brussels and, for that matter, all of Belgium.

Banks and bureaux de change

If you need to change money, Brussels' **banks** usually offer the best deals. Bank **opening hours** are generally from Monday to Friday 9am to 3.30pm with a few banks also open on Saturday mornings; all are closed on public holidays (see p.35). Outside regular banking hours, most major hotels, many travel agents and some hostels will change money at less generous rates and with variable commissions, as will the **foreign exchange kiosks** (*bureaux de change*) to be found in key locations across the city centre. These include the 24-hour CBC exchange at Grand-Place 7 and at all three of the city's main train stations, Nord (Mon–Fri 8am–8pm & Sat 9am–5pm); Centrale (Mon–Fri 9.30am–5pm); and Midi (daily 8am–8pm).

Wiring money

Having **money wired** from home using one of the companies listed below is never convenient or cheap, and should only be considered as a last resort – indeed it can actually be cheaper to have **your own bank** send the money through. For the latter, you need to nominate a receiving bank in Brussels and confirm the arrangement with them before you set the wheels in motion back home. The sending bank's fees are geared to the amount being transferred and the urgency of the service you require – for example standard transfers, taking five working days, start at around £20/US$40 for the first £2,000/US$3780 or so.

Money-wiring companies

Travelers Express/MoneyGram US ☎ 1-800/444-3010, Canada ☎ 1-800/933-3278, UK,

Ireland and New Zealand ☎ 00800/6663 9472, Australia ☎ 0011800/6663 9472, ⓦ www .moneygram.com.
Western Union US and Canada ☎ 1-800/CALL-CASH, Australia ☎ 1800/501 500, New Zealand ☎ 0800/005 253, UK ☎ 0800/833 833, Republic of Ireland ☎ 66/947 5603, ⓦ www.westernunion .com (customers in the US and Canada can send money online).

Post, phones and email

As you might expect, Belgium in general and Brussels in particular has an efficient postal system and a first-rate telephone network, including excellent mobile phone coverage. Telephone booths and mail boxes are liberally distributed across the city, and charges are reasonable too. Internet cafés are, however, surprisingly thin on the ground, partly because most of the better hotels now provide some sort of Internet facility.

Post

In Brussels, **post offices** are fairly plentiful and mostly open Monday to Friday 9am to 4 or 5pm, with the larger ones also open on Saturday mornings from 9am to noon. The main post office is on the first floor of the Centre Monnaie shopping centre, place de la Monnaie (Mon–Fri 8am–6pm & Sat 9.30am–3pm). They have a Poste Restante service; to collect items, you need your passport. Stamps are sold at a wide range of outlets including many shops and hotels. Mail to the US takes seven days or so, within Europe two to three days.

Telephones

You can make domestic and international **telephone calls** with equal ease from public and private phones. **Phone booths** are plentiful, though the irresistible rise of the mobile means that their numbers will not increase and may well diminish. The vast majority of phone booths take phone cards (called *télécards*) and credit cards,

but not cash; where this is not the case, they are of the usual European kind, where you deposit the money before you make your call. Most phone booths have English instructions displayed inside. **Télécards** can be bought at many outlets, including post offices, some supermarkets, railway stations and newsagents, and in several specified denominations, beginning at €5. The cheap-rate period for international calls is between 8pm and 7am during the week and all day at weekends. Finally, remember that although most hotel rooms have phones, there is almost always an exorbitant surcharge for their use. To make a **reverse-charge** or collect call, phone the international operator (they almost all speak English).

Telephone charge cards and credit-card calls

One of the most convenient ways of phoning home from abroad is by using a **telephone charge card** issued by your phone company

Useful telephone numbers and codes

International calls

Phoning abroad from Brussels

To Australia: ☎0061 + area code minus zero + number.
To Canada: ☎001 + area code + number.
To the Republic of Ireland: ☎00353 + area code minus zero + number.
To New Zealand: ☎0064 + area code minus zero + number.
To the UK: ☎0044 + area code minus zero + number.
To the US: ☎001 + area code + number.

Phoning Brussels from abroad

From the UK, Ireland and New Zealand: ☎00 + 32 (Belgium) + 2 (Brussels) + number.
From the US and Canada: ☎011 + 32 (Belgium) + 2 (Brussels) + number.
From Australia: ☎0011 + 32 (Belgium) + 2 (Brussels) + number.

Operator numbers in Belgium

Domestic directory enquiries ☎1307
International directory enquiries ☎1304
International operator assistance ☎1324

Emergency numbers in Belgium

Fire brigade & emergency medical assistance ☎100
Police ☎101

---

back home. Using a local access number and a PIN number, you can make calls from most hotel, public and private phones and these are subsequently charged to your home telephone number. Since most major charge cards are free to obtain, it's certainly worth getting one at least for emergencies. When you sign up for a card, double check that Belgium is covered – it almost certainly will be – and bear in mind that rates aren't necessarily cheaper than calling from a public phone.

In the **US and Canada**, AT&T, MCI, Sprint, Canada Direct and other North American long-distance companies all enable their customers to make **credit-card calls** while overseas, billed to your home number. Call your company's customer service line for details of the toll-free access code in Brussels. To call **Australia and New Zealand** from overseas, telephone charge cards such as Telstra Telecard or Optus Calling Card in Australia, and Telecom NZ's Calling Card can be used to make calls abroad, which are charged back to a domestic account or credit card.

Mobile phones

If you want to use your **mobile phone** in Brussels, you'll need to check cellular access with your phone provider before you set out. Also check out their **call charges** as these can be exorbitant, especially as you are likely to be charged higher rates for incoming calls that originate from back home as the people calling you will be paying the usual (national) rate. The same sometimes applies to **text messages**, though in most cases these can now be received with the greatest of ease – no fiddly codes and so forth – and at ordinary rates. In Brussels, the mobile network covers almost every corner of the city and works on GSM 900/1800. Note that mobiles bought in **North America** need to be **triband** to access the cellular system in Europe.

Email

One of the best ways to keep in touch while travelling is to sign up for a **free Internet email address** that can be accessed from anywhere, for example YahooMail or Hotmail – accessible through www.yahoo .com and www.hotmail.com respectively. Once you've set up an account, you can use these sites to pick up and send mail from any Internet café, or hotel with Internet access. In addition, www.kropla.com is a useful website giving details of how to plug your laptop in when abroad, as well as listing international phone codes and providing information about electrical systems in different countries.

The media

British newspapers and magazines are easy to get hold of in Brussels and neither is there much difficulty in finding American publications. Two of Britain's leading TV channels – BBC1 and BBC2 – are picked up by most of the city's hotels.

The press

British newspapers – from tabloid through to broadsheet – as well as the more popular **English-language magazines** are widely available either on the day of publication or the day after right across Brussels. Internationally distributed **American newspapers** – principally the *Wall Street Journal*, *USA Today* and the *International Herald Tribune* – are also easy to get hold of, though distribution is concentrated in and around the city centre and the EU Quarter. Train-station bookstands are usually an excellent bet for English-language newspapers and magazines.

The three main newspapers in **French-speaking Belgium** are the influential, independent *Le Soir*; the right-wing, very Catholic *La Libre Belgique*; and *La Dernière Heure*, which is noted for its sports coverage. **Flemish-speakers** rely on the leftish *De Morgen*, traditionally the favourite of socialists and trade unionists; the right-leaning *De Standaard*; and the populist, vaguely liberal *Het Laatste Nieuws*. There's also an **English-language weekly magazine**, *The Bulletin*, which primarily caters for the sizeable expat community resident in Brussels. Its news articles are interesting and diverse, picking up on key Belgian themes and issues, and its listings section is first rate. It also carries a fair-sized classified section – useful if you've just arrived for an extended stay and are looking for an apartment or even work.

TV and radio

British radio stations can be picked up in Brussels: you'll find BBC Radio 4 on 198kHz (1515m) long wave, the World Service on 648kHz (463m) medium wave and BBC Radio 5 Live on 909am and 693am. Shortwave frequencies and schedules for BBC World Service (www.bbc.co.uk /worldservice), Radio Canada (www.rcinet .ca) and Voice of America (www.voa.gov) are listed on their respective websites.

As far as **British TV** is concerned, BBC1 and BBC2 television channels are on most hotel room TVs. In addition, many bars and most hotels are geared up for (at least a couple of) the big pan-European **cable and satellite** channels: MTV, CNN, Eurosport and so forth. You can also almost invariably pick up all the Dutch and German stations, and often those from France and Italy too. **Domestic TV** is largely uninspiring, though the Flemish-language TV1 and Kanaal 2 usually run English-language films with subtitles, whereas the main Wallonian channels – RTBF 1 and RTBF 2 – mostly dub. For local news and current affairs in French, try the city's own **Télé–Brussels**; the Flemish equivalent is **TV Brussels**.

Opening hours and public holidays

Although there's recently been some movement towards greater flexibility, opening hours for shops, businesses and tourist attractions remain a little restrictive, rarely extending into the evening and with Sunday opening far from commonplace, except in the case of museums. In addition, travel plans can be disrupted on public holidays, when most things close down – apart from restaurants, bars and hotels – and public transport is reduced to a Sunday timetable. For the dates of festivals and special events, which can be similarly disruptive to the normal ebb and flow of the city, see pp.237–240.

Opening hours

Typical **business hours** (ie office hours) run from Monday to Friday 10am to 5pm, whereas regular **shopping hours** are Monday through Saturday 10am to 6 or 7pm. However, many smaller shops open late on Monday morning and/or close a tad earlier on Saturdays, most supermarkets and department stores are likely to have extended hours with late-night opening on Fridays (till 8 or 9pm) especially popular, and the tourist-orientated shops in and around the Grand-Place generally open seven days a week until into the early evening.

The majority of the city's **museums** are state-run and these almost invariably conform to a pattern: closed on Monday, and open Tuesday to Sunday from 10am to 5pm, though the most important usually open on Mondays during the summer months too. **Church** hours vary considerably, but the most visited are normally open Monday to Saturday from around 9am to 5pm, with more restrictive opening hours on Sunday. Most **restaurants** are open for dinner from about 6 or 7pm, and though many close as early as 9.30pm, a few stay open past 11pm; many open for a couple of hours at lunchtime too – say noon–2pm

Public holidays in Belgium

New Year's Day
Easter Sunday
Easter Monday
Labour Day (May 1)
Ascension Day (forty days after Easter)
Whit Sunday
Whit Monday
Belgium National Day (July 21)
Assumption (mid-August)
All Saints' Day (November 1)
Armistice Day (November 11)
Christmas Day

– and some close one day a week. **Clubs** generally function from 11pm to 4am during the week, though few open every night, and stay open until 5am on the weekend.

Precise opening hours for shops, museums, churches, restaurants and clubs – as well as many other attractions – are given in the Guide.

Public holidays

In Belgium, there are twelve national **public holidays** per year; most are keenly observed in the capital.

Crime and personal safety

There's little reason why you should ever come into contact with the Belgian police force. For one thing, it's statistically unlikely you'll be a victim of crime; for another the police generally keep a low profile, though they do blitz areas – especially the city's three main train stations – when they feel things are getting out of hand. As far as personal safety goes, it's generally possible to walk around Brussels without fear of harassment or assault, though the city does have its shady areas and wherever you are it's better to err on the side of caution late at night, when – for instance – badly lit or empty streets should be avoided.

In Belgium, there are two main types of police. The **Gendarmerie Nationale**, who wear blue uniforms with red stripes on their trousers, patrol the motorways and deal with major crime, whereas the municipal **Police**, in their dark blue uniforms, cover everything else. Many officers **speak English**, though a modicum of French can be invaluable. All the police are armed.

Petty crime

Almost all the problems tourists encounter in Brussels are to do with **petty crime** – pickpocketing and bag-snatching – rather than more serious physical confrontations, so it's as well to be on your guard and know where your possessions are at all times. Thieves often work in pairs and, although **theft** is far from rife, you should be aware of certain **ploys**, such as: the "helpful" person pointing out "birdshit" (actually shaving cream or similar) on your coat, while someone else relieves you of your money; being invited to read a card, map or paper to distract your attention; someone in a café making a move for your drink with one hand while the other is in your bag as you react; and if you're in a crowd, watch out for anyone getting unusually close.

Personal safety

Sensible **precautions** include carrying bags slung across your neck and not over your shoulder; not carrying anything in pockets that are easy to dip into; having photocopies of your passport, airline ticket and driving licence; leaving passports and tickets in the hotel safe; and noting down travellers' cheque and credit card numbers. When you're looking for a hotel room, never leave your bags unattended and if you have a car, don't leave anything in view when you park. Vehicle theft is still fairly uncommon, but luggage and valuables left in cars do make a tempting target. If you're on a bicycle, make sure it is well locked up – bike theft and resale is a big deal in urban Belgium. **At night**, you'd be well advised to avoid walking round the tougher, rougher parts of Brussels: several of the city's inner suburbs can get a bit scary – at least in parts – but, of the districts you're likely to visit, be cautious in the streets around the Gare du Midi and in Molenbeek. Using public transport, even late at night, isn't usually a problem, but if in doubt take a taxi.

If you are **robbed**, you'll need to go to the police to report it, not least because your insurance company will require a police report; remember to make a note of the report number – or, better still, ask for a copy of the statement itself. Don't expect a great deal of concern if your loss is relatively small – and don't be surprised if the process of completing forms and formalities takes ages. In the unlikely event that you're **mugged** or otherwise threatened, never resist, and try to reduce your contact with the robber to a minimum. Either just hand over what's wanted, or throw money in one direction and take off in the other. Afterwards, go straight to the police, who should be much more sympathetic and helpful on these occasions.

Minor offences

You ought to be aware of a couple of **offences** that you might commit unwittingly. In theory, you're supposed to carry some kind of official **identification** at all times, and the police can stop you in the streets and demand to see it. If you can't produce identification or otherwise prove your identity, you can be held at a police station even if this is your only "crime". Every Belgian carries an identity card (*carte d'identité*) as do most EU nationals, but for others a passport will suffice. In practice, however, it's extremely unlikely that you'll be stopped unless there's a particular reason – for example involvement in a road accident.

In Belgium, the laws on the possession of illegal **drugs** are fairly strict. Travellers arriving from Holland, where it is effectively legal to possess small amounts of cannabis for personal use, are sometimes blissfully unaware of the differences between the Benelux countries in this regard, which can mean a major hassle. If you're carrying dope, you'd be well advised to leave it in the Netherlands.

Being arrested

Should you be **arrested** on any charge, you have the right to contact your **consulate** or embassy – see p.241 for local contact details. Unfortunately, consular officials are notoriously reluctant to get involved, though most are required to assist you to some degree if you have your passport stolen or lose all your money. If you've been detained for a drugs offence, don't expect any sympathy or help.

Sexual harassment

In the normal course of events, **women travellers** are unlikely to feel threatened and intimidated or attract unwanted attention in almost any part of Brussels. The main exception is in the seedier areas of the city, where the atmosphere may feel frightening, especially late at night – but with common sense and circumspection you shouldn't have anything to worry about. The men who hang around nightclubs and bars pose no greater or lesser threat than similar operators at home, though the language barrier (where it exists) makes it harder to know whom to trust.

Travellers with disabilities

Brussels is not an easy destination for the disabled traveller. Lifts and ramps are few, steep steps and rough pavements are common – and, even when an effort has been made, obstacles are frequent. That said, attitudes have changed: new buildings are required by law to be fully accessible and the number of existing premises geared up for disabled travellers has increased dramatically in the last few years, especially with regard to the city's hotels.

Other signs of progress are the installation of Braille information panels in some métro stations, new trams with low-level access platforms, and the special, low-cost (€1.50), door-to-door minibus service operated by the city's public transport provider, STIB, for people with disabilities – call ☎02 515 23 65 (French and Dutch only).

Contacts for travellers with disabilities

In the UK and Ireland

Access Travel ☎01942/888 844, ⓦwww .access-travel.co.uk. Small, personal-service tour operator that can arrange flights, transfers and accommodation for Brussels city breaks.

Holiday Care ☎0845/124 9971 or 020/8760 0072, ⓦ www.holidaycare.org.uk. Provides an information pack for £2.50 which details transport options, accommodation, special services, tour operators and useful contacts for travelling around the Netherlands, Belgium and Luxembourg.

Irish Wheelchair Association ☎01/818 6400, ⓦ www.iwa.ie. Useful information about travelling abroad.

RADAR (Royal Association for Disability and Rehabilitation) ☎020/7250 3222 minicom or 020/7250 4119, ⓦ www.radar.org.uk. A good source of advice, with a useful website.

Tripscope ☎0845/7 58 56 41, ⓦ www.tripscope .org.uk. Registered charity providing free advice on international transport.

In the US and Canada

Access-Able ⓦ www.access-able.com. Online resource for travellers with disabilities.

Mobility International USA ☎541/343-1284, ⓦ www.miusa.org. Information and referral services, access guides, tours and exchange programmes.

Society for the Advancement of Travelers with Handicaps 347 5th Ave, New York, NY 10016 ☎212/447-7284, ⓦ www.sath.org. Non-profit educational organization with tips on travelling and links to airlines.

Wheels Up! ☎1-888/38-WHEELS, ⓦ www .wheelsup.com. Provides discounted airfare and tour prices and a free monthly newsletter. Comprehensive website.

In Australia and New Zealand

ACROD (Australian Council for Rehabilitation of the Disabled) ☎02/6282 4333 (also TTY), ⓦ www.acrod.org.au. Provides lists of travel agencies and tour operators.

Disabled Persons' Assembly ☎04/801 9100 (also TTY), ⓦ www.dpa.org.nz. Resource centre with lists of travel agencies and tour operators.

Gay and lesbian travellers

Gay and lesbian life in Brussels does not have a high international profile, especially in comparison with neighbouring Amsterdam. That said, there's still a vibrant scene, though more so for men than women. By and large, Belgium's hetero majority leave gays and lesbians unmolested, a pragmatic tolerance – or intolerance soaked in indifference – that has provided opportunities for legislative change. In 1998 Belgium passed a law granting certain rights to cohabiting couples irrespective of their sex, and gay marriage was legalised, after much huffing and puffing by the political right, in 2003. The legal age of consent for gay men is 16. You'll find more on the gay/lesbian scene on pp.234–236, "Gay and lesbian Brussels".

Contacts for gay and lesbian travellers

In the UK

Also check out **adverts** in the weekly paper *Pink Paper*, handed out free in gay venues.

ⓦ **www.gaytravel.co.uk** Online gay and lesbian travel agent, offering good deals on all types of holiday. Also lists gay- and lesbian-friendly hotels around the world.

Dream Waves Holidays ☎0870/042 2475,

ⓦ www.gayholidaysdirect.com. Specializes in exclusively gay holidays, including skiing trips and summer sun packages.

Madison Travel ☎01273/202 532, ⓦ www .madisontravel.co.uk. Established travel agents specializing in packages to gay- and lesbian-friendly mainstream destinations, and also to gay/lesbian destinations.

Respect Holidays ☎0870/770 0169, ⓦ www .respect-holidays.co.uk. Offers exclusively gay packages to all popular European resorts and cities.

In the US and Canada

Damron ☎1-800/462-6654 or 415/255-0404, ⓦwww.damron.com. Publisher of the *Men's Travel Guide*, a pocket-sized yearbook full of listings of hotels, bars, clubs and resources for gay men; the *Women's Traveler*, which provides similar listings for lesbians; and *Damron Accommodations*, which provides detailed listings of over 1000 accommodation options for gays and lesbians worldwide. All of these titles are offered at a discount on the website. No specific city guides – everything is incorporated in the yearbooks.

gaytravel.com ☎1-800/GAY-TRAVEL, ⓦwww.gaytravel.com. The premier site for trip-planning, bookings, and general information about international gay and lesbian travel.

International Gay & Lesbian Travel Association ☎1-800/448-8550 or 954/776-2626, ⓦwww.iglta.org. Trade group that can provide a list of gay- and lesbian-owned or -friendly travel agents, accommodation and other travel businesses.

In Australia and New Zealand

Gay and Lesbian Tourism Australia ⓦwww.galta.com.au. Directory and links for gay and lesbian travel in Australia and worldwide.

Parkside Travel ☎08/8274 1222, ⓔparkside@herveyworld.com.au. Gay travel agent associated with local branch of Hervey World Travel; all aspects of gay and lesbian travel worldwide.

Silke's Travel ☎1800/807 860 or 02/8347 2000, ⓦwww.silkes.com.au. Long-established gay and lesbian specialist, with the emphasis on women's travel.

Tearaway Travel ☎1800/664 440 or 03/9510 6644, ⓦwww.tearaway.com. Gay-specific business dealing with international and domestic travel.

The City

The City

The Grand-Place

One of Europe's most beautiful squares, the **Grand-Place** is tucked away amid the tangle of ancient cobbled lanes that lies at the heart of Brussels. It's the Gothic magnificence of the **Hôtel de Ville** – the town hall – which first draws the eye, but in its shadow is an exquisite sequence of late seventeenth-century **guildhouses**, whose gilded facades with their columns, scrolled gables and dainty sculptures encapsulate the Baroque ideals of exuberance and complexity. There's no better place to get the flavour of Brussels' past and, as you nurse a coffee watching the crowds from one of the pavement cafés, its Eurocapital present.

Originally marshland, the Grand-Place was drained in the twelfth century, and by 1350 a covered market for bread, meat and textiles had appeared, born of an economic boom underpinned by a flourishing cloth industry. The market was so successful that it soon expanded beyond the boundaries of the square – hence the names of the warren of narrow streets around it: rues au Beurre and des Bouchers, marchés aux Herbes, aux Poulets and aux Fromages. On the square itself, the city's merchants built themselves their headquarters, the guildhouses that cemented the Grand-Place's role as the commercial hub of the emergent city.

In the fifteenth century, with the building of the Hôtel de Ville, the square took on a civic and political function too, with the ruling dukes descending from their Upper Town residence to hold audiences and organize tournaments. Official decrees and pronouncements were also read here, and rough justice was meted out with public executions. In the 1480s, Brussels, along with the rest of the Low Countries, became a fiefdom of the **Habsburgs** and the role of the Grand-Place was transformed by that most Catholic of kings, **Philip II of Spain** (1555–98), who turned the square's public executions into religious events as he strove to crush the city's Protestants. These were the opening shots of a bitter religious war that was to rack the Low Countries for the next hundred years, although Brussels, after changing hands a couple of times, was finally secured by the Catholics in 1585. In victory, the Habsburgs were surprisingly generous, granting a general amnesty and promising to honour ancient municipal privileges. The city's economy revived and the Grand-Place resumed its role as a commercial centre. Of the square's medieval buildings, however, only parts of the Hôtel de Ville and the lower floors of two guildhouses survive today, the consequence of a 36-hour **French artillery bombardment**, which pretty much razed Brussels to the ground in 1695.

Unperturbed, the city's **guilds** swiftly had their headquarters rebuilt, using their control of the municipal council both to impose regulations on the sort of construction that was permitted and to ward off the Habsburg governor's notions of a royal – as distinct from bourgeois – main square. The council was not to be trifled with. In an early example of **urban planning**, it decreed:

GRAND-PLACE & AROUND

▲ Cathedral   ▲ Gare Centrale

N

0   100 m

RUE DE LOXUM
RUE DE CARDINAL MERCIER
RUE DE LA PUTTERIE
RUE CANTERSTEEN
RUE CANTERSTEEN
L'IMPERATRICE
DE
CARREFOUR DE L'EUROPE
BOULEVARD
RUE DE LA MONTAGNE
RUE DE L'INFANTE ISABELLA
RUE DE LA MADELEINE
GALERIE DE LA REINE
RUE DES BOUCHERS
Arenberg Galleries
PLACE ESPAGNE
Galerie Bortier
DUQUESNOY
IMPASSE DE SCHUDDEVELD
Théâtre de Toone
PETITE RUE DES BOUCHERS
RUE DE LA COLLINE
Maison des Ducs de Brabant
GALERIE AGORA
AUX FROMAGES
RUE DES EPERONNIERS
Actors' Studio
RUE DU MARCHE AUX HERBES
La Boutique Tintin
GALERIE AGORA
RUE DES PARENTS
RUE DES HARENGS
R CHAIR ET PAIN
Maison du Roi (Musée de la Ville de Bruxelles)
GRAND PLACE
Maison de L'Etoile
RUE DU MARCHE AGES
PLACE ST-JEAN
▼ Jacques Brel Fondation
Eglise St-Nicolas
RUE AU BEURRE
Roi d'Espagne
RUE DE CHARLES BUS
RUE DES BRASSEURS
Maison Dandoy
Maison du Renard
Hôtel de Ville
RUE DES CHAPELIERS
RUE DE LA VIOLETTE
RUE DU TABORA
RUE TETE D'OR
i
Musée de Costume & de la Dentelle
Bourse
RUE DE L'AMIGO
RUE DE L'ETUVE
RUE DU LOMBARD
Manneken Pis
RUE DU CHENE
RUE HENRI MAUS
Music Village
Brüsel
RUE DES PIERRES
Ancienne Belgique
RUE DE LA CHAUFFERETTE
AU CHARBON
RUE DES GRANDS CARMES
BOULEVARD ANSPACH
RUE BORGWAL
PLATTESTEEN
RUE DU MARCHE AU CHARBON
DU MIDI
MOINEAUX
Tels Quels
RUE BON SECOURS
RUE DES TEINTURIERS
RUE DES

"(We) hereby forbid the owners to build houses on the lower market [ie the Grand-Place] without the model of the facade . . . first being presented to the Council . . . Any construction erected contrary to this provision shall be demolished at the expense of the offender." By these means, the guilds were able to create a homogeneous Grand-Place, choosing to rebuild in a distinctive and flamboyant Baroque which made the square more ornate and more imposing than before. This magisterial self-confidence was, in fact, misplaced, as the factories that were soon to render the guilds obsolete were already colonizing parts of the city. The industrialization of the city effectively becalmed the Grand-Place and accidentally preserved it in its entirety.

The Hôtel de Ville (town hall)

From the south side of the Grand-Place, the newly scrubbed and polished **Hôtel de Ville** dominates proceedings, its 96-metre spire soaring high above two long series of robust windows, whose straight lines are mitigated by fancy tracery, striking gargoyles, solid statuettes and an arcaded gallery. The town hall dates from the beginning of the fifteenth century, when the town council decided to build itself a mansion that adequately reflected its wealth and power. The first part to be completed (in the 1410s) was the **east wing**, and the original entrance is still marked by the twin lions of the Lion Staircase, though the animals were only added in 1770. Work started on the **west wing** in 1444 and continued until 1480. Despite the gap, the wings are of very similar style, and you have to look hard to notice that the later wing is slightly shorter than its neighbour, allegedly at the insistence of Charles the Bold who – for some unknown reason – refused to have the adjacent rue de la Tête d'Or narrowed. The niches were left empty and the statues you see now – which represent leading figures from the city's past – are modern, part of a heavy-handed nineteenth-century refurbishment.

The tower of the Hôtel de Ville

By any standard, the **tower** of the Hôtel de Ville is quite extraordinary, its remarkably slender appearance the work of Jan van Ruysbroeck, the leading spire specialist of the day, who also played a pivotal role in the building of the cathedral (see p.71) and SS. Pierre et Guidon in Anderlecht (see p.122). Ruysbroeck had the lower section built square to support the weight above, choosing a design that blended seamlessly with the elaborately carved facade on either side – or almost: look carefully and you'll see that the main entrance is slightly out of kilter. Ruysbroeck used the old belfry porch as the base for the new tower, hence the misalignment, a deliberate decision and not a miscalculation prompting the architect's suicide, as legend would have it. Above the cornice protrudes an octagonal extension where the basic design of narrow windows flanked by pencil-thin columns and pinnacles is repeated up as far as the pyramid-shaped **spire**, a delicate affair surmounted by a gilded figure of **St Michael**, protector of Christians in general and of soldiers in particular.

Guided tours of the Hôtel de Ville

The tower is off-limits and forty-minute **guided tours** in English (April–Sept on Tues & Wed at 3.15pm & Sun at 10.45am & 12.15pm; Oct–March on Tues

△ The tower of the Hôtel de Ville

& Wed at 3.15pm; €3) are confined to a string of lavish official rooms used for receptions and town council meetings. The most dazzling of these is the sixteenth-century **Council Chamber**, decorated with gilt moulding, faded tapestries and an oak floor inlaid with ebony. The entrance chamber at the top of the first flight of stairs is also of interest for its assortment of royal portraits.

The Empress Maria Theresa of Austria is pictured side-saddle with her little feet (of which she was inordinately proud) poking out from her amazingly expensive lacy dress, while a gallant-looking **Charles II** (see below) sits astride his handsome steed, courtesy of Jan van Orley. This must have stretched Orley's imagination to the limit: Charles, the last of the Spanish Habsburgs, was – according to the historian J. H. Elliott – "a rachitic and feeble-minded weakling, the last stunted sprig of a degenerate line". Tours begin at the reception desk off the interior quadrangle; be prepared for the guides' overly reverential script.

The guildhouses of the Grand-Place

Flanking and facing the Hôtel de Ville are the **guildhouses** that give the Grand-Place its character, their slender, gilded facades swirling with exuberant, self-publicizing carvings and sculptures. Decorated with semicircular arches and classical motifs, scrollwork, supple bas-reliefs and statuettes, they represent the apotheosis of **Italian–Flemish architecture**, a melding of two stylistic traditions first introduced into the Low Countries by artists and architects returning from Italy in the early seventeenth century. Each guildhouse has a name, usually derived from one of the statues, symbols or architectural quirks decorating its facade – and the more interesting are described below. Most of the old guildhouses have ground-floor **cafés**, which spill out across the cobbled square. As you might expect, they all charge premium rates, but *La Brouette*, at nos. 2–3, with its tasteful repro furniture and fittings and open fire, is nonetheless particularly appealing and its first floor offers an attractive view of the square; a good second bet is *La Chaloupe d'Or* at no. 24, which is kitted out in similar style. All the Grand-Place cafés are very popular and are best visited early in the morning before about 10am, when the tourists arrive in force.

The health of Charles II

Philip IV of Spain (1605–65) had no fewer than fourteen children, but only one of his sons – **Charles II** (1661–1700) – reached his twenties. With women banned from the succession, the hapless, sickly Charles became king at the tender age of four and, much to everyone's surprise, survived to adulthood. After his first marriage in 1679, there were great hopes that he would be able to sire an **heir**, but none arrived, probably because Charles suffered from premature ejaculation. A second marriage, twenty years later, was equally fruitless and, as it became increasingly clear that Charles was unable to procreate, Europe focused on what was to happen when Charles died and the Spanish royal line died out. Every ambassador to the Spanish court wrote long missives home about the health of Charles, none more so than the English representative, **Stanhope**, who painted an especially gloomy picture: "He (Charles) has a ravenous stomach and swallows all he eats whole, for his nether jaw stands out so much that his two rows of teeth cannot meet…His weak stomach not being able to digest the food, he voids it in the same (whole) manner."

In the autumn of 1700, it was clear that Charles was dying and his doctors went to work in earnest, replacing his pillows with freshly killed pigeons and covering his chest with animal entrails. Surprise, surprise, this didn't work and Charles **died** on November 1, his death leading directly to the **War of the Spanish Succession** (1701–14).

△ Guildhouses of the Grand-Place

The west side of the Grand-Place: Nos. 1–7

On the west side of the square, at the end of the row, stands the **Roi d'Espagne**, at no. 1, a particularly fine building, which takes its name from the bust of

Charles II (see box p.47) on the upper storey, but was the headquarters of the guild of bakers. A Moorish and a Native American prisoner, symbolic trophies of war, flank the bust of Charles while balanced on the balustrade up above are allegorical statues of Energy, Fire, Water, Wind, Wheat and Prudence, presumably meant to represent the elements necessary for baking the ideal loaf. The guildhouse now holds the most famous of the square's bars, *Le Roy d'Espagne*, a surreal though somewhat dingy affair with animal bladders and marionettes hanging from the ceiling – and repro pikes and halberds in the toilets.

At nos. 2–3, the **Maison de la Brouette** was the tallow-makers' guildhouse, but it takes its name from the wheelbarrows etched into the cartouches. The figure at the top is St Gilles, the guild's patron saint. Next door, the three lower storeys of the **Maison du Sac**, at no. 4, escaped the French bombardment of 1695, but they are really rather unremarkable, unlike the upper storeys whose pilasters and caryatids resemble the ornate legs of Baroque furniture, an appropriate design given that this was the guildhouse of the carpenters and coopers.

The **Maison de la Louve**, at no. 5, also survived the French artillery, and was originally home to the influential archers' guild. The pilastered facade is studded with sanctimonious representations of concepts such as Peace and Discord, and the medallions just beneath the pediment carry the likenesses of four Roman emperors set above allegorical motifs indicating their particular attributes. Thus, Trajan is above the Sun, a symbol of Truth; Tiberius with a net and cage for Falsehood; Augustus and the globe of Peace; and Julius Caesar with a bleeding heart for Disunity. Above the door, there's a charming bas-relief of the Roman she-wolf suckling Romulus and Remus, while the pediment holds a relief of Apollo firing at a python; right on top, the Phoenix rises from the ashes.

The **Maison du Cornet**, at no. 6, headquarters of the boatmen's guild, is a fanciful creation of 1697 sporting a top storey resembling the stern of a ship. Charles II makes another appearance here – it's his head in the medallion, flanked by representations of the four winds and a pair of sailors.

The house of the haberdashers' guild, the **Maison du Renard**, at no. 7, displays animated cherubs in bas-relief playing at haberdashery on the ground floor, while a scrawny, gilded fox – after which the house is named – squats above the door. Up on the second storey a statue of Justice proclaims the guild's honest intentions and is flanked by statues symbolizing the four continents, suggesting the guild's designs on world markets – an aim to which St Nicolas, patron saint of merchants, glinting above, clearly gives his blessing.

The south side of the Grand-Place: Nos. 8–10

On the south side of the square, beside the Hôtel de Ville, the arcaded **Maison de l'Etoile** (no.8) is a nineteenth-century rebuilding of the medieval home of the city magistrate. In the arcaded gallery, the exploits of one **Everard 't Serclaes** are commemorated: in 1356 the Francophile Count of Flanders attempted to seize power from the Duke of Brabant, occupying the magistrate's house and flying his standard from the roof. 'T Serclaes scaled the building, replaced Flanders' standard with that of the Duke of Brabant, and went on to recapture the city for the Brabantines, events represented in bas-relief above a reclining statue of 't Serclaes. His effigy is polished smooth from the long-standing superstition that good luck will come to those who stroke it – surprising really as 't Serclaes was ultimately hacked to death by the count's mates in 1388.

Next door, the mansion that takes its name from the ostentatious swan on the facade, the **Maison du Cygne**, at no. 9, once housed a bar where Karl Marx regularly met up with Engels during his exile in Belgium. It was in Brussels in February 1848 that they wrote the Communist Manifesto, only to be deported as political undesirables the following month. Appropriately enough, the Belgian Workers' Party was founded here in 1885, though nowadays the building shelters one of the city's more exclusive restaurants.

The **Maison de l'Arbre d'Or**, at no. 10, is the only house on the Grand-Place still to be owned by a guild (the brewers') – not that the equestrian figure stuck on top gives any clues: the original effigy – of one of the city's Habsburg governors – dropped off and the present statue, picturing the eighteenth-century aristocrat Charles of Lorraine, was moved here simply to fill the gap. Inside, the small and mundane **Musée de la Brasserie** (April–Nov daily 10am–5pm; Dec–March Mon–Fri 10am–5pm, Sat & Sun noon–5pm; €4; ⊚www.beerparadise.be) has various bits of brewing paraphernalia; a beer is included in the price of admission.

The east and north sides of the Grand-Place: Nos. 13–27

The seven guildhouses **(nos. 13–19)** that fill out the east side of the Grand-Place have been subsumed within one grand edifice, the **Maison des Ducs de Brabant**, named after the nineteen busts of dukes of Brabant that grace the facade's pilasters. This building, more than any other on the Grand-Place, has the flavour of the aristocracy, as distinct from the bourgeoisie, and needless to say, it was much admired by the city's Habsburg governors.

The guildhouses and private mansions **(nos. 20–39)** running along the north side of the Grand-Place are not quite as distinguished as their neighbours, though the **Maison du Pigeon** (nos. 26–27), the painters' guildhouse, is of interest as the house where Victor Hugo spent some time during his exile from France – he was expelled after the crushing of the French insurrection of 1848. The house also bears four unusual masks in the manner of the green man of Romano-Celtic folklore. The adjacent **Maison des Tailleurs** (nos. 24–25) is appealing too; the old headquarters of the tailors' guild, it is adorned by a pious bust of St Barbara, their patron saint.

Maison du Roi and the Musée de la Ville de Bruxelles

Much of the northern side of the Grand-Place is taken up by the late nineteenth-century **Maison du Roi** (King's House), a fairly faithful reconstruction of the palatial Gothic structure commissioned by Charles V in 1515. The emperor had a point to make: the Hôtel de Ville was an assertion of municipal independence and Charles wanted to emphasize imperial power by erecting his own building directly opposite. With its angular lines, spiky pinnacles and lacy stonework, the original Maison du Roi was an impressive building, but although its replacement, which was completed in the 1890s, is still fairly grand, the arcaded galleries – which were an addition – interrupt the flow of the design. Charles spared no expense in the earlier construction. When it turned out that the ground was too marshy to support the edifice, the architects began again, sinking piles deep into the ground and stretching cattle hides between them to keep the stagnant water at bay.

Despite its name, no sovereign has ever taken up residence in the Maison du Roi, though this was where the Habsburgs sometimes stayed when they visited the city. They also installed their tax men and law courts here, and used it to hold their more important prisoners – the counts of Egmont and Hoorn (see p.90) spent their last night in the Maison du Roi before being beheaded outside in the Grand-Place. The building was also used as a sort of royal changing room:

△ The Maison du Roi

the future Philip II donned his armour here before joining a joust held in the Grand-Place, and the Archdukes Albert and Isabella dressed up inside before appearing on the balcony to shoot down a symbolic target that made them honorary members of the guild of crossbowmen.

Musée de la Ville de Bruxelles

The Maison du Roi now holds the **Musée de la Ville de Bruxelles** (Tues–Sun 10am–5pm; €3), a wide-ranging if patchy collection whose best sections feature medieval fine and applied art – not that you'll glean much from the scanty (French and Flemish) labelling.

The ground floor

To the **left of the entrance**, there's a room full of **Gothic sculpture** retrieved from various city buildings. Pride of place goes to the eight prophets, complete with heavy beards and eccentric headgear, who once decorated the porch of the Hôtel de Ville. Two rooms further on you'll find a small but charming sample of eighteenth-century **glazed earthenware**, for which the city was once internationally famous. The finest work is by Philippe Mombaers (1724–54), whose workshop, on rue de Laeken, is credited with developing table decorations in the form of vegetables or animals – hence the splendid turkey, cod-fish, duck and cabbage soup tureens and casserole dishes.

The first of the rooms to the **right of the entrance** boasts superb **altarpieces** – or retables – the intricacy of which was a Brussels speciality, with the city producing hundreds of them from the end of the fourteenth century until the economic slump of the 1640s. Their manufacture was similar to a production line, with panel- and cabinet-makers, wood carvers, painters and goldsmiths (for the gilding) working on several altarpieces at any one time. The standard format was to create a series of mini-tableaux illustrating Biblical scenes, with the characters wearing medieval gear in a medieval landscape. It's the extraordinary detail that impresses most – look closely at the niche carvings on the whopping **Saluzzo altarpiece** (*The Life of the Virgin and the Infant Christ*) of 1505 and you'll spy the candle-sticks, embroidered pillowcase and carefully draped coverlet of Mary's bedroom in the *Annunciation* scene, while the adjacent Nativity panel comes complete with a set of cute little angels. Up above, in a swirling, phantasmagorical landscape (of what look like climbing toadstools) is the *Shepherds Hear the Good News*. Also in this room is **Pieter Bruegel the Elder**'s *Wedding Procession*, a good-natured scene with country folk walking to church to the accompaniment of bagpipes.

The second room to the right is devoted to four large-scale **tapestries** from the sixteenth and seventeenth centuries. The earliest of the four – from 1516 – relates the legend of Notre Dame du Sablon, the tedious tale of the transfer of a much revered statue of the Virgin from Antwerp to Brussels (see p.90), though fortunately the tapestry is much better than the story. A second tapestry, dating from 1580, tells the Arthurian legend of Tristan and Isolde, but easily the most striking is the *Solemn Funeral of the Roman Consul Decius Mus*, based on drawings by Rubens. Decius was a heroic figure who had won a decisive victory against the Samnites, thus securing Roman control of Italy in the third century BC. In this extraordinary tapestry, he is shown laid out on a chaise-longue and surrounded by classical figures of muscular men and fleshy women. Even inanimate objects join in the general mourning – with the lion head of the chaise-longue, for instance, glancing sorrowfully at the onlooker.

The upper floors

The museum's upper floors are less diverting. The **first floor** has several relatively interesting scale models of Brussels, but the small thematic sections devoted to the city's historical development, both here and on the **second floor** above, are difficult to follow, their themes – intellectual life, political life and so on – inadequately explored. Nevertheless, several of the paintings, sketches and photographs displayed on the second floor are worth a second look, notably a curiously detailed N. van der Horst (1598–1646) canvas depicting the state arrival of the Spanish Infanta, Isabella, in Brussels in 1622. Here also is a crudely painted, anonymous sixteenth-century diptych depicting – and named after – the anti-Jewish myth behind the Saint Sacrement de Miracle (the Miracle of the Sacrament, see p.75). On the second floor, too, in a separate section, is a goodly sample of the **Manneken Pis**'s (see p.54) vast wardrobe – around one hundred sickeningly saccharine costumes ranging from Mickey Mouse to a maharajah, all of them gifts from various visiting dignitaries destined for the cheeky little statue that has become the city's mascot.

Around the Grand-Place – the Musée de Costume et de la Dentelle

In the 1890s, burgomaster **Charles Buls** spearheaded a campaign to preserve the city's ancient buildings. One of his rewards was to have a street named

Tapestry manufacture and design

Tapestry manufacture in Brussels began in the middle of the fifteenth century and soon came under the control of a small clique of manufacturers who imposed a rigorous system of quality control. This was codified even more precisely in 1528, when every new tapestry made in Brussels was obliged to bear the town's trademark – two "Bs" enclosed in a red shield. Brussels' tapestries were famous for their lavish raw materials – especially gold thread – and this also served to keep control of the industry in the hands of the few. Only rarely were weavers able to accumulate enough money to buy their materials, never mind their own looms.

The first great period of Brussels tapestry-making lasted until the middle of the sixteenth century, when religious conflict overwhelmed the city and many of its Protestant-inclined weavers migrated north to rival workshops. There was a partial revival at the beginning of the seventeenth century, but later the French occupation and the shrinking of the Spanish market led to diminishing production, with the industry finally fizzling out by the end of the eighteenth century.

Tapestry production was a cross between embroidery and ordinary weaving. It consisted of interlacing a wool weft above and below the strings of a vertical linen "chain", a process similar to weaving. However, the weaver had to stop to change colour, requiring as many shuttles for the weft as he had colours, as in embroidery. The design of a tapestry was taken from a painting to which the weaver made constant reference. Standard-size tapestries took six months to make and were produced exclusively for the very wealthy, the most important of whom would often insist on the use of gold and silver thread and the employment of the most famous artists of the day for the preparatory painting. Amongst many, Pieter Paul Rubens, Jacob Jordaens and David Teniers all had tapestry commissions.

after him, and this runs south from the Grand-Place in between the Maison de l'Etoile and the Hôtel de Ville to the corner of **rue des Brasseurs** (the first on the left), scene of a bizarre incident in 1873 when the French Symbolist poet Paul Verlaine shot and wounded his fellow poet and lover Arthur Rimbaud. This rash act earned him a two-year prison sentence – and all because Rimbaud had dashed from Paris to dissuade him from joining the Spanish army.

Moving on, you soon reach **rue de la Violette**, the second turn on the left, where, at nos. 4–6, you'll find the recently revamped **Musée de Costume et de la Dentelle** (Costume and Lace Museum; Mon–Fri, except Wed, 10am–12.30pm & 1.30–5pm, Sat & Sun 2–5pm; €3). Brussels was a lace-making centre for three hundred years, but the last of its lacemakers closed down in the 1930s and what you see on sale in the city today comes mostly from the Far East. At its peak, in the late nineteenth century, the city had no fewer than ten thousand lacemakers, all of them women, and the lace they made was renowned across Europe for the intricacy of its designs. The museum's permanent collection, which is firmly focused on lace rather than costume, is arranged chronologically over three floors, beginning on the top floor with the earliest pieces. The labelling is in Dutch and French, but a detailed English booklet available free at the reception gives all the background details you could ever want and then some; the museum also runs a programme of temporary exhibitions, mostly concentrating on historical costumes and/or the evolution of fashion right up to the present.

The **permanent collection** kicks off in style with a clutch of seventeenth-century portraits of the rich and powerful decked out in all their silk trimmings. The portrait of the Spanish queen Marguerite of Austria (item 1) is especially striking, though her iron-threaded ruff must have given her thunderous neck aches, while item 11, nearby, is an intriguing portrait of an unknown Dutch woman, who has adopted the boat-shaped neckline that came into fashion during the 1660s. Subsequent sections illustrate the influence Italian lace had on the city's lacemakers, the extraordinarily elaborate lacy fashions inspired by Louis XIV's desire to keep his nobles occupied (and impoverished), and the lighter, simpler Regency style that came to dominate the scene in the eighteenth century. The last half of the collection concentrates on lace from the 1840s onwards when large and complicated pieces – primarily for shawls, crinoline gowns, overskirts and bridal gear – became increasingly popular in a variety of styles, including Duchesse, Chantilly and *point de gaze* (or point de rose).

The Manneken Pis

From the foot of rue de la Violette, **rue de l'Etuve** runs south to the **Manneken Pis**, a diminutive statue of a pissing urchin stuck high up in a shrine-like affair protected from the hoards of tourists by an iron fence. The Manneken is supposed to embody the "irreverent spirit" of the city, or at least that is reputed to have been the intention of Jérôme Duquesnoy when he cast the original bronze statue in the 1600s to replace the medieval stone fountain that stood here before. It's likely that Duquesnoy invented the Manneken Pis, whose popularity blossomed during the sombre, priest-dominated years following the Thirty Years' War, but it's possible his bronze replaced an earlier stone version of ancient provenance. There are all sorts of folkloric tales about its origins, from lost aristocratic children recovered when they were taking a pee, to peasant lads putting out dangerous fires and – least likely of the lot – boys slashing on the city's enemies from the trees and putting them to flight. As a

△ Manneken Pis

talisman, it has certainly attracted the attention of thieves, notably in 1817 when a French ex-convict swiped it before breaking it into pieces. The thief and the smashed Manneken were apprehended, the former publicly branded on the Grand-Place and sentenced to a life of forced labour, while the fragments of the latter were used to create the mould in which the present-day Manneken was cast. It's long been the custom for visiting VIPs to donate a costume, and the little chap is regularly kitted out in different tackle – often military or folkloric gear, from C&W stetsons and chaps to golfers' plus fours and Donald Duck and Mickey Mouse outfits.

Onwards from the Manneken Pis

From the Manneken Pis, it's a short walk southeast to the Jacques Brel Foundation (see p.68) and the slope that leads to the Upper Town (see Chapter 2). Alternatively, you can double back to the Grand-Place to start an exploration of the Lower Town as outlined in the next chapter.

The Lower Town

T he **Lower Town** is the commercial centre of Brussels, a sprawling, bustling quarter that's home to most of the city's best restaurants, shops and hotels. At its heart is the Grand-Place (see Chapter One) and fanning out from here is a labyrinth of narrow, cobbled lanes and alleys whose layout remains essentially medieval, their names often revealing their original purpose as markets – rue du Marché aux Fromages, for example. This medieval street pattern is interrupted by the boulevards that were inserted during the nineteenth century, giving the Lower Town the shape it maintains today: bordered to the north, south and west by the boulevards of the petit ring, and running east to the foot of the steep slope which marks the start of the Upper Town (see Chapter Three), along the line of boulevards Berlaimont, L'Impératrice and L'Empereur. These nineteenth-century boulevards were part of a drive to modernize a city which had become – even by the standards of the day – notably squalid, a refit that included the demolition of acres of slum and the covering over of the fetid River Senne. Nevertheless, they did little to disturb the jostle and jangle that gave – and still give – the Lower Town its character, with almost every street crimped by tall and angular town houses. There's nothing neat and tidy about all of this, but that's what makes Brussels so intriguing – dilapidated terraces stand next to prestigious mansions and the whole district is dotted with superb buildings: everything from beautiful Baroque **churches** through to **Art Nouveau** department stores, one of which holds the enjoyable **Centre Belge de la Bande Dessinée** (Belgian Comic Strip Centre).

Northwest of the Grand-Place

Arguably the most diverting part of the Lower Town, the jumble of narrow streets and pocket-sized squares that spreads **northwest of the Grand-Place** to **place Ste-Catherine** is crowded by the elegant, though often down-at-heel, town houses of the late nineteenth-century bourgeoisie. This is the most fashionable part of the city, in an urban chic sort of way, and there are lots of great bars plus a couple of especially fine buildings, the Victorian **Bourse** and the Baroque church of **St-Jean Baptiste au Béguinage**.

The Church of St-Nicolas

Walking northwest out of the Grand-Place along **rue au Beurre**, you soon reach one of the city's best-known confectioners, **Maison Dandoy**, at no.

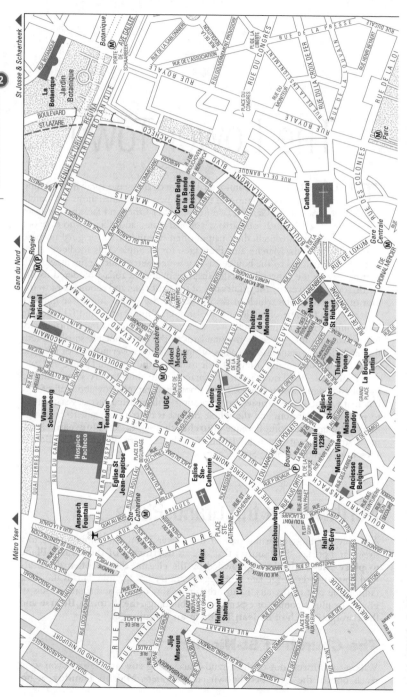

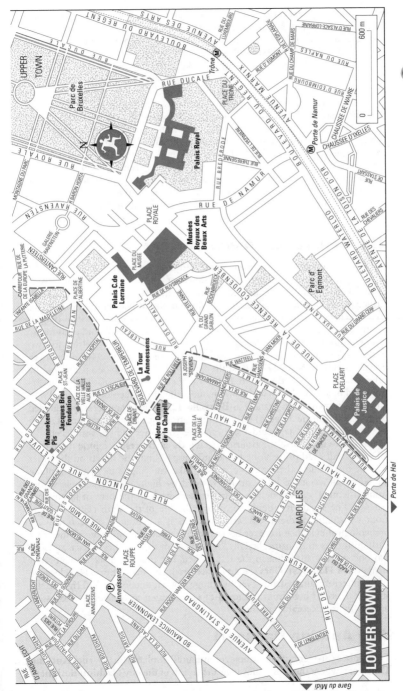

LOWER TOWN

600 m

0

31, whose tasty specialities are macaroons and "spekuloos", a sugary brown, cinnamon-flavoured biscuit that's prepared in a variety of traditional and intricate moulds. Close by, squeezed into its surroundings just across the street, is the church of **St-Nicolas** (currently closed for repairs, but normally Mon–Fri 8am–6.30pm, Sat 9am–6pm & Sun 9am–7.30pm; free), dedicated to St Nicholas of Bari, the patron saint of sailors, or, as he's better known, Santa Claus. The church dates from the twelfth century, but has been heavily restored on several occasions, most recently in the 1950s, when parts of the outer shell were reconstructed in a plain Gothic style. The church is unusual in so far as the three aisles of the nave were built at an angle to the chancel, in order to avoid a stream. It also carries a memento of the French bombardment of 1695 in the cannon ball embedded high up in the third pillar on the left of the nave. Otherwise, the gloomy interior hardly sets the pulse racing, although – among a scattering of objets d'art – there's a handsome, gilded copper reliquary shrine near the entrance. The shrine was made in Germany in the nineteenth century to honour a group of Catholics martyred by Protestants in Gorinchem in the Netherlands in 1572.

The Bourse and place St-Géry

Opposite St-Nicolas rises the grandiose **Bourse**, formerly the home of the city's stock exchange, a Neoclassical edifice of 1873 caked with garlands of fruit, fronds, languishing nudes and frolicking putti. This breezily self-confident structure sports a host of allegorical figures (Industry, Navigation, Asia, Africa, etc) which both reflect the preoccupations of the nineteenth-century Belgian bourgeoisie and, in their easy self-satisfaction, imply that wealth and pleasure are synonymous. The Bourse is flanked by sterling town houses, the setting for two of the city's more famous cafés, the Art Nouveau *Falstaff* (see p.194), on the south side at rue Henri Maus 17–23, and the fin-de-siècle *Le Cirio* (see p.202) on the other side at rue de la Bourse 18. In front of *Le Cirio* are the glassed-in foundations of a medieval church and convent, unearthed by archeologists in the 1980s and now known rather grandly as **Bruxella 1238**. There are occasional guided tours of the site (in English; €3), but they are only of specialist interest – the Maison du Roi on the Grand-Place can give you times and sell you tickets.

The square in front of the Bourse – **place de la Bourse** – is little more than a heavily trafficked pause along boulevard Anspach, but the streets on the other side of the boulevard have more appeal. Take rue Jules van Praet for **place St-Géry**, an attractive little square crowded by high-sided tenements whose stone balconies and wrought-iron grilles hark back to the days of bustles and parasols. The square is thought to occupy the site of the sixth-century chapel from which the medieval city grew, but this is a matter of conjecture – no archeological evidence has ever been unearthed and the only clue to the city's early history is in its name, literally "settlement in the marshes". Place St-Géry has one specific attraction in the refurbished, late nineteenth-century covered market, the **Halles St-Géry**, an airy glass, brick and iron edifice. The elegance of the interior is marred, however, by a huge stone fountain plonked right in the middle – moved here from the town of Grimbergen to the north of Brussels, apparently for decorative reasons.

Rue Antoine Dansaert

From place St-Géry, it's a couple of minutes' stroll north to **rue Antoine Dansaert**, where the most innovative and stylish of the city's **fashion designers** have set up shop amongst the careworn old houses that stretch up towards place du Nouveau Marché aux Grains. Amongst several outstanding boutiques on this street, two of the best are the ultra-chic Oliver Strelli, at no. 46, and Stijl, at no. 74, which showcases a bevy of big-name designers. There's also strikingly original furniture at Max, whose two shops face each other at nos. 90 and 103.

Place du Nouveau Marché aux Grains is a pleasant, open square lined with trees and decorated with a suitably pensive statue of **Jean-Baptiste van Helmont** (1578–1644), a Brussels-born physician and chemist who coined the word "gas" to explain the results of some of his experiments. Moving on from the square, there's a choice of routes: you can either double back to place Ste-Catherine (see below) or push on to the Jijé Museum.

The Jijé Museum

From place du Nouveau Marché aux Grains, it's another short hop to the **Musée Bande Dessinée Jijé**, at rue du Houblon 43 (Tues–Sun 10am–6pm; €6), the newer of the city's two comic strip museums. Unlike its sister museum, which attempts to chronicle the Belgian contribution to the comic strip (see p.65), this concentrates on the work of one artist, **Jijé**, the pen name of the prolific and influential Joseph Gillain (1914–80). Gillain specialized in tales of derring do, of cowboys and fighter pilots, Vikings and knights along with witty biographies and even adaptations of novels, and there are scores of examples of his work, all well presented and displayed. Comic-strip aficionados love the stuff, but to the untrained eye, Gillain's stagey realism has little of the instant appeal of, say, Tintin and if you don't read French most of the humour will pass you by. The permanent collection is supplemented by a lively programme of temporary exhibitions featuring the work of comic strip artists from around the world.

Place Ste-Catherine

Doubling back to rue Antoine Dansaert from the Jijé Museum, turn along rue du Vieux Marché aux Grains to reach **place Ste-Catherine**, which is,

△ Place Ste-Catherine

despite its dishevelled appearance, at the heart of one of the city's most fashionable districts, not least because of its excellent seafood restaurants. Presiding over the square is the **church of Ste-Catherine** (Mon–Sat 8.30am–5.30pm, Sun 8.30am–noon; free), a battered nineteenth-century replacement for the Baroque original, of which the creamy, curvy belfry beside the west end of the church is the solitary survivor. Venture inside Ste-Catherine and you'll spy – behind the glass screen that closes off most of the nave – a fourteenth-century Black Madonna and Child, a sensually carved stone statuette that was chucked into the Senne by Protestants, but landed rather fortuitously on a clod of peat and was fished out.

Quai aux Briques and the parallel **quai aux Bois à Brûler** extend northwest from place Ste-Catherine on either side of a wide and open area that was – until it was filled in – the most central part of the city's main **dock**. Strolling along this open area, you'll pass a motley assortment of nineteenth-century warehouses, shops, restaurants and bars which maintain an appealing canalside feel – an impression heightened in the early morning when the streets are choked with lorries bearing trays of fish for local restaurants. At the end of the old quays, the fanciful **water fountain**, with its lizards and dolphins, honours Burgomaster Anspach, a driving force in the move to modernize the city during the 1880s.

St-Jean Baptiste au Béguinage

Lying just to the east of quai aux Bois à Brûler, **place du Béguinage** is a good-looking piazza dominated by **St-Jean Baptiste au Béguinage** (normally Tues–Sat 10am–5pm, Sun 10am–8pm, but currently closed by fire damage; free), a supple, billowing structure dating from the second half of the seventeenth century. This beautiful church is the only building left from the Béguine convent founded here in the thirteenth century. The convent once crowded in on the church, and only since its demolition – and the creation of the star-shaped place du Béguinage in 1855 – has it been possible to view the exterior with any degree of ease. There's a sense of movement in each and every feature, a dynamism of design culminating in three matching gables where the upper portion of the central tower is decorated with pinnacles that echo those of the Hôtel de Ville. The church's light and spacious interior is lavishly decorated, the white stone columns and arches dripping with solemn-faced cherubs intent on reminding the congregation of their mortality. The nave and aisles are wide and open, offering unobstructed views of the high altar, but you can't fail to notice the enormous wooden **pulpit** featuring St Dominic preaching against heresy – and trampling a heretic under foot for good measure.

Hospice Pacheco

Around the back of the church, a short street (rue de l'Infirmerie) takes you through to a slender, tree-lined square framed by the austere Neoclassicism of the **Hospice Pacheco** (no access), built to house the destitute in the 1820s. It's a peaceful spot today, but the stern wall that surrounds the complex is a reminder of times when the hospice was more like a prison than a shelter, and draconian rules were imposed with brutal severity. The River Senne once flowed beside the hospice, but by the nineteenth century it had become intolerably polluted – to quote the Brussels writer Camille Lemonnier, "the dumping ground, not only of industry, but also of the houses lining the river: it was not unusual to see the ballooned stomach of a dog mixed pell mell with its own litter..." After an outbreak of cholera in 1866, which killed over 3500 city folk, the river was piped underground and paved over.

From the Hospice Pacheco, it's a five- to ten-minute walk east to the place des Martyrs (see p.65), north of the Grand-Place.

North of the Grand-Place

The busy streets between the Grand-Place and the Gare du Nord are not especially enticing, though **rue des Bouchers** does heave with restaurants and **rue Neuve** possesses many of the city's biggest shops and department stores. The prime architectural sight hereabouts is the **place des Martyrs**, a handsome square built by the Austrian Habsburgs in their pomp, whilst the most interesting attraction is the **Centre Belge de la Bande Dessinée** – the Belgian Comic Strip Centre. Belgian artists and writers produce the best comics in the world – or so they would argue – and the centre samples a vast range of their work, including the most famous comic strip character of the lot, **Tintin**, who first appeared as long ago as 1929.

△ Rue des Bouchers

Rue des Bouchers and the Galeries St-Hubert

Take rue des Harengs north from the Grand-Place and at the end, across the street, you'll see the (signed) ancient alley that leads through to the **Théâtre Royal de Toone**, at Impasse Schuddeveld 6, which puts on puppet plays in the bruxellois dialect known as Brusselse Sproek or Marollien. It's very much a city institution and there are regular performances from Tuesday to Saturday (see p.233) – as well as an excellent bar (see p.199). Another little alley leads west out of the Toone theatre into pedestrianized **petite rue des Bouchers**, which, along with **rue des Bouchers**, is the city centre's restaurant ghetto, its narrow cobblestoned lanes transformed at night into fairy-lit tunnels where several dozen restaurants vie for custom with elaborate displays of dull-eyed fish and glistening mollusks. The bad news is that these same restaurants have a reputation for charging over the odds.

Footsteps away are the **Galeries St-Hubert**, whose trio of glass-vaulted galleries – du Roi, de la Reine and the smaller des Princes – cut across rue des Bouchers. Opened by Léopold I in 1847, the galleries were one of Europe's first shopping arcades, and the pastel-painted walls, classical columns and cameo sculptures still retain an air of genteel sophistication – with the deluxe shops to match.

Théâtre de la Monnaie and the Hôtel Métropole

Emerging at the north end of the Galerie du Roi, you've a brief walk down rue de l'Ecuyer to **place de la Monnaie**, the drab and dreary modern square that's overshadowed by the huge **centre Monnaie**, housing offices, shops and the main post office. The only building of interest here is the **Théâtre de la Monnaie** (for tickets and performance information, see p.213), Brussels' opera house, a Neoclassical

△ Théâtre de la Monnaie

structure built in 1819 and with an interior added in 1856 to a design by Poelaert, the architect of the Palais de Justice (see p.93). The theatre's real claim to fame, however, is as the starting-point of the revolution against the Dutch in 1830: a nationalistic libretto in Auber's *The Mute Girl of Portici* sent the audience wild, and they poured out into the streets to raise the flag of Brabant, signalling the start of the rebellion. The opera told the tale of an Italian uprising against the Spanish, and with such lines as "To my country I owe my life, To me it will owe its liberty" one of the Dutch censors – of whom there were many – should really have seen what was coming, as a furious King William I pointed out.

On the far side of the centre Monnaie is traffic-clogged boulevard Anspach, which forks and widens at **place de Brouckère**, a busy junction that accommodates the **Hôtel Métropole** (see p.180), whose splendidly ornate lobby and bar date from 1895 and were once the haunt of the likes of Sarah Bernhardt and Isadora Duncan.

Rue Neuve and place des Martyrs

From place de la Monnaie, **rue Neuve** forges north, a workaday pedestrianized shopping street that's home to a string of big chain shops – Zara, H&M, Hema and so forth. About halfway up, turn east along rue St-Michel for the **place des Martyrs**, a cool, rational square superimposed on the city by the Habsburgs in the 1770s. Long neglected, the square is very much the worse for wear – work has at last started on a thoroughgoing refurbishment – but there's still no mistaking the architectural elegance of the ensemble, completed in the last years of Austrian control. The square's imposing centrepiece was added later. It comprises a stone plinth rising from an arcaded gallery inscribed with the names of those 445 insurrectionists who died in the Belgian revolution of 1830 and is surmounted by a female representation of Belgium, the Motherland.

Centre Belge de la Bande Dessinée (Belgian Comic Strip Centre)

Heading east from the place des Martyrs, it takes about five minutes to walk to the city's only surviving Horta-designed department store, the **Grand Magasin Waucquez**, situated amongst run-down offices and warehouses at rue des Sables 20. Recently restored after lying empty for thirty years, it's a wonderfully airy, summery construction, with light flooding through the glass and stained glass that encloses the expansive entrance hall. Completed in 1906, it was built for a textile tycoon, and exhibits all the classic features of Horta's work (see p.98) – from the soft lines of the ornamentation to the metal grilles, exposed girders and balustrades.

Around the entrance hall is a bookshop, a small display on the building's history, a reference library (Tues–Thurs noon–5pm, Fri noon–6pm, Sat 10am–6pm; free), and a café, the *Brasserie Horta*. From the hall, a flight of stairs leads up to the "museum" itself, the **Centre Belge de la Bande Dessinée** (Tues–Sun 10am–6pm; €6.20), whose displays are extensive and diverting. The labelling is almost exclusively in French and Dutch, but a free and very thorough English guidebook is available at the reception.

The Centre's Museum of the Imagination

The exhibits begin with a modest section outlining the processes involved in drawing comic strips and another on cartoon animation. There's also a small auditorium showing cartoons and documentaries about the comic strip, but you really get down to business on the next floor up with the grandly titled "**Museum of the Imagination**", which traces the development of the Belgian comic strip from its beginnings in the 1920s up until 1960 with examples of the work of all the leading practitioners. First up – appropriately enough, given his perennial popularity – is **Tintin**, the creation of Brussels-born **Georges Remi**, aka Hergé (1907–83). Remi's first efforts (non-Tintin) had been sponsored by a right-wing Catholic journal, *Le XXème Siècle*, and in 1929 when this same paper produced a kids' supplement – *Le Petit Vingtième* – Remi was given his first major break. Remi was asked to produce a two-page comic strip and the result was *Tintin in the Land of the Soviets*, a didactic tale about the evils of Bolshevism. Tintin's Soviet adventure lasted until May 1930, and to round it all off the director of *Le XXème Siècle* decided to stage a PR-stunt reception to celebrate Tintin's return. Remi – along with a Tintin lookalike – hopped on a train just east of Brussels and when they pulled into the capital they were mobbed by scores of excited children. Remi and Tintin never looked back. Remi decided on the famous quiff straight away, but other features – the mouth and expressive eyebrows – only came later. His popularity was – and remains – quite phenomenal: *Tintin* has been translated into sixty languages and over twenty million copies of the comic *Le Journal de Tintin*, Remi's own independent creation first published in 1946, have been sold.

Beyond the Tintin section appears the work of Remi's leading contemporaries and successors with each artist given his own section, however small. To fully appreciate what you see, it does help if you already know something about comic strips and have a working knowledge of French; cartoonists to look out for include the versatile **Jijé** (who has his own museum, see p.61) and **Edgar-Pierre Jacobs**, whose theatrical compositions and fluent combination of genres – science fiction, fantasy and crime – are displayed in his *Blake and Mortimer*. As with several others, Jacobs became popular after his work appeared in *Le Journal de Tintin*, while Belgium's oldest comic-strip paper, the *Le Journal de Spiro*, performed a similar service for the likes of **André Franquin**, the creator of the feckless anti-hero *Gaston Lagaffe*. Sadly, *Spiro* was also where *The Smurfs* first saw light of day, the creation of Peyo, in 1958.

On the top floor, the **Museum of Modern Comic Strips** looks at new trends and themes. The comic strip has long ceased to be primarily aimed at children, and now focuses on the adult (sometimes very adult) market. A series of regularly rotated displays ably illustrates some of the best of this new work and there's also a programme of temporary exhibitions. If all this leaves you with a taste for more, you can check out the city's excellent **comic shops**, detailed on p.217 in "Shopping".

Le Botanique

Heading north from the Centre Belge de la Bande Dessinée along **rue du Marais**, you'll soon hit the petit ring near the burgeoning skyscrapers of **place Rogier**, from where huge office blocks continue up rue du Progrès to the **Gare du Nord**. This is all predictable stuff – and predictably overpowering – but don't despair: on the north side of the boulevard, on **rue Gineste**, you can escape the concrete and glass, if not the rumble of the traffic, by walking into the **Jardin Botanique** (May–Sept daily 8am–8pm, Oct–April daily 8am–5pm; free), an attractive park whose woods, lawns and borders are decorated by statues and a tiny lake. The park meanders up to the carefully manicured formal gardens that front **Le Botanique**, an appealingly grandiose greenhouse dating from 1826. The building once housed the city's tropical gardens, but these were moved out long ago and the place has been turned into a Francophone cultural centre. Incidentally, although the gardens are a pleasant spot, dodgy characters haunt its precincts in the evening.

From Le Botanique, it's a short walk along rue Royale either south to the Colonne du Congrès (see p.89) or north into the St Josse neighbourhood (see below).

St Josse and Schaerbeek's Maison Autrique

Immediately to the north of Le Botanique, beyond the petit ring (and technically the limits of the Lower Town), lies **St Josse**, a largely residential district noted for its inexpensive Turkish restaurants, mostly dotted along chaussée de Haecht. The one architectural attraction hereabouts is the vast, domed **Eglise de Ste-Marie**, a real nineteenth-century whopper, standing tall at the head of rue Royale, its clumping cupola rising high above its heavy-duty buttresses.

The chaussée de Haecht cuts through St Josse bound for the next suburb to the north, **Schaerbeek** (Schaarbeek in Flemish), where, in 1893, Victor Horta (see p.98) undertook one of his earliest commissions, the **Maison Autrique**, at chaussée de Haecht 266 (Wed–Sun noon–6pm; €5; ⓦwww .autriche.be). Faced with a ponderous old mansion, Horta redesigned the exterior in bold style, using contrasting types of stone which he etched with a swirling filigree of decoration before rounding it all off with a top-floor beamed gallery with curved stone lintels. By comparison, the interior modifications were – at least by the standard of some of his later confections – really rather modest, being largely confined to the creation of a mosaic floor in the foyer, the insertion of ornately decorated stained-glass skylights into the stairway landings and the amalgamation of the two main ground-floor rooms into one, complete with an exposed girder, one of Horta's favourite design features.

It's a fun place to explore, especially as space has been given over to the unexpected bits and pieces discovered when the house was restored in the 1990s. These relate to two of the house's more eccentric occupants. One was an obscure French painter by the name of Augustin Desombre (1869–1912), a tormented soul who walled himself up here and left behind a small collection of paintings and a crude and very large early camera. The other was an inventor named Axel Wappendorf, who retreated to the attic to invent away surrounded by all sorts of clobber – the museum has kitted out the attic in an appropriately cluttered style.

To get to the Maison Autrique, take **tram** #92 or #93 and get off beyond avenue Rogier, a five-minute journey from Le Botanique.

South of the Grand-Place

Few tourists venture into the old working-class districts **south of the Grand-Place**, either into the increasingly gentrified **Quartier Marolles**, to either side of rue Blaes, or further south to the impoverished area around the **Gare du Midi**. There are, however, a couple of interesting attractions on the northern periphery of the Quartier Marolles – the beautiful church of **Notre-Dame de la Chapelle** and the **Fondation internationale Jacques Brel**, celebrating the country's leading balladeer. Furthermore, the Marolles holds several atmospheric bars and restaurants and has an excellent **market**.

The Fondation internationale Jacques Brel

Strolling south from the Grand-Place along rue de l'Etuve, turn left up rue du Lombard and you'll soon reach **place St-Jean**, where the memorial in the middle of the square commemorates the remarkable **Gabrielle Petit**. Equipped with a formidable – some say photographic – memory, Petit played a leading role in the Belgian Resistance movement during the German occupation of World War I. Caught, she refused to appeal, even though as a woman her sentence would almost certainly have been commuted. Instead, she declared that she would show the Germans how a Belgian woman could die. And that is precisely what she did: the Germans shot her by firing squad in 1916.

Just to the south of the square, the good-looking place de la Vieille-Halle aux Blés is home to the **Fondation internationale Jacques Brel** (Tues–Sun 10.30am–5pm; €5; ⊛www.jacquesbrel.be), a small but inventive museum celebrating the life and times of the Belgian singer Jacques Brel (1933–78). Brel became famous in the 1960s as a singer of mournful *chansons* about death and love and he still reaches into the very depths of many a French-speaking soul. The museum begins by showing a rare, televised interview with Brel, a full thirty-minute conversation in French, of course, and with Dutch subtitles. Beyond, a small cinema features an hour-long recording of one of his later concerts in all its emotional intensity.

From the Fondation, it's a short walk south to **boulevard de l'Empereur**, a busy carriageway that chews up this part of the centre. Across the boulevard, you'll spy the crumbling brickwork of **La Tour Anneessens**, a chunky remnant of the medieval city wall, while to the south looms the Baroque pepper pot spire of Notre-Dame de la Chapelle.

Notre-Dame de la Chapelle

The city's oldest church, founded in 1134, **Notre-Dame de la Chapelle** (June–Sept Mon–Sat 9am–5pm & Sun 8am–7.30pm; Oct–May daily 12.30–4.30pm; free) is a sprawling, broadly Gothic structure that boasts an attractive if somewhat incongruous Baroque bell tower, added after the French artillery bombardment of 1695 had damaged the original. Inside, heavyweight columns with curly-kale capitals support the well-proportioned **nave**, whose central aisle is bathed in light from the soaring clerestory windows. Amongst the church's assorted bric-à-brac, the **pulpit** is the most arresting, an extraordinarily flashy affair consisting of an intricately carved hunk of timber showing Eli in the desert beneath the palm trees. The prophet looks mightily fed up, but then he hasn't quite realized that there's an angel beside him with manna (bread). Also of interest is the statue of **Our Lady of Solitude**, in the second chapel of the nave's north side-aisle – to the left of the entrance. The Flemings were accustomed to religious statues whose clothing formed part of the original carving. It was the Spaniards who first dressed their statues in finery – and this is a much-revered example, gifted to the church by the Spanish Infanta in the 1570s. The church's main claim to fame, however, is the **memorial plaque to Pieter Bruegel the Elder**. It was made by his son Jan and is located high up on the wall on the right-hand side of the south side-aisle's fourth chapel; the other plaque and bronze effigy in the chapel were added in the 1930s. Pieter

△ Notre-Dame de la Chapelle

is supposed to have lived and died just down the street from the church at **rue Haute 132**.

After visiting Notre-Dame de la Chapelle, the obvious route is to press on into the Quartier Marolles – alternatively, you could backtrack north to rue de Rollebeek, a pleasant pedestrianized lane dotted with cafés and restaurants that clambers up to the place du Grand Sablon (see p.92) in the Upper Town.

The Quartier Marolles

South of Notre-Dame de la Chapelle, **rue Blaes**, together with the less appealing **rue Haute**, form the double spine of the **Quartier Marolles**, stacked on the slopes below the Palais de Justice (see p.93). This old working-class district is the linguistic heartland of **Brusselse Sproek** or Marollien, a traditional dialect based on Flemish, which has, over the centuries, been influenced by the languages of the city's overlords. Relatively few people speak it today, indeed there is a danger it will die out altogether, which is a pity as it's a colourful, ribald dialect. If you want to have a go yourself, you could make a start with *dikenek*, "big mouth"; *schieve lavabo*, "idiot" (literally "a twisted toilet"); or *fieu,* "son of a bitch".

The Quartier Marolles grew up in the seventeenth century as a centre for artisans working on the mansions of the nearby neighbourhood of Sablon. Industrialized in the eighteenth century, Marolles remained a thriving working-class district until the 1870s, when the paving-over of the Senne led to the riverside factories closing down and moving out to the suburbs. The workers and their families followed, initiating a long process of decline, which turned the district into an impoverished slum. Things finally started to change in the late 1980s, when outsiders began to snaffle up property here, and although the quartier still has its rougher moments, rue Blaes – or at least that part of it from Notre-Dame de la Chapelle to place du Jeu de Balle – is now lined with antique and interior-design shops. It's a good location as **place du Jeu de Balle**, the square at the heart of Marolles, has long been home to the city's best **flea market** (daily 7am–2pm). The market is at its most hectic on Sunday mornings, when the square and its immediate surroundings are swamped by pile after pile of rusty junk alongside muddles of eccentric bric-à-brac – everything from a chipped buddha, a rococo angel or African idol, to horn-rimmed glasses, a top hat or a stuffed bear.

If you've ventured as far south as the place du Jeu de Balle, then the Gare du Midi area (see below) is within easy walking distance – another ten minutes or so to the west. Much better, you're also within comfortable striking distance of the Porte de Hal and St Gilles, a five- to ten-minute walk south (see p.95).

Gare du Midi

Just outside the petit ring, the **Gare du Midi** is now the city's busiest train station, the terminus of most international services including those operated by Eurostar from the UK. The station has already been expanded and modernized on several occasions, but work continues with the construction of more platforms and facilities. The area around the station, however, is a severely depressed and at times seedy quarter with an uneasy undertow by day and sometimes overtly threatening feel at night. The only good time to visit the district is on a **Sunday morning**, when a vibrant souk-like **market** (see p.221) is held under the station's rail arches and along boulevard du Midi.

The Upper Town

From the heights of the **Upper Town**, the Francophile ruling class long kept a beady eye on the proletarians down below, and it was here they built their palaces and mansions, churches and parks. Political power is no longer concentrated hereabouts, but the wide avenues and grand architecture of this aristocratic quarter – the bulk of which dates from the late eighteenth and nineteenth centuries – have survived largely intact, lending a stately, dignified feel that's markedly different from the cramped bustle of the Lower Town below.

The Lower Town ends and the Upper Town begins at the foot of the sharp **slope** which runs north to south from one end of the city centre to the other, its course marked – in general terms at least – by a traffic-choked **boulevard** that's variously named Berlaimont, L'Impératrice and L'Empereur. This slope is home to the city's **cathedral**, a splendid Gothic edifice that's recently been restored, but otherwise is little more than an obstacle to be climbed by a series of stairways. Among these the most frequently used are the covered walkway running through the **Galerie Ravenstein** shopping arcade behind the Gare Centrale, and the open-air stairway that climbs up through the stolid, modern buildings of the **Mont des Arts**, a steep slope named by Léopold II in anticipation of a fine art museum he intended to build there; the project was never completed, and the land was only properly built upon in the 1950s.

Above the rigorous layout of the Mont des Arts lie the **rue Royale** and **rue de la Régence**, which together form the Upper Town's spine, a suitably smart location for the outstanding **Musées Royaux des Beaux Arts**, argu-ably the best of Belgium's many fine art collections, as well as the surpris-ingly low-key **Palais Royal**. Here, also, are the entertaining **Musée des Instruments de Musique (MIM)** and the enjoyable salons of the **Palais de Charles de Lorraine**. Further south, rue de la Régence clips through the well-heeled **Sablon district**, whose antique shops and chic bars and cafés fan out from the medieval church of **Notre-Dame du Sablon**. Beyond this is the monstrous **Palais de Justice**, traditionally one of the city's most disliked buildings.

The Cathedral

It only takes a couple of minutes to walk from the Grand-Place to the east end of rue de la Montagne, where a short slope climbs up to the **Cathedral**

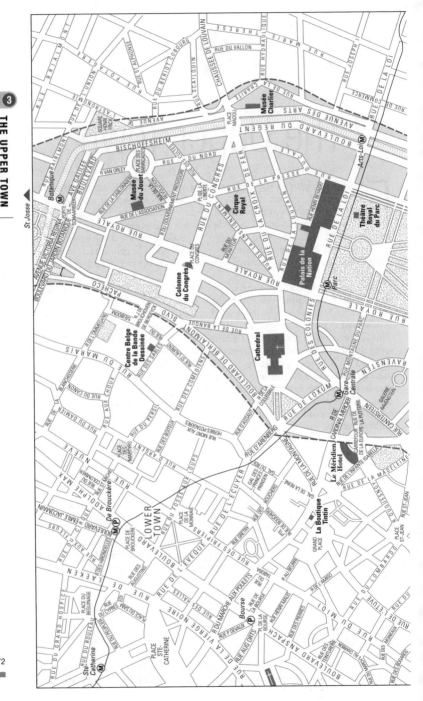

St Josse

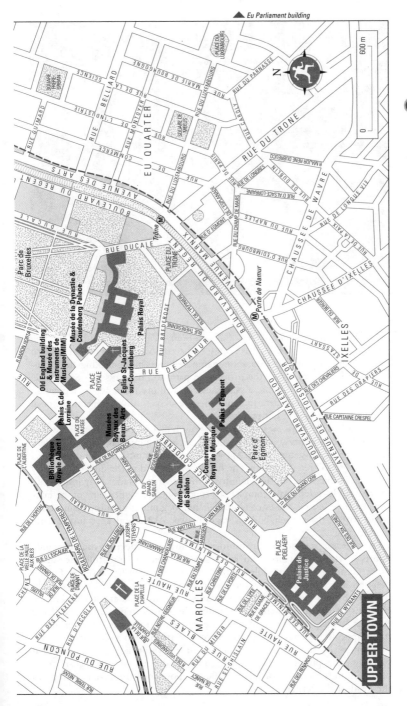

▲ Eu Parliament building

UPPER TOWN

△ The Cathedral

(Mon–Fri 8am–6pm, Sat & Sun 8.30am–6pm; free), a fine Gothic building whose commanding position has been sorely compromised by a rash of modern office blocks. Begun in 1215, and three hundred years in the making, the cathedral is dedicated jointly to the patron and patroness of Brussels – St Michael the Archangel, and St Gudule, a vague, seventh-century figure whose reputation was based on her gentle determination: despite all sorts of shenanigans, the devil could never put her off her prayers.

The cathedral sports a striking twin-towered, whitestone **facade**, whose central double doorway and twin side-doors are trimmed by fanciful tracery and adorned with statues of the Apostles, angels and saints and – on the central column – the Three Wise Men. The facade was erected in the fifteenth century in High Gothic style, but the intensity of the decoration fades away inside with the airy triple-aisled **nave**, completed a century before. Other parts of the interior illustrate several phases of Gothic design, beginning with the chancel, the oldest part of the church, built in stages between 1215 and 1280 in the Early Gothic style.

The interior is short on furnishings and fittings, reflecting the combined efforts of the Protestants, who ransacked the church (and stole the shrine of St Gudule) in the middle of the seventeenth century, and the French Republican Army, who wrecked the place a century later. Unfortunately, neither of them dismantled the ponderous sculptures that are attached to the columns of the nave – clumsy seventeenth-century representations of the Apostles, which only serve to dent the nave's soaring lines. Another, much more appealing survivor is the massive oak **pulpit**, an extravagant chunk of frippery by the Antwerp sculptor Hendrik Verbruggen. Among several vignettes, the pulpit features Adam and Eve, dressed in rustic gear, being chased from the Garden of Eden, while up above the Virgin Mary stamps on the head of the serpent.

The stained-glass windows

The cathedral also boasts some superb sixteenth-century **stained-glass windows**, starting above the main double doors with the hurly burly of the *Last Judgment*. Look closely and you'll spy the donor in the lower foreground with an angel on one side and a woman with long blonde hair (symbolizing Faith) on the other. Each of the main colours has a symbolic meaning with green representing hope, yellow eternal glory and blue heaven.

There's more remarkable work in the **transepts**, where the stained glass is distinguished by the extraordinary clarity of the blue backgrounds. These windows are eulogies to the Habsburgs – in the south transept, Charles V kneels alongside his wife beneath a vast triumphal arch as their patron saints present them to God the Father, and in the north transept Charles V's sister, Marie, and her husband, King Louis of Hungary, play out a similar scenario. Both windows were designed by Bernard van Orley (1490–1541), long-time favourite of the royal family and the leading Brussels artist of his day.

Chapelle du Saint Sacrement de Miracle

Just beyond the north transept, flanking the choir, the cathedral treasury (see below) is displayed in the Flamboyant Gothic **Chapelle du Saint Sacrement de Miracle**, named after a shameful anti-Semitic legend whose key components were repeated again and again across medieval Christendom. Dating back to the 1360s, this particular version begins with a Jew from a small Flemish town stealing the consecrated Host from his local church. Shortly afterwards, he is murdered in a brawl and his wife moves to Brussels, taking the Host with her. The woman then presents the Host at the synagogue on Good Friday and her fellow Jews stab it with daggers, whereupon it starts to bleed. Terrified, the Jews disperse and the woman tries to save her soul by giving the Host to the city's cathedral – hence this chapel, which was built to display the retrieved Host in the 1530s. The four **stained-glass windows** of the chapel retell the tale, a strip cartoon that unfolds above representations of the aristocrats who paid for the windows. The workmanship is delightful – based on designs by van Orley and his one-time apprentice Michiel van Coxie (1499–1592) – but the effects of this unsavoury legend on the congregation are not hard to imagine.

Le trésor (treasury)

Inside the Chapelle du Saint Sacrement de Miracle, the cathedral **treasury** (Mon–Fri 10am–12.30pm & 2–5pm, Sat 10.30am–12.30pm & 2–3.30pm, Sun 2–5pm; €1) is smartly turned out, but the exhibits themselves are, for the most part, a fairly plodding assortment of monstrances and reliquaries. The main exception is a splendid Anglo-Saxon reliquary of the **True Cross** (item 5), recently winkled out of the ornate, seventeenth-century gilded silver reliquary Cross (item 4) that was made to hold it. There's also a flowing altar painting, *The Legend of Ste Gudule*, by Michiel van Coxie (item 3), who spent much of his long life churning out religious paintings in the High Renaissance style he picked up when he visited Italy early in his career. Behind the chapel's high altar, look out also for the more-than-usually ghoulish **skull** of St Elizabeth of Hungary (1207–31). In her short life, this Hungarian princess managed to squeeze in just about everything you need to get canonized. She was a faithful wife (whose husband died on a Crusade), a devoted mother, and a loyal servant of the church, renouncing the world to become a nun and devote herself to the care of the poor and sick.

Chapelle de Notre-Dame de la Délivrance and the crypt

Opposite the treasury, next to the south transept, the **Chapelle de Notre-Dame de la Délivrance** dates from the middle of the seventeenth century, its stained-glass windows depicting scenes from the life of the Virgin on the upper level with the donors posing down below. The windows were designed by Théodore van Thulden, one of Rubens' pupils, and commissioned by the Infanta Isabella in 1649 – perhaps as spiritual compensation for the drubbing the Habsburgs had recently received from the Dutch, who had secured their independence from Spain the year before.

Back in the north side-aisle, near the double doors, a stairway leads down to the Romanesque **crypt** (on request; €2.50), which gives an inkling – but little more – as to the layout of the first church built on this site in the eleventh century.

South to the Musée des Beaux-Arts and the Musée du Cinéma

Just to the south of the cathedral, along boulevard de l'Impératrice, the carrefour de l'Europe roundabout is dominated by the curving, modern stonework of **Le Meridien Hotel** (see p.179), one of the city's more successful modern buildings. Opposite is the **Gare Centrale**, a bleak and somewhat surly Art Deco creation seemingly dug deep into the slope where Lower and Upper Town meet. Behind the station, on the far side of rue Cantersteen, the **Galerie Ravenstein** shopping arcade is traversed by a covered walkway. A classic piece of 1950s design, the arcade carries cheerfully bright decorative panels and an airy atrium equipped with a water fountain. It has, unfortunately, seen better days as witnessed by all the empty shops, but its walkway is still an agreeable way to climb up to rue Ravenstein.

The latter is home to the **Palais des Beaux Arts**, a severe, low-lying edifice designed by Victor Horta during the 1920s in complete contrast with his flamboyant earlier works (see p.98). The building holds a theatre and concert hall and hosts numerous temporary exhibitions, mostly of modern and contemporary art. Part of the complex – though it also has its own entrance a few metres up the stairway at the side – accommodates the **Musée du Cinéma** (daily except Thurs 5.30–10.30pm, Thurs 2.30–9pm; €2; @www.cinematheque.be), which has displays on the pioneering days of cinema and shows old movies most evenings. The programme changes during special festivals and events, but normally one projection room presents two silent films with piano accompaniment nightly, while the other shows three early "talkies".

From the Musée du Cinéma, you can either climb the steps up to rue Royale near the Palais Royal (see p.79), or stroll south along rue Ravenstein

△ Mont des Arts

to the top of the Mont des Arts and the Musée des Instruments de Musique (see p.78).

Place de l'Albertine and the Mont des Arts

The wide stone **stairway** that cuts up through the sombre 1940s and 1950s government buildings of the steeply sloping **Mont des Arts** also climbs the slope marking the start of the Upper Town, serving as an alternative to the Galerie Ravenstein (see above). The stairs begin on **place de l'Albertine**, which is overlooked by a large and imposing statue of **King Albert I**, depicted in military gear on his favourite horse. Easily the most popular king Belgium has ever had, Albert became a national hero for his determined resistance to the Germans in World War I and there was a genuine outpouring of popular grief when he died in a climbing accident near Namur, in southern Belgium, in 1934. Opposite him, across the square, there used to be a statue of his wife, Queen Elizabeth, but temporarily at least this has disappeared into some municipal vault or other – bad news for poor old Albert.

The stairway clambers up the hill to a wide **piazza**, equipped with water fountains, footpaths and carefully manicured shrubbery, and then it's on up again, offering splendid **views** over the Lower Town with the fanciful tower of the Hôtel de Ville soaring high above its surroundings. Beyond, at the top of the stairs, is rue Ravenstein and MIM (see below) and on the right, up a short flight of steps, is the place du Musée.

The place du Musée and Palais de Charles de Lorraine

Just off the Mont des Arts, the **place du Musée** is a handsome cobbled square edged by a crisp architectural ensemble of sober Habsburg symmetry, whose sweeping stonework dates back to the eighteenth century. The elongated facade that bends round the square was originally covered with a jungle of Neoclassical decoration – cherubs, statues, military insignia in the Roman style and trailing garlands – and although much has disappeared, enough remains to suggest its original appearance. Two sides of the square are now part of the Musées Royaux des Beaux Arts (see p.80), as is the hole in the middle, which allows light to reach the museum's subterranean floors, but on the north side are the five salons of the **Palais de Charles de Lorraine** (Tues–Fri 1–5pm & Sat 10am–5pm; €3), the surviving portion of the lavish suite of apartments designed for Charles de Lorraine, the Austrian who served as Brusssels' governor-general from 1749 to 1780. The salons reflect Charles's avowed enthusiasm for the Enlightenment: he viewed himself as the epitome of the civilized man and fully supported the reforms of his emperor, Joseph II (1741–90), though these same reforms – especially the move towards a secular society – created pandemonium amongst his fiercely Catholic Flemish and Wallonian subjects.

The palais begins in style with a statue of **Hercules**, the symbol of strength and courage, guarding a sweeping staircase. There's no false modesty here: if any of his guests bothered to look – and be sure they did – they'd see that Charles was at pains to associate himself with Hercules, whose club is inscribed with the Cross of Lorraine, the Teutonic Cross (Charles was a Grandmaster of the Teutonic Order) and the letter "C" (after his name). Neither does it end there: at the feet of Hercules is a salamander, a creature that had long been linked with alchemy, one of Charles's keenest interests. At the top of the staircase behind Hercules, the **doorway** has its own guardian, a cherub with a finger on his mouth and sitting on a sphinx – as in silence and secrets – and just beyond is a lavish **rotunda** decorated with stucco Roman military insignia to emphasize Charles's military prowess. The rotunda boasts an intricate marble floor with chequer-board tiles surrounding a star-shaped central feature consisting of lots of different types of marble, but here again it's all about good old Charles who prided himself on his knowledge of geology. The rotunda leads to five inter-connecting **salons**, each of which holds a miscellany of eighteenth-century bygones illustrative of one or other of Charles's many interests. The first room is mechanical, the second horological and geographical, the third is devoted to hunting and leisure, the fourth is musical and the fifth has a cabinet of porcelain. Few of these bygones were actually owned by Charles, but it is an enjoyable collection, the most interesting pieces being his Masonic trinkets and baubles.

Charles had his own private chapel next door – he was a well-known rake, so presumably it was handy for confession – and this could once be reached from the rotunda, but today you have to go back outside the palais to gain access to what is now the **Eglise Protestante de Bruxelles** (Sun 10.30–11.30am, during services, and by appointment on ☎02 513 23 25). Charles decorated the chapel in suitably ornate style, dripping with delicate stuccowork and glitzy chandeliers, and these have survived it being passed on to the city's Protestants in 1804.

Le Musée des Instruments de Musique (MIM)

Metres from the place du Musée, at rue Montagne de la Cour 2, the **Old England building** is a whimsical Art Nouveau confection, all glass and wrought-iron, that started life as a store, taking its name from the eponymous British company who had the place built as their Brussels headquarters in 1899. It has recently been refurbished to house the entertaining **Musée des Instruments de Musique** (Tues–Fri 9.30am–5pm, Sat & Sun 10am–5pm; €5 plus extra charge for exhibitions; ⍟www.mim.fgov.be), a prestige development that works very well. Spread over three floors, the museum's permanent collection features several hundred musical instruments, with an international assortment of traditional folk-music instruments on the ground floor and European instruments – from antique trumpets and trombones to eighteenth-century Italian violins and clavichords – up above. The special feature is the **infrared headphones**, which are cued to play music to match the type of instrument you're looking at. This is really good fun, especially in the folk music section where – for example – you can hear the sound made by a whopping Tibetan temple trumpet and, amongst all sorts of bagpipes, the whine of the medieval Cornemuse, as featured in the paintings of Pieter Bruegel the Younger. One word of caution, however: middle-aged parents will no doubt spot the dreaded ocarine, a slug-shaped instrument that was once popular with children and drove many an adult to despair; the good news is that there's no sight of that other instrument of audio torture, the kazoo.

Aside from the permanent collection, one floor of the museum is devoted to temporary exhibitions (which may increase the cost of admission), another holds a concert hall and there's a very good shop selling CDs and books.

When you've had your fill, head up to the top-floor **restaurant** for refreshments, where you'll be rewarded with superb views over the city.

Place Royale

Composed and self-assured, the **place Royale** forms a fitting climax to rue Royale, the dead straight backbone of the Upper Town which runs 2km north to the suburb of St Josse (see p.67). Precisely symmetrical, the square is framed by late eighteenth-century mansions, each an exercise in architectural restraint, though there's no mistaking their size nor the likely cost of their construction.

Pushing into this understated opulence is the facade of the **church of St-Jacques sur Coudenberg** (Tues–Sat 1–6pm, Sun 9am–6pm; free), a fanciful, 1780s version of a Roman temple with a colourfully frescoed pediment representing Our Lady as Comforter of the Afflicted. Indeed, the building was so secular in appearance that the French Revolutionary Army had no hesitation in renaming it as a Temple of Reason. The church's soaring interior is a well-lit affair with a splendid coffered ceiling; you'll also find, amidst a fairly predictable assortment of furnishings and fittings in the transept, two large and dramatic paintings of the Crucifixion by Jean-François Portaels (1818–95), one-time director of the city's fine art academy.

The French Revolutionary Army also destroyed the statue of a Habsburg governor that originally occupied the middle of the place Royale; its replacement – a dashing equestrian representation of **Godfrey de Bouillon**, one of the leaders of the first Crusade – dates from the 1840s. The statue has Godfrey, all rippling muscles and tree-trunk legs, rushing into battle in a supposedly heroic manner, but the sculptor wasn't quite up to his brief. Godfrey is supposed to be staring determinedly into the distance, but instead it looks as if he needs specs.

Once you've reached the Place Royale, the obvious option is to visit the Musées Royaux des Beaux Arts (see below). But, if that doesn't appeal, there is a choice of walking routes: it's a short stroll south along rue de la Régence to the Sablon neighbourhood (see p.90), one of the city's swankier quarters; or you can walk round to the Palais Royal (see p.86) and then the fine art of the Musée Charlier (see p.89).

The Musées Royaux des Beaux Arts

A few metres from place Royale, at the start of rue de la Régence, the **Musées Royaux des Beaux Arts** (Tues–Sun 10am–5pm; €5) comprises two interconnected museums, one displaying modern art, the other older works. Together they make up Belgium's most satisfying, all-round collection of fine art, with marvellous collections of work by – amongst many – **Pieter Bruegel the Elder**, **Rubens** and the surrealists **Paul Delvaux** and **René Magritte**.

Both museums are large, and to do them justice you should see them in separate visits. Finding your way around is made easy by the detailed English-language, colour-coded **museum plan** issued with admission. The older paintings – up to the beginning of the nineteenth century – are exhibited in the **Musée d'Art Ancien**, where the **blue** area features paintings of the fifteenth and sixteenth centuries, including the Bruegels, and the **brown** area concentrates on paintings of the seventeenth and eighteenth centuries, with the collection of Rubens (for which the museum is internationally famous) as the highlight. The **orange** area comprises the small and undistinguished Gallery of Sculptures. The **Musée d'Art Moderne** has a **yellow** area devoted to ninteeth-century works, notably the canvases of Ostend-born **James Ensor**, and a **green** area, whose eight subterranean levels cover the twentieth century.

The Musée d'Art Ancien also hosts, in the **red** area, a prestigious programme of **temporary exhibitions**. A supplementary admission fee is usually payable for these and for the most popular you'll need to buy a ticket ahead of time; the ticket may specify the time of admission. The larger exhibitions may cause some disruption to the permanent collection, so treat the room numbers we've given with a little caution. Inevitably, the account below just scratches the surface; the museum's bookshop sells a wide range of detailed texts including a well-illustrated guide to the collections for €15, and an English **audioguide** is available at the ticket desk for an extra €2.50.

Musée d'Art Ancien

Well presented, if not exactly well organized, the **Musée d'Art Ancien** is saved from confusion by its colour-coded zones – blue, brown, orange and red. It's a large collection and it's best to start a visit with the **Flemish primitives** in the **blue** section.

Rogier van der Weyden and Dieric Bouts

Rooms 11 and 12 hold several paintings by **Rogier van der Weyden** (1399–1464), who moved from his hometown of Tournai (in today's southern Belgium) to Brussels in the 1430s, becoming the city's official painter shortly afterwards. When it came to portraiture Weyden's favourite technique was to highlight the features of his subject – and tokens of rank – against a black background. His *Portrait of Antoine de Bourgogne* (Room 11) is a case in point, with Anthony, the illegitimate son of Philip the Good, casting a haughty, tight-lipped stare to his right while wearing the chain of the Order of the Golden Fleece and clasping an arrow, the emblem of the guild of archers. In this room also is Weyden's *Pietà*, whose solemnity is modified by the brightening dawn sky.

In **Room 13**, the two panels of the *Justice of the Emperor Otto* are the work of Weyden's contemporary, the Leuven-based **Dieric Bouts** (1410–75). The story was well known: in revenge for refusing her advances, the empress accuses a nobleman of attempting to seduce her. He is executed, but the man's wife remains convinced of his innocence and subsequently proves her point by means of an ordeal by fire – hence the red hot iron bar she holds in her hand. The empress then receives her just desserts, being burnt at the stake on the hill in the background.

Hans Memling and the Master of the Legends of St Lucy and St Barbara

Room 14 has some fine portraits by **Hans Memling** (1430–94) as well as his softly hued *Martyrdom of St Sebastian*. Legend asserts that Sebastian was an officer in Diocletian's bodyguard until his Christian faith was discovered, at which point he was sentenced to be shot to death by the imperial archers. Left for dead by the bowmen, Sebastian recovered and Diocletian had to send a bunch of assassins to finish him off with cudgels. The tale made Sebastian popular with archers across Western Europe, and Memling's picture – showing the trussed up saint serenely indifferent to the arrows of the firing squad – was commissioned by the guild of archers in Bruges around 1470. In the same room, the anonymous artist commonly referred to as the **Master of the Legend of St Lucy** weighs in with a finely detailed and richly allegorical *Madonna with Saints*, where, with the city of Bruges in the background, the Madonna presents the infant Jesus for the adoration of eleven holy women. Decked out in elaborate medieval attire, the women have blank, almost expressionless faces, but each bears a token of her sainthood which would have been easily recognised by a medieval congregation. St Lucy, whose assistance was sought by those with sight problems, holds two eyes in a dish.

In **Room 15**, there's more early Flemish art in the shape of the *Scenes from the Life of St Barbara*, one panel from an original pair by the **Master of the Legend of St Barbara**. One of the most popular of medieval saints, Barbara, so the story goes, was a woman of great beauty whose father locked her away in a tower to keep her away from her admirers. The imprisoned Barbara became a Christian whereupon her father, Dioscurus, tried to kill her, only to be thwarted by a miracle that placed her out of his reach – a part of the tale that's ingeniously depicted in this painting. Naturally, no self-respecting saint could escape so easily, so later parts of the story have Barbara handed over to the local prince, who tortures her for her faith. Barbara resists and the prince orders Dioscurus to kill her himself, which he does only to be immediately incinerated by a bolt of lightning.

School of Hieronymus Bosch

Moving on, **Room 17** boasts a copy of the **Hieronymus Bosch** *Temptations of St Anthony* that's in the Museu Nacional in Lisbon. No one is quite sure who painted this triptych – it may or may not have been one of Bosch's apprentices – but it was certainly produced in Holland in the late fifteenth or early sixteenth century. The painting refers to St Anthony, a third-century nobleman who withdrew into the desert, where he endured fifteen years of temptation before settling down into his long stint as a hermit. It was the temptations that interested Bosch – rather than the ascetic steeliness of Anthony – and the central panel has an inconspicuous saint sticking desperately to his prayers surrounded by all manner of fiendish phantoms. The side panels develop the theme: to the right Anthony is tempted by lust and greed, and on the left Anthony's companions help him back to his shelter after he's been transported through the skies by weird-looking demons.

Lucas Cranach, Gerard David, Matsys and Bernard van Orley

Next door, **Room 18** holds works by Martin Luther's friend, the Bavarian artist **Lucas Cranach** (1472–1553), whose *Adam and Eve* presents a stylized, Renaissance view of the Garden of Eden with an earnest-looking Adam on the other side of the Tree of Knowledge from a coquettish Eve, painted with legs entwined and her teeth marks visible on the apple. **Room 21** displays a couple of panels by **Gerard David** (1460–1523), a Bruges-based artist whose draughtsmanship may not be of the highest order, but whose paintings do display a tender serenity, as exhibited here in his *Adoration of the Magi* and *Virgin and Child*.

In **Room 22**, **Quentin Matsys** (1465–1530) is well represented by the *Triptych of the Holy Kindred*. Matsys' work illustrates a turning point in the development of Flemish painting, and in this triptych, which was completed in 1509, Matsys abandons the realistic interiors and landscapes of his Flemish predecessors in favour of the grand columns and porticos of the Renaissance. Notice that each scene is rigorously structured, its characters – all relations of Jesus – assuming lofty, idealized poses.

Room 26 has several works by **Bernard van Orley** (1488–1541), a long-time favourite of the Habsburg officials in Brussels until his Protestant sympathies put him in the commercial dog house. A versatile artist, Orley produced action-packed paintings of Biblical scenes, often back-dropped by classical buildings in the Renaissance style, as well as cartoon designs for tapestries and stained-glass windows. His designs were used for several of the Cathedral's windows (see p.75). The pick of his paintings displayed here are the *Haneton Triptych*, whose crowded central panel is an intense vision of the Lamentation, and the *Triptych of the Virtue of Patience*, which tells the tale of Job. At the top of the left-hand panel, Satan challenges God to test Job, his faithful follower. God accepts the challenge and visits calamities on Job – at the bottom of the left-hand panel his sheep, horses, cattle and (peculiar-looking) camels are stolen. Even worse, the fearful central panel shows the roof falling in on Job's family while they are eating and only on the right-hand panel is order restored with God telling Job he has passed the test.

Pieter Bruegel the Elder

The museum's collection of works by the Bruegel family, notably **Pieter the Elder** (1527–69), is focused on **Room 31**. Often regarded as the finest Netherlandish painter of the sixteenth century, little is actually known of Pieter the Elder's life, but it's likely he was apprenticed in Antwerp and he certainly moved to Brussels in the early 1560s. He also made at least one long trip to Italy, but judging by his oeuvre, he was – unlike most of his "Belgian" contemporaries – decidedly unimpressed by Italian art. He preferred instead to paint in the Netherlandish tradition and his works often depict crowded Flemish scenes in which are embedded religious or mythical stories. This sympathetic portrayal of everyday life revelled in the seasons and was worked in muted browns, greys and bluey greens with red or yellow highlights. Typifying this approach, and on display here, are the *Adoration of the Magi* and the *Census at Bethlehem*, two particularly absorbing works – his son, Pieter (1564–1638), repeated the *Census* on several occasions – with the traditionally momentous events happening, almost incidentally, among the bustle of everyday life. The versatile Pieter also dabbled with the lurid imagery of Bosch, whose influence is seen most clearly in the *Fall of the Rebel Angels*, a frantic panel painting which had actually been attributed to Bosch until Bruegel's signature was discovered hidden under the frame. The *Fall of Icarus* is, however, his most haunting work, its mood perfectly captured by Auden in his poem *Musée des Beaux Arts*:

In Bruegel's Icarus, *for instance: how everything turns away*
Quite leisurely from the disaster; the ploughman may
Have heard the splash, the forsaken cry,
But for him it was not an important failure; the sun shone
As it had to on the white legs disappearing into the green
Water; and the expensive delicate ship that must have seen
Something amazing, a boy falling out of the sky,
Had somewhere to get to and sailed calmly on.

Rubens and his contemporaries

Apprenticed in Antwerp, **Rubens** (1577–1640) spent eight years in Italy studying the Renaissance masters before returning home, where he quickly completed a stunning series of paintings for Antwerp Cathedral (see p.150). His fame spread far and wide and for the rest of his days Rubens was inundated with work, receiving commissions from all over Europe. In **Room 52**, the popular misconception that Rubens painted nothing but chubby nude women and muscular men is dispelled with a clutch of fine portraits, each aristocratic head drawn with great care and attention to detail – in particular, note the exquisite ruffs adorning the Archdukes Albert and Isabella. In this room also are a series of Rubens' preparatory sketches and paintings, most memorably his *Studies of a Negro's Head*, a wonderfully observed preparation for the black magus in the *Adoration of the Magi*, a luminous work that's one of several huge canvases exhibited next door in **Room 53**. Other works of Rubens' here include the *Ascent to Calvary*, an intensely physical painting, capturing the confusion, agony and strain as Christ struggles on hands and knees under the weight of the cross. There's also the bloodcurdling *Martyrdom of St Lieven*, whose cruel torture – his tongue has just been ripped out and fed to a dog – is watched from on high by worried cherubs and angels.

Next door, in **Room 54**, is a modest sample of Dutch painting, including a couple of sombre and carefully composed **Rembrandt**s (1606–69). One of them – the self-assured *Portrait of Nicolaes van Bambeeck* – was completed in 1641, when the artist was finishing off his famous *Night Watch*, now exhibited in Amsterdam's Rijksmuseum. Several of Rembrandt's pupils feature here too, principally Nicolaes Maes (1634–93), who is well represented by the delicate *Dreaming Old Woman*. There are also several canvases by Rembrandt's talented contemporary, Frans Hals (1580–1666), notably his charming *Three Children and a Cart drawn by a Goat*.

The distinctive paintings of two of Rubens' pupils, Anthony van Dyck (1599–1641) and Jacob Jordaens (1593–1678), are also displayed in this part of the museum, with the studied portraits of the former appearing in **Room 63** and the big and brassy canvases of Jordaens dominating **Room 66**. Like Rubens, Jordaens had a bulging order-book and for years he and his apprentices churned out paintings by the cartload. His best work is generally agreed to have been completed early on – between about 1620 and 1640 – and there's evidence here in the two versions of the *Satyr and the Peasant*, the earlier work clever and inventive, the second a hastily cobbled together piece that verges on buffoonery.

Musée d'Art Moderne

To reach the **Musée d'Art Moderne** you'll need to use the underground passageway which leads from behind the museum entrance to **Level-2** of the **yellow** area, whose **nineteenth-century**, mostly Belgian paintings are spread over five small floors – two underground and three above. Note, however, that at the time of writing, this yellow area was undergoing a thoroughgoing revamp, which may – or may not – result in wholesale changes as to which of its paintings go where.

Another **stairway** on Level –2 of the yellow area proceeds down to the six subterranean half-floors that constitute the **green** area of **twentieth-century** works. The green area is comparatively small and has an international flavour, with the work of Belgian artists – including René Magritte and Paul Delvaux – supplemented by the likes of Dalí, Picasso, Chagall, Henry Moore, Miró, Matisse and Francis Bacon.

Social Realists

Level –2 features the work of the **Social Realists**, whose paintings and sculptures championed the working class. One of the early figures in this movement was Charles de Groux (1825–70), whose paternalistic *Poor People's Pew* and *Benediction* are typical of his work. Much more talented was Constantin Meunier (1831–1905), who is well represented here by two particularly forceful bronzes, *Firedamp* and the *Iron Worker*. Look out also for the stirring canvases of their mutual friend Eugene Laermans (1864–1940), who shifted from the Realist style into more Expressionistic works, as in the overtly political *Red Flag* and *The Corpse*, a sorrowful vision that is perhaps Laermans' most successful painting. If the Meunier bronzes whet your interest, you might consider visiting the Musée Meunier (see p.102).

David and his contemporaries

Skipping the uninspiring nineteenth-century works of **Level –1**, press on up to **Level +1**, where the obvious highlight is Jacques-Louis **David**'s famous *Death of Marat*, a propagandist piece of 1793 showing Jean-Paul Marat, the French revolutionary hero, dying in his bath after being stabbed by Charlotte Corday. David (1748–1825) has given Marat a perfectly proportioned, classical torso and a face which, with its large hooded eyes, looks almost Christ-like, the effect heightened by the flatness of the composition and the emptiness of the background. The dead man clasps a quill in one hand and the letter given to him by Corday in the other, inscribed "my deepest grief is all it takes to be entitled to your benevolence". The other note, on the wooden chest, is written by Marat and begins: "You will give this warrant to that mother with the five children, whose husband died for his country". This was David's paean to a fellow revolutionary for, like Marat, he had voted for the execution of Louis XVI, was a member of the revolutionary Convention, which commissioned this picture, and was an avowed Jacobin – the deadly rivals of the Girondins, whom Corday supported. David was also a leading light of the Neoclassical movement and became the new regime's Superintendent of the Fine Arts. He did well under Napoleon, too, but after Waterloo, David, along with all the other regicides, was exiled, ending his days in Brussels.

Symbolism and James Ensor

The Symbolists are clustered on **Level +2** and amongst them are the disconcerting paintings of Fernand Khnopff (1858–1921), a founding member of the Les XX art movement (see p.107). Khnopff painted his sister, Marguerite, again and again, using her refined, almost plastic, beauty to stir a vague sense of passion – for she's desirable and utterly unobtainable in equal measure. His haunting *Memories of Lawn Tennis* is typical of his oeuvre, a work without narrative, a dream-like scene with each of the seven women bearing the likeness of Marguerite. In *Caresses* Marguerite pops up once more, this time with the body of a cheetah pawing sensually at an androgynous youth. Also exhibited here – and a real surprise – is *Psyche's Wedding*, a delightful painting by that forerunner of Art Nouveau, the Englishman Edward Burne-Jones (1833–98). Antoine Wiertz, who has a museum all to himself near the EU Parliament building (see p.114), pops up too, his *La Belle Rosme* a typically disagreeable painting in which the woman concerned faces a skeleton.

In a separate section on Level +2 is a superb sample of the work of **James Ensor** (1860–1949). Ensor, the son of an English father and Flemish mother, spent nearly all of his long life working in Ostend, his home town. His first paintings were serious-minded portraits and landscapes, but in the early 1880s he switched to a more Impressionistic style, delicately picking out his colours as in *The Lady in Blue*. It is, however, Ensor's use of masks that sets his work apart – ambiguous carnival masks with the sniff of death or perversity. His *Scandalized Masks* of 1883 was his first mask painting, a typically unnerving canvas that works on several levels, whilst his *Skeletons quarrelling for a Kipper* (1891) is one of the most savage and macabre paintings you're ever likely to see.

Impressionism and Post-Impressionism

Pressing on, **Level +3** has a sprinkling of French Impressionists and Post-Impressionists – Monet, Seurat, Gauguin – alongside the studied pointillism of Théo van Rysselberghe (1862–1926), a versatile Brussels artist and founder member of Les XX (see p.107). Henry van de Velde (1863–1957), another member of Les XX, changed his painting style as often as Rysselberghe, but in the late 1880s he was under the influence of Seurat – hence *The Mender*.

Cubists, Expressionists and Fauvists

A stairway leads down from yellow-coded Level –2 to the **green area**, whose six subterranean half-floors (Levels –3 to –8) hold a diverse collection of modern art and sculpture. It's a challenging collection of international dimensions that starts – at the entrance to **Level −3/4** – as it means to continue with a lumpy, uncompromising Henry Moore and an eerie Francis Bacon, *The Pope with Owls*. Beyond lies an assortment of works by Picasso, Braque and Matisse, a Dufy or two, a battery of Rik Wouters, and several fanciful paintings by Chagall. Another highlight is Léon Spilliaert's evocations of intense loneliness, from monochromatic beaches to empty rooms and train cars. Spilliaert (1881–1946) lived in Ostend, the setting for much of his work, including a piercing *Self-Portrait* of 1907. Another noteworthy Belgian is Constant Permeke (1886–1952), whose grim and gritty Expressionism is best illustrated by *The Potato Eater* of 1935.

Surrealism – Delvaux and Magritte

Level −5/6 is given over to the Surrealists. There's a fine Dalí, *The Temptation of St Anthony*, a hallucinatory work in which spindly-legged elephants tempt the saint with fleshy women, and a couple of haunting de Chirico paintings. Amongst the Belgian Surrealists, Paul Delvaux is represented by his trademark themes of ice-cool nudes set against a disintegrating backdrop as well as trains and stations – see the *Evening Train* and the *Public Voice*. Even more elusive is the gallery's collection of paintings by **René Magritte** (1898–1967), perplexing works whose weird, almost photographically realized images and bizarre juxtapositions aim to disconcert. Magritte was the prime mover in Belgian surrealism, developing, by the time he was thirty, an individualistic style that remained fairly constant throughout his entire career. It was not, however, a style that brought him much initial success and, surprising as it may seem today, he remained relatively unknown until the 1950s. The museum has a substantial sample of his work, amongst which two of the more intriguing pieces are the baffling *Secret Player* and the subtly discordant *Empire of Lights*. For over twenty years, Magritte lived in Jette and his old home and studio are now a museum (see p.126).

Contemporary art

Down on **Level −7/8**, there's some pretty incomprehensible modern stuff, featuring an international range of artists. Here the paintings usually play second fiddle to the installations, a regularly rotated bunch comprising everything from photography, sculptures and mixed montages through to the indeterminate. All the same, you're likely to spot the swirling abstracts of Brussels-born and Paris-based Pierre Alechinsky (born in 1927), as well as the tongue-in-cheek work of Marcel Broodthaers (1924–76), famously his *Red Mussels Casserole*.

The Palais Royal

Just to the north of the Musées Royaux des Beaux Arts, around the corner from place Royale, is the long and architecturally repetitive **Palais Royal** (late July to early Sept Tues–Sun 10.30am–4.30pm; free), a sombre conversion of some late eighteenth-century town houses begun by King William I, the Dutch royal who ruled both Belgium and the Netherlands from 1815 to 1830. The Belgian rebellion of 1830 polished off the joint kingdom and since then the kings of independent Belgium haven't spent much money on the palace. Indeed, although it remains their official residence, the royals have lived elsewhere (in Laeken, see p.128) for decades and it's hardly surprising, therefore, that the **palace interior** is formal and unwelcoming. It consists of little more than a predictable sequence of opulent rooms – all gilt trimmings, parquet floors, and endless royal portraits, though the tapestries designed by Goya and the magnificent chandeliers of the Throne Room make a visit (just about) worthwhile.

Belgium's kings

Léopold I (1831–65). Foisted on Belgium by the great powers, Léopold, the first King of the Belgians, was imported from Germany, where he was the prince of Saxe-Coburg – and the uncle of Queen Victoria. Despite lacking a popular mandate, Léopold made a fairly good fist of things, keeping the country neutral as the great powers had ordained.

Léopold II (1865–1909). Energetic and forceful, Léopold II – son of Léopold I – encouraged the urbanization of his country and promoted its importance as a major industrial power. He was also the man responsible for landing Brussels with such pompous monuments as the Palais de Justice and for the imposition of a particularly barbaric colonial regime on the peoples of the Belgian Congo – now the Republic of Congo.

Albert I (1909–34). Easily the most popular of the dynasty, Albert's determined resistance to the German invasion of World War I, when the Germans occupied almost all of the country, made the king a national hero whose untimely death, in a climbing accident, traumatized the nation. Albert was the nephew of Léopold II and the father of Léopold III.

Léopold III (1934–51). In contrast to his father, Léopold III had the dubious honour of becoming one of Europe's least popular monarchs. His first wife died in a suspicious car crash; he nearly lost his kingdom by remarrying (anathema in a Roman Catholic country); and he was badly compromised during the German occupation of World War II. During the war, Léopold remained in Belgium rather than face exile, fuelling rumours that he was a Nazi collaborator – though his supporters maintained that he prevented thousands of Belgians from being deported. After several years of heated postwar debate, during which the king remained in exile, the issue of his return was finally put to a referendum in 1950. Just over half the population voted in Léopold's favour, but there was a clear French/Flemish divide, with opposition to the king concentrated in French-speaking Wallonia. Fortunately for Belgium, Léopold abdicated in 1951 in favour of his son, Baudouin.

Baudouin I (1951–93). A soft spoken family man, Baudouin did much to restore the popularity of the monarchy, not least because he was generally thought to be even-handed in his treatment of the French- and Flemish-speaking communities. He also hit the headlines in April 1990 by standing down for a day so that an abortion bill (which he as a Catholic had refused to sign) could be passed. Childless, he was succeeded by his brother.

Albert II (post-1993). Born in 1934, the present king was the younger brother of Baudouin. Impeccably royal, from his Swiss finishing school to his aristocratic Italian wife, Queen Paola, Albert is a steady chap who looks like an avuncular bank manager, though – horror, scandal – his wife was the first Belgian royal to be photographed in a swimming costume and, even worse, it was a bikini. Albert has proved to be a safe pair of hands, becoming a national figurehead in the manner of his predecessor and steering a diplomatic course through the shoals of Flemish–Wallonian antagonisms. The royal family is one of Belgium's few unifying forces and any slip off the linguistic/inter-community tightrope is always magnified out of all proportion, like the (admittedly ill-advised) comments criticizing the Flemish nationalists made by Crown Prince Philippe in late 2004.

The Musée de la Dynastie and Palais Coudenberg

One of the mansions that makes up the Palais Royal, the **Hôtel Bellevue**, at the corner of place des Palais and rue Royale, has been turned into the **Musée de la Dynastie** (April–Sept Tues–Sun 10am–6pm; Oct–March Tues–Sun 10am–5pm; museum €3, Coudenberg €4, combined ticket €5), which tracks the brief history of the Belgian royal family. It's all very professionally done, comprising a brisk chronological trawl juiced up by a wide range of personal artefacts – clothes, shoes, letters and the like – donated by the royals, with separate sections on each of the country's monarchs. There is a particularly detailed section on King Baudouin, who seems to have been a kind and gentle soul, but the museum almost always dodges the controversies that have surrounded several of Belgium's kings. It is particularly shameless in its treatment of Léopold II: apparently, he loved to travel and was quite an adventurer, attributes which his Congolese victims (of whom there is scarcely a mention) would have been hard pressed to appreciate. The museum is currently being refurbished, but it is unlikely to adopt a less fawning, more investigative stance.

The museum also gives access to the labyrinth of caves, cellars and vaults that make up the scant remains of the **Coudenberg Palace**, which once occupied the top of the hill on what is now place Royale. A castle was built here in the eleventh century and enlarged on several subsequent occasions, but it was badly damaged by fire in 1731 and the site was levelled off in 1775. The foundations were, however, left untouched and, now cleared of debris, they have been opened up to visitors, who can wander round guided by an especially detailed booklet issued at the reception – though you still need a vivid imagination to get much out of a visit. The main highlight, and one spot where you do get a sense of what was here before, is amongst the capacious foundations of the **Aula Magna**, or great hall, built by the spendthrift Philip the Good, Duke of Burgundy, in the 1450s, though on this particular occasion the duke made the city council pay the bills. There's also a modest display of artefacts unearthed during the archeological excavations – pieces of pottery, glass, majolica and so forth.

Parc de Bruxelles and place du Trône

Opposite the Palais Royal, the **Parc de Bruxelles** is the most central of the city's larger parks, along whose tree-lined footpaths civil servants and office workers stroll at lunchtime, or race to catch the métro in the evenings. They might well wish the greenery was a bit more interesting. Laid out in the formal French style in 1780, the park undoubtedly suited the courtly – and courting – rituals of the times, but today the straight footpaths and long lines of trees can merely seem tedious, though the classical statues dotted hither and thither do cheer things up.

Beside the park's southeast corner stands the **Palais des Académies**, a grand edifice that once served as a royal residence, but now accommodates the Francophone Academy of Language and Literature. Just beyond is the **place du Trône**, where the heavy-duty equestrian statue of Léopold II was the work of Thomas Vinçotte, whose skills were much used by the king – look out for Vinçotte's chariot on top of the Parc du Cinquantenaire's triumphal arch (see p.117).

From place du Trône, it's a ten-minute walk north along avenue des Arts to the Musée Charlier (see below), or you can double back to the Musées Royaux des Beaux Arts and stroll south along rue de la Régence to reach the well-heeled Sablon district (see p.90). Alternatively, it's a few minutes' stroll east to the EU Parliament building and the EU Quarter, covered in Chapter 000.

Musée Charlier

The enjoyable **Musée Charlier** (Tues–Fri noon–5pm; €5; ⓦwww.charlier museum.be), just off the petit ring near place Madou at avenue des Arts 16, illustrates the artistic tastes of Belgium's upper middle class at the end of the nineteenth century. It holds the fine and applied art collection of a certain Henri van Cutsem, a wealthy businessman who bought two adjacent proper-ties here in 1890. Cutsem merged and modified the two buildings so that he could display his collection to best effect, even going to the trouble of having Victor Horta install glass roofs, and he subsequently bequeathed the house and its contents to a sculptor he knew and admired, **Guillaume Charlier** (1854–1925). Charlier kept the collection pretty much intact and so it remains today, comprising everything from Belgian tapestries and antique French furni-ture through to Chinese porcelain and paintings by a number of Belgian artists, mostly lesser-known figures but with one or two major artists represented too.

Each of the dozen or so rooms is crammed with Cutsem's bits and pieces, and it's this jumbled diversity which is the museum's principal charm. Nevertheless, there are one or two artistic highlights, beginning with James Ensor's *Flowers and Butterflies*, and Eugene Laermans' *The Promenade*, showing peasants out walking; both are on display in the Concert Room.

Place de la Liberté and place des Barricades

From the Musée Charlier, it's a five-minute walk west across the boulevard to **place de la Liberté**, a leafy little square decorated with a statue of Charles Rogier (1800–85), a member of the insurrectionist Provisional Government of 1830 who went on to become a railway tycoon. The square is at the heart of one of the more attractive parts of the city centre, a pocket-sized district where the mansions of the nineteenth-century bourgeoisie, built with dignified balco-nies and wrought-iron grilles, overlook wide, straight streets and fetching little piazzas. One of these squares, the somewhat careworn **place des Barricades**, is named after the impromptu barricades that were erected here against the Dutch in 1830, and in the middle is a statue of a long-forgotten rebel leader, one Hector Goffart. Another, much more famous rebel, **Victor Hugo** (1802–85), lived on the square, at no.4, from 1866 to 1871 – the house carries a plaque. Hugo had been exiled from France for supporting the revolution of 1848 and was only allowed to return after the fall of the Second Empire in 1870 – a fate he shared with other literary lights, notably Dumas and Baudelaire.

Colonne du Congrès

At the west end of rue du Congrès, the 47-metre-high **Colonne du Congrès**, on place du Congrès, was erected in 1850 to commemorate the country's first national parliament. The column sports a statue of Léopold I on top and four allegorical female figures down below, representing the freedoms enshrined in the Constitution – of worship, association, education and the press. The lions were added later, guarding the tomb of the unknown soldier, in front of which burns the eternal flame honouring Belgium's dead of the two World Wars. The column dominates a large and bleak **belvedere** that offers a singularly unflattering view over the Lower Town. Even worse, the belvedere is flanked by blank glass and concrete office buildings, whose uncompromising lines must have looked great on the plans, but make the place feel unfriendly if not downright hostile, especially in the chill of a winter wind.

From the Colonne du Congrès, it's a five- to ten-minute walk north along rue Royale to Le Botanique (see p.66), or five minutes' walk west via concrete walkways down to the entertaining Centre Belge de la Bande Dessinée – the Belgian Comic Strip Centre (see p.65).

The Sablon district

The **Sablon district** anchors the southern end of the Upper Town and in its midst is **place du Petit Sablon**, a small rectangular area which was laid out as a public garden in 1890 after previous use as a horse market. The wrought-iron fence surrounding the garden is decorated with 48 **statuettes** representing the medieval guilds and inside, near the top of the slope, are ten more – slightly larger – statues honouring some of the country's leading sixteenth-century figures. The ten are hardly household names in Belgium never mind anywhere else, but one or two may ring a few bells: Mercator, the geographer and cartographer responsible for Mercator's projection of the earth's surface; William the Silent, the founder of the Netherlands; and the painter Bernard van Orley. Here also, on top of the fountain, are the figures of the counts **Egmont and Hoorn**, clasping each other in brotherly fashion, as befits two men who were beheaded together on the Grand-Place for their opposition to the Habsburgs in 1568 (see p.51).

Count Egmont is further remembered by the **Palais d'Egmont** (no admission) at the back of the square. This elegant structure was originally built in 1534 for Françoise of Luxembourg, mother of the executed count. It was remodelled on several subsequent occasions and in 1972 it was where Britain signed the treaty admitting it to the EEC.

Notre-Dame du Sablon

Opposite the foot of the park, the fifteenth-century church of **Notre-Dame du Sablon** (Mon–Fri 9am–6pm, Sat & Sun 10am–5pm; free) began life as a

△ Notre-Dame du Sablon

chapel constructed for the guild of archers in 1304. Its fortunes were, however, transformed when a much-revered statue of Mary, purportedly with healing powers, was brought here by boat from Antwerp in 1348. The chapel soon became a centre of pilgrimage and a proper church – in high Gothic style – was built to accommodate its visitors, and it's this handsome structure that survives today. Recently scrubbed and polished, the sandy hues of the church's exterior stonework are now revealed to full advantage, all imposing buttresses, slender parapets, screeching gargoyles and delicate pinnacles.

Inside, the triple-aisled **nave** is dark and gloomy, making it hard to pick out the Gothic detail, but there's no missing the lofty vaulted ceiling or the fancily carved stone tracery of the windows. The statue of Mary is long gone – the Protestants chopped it up in 1565 – but two carvings of the legendary boat and its passengers recall the story, one in the nave, the other above the inside of the present, rue de la Régence entrance. The woman in the boat is one Béatrice Sodkens, the pious creature whose visions prompted her to procure the statue and bring it to Brussels. The occasion of its arrival in the city is still celebrated annually in July by the **Ommegang** procession (see p.239). Look out, also, for the grotesque **tombstone** of Claude and Jacqueline Bouton, members of Charles V's entourage, which, resting against the wall near the old main entrance, displays two graphically realistic skeletons. More conspicuous is the black and white marble facade of the **funerary chapel** in the transept beside the current entrance – a Baroque mausoleum for the earthly remains of the Tour and Taxis family, local worthies who founded the Belgian postal system.

△ Hunting for bargains on the place du Grand Sablon

Place du Grand Sablon

Behind the church, the **place du Grand Sablon** is one of Brussels' most popular squares, a sloping wedge of cobblestones flanked by tall and slender town houses of every architectural persuasion, from modest crowstep gables through to grand Neoclassical facades and the occasional Art Nouveau extravagance. The square serves as the centre of one of the city's wealthiest districts, and is busiest at weekends, when an **antiques market** (Sat 9am–6pm, Sun 9am–2pm) clusters below the church. Many of the shops on Sablon and the surrounding streets are devoted to antiques and art, and you could easily spend an hour or so window-browsing from one to another – or you can soak up the atmosphere eating or drinking in one of Sablon's many cafés.

Palais de Justice and place Louise

From place du Grand Sablon, follow rue Ernest Allard up the hill to **place Poelaert**, named after the architect who designed the immense **Palais de Justice** that dwarfs the square and everything around it. Opened in 1883, it's a real monster of a building, decorated with an eccentric mix of Greek, Roman, Egyptian and Assyrian motifs and capped with a gigantic crown which has recently been restored at colossal expense – when blowing the whole thing up would perhaps have been a better idea. It's possible to wander into the main hall of the building, a sepulchral affair with tiny audience tables where lawyers huddle with their clients, but really it's the size alone that impresses. During the construction of the palais, several thousand townsfolk were forcibly evicted to make the necessary space, and Poelaert became one of the most hated men in the capital. Indeed, when he went insane and died in 1879, it was widely believed a *steekes* (witch) from the Marolles had been sticking pins into an effigy of him. The square is also the site of two **war memorials**: the one on the corner of rue de la Regence, dating to 1923, pays tribute to the Anglo-Belgian alliance; the other in the middle of the square commemorates Belgian dead with Art Déco soldiers following an Art Déco angel.

A stone's throw from the Palais de Justice, **place Louise**, part square, part traffic junction, heralds the start of the city's most exclusive shopping district. It's here and in the immediate vicinity that you'll find designer boutiques, jewellers and glossy shopping malls. The glitz spreads east along boulevard de Waterloo and south down the northernmost section of avenue Louise, which is described on pp.101–103.

4

St Gilles, Avenue Louise and Ixelles

Cobwebbed by tiny squares and narrow streets, home to a plethora of local bars and some of the capital's finest Art Nouveau houses, the neighbouring districts of St Gilles and Ixelles, just south of the petit ring, make a great escape from the hustle and bustle of the city centre. This is Brussels without the razzmatazz and tourists are few and far between, especially in **St Gilles**, the smaller of the two *communes*, which is often regarded as little more than an example of inner-city decay. Frankly, this is true enough of its most westerly section, comprising the depressing immigrant quarters of the Gare du Midi, but St Gilles gets very much more appealing the further east it spreads, its run-down streets soon left behind for refined avenues interspersed with dignified squares.

Ixelles, for its part, is one of the city's most interesting and exciting outer areas, with a couple of enjoyable museums, and a diverse street-life and café scene. Typified by its cheek-by-jowl diversity, Ixelles has long attracted artists, writers and intellectuals of many persuasions – Karl Marx, Auguste Rodin and Alexandre Dumas all lived here – and even today it retains an arty, sometimes Bohemian feel. Ixelles is divided in two by **avenue Louise**, whose character is entirely different, as befits an administrative anomaly: the boulevard is counted as part of the city centre, and has been home to the haute bourgeoisie ever since Léopold II had the avenue laid out in the 1840s. It's here you'll find some of the city's most expensive shops and hotels, pricey jewellers, slick office blocks and the interesting **Musée Constantin Meunier**, sited in the sculptor's old house and studio.

More than anything else, however, it's the dazzling array of **Art Nouveau buildings** clustering the streets of both St Gilles and Ixelles that really grab the attention. Many of the finest examples are concentrated on and around the boundary between the two *communes* – in between chaussée de Charleroi and avenue Louise. Here you'll find Horta's own house, now the glorious **Musée Horta**, as well as examples of the work of Paul Hankar and Armand van Waesberghe. Access to most of the city's Art Nouveau buildings is restricted, so you can either settle for the view from outside, or take one of ARAU's **Art Nouveau tours** (see p.30).

St Gilles

One of the smallest of the city's *communes*, **St Gilles** is also one of the most varied, stretching from the impoverished, sometimes threatening streets around the **Gare du Midi** to the affluent precincts of avenue Louise. Generations of political and economic refugees from the Mediterranean and North Africa have established themselves here, but as the tide of gentrification rolls remorselessly on from east to west, so the district's demographic make-up is being transformed. The prettiest part of St Gilles is just to the south of the **Porte de Hal**, and there is one star attraction, the **Musée Victor Horta**.

Porte de Hal and the Hôtel Winssinger

The imposing **Porte de Hal**, standing on the edge of St Gilles at the southern tip of the petit ring, is the only one of the city's seven medieval gates to have survived – the rest were knocked down by Napoleon, but this one was left untouched primarily because it was a prison. The gate is a ponderous, heavily fortified affair, with towers and turrets, battlements and machicolations, and – although it was clumsily remodelled in the 1870s – it gives a good idea of the strength of the city's former defences.

Heading south from the gateway, down the **chaussée de Waterloo**, you're soon in the heart of St Gilles, with the elaborate Art Nouveau houses of **rue Vanderschrick** running off to the right and culminating in a popular Art Nouveau café, *La Porteuse d'Eau* (see "Drinking", p.204). Turn left here, up avenue Jean Volders, and it's a few metres to the **parvis de St Gilles**, a particularly attractive square that is the site of a lively fruit and vegetable **market** (Tues–Sun 6am–noon). One side of the square is overlooked by the soaring stone facade of a nineteenth-century parish church, the other by the sweeping curve of a matching pair of tenement buildings, where each apartment is equipped with its own mini-balcony and wrought-iron grille. From here, it's a short stroll east via rues Jourdan and de la Victoire to Victor Horta's **Hôtel Winssinger**, at rue de l'Hôtel des Monnaies 66. Dating from the 1890s, Horta's most creative period, the building sports a wide facade, with multiple ground-floor windows set against striped bands of stone. Up above are a series of delicate balconies and the stylistic centrepiece, an ornate bow window.

The Barrière de St Gilles to the Maison and Atelier Dubois

From the Hôtel Winssinger, push on south down rue de l'Hôtel des Monnaies until you reach the **Barrière de St Gilles** – a seven-road junction that was, until the middle of the nineteenth century, the site of a toll gate. Close by, south again up avenue Paul Dejaer, is the *commune*'s **Hôtel de Ville**, a heavy-duty, pseudo-Renaissance edifice, and behind that, at the top end of avenue Jef Lambeaux, rises the ersatz medieval castle (built in the nineteenth century), which holds the **prison**.

Heading east from the prison, take the first right off avenue Ducpétiaux and then the second on the left – avenue de la Jonction – to reach the **Hôtel Hannon**, a fine Art Nouveau edifice designed by the architect Jules Brunfaut in 1903 and located on the corner of avenue Brugmann. The windows, equipped with Tiffany glass, are a special highlight here – flowing, beautifully carved extravagances set against a facade whose brickwork is decorated with

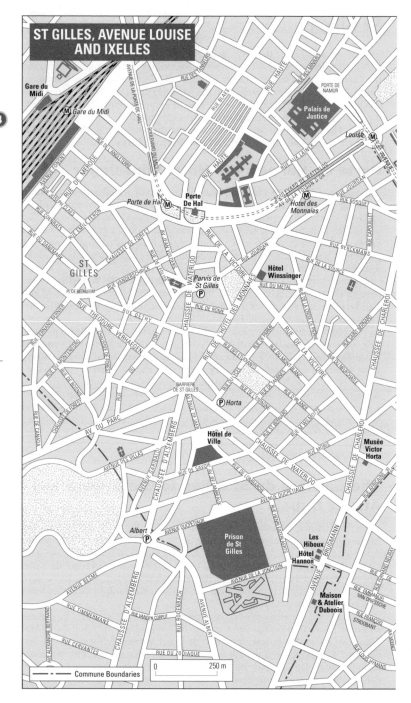

ST GILLES, AVENUE LOUISE AND IXELLES

Gare du Midi

Ⓜ Gare du Midi

AVENUE DE LA PORTE DE HAL

RUE DES VANDERS

RUE BLAES

RUE HAUTE

RUE DES VANDRE

PORTE DE NAMUR

Palais de Justice

Louise Ⓜ

RUE DE MÉRODE

AVENUE ONSNY

RUE JOSEPH CLAES

RUE DE L'ANGLETERRE

BOULEVARD DU MIDI

RUE HAUTE

RUE AUX LAINES

RUE JOURDAN

RUE DE LA VICTOIRE

BOULEVARD DE WATERLOO

Porte de Hal Ⓜ

Porte De Hal

AV DE LA TOISON D'OR

Hôtel des Monnaies Ⓜ

RUE BOSQUET

RUE CAPOUILLET

RUE COENRAETS

RUE ÉMILE FÉRON

RUE DU DANEMARK

ST GILLES

PL. DE BETHLÉEM

RUE VANDERSCHRICK

CHAUSSÉE DE FOREST

CHAUSSÉE DE WATERLOO

RUE DE L'ÉGLISE

RUE DE L'HÔTEL DES MONNAIES

Parvis de St Gilles Ⓟ

RUE JOURDAN

RUE BERCKMANS

RUE DE LA SOURCE

Hôtel Winssinger

RUE DU METAL

RUE FERNAND BERNIER

RUE THÉODORE VERHAEGEN

RUE DETHY

CHAUSSÉE DE FOREST

RUE DE ROME

RUE DE PRANT

RUE DES ETUDIANTS

RUE DU FORT

RUE DUMONT BLANC

RUE DE LA VICTOIRE

RUE SAINT-BERNARD

CHAUSSÉE DE CHARLEROI

RUE DE MONTENEGRO

RUE DE BOSNIE

CHAUSSÉE DE FOREST

BARRIÈRE DE ST GILLES

Ⓟ Horta

RUE JEAN ROBIE

RUE DE DANNES

RUE DE L'ESPAGNE

RUE DE FRANCE

RUE J. LECLERQ

RUE DE CANADA

AV DU PARC

Hôtel de Ville

RUE S. BERNARD

RUE M. WILMOTTE

CHAUSSÉE DE WATERLOO

RUE MORIS

Musée Victor Horta

CHAUSSÉE DE CHARLEROI

RUE AFRICAINE

AVENUE DES VILLAS

CHAUSSÉE D'ALSEMBERG

AVENUE GARIBALDI

RUE DE SAVOIE

RUE DE L'AQUEDUC

RUE DE LOMBARDIE

AVENUE DUCPÉTIAUX

RUE HENRI FACQUEZ

Les Hiboux Hôtel Hannon

AVENUE BRUGMANN

Albert Ⓟ

AVENUE DUCPÉTIAUX

Prison de St Gilles

AVENUE BESME

AVENUE DE LA JONCTION

Maison & Atelier Dubois

RUE EMMANUEL VAN DRIESSCHE

RUE FRANÇOIS STROOBANT

RUE ALEXANDRE BERTRAND

RUE TIMMERMANS

CHAUSSÉE D'ALSEMBERG

RUE VANDEN CORPUT

RUE ROOSENBACH

AVENUE ALBERT

RUE DU ZODIAQUE

RUE CERVANTES

RUE LOUIS HYMANS

0   250 m

––– · ––– Commune Boundaries

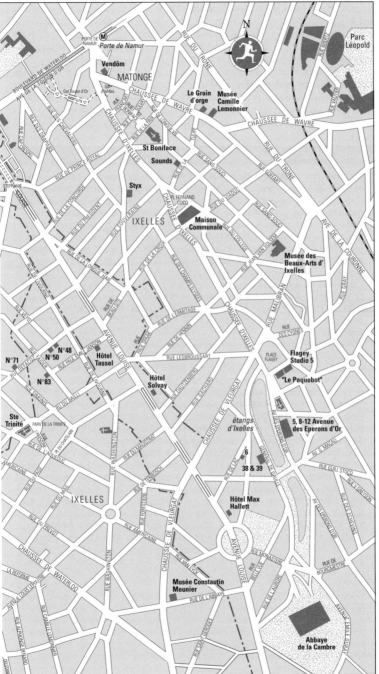

N

Parc Léopold

PORTE DE NAMUR
Porte de Namur
MATONGE
Vendôm
Gal Toison d'Or
BOULEVARD DE WATERLOO
AVE DE LA TOISON D'OR
RUE DES DRAPIERS
CHAUSSEE DE WAVRE
RUE DU TRONE
Le Grain d'orge
Musée Camille Lemonnier
CHAUSSEE DE WAVRE
Gare d'Ixelles
CHAUSSEE DIXELLES
RUE DES CHEVALIERS
RUE DE PRINCE ROYAL
St Boniface
Sounds
RUE DU VIADUC
RUE DU TRONE
STEPHANIE
Styx
RUE DE LA PONCHODE
RUE DE LA LONGUE HAIE
CH. FERNAND COCO
IXELLES
Maison Communale
CHAUSSEE DIXELLES
RUE VAN VOLSEM
Musée des Beaux-Arts d'Ixelles
RUE GRAY
RUE DE LA CROIX
RUE DES CHAMPS ELYSEES
RUE MALIBRAN
RUE DE L'ERMITAGE
RUE DES CYGNES
AVENUE LOUISE
N°71
N°48
N°50
Hôtel Tassel
RUE LESBROUSSART
PLACE FLAGEY
Flagey Studio 5
N°83
Hôtel Solvay
RUE DARIMON
RUE RAMBAND
"Le Paquebot"
Ste Trinité
PARV DE LA TRINITE
RUE SIMONIS
RUE DU BAILLI
étangs d'Ixelles
5, 8-12 Avenue des Eperons d'Or
AV G MACAU
RUE GUILL STOCO
AMERICAINE
RUE WASHINGTON
6
38 & 39
CHAUSSEE DE VLEURGAT
IXELLES
RUE DU PREVOT
RUE AMERICAINE
Hôtel Max Hallett
AVENUE LOUISE
RUE DE BOURGMESTRE
CHAUSSEE DE WATERLOO
LA REFORME
AVENUE LOUISE
RUE CAMILLE LEMONNIER
Musée Constautin Meunier
RUE DE L'ABBAYE
Abbaye de la Cambre
AVENUE EMILE DURAY

97

Bois de la Cambre ▼

strips of stone. Next door, **Les Hiboux** – The Owls' House – is a more modest red-brick affair, but it does carry some attractive wrought-iron grilles and stained-glass windows, plus an sgraffiti panel depicting two perky little owls – **sgraffiti** being the decorative technique in which one colour is laid over another and the top coat then partly etched away to create the design.

Five minutes' walk away to the south, at avenue Brugmann 80, is Victor Horta's **Maison and Atelier Dubois**. Completed in 1906, towards the end of Horta's Art Nouveau period, the building is much simpler than some of his earlier works, though it still bears several of his familiar trademarks: a well-lit interior, exquisite carpentry in mahogany and oak, a mosaic floor, and a marble

Victor Horta

The son of a shoemaker, **Victor Horta** (1861–1947) was born in Ghent, where he failed in his first career, being unceremoniously expelled from the city's music conservatory for indiscipline. He promptly moved to Paris to study architecture, returning to Belgium in 1880 to complete his apprenticeship in Brussels with Alphonse Balat, architect to King Léopold II. Balat was a traditionalist, responsible for the classical facades of the Palais Royal – amongst many other prestigious projects – and Horta looked elsewhere for inspiration. He found it in the work of William Morris, the leading figure of the English Arts and Crafts movement, whose designs were key to the development of **Art Nouveau**. Taking its name from the Maison de l'Art Nouveau, a Parisian shop which sold items of modern design, Art Nouveau rejected the imitative architectures which were popular at the time – Neoclassical and neo-Gothic – in favour of an innovative style that was characterized by sinuous, flowing lines. In England, Morris and his colleagues had focused on book illustrations and furnishings, but in Belgium Horta extrapolated the new style into architecture, experimenting with new building materials – steel and concrete – as well as traditional stone, glass and wood.

In 1893, Horta completed the curvaceous **Hôtel Tassel** (see p.101), Brussels' first Art Nouveau building – "hôtel" meaning town house. Inevitably, there were howls of protest from the traditionalists, but no matter what his opponents said, Horta never lacked for work again. The following years – roughly 1893 to 1905 – were Horta's most inventive and prolific. He designed over forty buildings, including the **Hôtel Solvay** (see p.102) and the **Hôtel Winssinger** (see p.95) as well as his own beautifully decorated house and studio, now the **Musée Victor Horta** (see p.99). The delight Horta took in his work is obvious, especially when employed on private houses, and his enthusiasm was all encompassing – he almost always designed everything from the blueprints to the wallpaper and carpets. He never kept a straight line or sharp angle where he could deploy a curve, and his use of light was revolutionary, often filtering through from above, atrium-like, with skylights and as many windows as possible. Curiously, Horta also believed that originality was born of frustration, and so he deliberately created architectural difficulties, pushing himself to find harmonious solutions. Horta felt that the architect was as much an artist as the painter or sculptor, and so he insisted on complete stylistic freedom. It was part of a well-thought out value system that allied him with both Les XX (see p.107) and the Left; as he wrote, "My friends and I were reds, without however having thought about Marx or his theories."

Completed in 1906, the **Maison and Atelier Dubois** (see above) and the **Grand Magasin Waucquez** department store (p.65) were transitional buildings signalling the end of Horta's Art Nouveau period. His later works were more Modernist constructions, whose understated lines were a far cry from the ornateness of his earlier work. In Brussels, the best example of his later work is the Palais des Beaux-Arts of 1928 (see p.76).

staircase. The building is not open to the public, but the exterior – a modest but subtle facade with curvaceous windows set off by the careful use of wrought iron – is mightily impressive.

Doubling back along avenue Brugmann, it's a short stroll to the **chaussée de Charleroi**, within easy striking distance of the Musée Victor Horta.

Musée Victor Horta

The **Musée Victor Horta** (Tues–Sun 2–5.30pm; €5; Ⓦwww.hortamuseum .be), just off the chaussée de Charleroi at rue Américaine 25, occupies the two houses Horta designed as his home and studio at the end of the nineteenth

△ Musée Victor Horta

century, and was where he lived until 1919. The only Horta house fully open to the public, the museum was opened in the late 1960s as part of a sustained campaign to stop the destruction of Brussels' architectural heritage and to publicize the charms of Art Nouveau. From the outside the building is quite modest, a dark, narrow terraced house with a fluid facade and almost casually knotted and twisted ironwork, but it is for his interiors that Horta is especially famous. Inside is a sunny, sensuous dwelling exhibiting all the architect's favourite flourishes in wrought iron and stained glass alongside ornate furniture and panelling made from several different types of timber.

The main unifying feature is the **staircase**, a dainty spiralling affair that runs through the centre of the house, illuminated by a large skylight. Decorated with painted motifs and surrounded by mirrors, it is one of Horta's most magnificent and ingenious creations and it gives access to a sequence of wide, bright rooms, most memorably the **dining room**, an inventive blend of white enamelled brickwork and exposed structural metal arches above a parquet floor. Lining the walls of this room are six bas-reliefs carved by Pierre Braecke, five of which portray the arts represented by the muses above the dresser: painting, music, sculpture, literature, and architecture – with the sixth holding out a model of the Aubecq mansion, built by Horta in 1899 and demolished in 1950. Also of interest is the modest but enjoyable selection of **paintings**, many of which were given to Horta by friends and colleagues, including works by Félicien Rops and Joseph Heymans.

To **get to** the museum from the city centre by public transport, take **tram** #91 from place Louise or #92 from either place Louise, rue de la Régence or rue Royale.

Western Ixelles

Wedged in between the chaussée de Charleroi and avenue Louise, **western Ixelles** is one of the most fashionable parts of the city, its more prosperous inhabitants occupying graceful late nineteenth- and early twentieth-century town houses, usually of stone and often with attractive grilled balconies. The district holds a fine sample of Art Nouveau houses, with the pick of them on or in the vicinity of **rue Defacqz** and **rue Faider**.

The church of Ste-Trinité and place du Châtelain

Heading east from the Musée Victor Horta, take the first turning on the left – rue Africaine – for the parvis de la Trinité, the site of the sulky **church of Ste-Trinité**, a run-down but still domineering Baroque structure whose heavy-duty stonework fills out the square. The church's most interesting feature is the extravagant main facade, which was originally part of the church of St Augustin (1620), demolished to make way for place de Brouckère in 1896. The facade was moved here block by block and although pollution and years of neglect have left their mark, it remains – with its swirling lines, pointed pediments and pilasters – an impressive structure. There are vague plans to restore the church, but at the moment it remains firmly closed – a shame because the stained-glass windows are allegedly quite stunning.

Just to the east of the church – along rue de l'Amazone – is **place du Châtelain**, a pleasant, tapering square lined with bars and cafés. Best known for its Wednesday afternoon food **market** (2–7pm) – where you can buy home-made wines, fine cheeses and a mouthwatering selection of cakes and pastries – it's also a relaxing place for a quiet drink or a spot of lunch. Incidentally, *Le Pain de Châtelain* serves what many locals regard as the best croissants in town.

Rue Defacqz: the Art Nouveau of Paul Hankar

From place du Châtelain, it's a short stroll northwest up rue Simonis to **rue Defacqz**, the site of several charming Art Nouveau houses. Three were designed by **Paul Hankar** (1859–1901), a classically trained architect and contemporary of Horta, who developed a real penchant for **sgraffiti** – akin to frescoes – and multicoloured brickwork. Hankar was widely regarded as one of the most distinguished exponents of Art Nouveau and his old home, at **no. 71**, is marked by its skeletal metalwork, handsome bay window and four sgraf-fiti beneath the cornice – one each for morning, afternoon, evening and night. Hankar designed his home in the early 1890s, making it one of the city's earliest Art Nouveau buildings. **Number 50** is a Hankar creation too, built for another painter, René Janssens, in 1898, and noteworthy for its fanciful brickwork. Next door, at **no. 48**, the house Hankar constructed for the Italian painter Albert Ciamberlani in 1897 sports a fine, flowing facade, decorated with rapidly fading sgraffiti representing the Ages of Man.

Rue Faider and the Hôtel Tassel

There are more Art Nouveau treats in store on neighbouring **rue Faider**, where **no. 83** boasts a splendidly flamboyant facade with ironwork crawling over the windows and frescoes of contented pre-Raphaelite women, all to a design by **Armand Van Waesberghe**. Directly opposite is rue Paul Emile Janson at the bottom of which, at no. 6, is the celebrated **Hôtel Tassel**, the building that made **Horta**'s reputation. The sinuous facade is appealing enough, with its clawed columns, stained glass and spiralling ironwork, but it was with the interior that Horta really made a splash, an uncompromising fantasy featur-ing a fanciful wrought-iron staircase and walls covered with linear decoration. It's also a striking example of the way in which Horta tailor-made his houses to suit the particular needs of clients. In this case it was built for an amateur photographer and includes a studio and projection room.

At the end of rue Paul Emile Janson you hit avenue Louise, where a right turn will take you to another couple of vintage Horta buildings: the Hôtel Solvay and, a little further down the avenue, the Hôtel Max Hallet (see below).

Avenue Louise

Named after the eldest daughter of its creator, King Léopold II, **avenue Louise** slices southeast from the petit ring, its beginnings lined with some of the city's most expensive shops and boutiques. Further along, the shops give way to plush apartment blocks, the most visible part of the wealthy residential area which occupies the side-streets to either side of the avenue. It's here you'll find Horta's **Hôtel Solvay** and **Hôtel Max Hallet**, as well as the diverting **Musée Constantin Meunier**, which displays a large sample of the work of the late

△ High fashion on Avenue Louise

nineteenth-century sculptor, and the **Abbaye de la Cambre**, whose pleasant gardens and old brick buildings are sited in what has now become a diplomatic zone right at the end of the avenue.

Horta's Hôtel Solvay and Hôtel Max Hallet

The **Hôtel Solvay** at no. 224 Avenue Louise (a couple of hundred metres south of the corner with rue Paul Emile Janson) is another Horta extravagance which, like the Musée Horta (see p.99), contains most of its original furnishings and fittings. The 33-year-old Horta was given complete freedom and unlimited funds by the Solvay family (who made a fortune in soft drinks) to design this opulent town house, whose facade is graced by bow windows, delicate metalwork and contrasting types of stone. Inside, Horta commissioned an artist to paint a scene from the Solvay's summer cottage on the first staircase landing, but typically chose the dominant colours himself.

Also on avenue Louise, five minutes' further along at no. 346, is Horta's **Hôtel Max Hallet**, a comparatively restrained structure of 1904, where what was originally a very ordinary, domestic facade is decorated with elegant doors and windows and an elongated stone balcony with a wrought iron balustrade. Just beyond, the modern **sculpture** stranded in the middle of the traffic island looks like a set of elephant tusks, but is in fact a representation of the "V" for Victory sign of World War II. Named *Phénix 44*, it's the work of Olivier Strebelle.

From the Max Hallet residence, it's a quick tram ride north (#93 or #94) to the smart commercialism of place Louise or a five- to ten-minute stroll south to the Musée Constantin Meunier (see below).

The Musée Constantin Meunier

The **Musée Constantin Meunier** (Tues–Fri 10am–noon & 1–5pm, plus alternate weekends – call for schedule ☏02 648 44 49; free) is at rue de l'Abbaye

59, just off avenue Louise, about 500m beyond Victor Horta's Hôtel Max Hallet (see p.102). It's housed on the ground floor of the former home and studio of Brussels-born Constantin Meunier, who lived here from 1899 until his death at the age of 74 just six years later. Meunier began as a painter, but it's as a sculptor that he's best remembered, and the museum has a substantial collection of his dark and brooding bronzes.

The museum's front room holds a couple of Meunier's paintings and statues, but the collection doesn't really warm up until you reach the corridor behind it, where there are a handful of watercolours, a bronze or two and several interesting sketches of London made during one of the artist's many visits to England. The largest and most important sculptures and paintings are, however, in the old studio at the back, including a series of life-size bronzes of muscular men with purposeful faces, all standing around looking heroic – *Le Moissonneur* (The Reaper), *Le Semeur* (The Sower) and *Le Marteleur* (The Metalworker) are typical. Among the paintings in the studio, there are several gritty industrial scenes like the coalfield of *Black Country Borinage* and the gloomy dockside of *The Port*, one of Meunier's most forceful works. Much stranger is Meunier's attempt to equate the harsh life of the Belgian miner with the sufferings of Christ in his *Triptych of the Mine: Descent, Calvary and Resurrection*, a moody but ultimately unapproachable work. Meunier was angered by the dreadful living conditions of Belgium's working class, particularly (like van Gogh before him) the harsh life of the coal miners of the Borinage. This anger fuelled his art, which asserted the dignity of the worker in a style that was to be copied by the Social Realists of his and later generations. According to historian Eric Hobsbawm's *Age of Empire*, "Meunier invented the international stereotype of the sculptured proletarian."

To **get to** the museum by public transport from the city centre, take **tram** #93 or #94 from place Louise, rue de la Régence or rue Royale.

The Abbaye de la Cambre

In a lovely little wooded dell just to the east of avenue Louise, a ten-minute walk from the Meunier Museum – and readily approached via rue de l'Aurore – lies the postcard-pretty **Abbaye de la Cambre** (open access; free). Of medieval foundation, the abbey was suppressed by the French Revolutionary army at the beginning of the nineteenth century, but the soldiers left its eighteenth-century brick buildings standing and, after many toings and froings, they are now used as offices by several government departments. An extensive complex, the main courtyard is especially attractive and it serves as the entrance to the charming **abbey church** (Mon–Fri 9am–noon & 3–6pm; free), whose nave, with its barrel vaulting and rough stone walls, is an exercise in simplicity. The church is an amalgamation of styles, but Gothic predominates except in the furnishings of the nave, where beautifully carved Art Deco wooden panelling frames a set of religious paintings of the Stations of the Cross. The church also holds one marvellous painting, Albert Bouts' *The Mocking of Christ*, an early sixteenth-century work showing a mournful, blood-spattered Jesus. Around the abbey's buildings are walled and terraced gardens plus the old abbatical pond, altogether an oasis of peace away from the hubbub of avenue Louise. To **get to** the abbey, take tram #93, #94 along avenue Louise.

From the abbey, it's a brief walk south to the Bois de la Cambre (see below) and five minutes or so to the mini-lakes and Art Nouveau houses of the étangs d'Ixelles (see p.107).

△ Guarding the entrance to the Abbaye de la Cambre

Bois de la Cambre

Beyond the abbey, at the end of avenue Louise, the **Bois de la Cambre** is unpleasantly crisscrossed by the main commuter access roads in its upper reaches, but a good deal more agreeable around the lake that lies further to the south. It's Brussels' most popular park, bustling with joggers, dog-walkers, families and lovers at weekends, and is the northerly finger of the large **Forêt**

de Soignes, whose once mighty woodland bears a clutch of dual carriageways, and, more promisingly, scores of quiet footpaths.

Eastern Ixelles

Eastern Ixelles radiates out from the petit ring, its busy streets spined by the workaday **chaussée d'Ixelles**, whose long string of shops meanders down to **place Fernand Cocq** and ultimately **place Eugène Flagey**. It's the general flavour that appeals hereabouts rather than any specific sight, though there are a few exceptions, notably the first-rate **Musée des Beaux-Arts d'Ixelles**, whose forte is modern Belgian art; the good-looking **church of St Boniface**; and – less compellingly – the accumulated *objets d'art* of the **Musée Camille Lemonnier**.

South along the chaussée d'Ixelles to St Boniface

From the big and hectic square that is the **Porte de Namur**, it's a short walk south down past the shops of the **chaussée d'Ixelles** to **rue Ernest Solvay**, a side-street on the left. Turn here and then take the first right along **rue St Boniface**, a particularly engaging street that's home to a number of laid-back café-bars including the immensely popular *L'Ultime Atome* (see "Cafés", p.197). The far end of rue St-Boniface is blocked by the imposing gabled facade of the **Eglise de St Boniface**, a largely Gothic structure, which, with its soaring buttresses, dates back to the fifteenth century. The outside of the church is in a sorry state of disrepair, but the interior is in good nick, its triple-aisled nave supported by mighty columns and illuminated by an impressive spread of stained-glass windows.

Musée Camille Lemonnier

The **Musée Camille Lemonnier** (Mon & Thurs 2–4pm, Wed & Fri 10am–noon & 2–4pm; free), a brief walk east of St-Boniface at chaussée de Wavre 150, is dedicated to the eponymous Belgian intellectual, writer, dramatist and essayist, who was an influential member of the city's cultural elite for almost fifty years. A sharp-witted Francophone, Lemonnier (1844–1913) started out writing for a literary review, the *Journal des Artistiques*, and subsequently turned his hand to novels, books of art criticism – including the *Histoire de Beaux-Arts en Belgique* (1887) – and political texts. There were also monographs on the artists of the day – for instance Henri de Braekeleer, Alfred Stevens and Constantin Meunier – as well as oodles of stuff on the avant-garde Les XX (see p.107). Inevitably, Lemonnier's acid tongue created hostility and bitter arguments punctuated his career, most disagreeably with the artist James Ensor.

Set up by Camille's daughter Louise in 1946, the **museum** is housed in an attractive late nineteenth-century building and holds an eclectic collection of *objets d'art*, everything from sculptures and paintings to gilded books. In the main room upstairs are paintings by Louise, hanging alongside portraits of her father by Emile Claus, Constantin Meunier and Isidore Verheyden. Other paintings of note include *The Fair* by Victor Gilsoul, and the bleak *Hunter in the Snow* by Emile Verheyden, Lemonnier's cousin. The finest of the sculptures are *The*

Foolish Song by Jef Lambeaux and *Eternal Spring* by Auguste Rodin. Incidentally, several of our readers have complained that they were unable to gain admission to the Musée Camille Lemonnier during its listed opening hours. To double check, call ☎02 512 29 68.

Place Fernand Cocq

From the Musée Camille Lemonnier, rue de la Tulipe leads south back to the chaussée d'Ixelles and **place Fernand Cocq**, a small, refreshingly leafy square named after a one-time Ixelles burgomaster, and lined with a good selection of bars, including *Volle Gas* (see p.193) and *L'Amour Fou* (see p.204). The square's centrepiece is the **Maison communale**, a sturdy Neoclassical building designed by the Flemish architect Vanderstraeten for the opera singer **Maria Malibran**, née Garcia (1808–36), and her lover, the Belgian violinist Charles de Bériot. Malibran was one of the great stars of her day and her contralto voice created a sensation when she first appeared on the stage in London in 1825. Her father, one Manuel Garcia, trained her and organized her tours, but pushed his daughter into a most unfortunate marriage in New York. Mr Malibran turned out to be bankrupt and Maria pluckily left husband and father behind, returning to Europe to pick up her career. She was fantastically successful and had this Ixelles mansion built for herself and Bériot in 1833. After her death, the house lay uninhabited until it was bought by the Ixelles *commune* in 1849; the gardens in which Maria once practised have been reduced to a small park that now fronts the house.

Musée des Beaux-Arts d'Ixelles

The excellent **Musée des Beaux-Arts d'Ixelles** (Tues–Fri 1–6.30pm, Sat & Sun 10am–5pm; free, except during exhibitions), rue Jean van Volsem 71, is located about ten minutes' walk southeast of place Fernand Cocq, via rue du Collège. Established in an old slaughterhouse in 1892, the museum was enlarged and refurbished a few years back and since then it has built up an excellent reputation for the quality of its temporary exhibitions, ranging from Belgian surrealism through to Russian modernism. The permanent collection is mainly late nineteenth- and early twentieth-century Belgian material, but it tends to play second fiddle to the exhibitions and is regularly chopped and changed, so although we mention some of the paintings you're likely to see, there are no guarantees. The museum's temporary exhibitions are almost always held in the **main auditorium**, a substantial warehouse-like affair ringed by two elevated galleries and located to the right of the entrance. The permanent collection is displayed in the long, single-storey **wing** that leads off from this auditorium.

Highlights of the **permanent collection** include several exquisite pointillist canvases, the pick of which is Theo van Rysselberghe's (1862–1926) charming painting of three women having tea in the garden and the playful primitivism of Gustave de Smet (1877–1943), who has around a dozen paintings here. There's also a wonderful collection of haunting works by Charles Herman, one of a group of Belgian realists who struggled to get their work exhibited in the capital's salons, which until the late 1870s would contemplate only Romantic and Neoclassical works. Look out, also, for the large collection of posters featuring the work of Toulouse-Lautrec (1864–1901) – thirty of his total output of thirty-two are owned by the museum.

Among the more modern artists featured are well-known figures like the surrealist Paul Delvaux (1897–1994) and Marcel Broodthaers (1924–76),

Les XX

Founded in 1883, **Les XX** was an influential group of twenty Belgian painters, designers and sculptors, who were keen to bring together all the different strands of their respective crafts. For ten years, they staged an annual exhibition showcasing both domestic and international talent and it was here that Cézanne, Manet and Gauguin were all exhibited at the very beginning of their careers. With members as diverse as the painter Ensor and the architect-designer Henri van de Velde, Les XX never professed to be united by the same artistic principles, but several of its members, including Theo van Rysselberghe, were inordinately impressed by the Post-Impressionism of Seurat, whose pointillist *The Big Bowl* created a sensation when it was exhibited by Les XX in 1887.

Les XX – and the other literary-artistic groupings which succeeded it – were part of a general **avant-garde** movement which flourished in Brussels at the end of the nineteenth century. This avant-garde was deeply disenchanted with Brussels' traditional salon culture, not only for artistic reasons but also because of its indifference to the plight of the Belgian working class. Such political views nourished close links with the fledgling **Socialist movement**, and Les XX even ran the slogan "art and the people have the same enemy – the reactionary bourgeoisie". Indeed, the Belgian avant-garde came to see art (in all its forms) as a vehicle for liberating the Belgian worker, a project regularly proclaimed in *L'Art Moderne*, their most authoritative mouthpiece.

who pops up with an eerily abstracted *Winter Landscape*, through to less familiar names such as Edgar Tytgat and Constant Permeke. There is also a healthy sample of the work of René Magritte (1898–1967), perhaps most persuasively *La Corde Sensible*, in which an over-sized cup and cloud are set against a mountainous backdrop; for more on Magritte, see p.127.

Finally, the museum possesses a smattering of **sculptures**, with the main event being Rodin's *La Lorraine* and *J.B. Willems*. Rodin (1840–1917) used to have a studio in Ixelles, at rue Sans Souci 111, and this was where he designed his first major work, *The Age of Bronze*. When it was exhibited in 1878, there was outrage: Rodin's naturalistic treatment of the naked body broke with convention and created something of a scandal – he was even accused of casting his sculptures round live models.

To **get to** the museum by public transport, take **bus** #71 linking Bruxelles-Centrale station with Porte de Namur, the chaussée d'Ixelles and place Eugène Flagey, and walk up from there.

South to the étangs d'Ixelles

From the Musée des Beaux-Arts d'Ixelles – as well as place Fernand Cocq (see p.106) – it's an uneventful ten minutes' walk south to **place Eugène Flagey**, whose fortunes are on the up after a long period of neglect: by the 1990s, the square had become a bare, dispiriting expanse, but it is now in the middle of a major revamp and the chain of 1930s modernist buildings that fringes its southern side has new life and purpose. The largest is the former National Broadcasting Institute, a sweeping structure of yellow brick and acres of glass that was completed in 1937. It is, perhaps, hard to fathom quite why, but the building is regarded with some warmth by the locals, who call it **le paquebot** for its resemblance to a luxury liner.

To the southwest of place Eugène Flagey lie the **étangs d'Ixelles**, two little lakes – really large ponds – that are flanked by several handsome Art Nouveau

The EU Quarter and around

A s Belgium thrived during the nineteenth century, Brussels began to expand beyond the petit ring, Léopold II in particular building smart residential areas to the east that incorporated the grandiloquent monuments and parks that he felt were a fitting reflection of his young nation's new-found status amongst the world's leading industrial nations. Much of the essentials of Léopold's grand design have survived, most notably the Parc du Cinquantenaire, and they provide the district's key attractions; but it's been somewhat contaminated by the uncompromising office blocks and wanton speculation of the **EU Quarter**, known properly as the Quartier des Institutions Européennes – home to the **European Commission**, whose civil servants support and advise the EU's ultimate decision-making body, the **Council of Ministers**, and part of the **European Parliament** (which also sits in Strasbourg). This part of town is hard to like: the streets groan with traffic and a vast building programme has turned whole blocks into dusty construction sites, interspersed with rundown and boarded-up terraces looking over scraps of waste ground. Walking around the district, you can't help but get the feeling of "Europe" as a huge, unfinished project: there's so much construction going on, so much money being spent; and the buildings are so overblown with their own sense of self-importance. But the odd isolated island of charm survives, and there has been a recent wave of repentance in the EU, with the result that its most recent buildings are not quite the inhumane monsters of before (witness the refurbishment of the much-hated Berlaymont). Nonetheless, despite recent efforts to create a more friendly, human-scale environment, it's not the city's most appealing quarter and to enjoy a visit you'll need to know what you want to see and to follow a clear itinerary – one which allows you to avoid, as much as possible, rues de la Loi and Belliard, the two wide boulevards that serve as the area's main thoroughfares. The best place to start is in the vicinity of **Parc Léopold**, just a few minutes' stroll from the petit ring, where you'll find the intriguing **Musée Wiertz**, exhibiting the huge and eccentric paintings of the eponymous artist, footsteps from the gleaming **European Parliament building**. Below the park, around **place Jourdan**, there are a few streets that retain some of the charm that has been otherwise swept away, and it's just a ten-minute walk from here to the **Parc du Cinquantenaire**, with its triumphal arch built to celebrate the

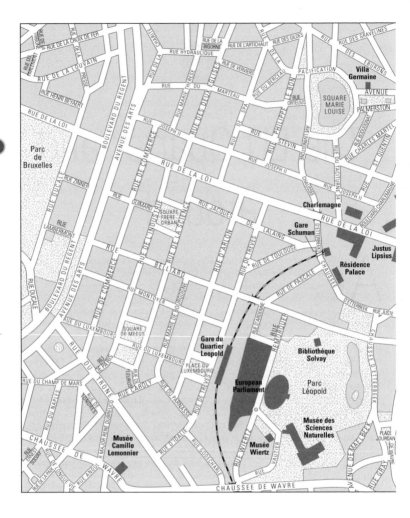

golden jubilee of Belgian independence and three large and rather old-fashioned museums.

Square de Meeus and place du Luxembourg

Place du Trône, with its double lion gates and sooty, life-size statue of Léopold II, perched on his horse, makes a fittingly grand start to any tour of the EU Quarter. From here **rue du Luxembourg** heads east, bisecting **Square de Meeus**, a small city park whose northern half contains a modest

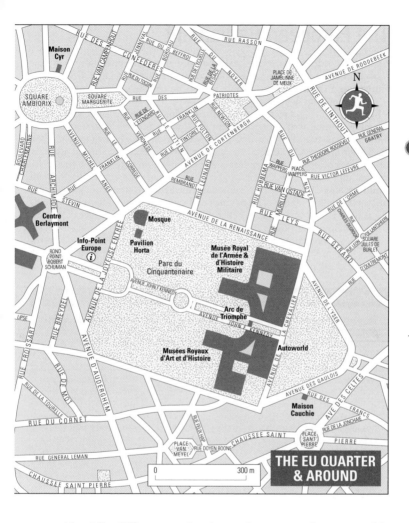

Within the map:

Maison Cyr

SQUARE
AMBIORIX

SQUARE
MARGUERITE

RUE DES CONFEDERES

PLACE DE
JAMBLINNE
DE MEUX

AVENUE DE ROODEBEEK

N

Centre
Berlaymont

Info-Point
Europe
(i)

ROND
POINT
ROBERT
SCHUMAN

Mosque

Pavilion
Horta

Parc du
Cinquantenaire

AVENUE DE LA RENAISSANCE

Musée Royal
de l'Armée &
d'Histoire
Militaire

SQUARE
JULES DE
BURLET

Arc de
Triomphe

Musées Royaux
d'Art et d'Histoire

Autoworld

Maison
Cauchie

THE EU QUARTER
& AROUND

0   300 m

memorial to Julien Dillens, a popular nineteenth-century sculptor responsible for the effigy of Everard 't Serclaes on the Grand-Place. A leafy, well-proportioned open space, it must have been nice before it became surrounded by the undistinguished boxy office blocks of Euroland. Just along the street, the **place duLuxembourg** is a scruffier, more characterful square, overlooked by the ever-burgeoning buildings of the European Parliament, just across the railway tracks. The square's fortunes are on the up, with fashionable cafés moving in as its three-storey, stone-trimmed houses are refurbished. In the middle of the square, a statue remembers John Cockerill (1790–1840), a British entrepreneur who built a steel-making empire in southern Belgium, particularly Liège. His pioneering efforts certainly transformed the local economy – and his company still exists today – but the loyal workers at his feet stretch the point somewhat, as does the statue's inscription: *Au père des ouvriers* ("To the father of the workers").

The European Parliament

On the far side of place du Luxembourg, behind the once tatty but now modernized Gare du Quartier Léopold station, rises the veritable cliff-face of the **European Parliament** – accessible by way of a walkway through the station – a glass, stone and steel whopper equipped with a curved glass roof that rises to a height of 70m. Completed in 1997, the building contains a large, semicircular assembly room as well as the offices of the President of the Parliament and the General Secretariat. The structure has its admirers, but it's known locally as the *caprices des dieux* or "whims of the gods", after its undeniably fanciful assertion of its own power, and its resemblance to a well-known supermarket cheese. It's divided into two wings: the first, nearest the station, is known as the **Spinelli building**, and houses the MEPs' offices and the library; it also has an information office which dishes out EU propaganda and can answer questions on the building and advise on tours. On the other side of rue Wiertz, the smaller of the two wings, the **Spaak building**, is home to the horseshoe-shaped debating chamber, committee rooms and the press centre, and is visitable on free guided **tours**. Depending on what's happening in the Parliament, these leave from the Spaak building's north entrance (Mon–Thurs 10am & 3pm, Fri 10am; tours take about

The European Union

The **European Union** is operated by three main institutions, each of which does most of its work in Brussels:

The **European Parliament** sits in Strasbourg, but meets in Brussels for around six two-day plenary sessions per year. It's the only EU institution to meet and debate in public, and has been directly elected since 1979. There are currently 736 MEPs, and they sit in political blocks rather than national delegations; members are very restricted on speaking time, and debates tend to be well-mannered consensual affairs, sternly controlled by the President, who – along with 14 Vice-Presidents – is elected for two and a half years, by Parliament itself. The President (or a Vice-President) meets with the leaders of the political groups to plan future parliamentary business. Basically the Commission submits legislation to Parliament, and it's debated first by committees, who meet in Brussels every month. Their work is then presented to the EP's plenary sessions, which consider the legislation at the same time as the European Commission. If – and only if – they can agree, then the legislation is adopted.

The **Council of Ministers** consists of the heads of government of each of the member states and the President of the European Commission (see below). They meet regularly in "European Summits". Most Council meetings are not, however, attended by the heads of government, but by a delegated minister. There are complex rules regarding decision-making: some subjects require only a simple majority, others need unanimous support. This political structure is underpinned by scores of committees and working parties made up of both civil servants and political appointees. These committees and working parties are based in Brussels. The Council of Ministers' HQ is the Justus Lipsius building on rue de la Loi.

The **European Commission** acts as the EU's executive arm and board of control, managing funds and monitoring all manner of agreements. The twenty Commissioners are political appointees, nominated by their home country, but once they're in office they are accountable to the European Parliament. The president of the Commission is elected by the European Parliament for a three-year period of office. Over 10,000 civil servants work for the Commission, whose headquarters are in Brussels, in the Berlaymont and adjacent Charlemagne building on rue de la Loi.

△ The European Parliament

30min, and you'll need to take ID). They're fairly cursory affairs, more or less a look at the debating chamber and the stairwell outside, with the aid of headphones that take you through the whole thing and explain how the EU works. It's not exactly essential viewing, but you do learn something of the purpose of the building – which, amazingly enough, is here mainly to house the Parliament's various committees (most of the debates take place in Strasbourg).

△ Musée Wiertz

Musée Wiertz

Five minutes' walk from the European Parliament building, up the slope at rue Vautier 62, the **Musée Wiertz** (Tues–Fri 10am–noon & 1–5pm; alternate weekends 10am–noon & 1–5pm; free) is a small museum devoted to the works of one of the city's most distinctive, if disagreeable, nineteenth-century artists. Once immensely popular – so much so that Thomas Hardy in *Tess of the d'Urbervilles* could write of "the staring and ghastly attitudes of a Wiertz museum" – **Antoine-Joseph Wiertz** (1806–65) painted religious and mythological canvases, featuring gory hells and strapping nudes, as well as fearsome scenes of human madness and suffering. The core of the museum is housed in his studio, a large, airy space that was built for him by the Belgian state on the understanding that he bequeath his work to the nation. Pictures include *The Burnt Child*, *The Thoughts and Visions of a Severed Head* and a small but especially gruesome *Suicide* – not for the squeamish. There are also a number of smaller, quite elegantly painted quasi-erotic pieces featuring coy nudes, and a colossal *Triumph of Christ*, a melodramatic painting of which Wiertz was inordinately proud. Three adjoining rooms contain further macabre works, such as *Premature Burial* and *Hunger, Folly, Crime*, in which a madwoman is pictured shortly after hacking off her child's leg and throwing it into the cooking pot. Mercifully, there's some more restrained stuff here too, including several portraits and more saucy girls in various states of undress. It's strong stuff, and technically accomplished – after all Wiertz was a good painter. But he eventually came to believe that he was a better painter than Rubens and Michelangelo. Judge for yourself.

Muséum des Sciences Naturelles

Follow rue Vautier up the hill from the Wiertz museum and you come to the **Muséum des Sciences Naturelles**, at rue Vautier 29 (Tues–Fri 9.30am–4.45pm, Sat & Sun 10am–6pm; €4; ⊛www.sciencesnaturelles.be), which holds the city's natural history collection. It's a large, sprawling museum, and is currently undergoing a much-needed restoration to its mixture of late nineteenth-century and 1960s galleries. When fully open, you can expect to find sections devoted to crystals and rocks and rodents and mammals on the ground floor; insects and crustaceans upstairs; and, perhaps most impressive of all, a man and dinosaur section with a fine set of iguanodon skeletons – two-legged herbivores discovered in the coal mines of Hainaut in the late nineteenth century. Other museum highlights include a first-rate collection of tropical shells, a section comparing the Arctic and Antarctic, and a whale gallery featuring eighteen skeletons, including the enormous remains of a blue whale.

Parc Léopold and around

On rue Vautier, almost opposite the Musée Wiertz, a scruffy back entrance leads into the rear of **Parc Léopold**, a hilly enclave landscaped around a lake. The park is pleasant enough, but its open spaces were encroached upon years ago when the industrialist Ernest Solvay began constructing the educational and research facilities of a prototype science centre here. The result is a string of big old buildings that spreads along the park's western periphery. The most interesting is the first you'll come to, the newly refurbished **Bibliothèque Solvay** (no set opening times), a splendid barrel-vaulted structure with magnificent mahogany panelling. Down below the library and the other buildings, at the bottom of the slope, is the main entrance to Parc Léopold, where a set of stumpy stone gates bear the legend "Jardin royal de zoologie". Léopold wanted the park to be a zoo, but for once his plans went awry. Leave the park by this front entrance and you're on rue Belliard, a block from rue de la Loi – the two traffic-choked main arteries of the EU Quarter, neither of which hold much interest for themselves, but which serve as a route through to the Parc du Cinquantenaire (see p.117). You'll need fortification first, though, for which one of the cafés or restaurants that fringe the pleasant triangle of nearby **place Jourdan** – or its fine and famous long-established *frites* stand – should prove a very welcome standby.

Rue de la Loi, rue Belliard and around

The office blocks of the EU are concentrated along and between the two wide boulevards – **rue de la Loi** and **rue Belliard** – which Léopold II built to connect his Parc du Cinquantenaire with the city centre. It's not an interesting area to visit: the EU remains committed to modernistic, state-of-the-art high-rises and street-level here is dominated by offputting lobbies and lines of traffic – not a shop, not a café in sight. The hub of the area, around

rondpoint Schuman, is a little more lively, home to the EU's most notorious construction, the **Centre Berlaymont**, a huge office building that was widely praised for its ground-breaking design – shaped like a giant cross of St Andrew – when it opened in 1967, but in 1991 was abandoned for health and safety reasons when it was discovered the building was riddled with asbestos and (ironically) contravened EU regulations. It has recently reopened after a refurbishment that took twelve years, and certainly looks a lot better – just as well, given its role as home to the executive council of the EU, the European Commission. It remains probably the best-known symbol of the EU, and has recently been acquired from the Belgian state by the EU for around €550 million. Next door, the huge **Charlemagne building** houses the rest of the European Commission's bloated bureaucracy, while opposite, housing the Council of Ministers, is the more recent boxy cream-coloured **Justus Lipsius building**, constructed in the mid-Nineties and almost as bland and nondescript as the Berlaymont is flamboyant. Almost next door, the Art Deco **Résidence Palace** is under renovation and will soon be open as the world's largest press centre. Finally, the **Info-Point Europe** office at rue de la Loi 244 (Mon–Fri 9am–4pm), between rondpoint Schuman and the Cinquantenaire park, has more information on the EU than anyone could ever want or need.

Although EU buildings dominate this segment of the city, not everything is on such a large scale. Just behind Berlaymont, **rue Archimède** has a pleasant stretch of shops and cafés serving the Eurocrats and ex pats, and it leads through to two pleasant and leafy plazas – squares Ambiorix and Marie-Louise – which were laid out in the 1870s on what had previously been marshland. By the end of the century, they formed, along with the short avenue Palmerston which linked them, one of the city's most fashionable suburbs, where the residences of the bourgeoisie included several splendid examples of Art Nouveau – none, unfortunately, open to visitors. Nowadays, **square Ambiorix** is largely overshadowed by modern apartments, but you shouldn't miss the superb facade of the **Maison Cyr**, on the far side of the square at no. 11, one of the city's most ornate Art Nouveau buildings and the one-time home of the painter Georges de Saint-Cyr. The house itself is almost impossibly narrow, but its spidery balconies and swirling window frames make a flamboyant artistic statement nonetheless. "I daresay I have commissioned one of the most beautiful houses on the square," the painter observed modestly – but with some justification. Just below here, on avenue Palmerston, the **Villa Germaine**, at no. 24, exhibits striking floral patterned tiles and multicoloured bricks, while down at the foot of the street are three wonderfully subtle buildings by Victor Horta: no. 2 is a charming corner house with a delicately carved, fluted stone facade, completed a few years after the adjoining no. 4, which has a functional design of riveted cast-iron softened by arched lintels and mosaics; together they're known as the **Hôtel van Eetvelde**. And finally there's the austere facade of no. 3, across the street, whose white and grey stone trimmings lead round to an exuberant side-entrance.

The south side of **square Marie-Louise** is occupied by a series of big old houses whose stone trimmings, balconies, dormer windows and high gables jostle each other. Just off the square, back towards rue de la Loi, rue du Taciturne 34 is a lavish structure with an elegant facade of intricate window grilles and tiny black columns. It was designed by Paul Saintenoy, who was also responsible for the Old England building at the top of rue Ravenstein. If you want to see more of this sort of architecture, see p.120 for the Maison Cauchie, and pp.98–100 for more of the work of Victor Horta.

Le Cinquantenaire

The wide and largely featureless lawns of the **Parc du Cinquantenaire** slope up towards a gargantuan triumphal **arch** surmounted by a huge and bombastic bronze entitled *Brabant Raising the National Flag*. The arch, along with the two heavyweight stone buildings it connects, comprise **Le Cinquantenaire**, which

△ The Musées Royaux d'Art et d'Histoire

was placed here by Léopold II for an exhibition to mark the golden jubilee of the Belgian state in 1880. By all accounts the exhibition of all things made in Belgium and its colonies was a great success, and the park continues to host shows and trade fairs of various kinds, while the buildings themselves – a brief walk from Métro Merode – contain extensive collections of art and applied art, weapons and cars, displayed in three separate museums.

The only thing to see in the park itself is the **Pavillon Horta** (Tues–Fri 2.30–3.30pm; €2, tickets from the Museé Royaux d'Art et d'Histoire), a grey, graffitied Neoclassical box that is subtitled the "pavilion of human passions", due to the sculpture inside, by Jef Lambeaux, from 1886, which shows writhing naked figures overlooked by a shrouded depiction of death. Designed specifically to hold the sculpture, this was Horta's first public commission and shows no hint of the later organic decorative work for which he became known. In fact, the building was closed three days after opening due to the controversy the no-holds-barred work caused. The big cream-coloured building next door is Brussels' main **mosque**, built in 1978 in a modern Arabic style by a Tunisian architect but not in fact a symbol of the city's new multiculturalism – it was, rather, a replacement for an earlier building that dated from 1897.

Musées Royaux d'Art et d'Histoire

The **Musées Royaux d'Art et d'Histoire**, on the south side of the south wing of the Cinquantenaire complex (Tues–Fri 9.30am–5pm, Sat & Sun 10am–5pm; €4; ⊛www.kmkg-mrah.be), is made up of a maddening and badly labelled maze of pottery, carvings, furniture, tapestries, glassware and lacework from all over the world. There's almost too much to absorb in even a couple of visits, and there's no plan, which makes it even harder to select the bits that interest you most. There are enormous galleries of mostly run-of-the-mill Greek, Egyptian and Roman artefacts, an assortment of Far Eastern art and textiles, medieval and Renaissance carving and religious artefacts, and a decent collection of glasswork from all eras. But perhaps the best thing to do with a large, disorganized museum of this nature, is to wander freely and stop when something catches your eye.

To the right of the entrance hall, the **European decorative arts** sections have perhaps the most immediacy, featuring everything from Delft ceramics, altarpieces, porcelain and silverware through to tapestries, and Art Deco and Art Nouveau furnishings. It's all a little bewildering, however, with little to link one set of objects to another. The ground level also has glassware from Roman times to the nineteenth century alongside a Gothic-style cloister, next to which are some striking fifteenth- and sixteenth-century **altarpieces** from Brussels and Antwerp churches, notably the *Passion Altarpiece*, animated with a mass of finely detailed wooden reliefs. Carved in Brussels in the 1470s, it's quite different from the *Passion Altarpiece* in the next room, made in Antwerp some fifty years later and much more extravagant, sporting a veritable doll's house of figures. Seek out, too, *The Triumph of the Virtues*, a set of eight Brussels **tapestries** dating from the middle of the sixteenth century, the heyday of the city's tapestry industry, as well as less languid earlier works manufactured during the fifteenth century in Tournai, southern Belgium, depicting scenes of tense and often violent drama as in the *Battle of Roncesvalles*, in which Christians and Moors slug it out in a fearsome, seething battle scene. Other sixteenth-century Brussels tapestries include *The Legend of Notre Dame of Sablon* (see p.90), while there are also some fine alabasters from Mechelen, just north of Brussels, and a delightful double bed – a fancy, canopied affair produced for a Swiss burgher in the 1680s. Finally, don't leave without poking your nose round the **Art Nouveau** sections, where the display cases were designed by Victor Horta for a firm of jewellers, and now accommodate the celebrated *Mysterious Sphinx*, a ceramic bust of archetypal Art Nouveau design. It was the work of Charles van der Stappen in 1897. **Upstairs** there's more glassware, including some nice twentieth-century pieces, all presided over by a giant equestrian statue of Léopold II.

Back on the ground floor, on the other side of the entrance hall, there's an excellent **shop** – certainly the best-organized bit of the museum – and, beyond, halls devoted to ancient civilizations. The **Roman collection** focuses on a giant hunting mosaic from 415 AD, which you can view from above and from ground level – it's very vivid and well preserved, showing hunters spearing tigers and chasing lions with dogs. There are also busts of emperors and dignitaries, including a full-length bronze of Septimus Severus, and a number of floor mosaics from villas in Syria. On the same floor at the moment the **Greek collection** consists mainly of Greek and Hellenistic pottery, while upstairs the **Egyptian section** has an array of funerary stelae, sculptures and ancient furniture. On the other side of the main staircase, the **Asian section** is probably better, with a particularly strong collection of Chinese and Indonesian artiefacts: stone buddhas and bodhisattvas, puppets and theatrical masks, and a huge lacquered Chinese bed – which after this lot you might be tempted to sink into.

Autoworld

Housed in a vast hangar-like building in the south wing of Le Cinquantenaire, **Autoworld** (April–Sept daily 10am–6pm; Oct–March daily 10am–5pm; €6; ⓦwww.autoworld.be) is a chronological stroll through the short history of the automobile, with a huge display of vintage vehicles, beginning with early turn-of-the-century motorized cycles and Model Ts. Perhaps inevitably, European varieties predominate: there are lots of vehicles from Peugeot, Renault and Benz, and homegrown examples, too, including a Minerva from 1925 which once belonged to the Belgian monarch. American makes include early Cadillacs, a Lincoln from 1965 that was also owned by the Belgian royals, and some great gangster-style Oldsmobiles; among the British brands, there's a mint-condition Rolls-Royce Silver Ghost from 1921, one of the first Austins, and, from the modern era, the short-lived De Lorean sports car. Upstairs is a collection of assorted vehicles that don't fit into the main exhibition. It's a bit of a mish-mash, but worth a brief look for some early Porsches and Volvos, classic 1960s Jags and even a tuk-tuk from Thailand. The museum's major drawback is its lack of recent vehicles – few cars date from after the mid-1970s. That said, there's good English labelling, at least on the downstairs exhibits, and a decent museum shop, with lots of automobile-related gear, including a great selection of model cars. Its restaurant is also a bonus if you're flagging.

Musée Royal de l'Armée et d'Histoire militaire

In the north wing of Le Cinquantenaire, on the other side of the triumphal arch from the other two museums, the **Musée Royal de l'Armée et d'Histoire Militaire** (Tues–Sun 9am–noon & 1–4.45pm; free; ⓦwww.klm-mra.be) traces the history of the Belgian army from independence to the present day by means of weapons, uniforms and paintings. It's a great museum in its way, with large and well – if rather stuffily – displayed collections. There are also sections dealing with "Belgian" regiments in the Austrian and Napoleonic armies, and, more interestingly, the volunteers who formed the nucleus of the 1830 revolution. The hall devoted to World War I is excellent, with uniforms and kit from just about every nationality involved in the conflict, together with a fearsome array of field guns, tanks and a German Fokker replica (in red, naturally). The courtyard outside has a squadron of tanks from the 1940s – British, American and German – while the largest hall is devoted to aviation, and not just military either, with a Sabena Caravelle among its extensive collection, although the highlights are inevitably the jet fighters – a Belgian airforce F16, a Mirage and MIG23, and the obligatory Hurricane and Spitfire. The big Hall Bordiau overlooking the park covers World War II, and depicts the build-up to the war, including the Belgian experience of fascism and Flemish collaboration, plus it has some great blown-up photographs of the end of the conflict and liberation. Finally, a nice bonus to the museum is the fact that you can get out onto the **triumphal arch** and enjoy extensive views over the city from its terrace. And military buffs will enjoy the books and models in the museum shop. All in all, much more interesting than you might expect.

Maison Cauchie

Visible through the trees from the Cinquantenaire museums, the facade of the **Maison Cauchie**, rue des Francs 5 (open first weekend of each month 11am–1pm & 2–6pm; €7), is the epitome of the decorative Art Nouveau tradition, and considered to be one of the finest examples of the style in Brussels. Paul Cauchie, who had the house built in 1905, was a designer and painter who specialized in the "sgraffiti" style that decorated the facades of Art Nouveau houses, and the twenty-metre-high frontage is a literal advertisement for his work, elegantly decorated with nine muses evoking the arts. You have to take a tour to see inside, but it's small enough, the basement and former studio displaying paintings by Cauchie and his contemporaries, and detailing the evolution of the house, while the first floor shows the living quarters pretty much as they were when Cauchie died in 1952.

The Outlying Districts

B russels pushes out in all directions from the city centre and the inner suburbs, its present-day perimeter – marked by the ring road, the RO – enclosing no fewer than nineteen *communes*. Within this circle, the city's **Outlying Districts** are little known by tourists but they do hold a handful of first-rate attractions as well as some lesser sights. All of the places mentioned are within easy reach of the centre by public transport.

On the western edge of the city centre, the gritty *commune* of **Anderlecht** comes top in the order of places to visit, a tight-knit working-class suburb that has a small-town provincial feel and is home to one of Europe's most famous football teams (see p.226). It's also the location of the Maison d'Erasme, where Erasmus holed up for a few months in 1521, and the Musée Bruxellois de la Gueuze, devoted to the production of the eponymous brew. **Koekelberg**, just to the north, is less well endowed but is the site of the colossal Basilique du Sacré Coeur, visible from just about everywhere in Brussels, while **Jette**, next door, boasts the enjoyable Musée René Magritte, sited in the artist's old home and studio. To the north, **Heysel** is best known as the location of the infamous Heysel stadium, scene of the 1985 Liverpool-Juventus football crowd disaster, but it's also home to the Atomium, whose giant metal balls are virtually the symbol of the city, and other attractions that might suit kids. Next door is leafy **Laeken**, whose sprawling parkland is dotted with the accoutrements of the Belgian royals – their greenhouses, statues and monuments, as well as the main palace and a couple of regal follies, a Japanese tower and a Chinese pavilion.

South of the city centre, the small town of **Tervuren** is the site of the Musée Royal de l'Afrique Centrale, whose assorted African artefacts were first brought together by Léopold II, while a little way west of here lies the **Forêt de Soignes**, a great chunk of forest criss-crossed by footpaths and scattered with picnic sites. Further west still, prosperous and leafy **Uccle** sports the marvellous house and art collection of the Musée David et Alice van Buuren.

The western suburbs

Brussels' **western suburbs** are a rather dreary collection of grey, industrial districts that on first impressions seem to have little to recommend them. But there are one or two highlights that can make a trip out to this part of town worthwhile – and the good thing is that the public transport connections make it easy to be selective. The centre of Anderlecht is easily accessed by métro (to

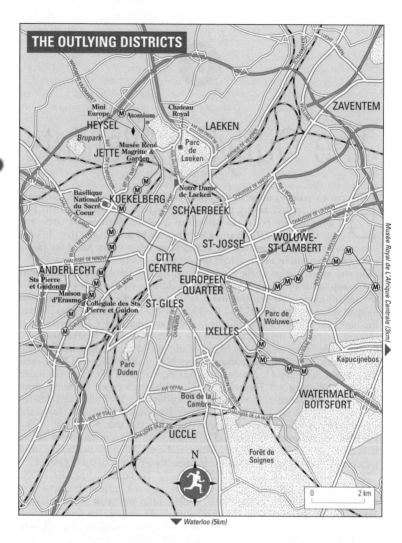

THE OUTLYING DISTRICTS

ZAVENTEM

Mini Europe · Atomium · Château Royal · HEYSEL · LAEKEN

Brupark

JETTE · Musée René Magritte & Garden · Parc de Laeken

Basilique Nationale du Sacré Coeur · KOEKELBERG · Notre Dame de Laeken · SCHAERBEEK

ST-JOSSE · WOLUWE-ST-LAMBERT

CITY CENTRE

ANDERLECHT · Sts Pierre et Guidon · EUROPEEN QUARTER

Maison d'Erasme · Collégiale des Sts Pierre et Guidon · ST-GILES · Parc de Woluwe

IXELLES · Kapucijnebos

Parc Duden · WATERMAEL-BOITSFORT

Bois de la Cambre

UCCLE · Forêt de Soignes

N

0   2 km

▼ Waterloo (5km)

St Guidon on line #1B), and is well connected to its neighbours further north by a mixture of tram (line #19) and métro (line #1B and #1A).

Anderlecht

No one could cliam **ANDERLECHT** is beautiful, but it has its attractive nooks and crannies, particularly in the vicinity of the métro station, where the area around the place de la Vaillance has the feel of a small Belgian town – a pleasant triangular plaza flanked by little cafés and the whitestone tower and facade of the **church of Sts Pierre et Guidon** (Mon–Fri 9am–noon & 2.30–6pm; free). The facade, which mostly dates from the fifteenth century, is unusually long and slender, its stonework graced by delicate flourishes and a fine set of gargoyles. Inside, the church has a surprisingly low and poorly lit nave, in a corner of which is a vaulted chapel dedicated to St Guido, otherwise known as St Guy, a local figure who was around at the end of the tenth century. Of peasant origins, Guido entered the priesthood but he invested all of his church's money in an enterprise that went bust and spent the next seven years as a pilgrim, a sackcloth-and-ashes figure who walked to Rome and Jerusalem and in between devoted most of his time to prayer and charitable works. Inside the church, a chapel contains a breezy *Miracle of St Guido* by Gaspard de Crayer, a local seventeenth-century artist who made a tidy income from religious paintings in the style of Rubens. Elsewhere in the church, several of the walls are decorated with late medieval murals and although these are incomplete and difficult to make out in the prevailing gloom, one or two make interesting viewing. On the north wall of the nave look out for the martyrdom of St Erasmus – who is having his guts ripped out – and opposite, in the Chapelle de Notre Dame de Grâce, the recently restored scenes from the life of St Guido. The chancel is of interest too – it was designed by Jan van Ruysbroeck, who was also responsible for the tower of the Hôtel de Ville (see p.45), and it contains two contrasting tombs. The earlier effigy, a recumbent knight wearing his armour, is conservative and formal, whereas the kneeling figure opposite is dressed in lavish, early Renaissance attire, his helmet placed in front of him as decoration.

The Béguinage

Behind the church, off rue du Chapelain, the two buildings of the **Béguinage** (Tues–Sun 10am–noon & 2–6pm; €1.25) face each other across a small courtyard, a world apart from the rest of Anderlecht, let alone Brussels. Founded originally in the mid-thirteenth century, this is Brussels' oldest surviving *béguinage* (a kind of convent, but inhabited by single female members of the lay community), dating from the sixteenth century, and is now a small museum, with its rooms remodeled much as they would have looked when they were built. It's a low-key attraction, but is sensitively done, with a small, Anderlecht-centred selection of artisanal and domestic artefacts on one side, and a set of period rooms on the other – an old kitchen, rooms that would have been used for lacemaking, an old sweetshop and cases showing prayers to St Guido, with cast-iron limbs and models of pigs and cows (he's the patron saint of peasants and farm animals).

Maison d'Erasme

From Sts Pierre et Guidon, it's just a couple of minutes' walk to the **Maison d'Erasme**, at rue du Chapitre 31 (Tues–Sun 10am–5pm; €1.25); turn left out of the béguinage and it's on the right. With its pretty dormer windows and sturdy symmetrical lines, this is Anderlecht's most medieval corner, a largely sixteenth-century gabled Flemish house set in its own walled garden. The oldest parts actually date from 1468, when it was built to accommodate important visitors to the church, easily the most celebrated of which was Desiderius Erasmus, who lodged here for five months in 1521. It's immaculately preserved, and hosts a variety of period exhibitions squeezed into half a dozen clearly signed rooms, but it contains none of Erasmus' actual belongings. To get the most out of a visit you should borrow the (English-language) catalogue from reception. There are lots of portraits of Erasmus, including one by Quentin Matsys in the old study, and a varied array of ancient books, including a good sample of first editions of Erasmus' work in the upstairs

By any measure, Desiderius **Erasmus** (1466–1536) was a remarkable man. Born in Rotterdam, the illegitimate son of a priest, he was orphaned at the age of thirteen and defrauded of his inheritance by his guardians, who forced him to become a monk. He hated monastic life and seized the first opportunity to leave, becoming a student at the University of Paris in 1491. Throughout the rest of his life Erasmus kept on the move, travelling between the Low Countries, England, Italy and Switzerland, and everywhere he went, his rigorous scholarship, sharp humour and strong moral sense made a tremendous impact. He attacked the abuses and corruptions of the Church, publishing scores of polemical and satirical essays which were read all over Western Europe. He argued that most monks had "no other calling than stupidity, ignorance . . . and the hope of being fed." These attacks reflected Erasmus' determination to reform the Church from within, both by rationalizing its doctrine and rooting out hypocrisy, ignorance and superstition. He employed other methods too, producing translations of the New Testament to make the Scriptures more widely accessible, and co-ordinating the efforts of like-minded Christian humanists. The Church authorities periodically harassed Erasmus but generally he was tolerated, not least for his insistence on the importance of Christian unity. Luther was less indulgent, bitterly denouncing Erasmus for "making fun of the faults and miseries of the Church of Christ instead of bewailing them before God." The quarrel between the two reflected a growing schism amongst the reformers that eventually led to the Reformation.

Salle Blanche, alongside an intriguing cabinet of altered and amended texts: some show scrawled comments made by irate readers, others are the work of the Inquisition and assorted clerical censors. The best paintings are in the *Salle Renaissance*, which boasts a charmingly inquisitive *Adoration of the Magi* by Hieronymus Bosch, a gentle *Nativity* by Gerard David, and a hallucinatory *Temptation of St Anthony* by Pieter Huys, a follower of Bosch – though it's hard not to feel that the freakish beasts populating his painting are as much to titillate as terrify. All in all the place has a peaceful and authentic atmosphere – something that is only enhanced by the calm of the walled garden, which feels a million miles from central Brussels.

Musée Bruxellois de la Gueuze

The **Musée Bruxellois de la Gueuze**, at rue Gheude 56 (Mon–Fri 8.30am–5pm, Sat & Sun 10am–5pm; €3.50; ⓦwww.cantillon.be), is ten minutes' walk north of the Gare du Midi métro station, via avenue Paul Henri Spaak and rue Limnander; to get there direct from the Maison d'Erasme, take tram #56 from the St Guidon métro station to the Gare du Midi. Founded in 1879, the museum is home to the **Cantillon Brewery**, the last surviving Gueuze brewery in Brussels. Gueuze is a Brussels beer speciality, and it's still brewed here according to traditional methods: the beer, made only of wheat, malted barley, hops and water, is allowed to ferment naturally, reacting with natural yeasts peculiar to the Brussels air, and is bottled for two years before it's ready to drink. The museum gives a fairly dry explanation of the brewing process, but the brewery itself is mustily evocative, with huge vats in which the ingredients are boiled before being placed in large oak barrels where the fermentation process begins. The results can be sampled at the tasting session at the end of your visit – and of course bought to take home and enjoy.

Koekelberg and Jette

North of Anderlecht, **KOEKELBERG** and **JETTE** merge into each other, fairly nondescript neighbourhoods for the most part that wouldn't merit a second glance if it weren't for the city's largest church and the former home of René Magritte. You can reach the basilica by taking métro line #2 to Simonis at the end of the line and walking for ten minutes through the Elisabeth Park, or by taking tram #49 from Anderlecht. To get to the Magritte museum from the basilica, you can walk or ride one stop up to métro station Belgica and then take tram #18.

The Basilique du Sacré Coeur

Commissioned by the man responsible for so much of the capital's grandiose architecture, Léopold II, the **Basilique du Sacré Coeur** (church daily: Easter

△ Basilique du Sacré Coeur

to Oct 8am–6pm; Nov to Easter 8am–5pm; free; dome daily: Easter to Oct 9am–5.15pm; Nov to Easter 10am–4.15pm; €3), is a huge structure – 140m long with a 90-metre-tall dome – which dominates its surroundings, and indeed the whole of Brussels. Begun in 1905 and still in part unfinished, the basilica was conceived as a neo-Gothic extravagance in imitation of the basilica of the Sacré Coeur in Montmartre, Paris – a structure which had made the Belgian king green with envy, and had him even more determined to build Brussels into a capital worthy of taking its place with the best of Europe. The construction costs, however, proved colossal and the plans had to be modified; the result is this amalgamation of the original neo-Gothic design with Art Deco features added in the 1920s. Inside it's undeniably impressive, with a modern sensibility that works well with the soft brown bricks and the gently filtered light – the atmosphere is more soothing, and the church cosier, than you might expect from outside. And once you've seen the church, climb up to the top of the dome for some rip-roaring views of the city.

The Musée René Magritte

To the north, Koekelberg fades into the prosperous suburb of Jette, home to the renowned **Musée René Magritte**, rue Esseghem 135 (Wed–Sun 10am–6pm; €7), which contains a plethora of the surrealist's paraphernalia, as well as a modest collection of his early paintings and sketches. Magritte lived with his wife Georgette on the ground floor of this modest house for 24 years, from 1930 to the mid-1950s, an odd location for what was effectively the headquarters of the surrealist movement in Belgium, most of whose leading lights met here every Saturday to concoct a number of shocking and subversive books, magazines and images.

The **ground floor** of the museum has been faithfully restored to recreate the artist's studio and living quarters, using mostly original ornaments and furniture, with the remainder carefully replicated from photographs. Hung behind a glass display near the indoor studio is the famous bowler hat which crops up in several of Magritte's paintings. Many features of the house itself also appear in a number of his works: the sash window, for instance, framed the painting entitled *The Human Condition*, while the glass doors to the sitting room and bedroom appeared in *The Invisible World*. Other parts of the interior, including the fireplace and staircase, as well as the lamppost in front of the house, also featured prominently in the painter's works. Magritte built himself a studio – which he named Dongo – in the garden, and it was here he produced his bread-and-butter work, such as graphics and posters, though he was usually unhappy when working on such mundane projects, and his real passions were painted in the dining-room studio, where the only work of art by another artist he possessed at the time – a photo by Man Ray – is still displayed.

You have to take off your shoes to visit the **first and second floors** of the house, which were separate apartments when the Magrittes lived here, but now are taken up by letters, photos, telegrams, lithographs, posters and sketches pertaining to the artist and his time here, all displayed in chronological order – the blue rug he had made for the bedroom, work by other surrealists, and lots of letters and telegrams, posters and prints. There are two fine posters announcing the world film and fine arts festivals which took place in Brussels in 1947 and 1949, as well as Magritte's first painting, a naive landscape which he produced at the tender age of 12. Finally there are a number of personal objects displayed in the **attic**, which he also rented, including the easel he used at the end of his life. Overall, it's a fascinating glimpse into the life of one of the most important artists of the twentieth century.

René Magritte (1898–1967) is easily the most famous of Belgium's modern artists, his disconcerting, strangely haunting images a familiar part of popular culture. Born in a small town just outside Charleroi, in southern Belgium, in 1915 he entered the Royal Academy of Fine Arts in Brussels and was a student there until 1920. His appearances were few and far between at the Academy as he preferred the company of a group of artists and friends fascinated with the Surrealist movement of the 1920s. Their antics were supposed to incorporate a serious intent – the undermining of bourgeois convention – but the surviving home movies of Magritte and his chums fooling around don't appear very revolutionary today.

Initially, Magritte worked in a broadly Cubist manner, but in 1925, influenced by the Italian painter Giorgio de Chirico, he switched over to Surrealism and almost immediately stumbled upon the themes and images that would preoccupy him for decades to come. The hallmarks of his work were striking, incorporating startling comparisons between the ordinary and the extraordinary, with the occasional erotic element. Favourite images included men in bowler hats, metamorphic figures, enormous rocks floating in the sky, tubas, fishes with human legs, bilboquets (the cup and ball game), and juxtapositions of night and day – one part of the canvas lit by artificial light, the other basking in full sunlight. He also dabbled in word paintings, mislabelling familiar forms to illustrate (or expose) the arbitrariness of linguistic signs. His canvases were devoid of emotion, deadpan images that were easy to recognize but perplexing because of their setting – perhaps most famously, the man in the suit with a bowler hat and an apple for a face.

He broke with this characteristic style on two occasions, once during the War – in despair over the Nazi occupation – and again in 1948, to revenge long years of neglect by the French artistic establishment. Hundreds had turned up to see Magritte's first Paris exhibition, but they were confronted with crass and crude paintings of childlike simplicity. These so-called "vache" paintings created a furore, and Magritte beat a hasty artistic retreat behind a smokescreen of self-justification. These two experiments alienated Magritte from most of the other Surrealists but in the event this was of little consequence as he was later picked up and popularized by an American art dealer, Alexander Iolas, who made him very rich and very famous. The Magrittes left their house in Jette in the late-Fifties, moving to a larger place that better reflected Magritte's status as a successful artist. He died in 1967, shortly after a major retrospective of his work at the Museum of Modern Art in New York which confirmed his reputation as one of the great artists of the century. You can see more of Magritte's work at the Musées Royaux des Beaux Arts (see p.80).

The northern suburbs

The main interest in Brussels' **northern suburbs** lies in the districts of **Heysel** and **Laeken** beyond the Gare du Nord, north of the centre – accessible by way of tram #19 from Jette, or métro line #1B to Heysel or Bockstael, or tram #81 from the Gare du Nord.

Heysel

Lying northwest of the city centre, **HEYSEL**, a 500-acre estate bequeathed to the authorities by Léopold II in 1909, is a theme park without a theme, a large, mainly green area with a diverse array of attractions, of which the **Atomium** (daily: April–Aug 9am–8pm; Sept–March 10am–6pm), a curious model of a molecule expanded 165 billion times, built for the 1958 World Fair in Brussels, is perhaps the most visually recognizable. Just reopened after an extensive renovation, the structure is something of a symbol of the city, and it's looking better than it has for some time, with a visitors' centre and state-of-the-art exhibitions – not to mention an excellent restaurant with superb views.

The Atomium borders a large trade fair area – the **Parc des Expositions**, where they held the World Fairs of 1935 and 1958 – and the **Stade du Roi Baudouin**, formerly the infamous Heysel football stadium (see p.226) in which 39 – mainly Italian – supporters were crushed to death when a sector wall collapsed in 1985. It's now the Belgian national stadium, with a capacity of 50,000: international fixtures are held here, and it was the main Belgian venue for Euro 2000, which Belgium hosted jointly with Holland.

The **Bruparck leisure complex** is also close by, and is a handy place to take kids, with **Océade**, a water funpark with slides, a swimming pool, wave pool and suchlike (Wed–Fri 10am–6pm, Sat & Sun 10am–9pm; €13.80, children €11.20; ⓦwww.oceade.be); a gigantic cinema complex called **Kinepolis**; and **Mini-Europe** (March 19–June daily 9.30am–6pm; July & Aug 9am–8pm; Sept 9.30am–6pm; Oct–Jan 8, 10am–6pm; €11.80, children €8.80, €18.40/15.90 for Mini Europe & Océade; ⓦwww.minieurope.com), where you can see scaled-down models of selected European landmarks and destinations – Big Ben, Venice, Vesuvius and more. In the middle of all this is a "village" with loads of places to eat a huge variety of ethnic cuisines; you can also drink and dance in various bars and of course there are plenty of souvenir shops

Laeken

Bordering Heysel on the east, around 3km north of the city, leafy **LAEKEN** is home to the royal family, who occupy a large out-of-bounds estate and have colonized the surrounding parkland with their monuments and memorials. From the south, Laeken is best approached on tram #23 or #52. Get off at the Araucaria tram stop, at Laeken's top end, just behind the **Pavillon**

△ Pavillon Chinois

Chinois (Tues–Sun 9.30am–5pm; €3, joint ticket with Tour Japonaise, free first Wed of each month), just off avenue Jules van Praet. This elegant and attractive replica of a Chinese pavilion was built by Léopold II after he had seen one at the World Fair in Paris in 1900. The king intended his creation to be a fancy restaurant, but this never materialized and the pavilion now houses a first-rate collection of Chinese and Japanese porcelain. Across the road, and reached by a tunnel from beside the pavilion, is the matching **Tour Japonaise** (same times as Pavillon Chinois; €3, joint ticket with Pavillon Chinois, free first Wed of each month), another of Léopold's follies, this time a copy of a Buddhist pagoda with parts made in Paris, Brussels and Yokohama, and now in use as a venue for temporary exhibitions – usually items from the Far Eastern collection of the Musées Royaux d'Art et d'Histoire (admission extra).

Around the corner behind the railings, along the congested avenue du Parc Royal, is the sedate **Château Royal** (no entry), the principal home of the Belgian royal family. Built in 1790, its most famous occupant was Napoleon, who stayed here on a number of occasions and signed the declaration of war on Russia here in 1812. In front of the château are the **Serres Royales**, several enormous greenhouses built for Léopold II, covering almost four acres and sheltering a mind-boggling variety of tropical and Mediterranean flora. They're pretty fantastic, but the problem is that they're only open to the public during April and May (admission €2), when the queues to see them can be daunting.

Opposite the front of the royal palace, a wide footpath leads up to the fanciful neo-Gothic monument erected in honour of Léopold I, the focal point of the pretty **Parc de Laeken**, which is also home to the Stuyvenbergh Castle, once the residence of Emperor Charles V's architect, Louis Van Bodeghem, although now used to accommodate high-ranking foreign dignitaries.

One kilometre further south along avenue du Parc Royal is the **Cimitière de Laeken** the last resting place of many influential Belgians including the artist Jef Dillen, whose tomb is marked by a copy of Rodin's *The Thinker*, and Maria Felicia Garcia, the famous Spanish soprano better known as Maria Malibran. The architect Joseph Poelaert (who designed the Palais de Justice), also lies here – fittingly perhaps, because he also designed the neo-Gothic church of Notre Dame de Laeken that stands at the cemetery's entrance, built in memory of Belgium's first Queen, Louise-Marie. Most of the country's royals are buried here, in the Royal Crypt.

The southern suburbs

Brussels is a green city and nowhere more so than in its **southern suburbs**, which ease gradually through the wild expanse of the **Forêt de Soignes** and leafy suburbs like Tervuren, Uccle, Woluwe St Pierre and into the countryside beyond. Tram #44 connects Montgomery métro station with **Tervuren**, a lovely trip which takes you down the chestnut tree-lined avenue de Tervuren and into the Forêt de Soignes before reaching the terminus at Tervuren town. The Forêt de Soignes is also accessible from the park just to the north, the Bois de la Cambre, although you have to cross the unpleasant chaussée de la Hulpe before you reach the forest's peaceful, winding footpaths, or by taking métro line #1A to the end of the line at Herrmann-Debroux – which in turn is connected with **Uccle** by bus #41.

The Forêt de Soignes

Some 5km southeast of the city, the leafy suburbs are left behind for the dense beech woodland of the **Forêt de Soignes**, one of Belgium's most beautiful national parks. Originally a royal domain used for hunting, it once covered over 27,000 acres; sadly, more than a century and a half of development has taken its toll. In the 1820s the king of the Netherlands gave the forest to the "General Society for promoting National Industry" and large parts of the forest were subsequently sold off, before it was turned over to the government in 1843. Further depletion followed when sections of the forest were cleared to make way for country estates, agricultural complexes and country houses, and in 1861 a huge slice was carved off to create a large urban park, now known as the **Bois de la Cambre**. Today just over one-third of the original forest remains.

What's left stretches from the Bois de la Cambre in its most northerly reaches, 10km southeast to La Hulpe, and from Uccle in the west, some 9km east to the Arboretum Géographique which lies less than a kilometre south of Parc de Tervuren. Despite the piecemeal development, it still remains one of the region's most attractive spaces, and is a popular escape for walkers and cyclists, as well as horse riders, golfers and anglers.

Tervuren

Six kilometres southeast of the city, the small town of **TERVUERN** is one of the prettiest (and greenest) places in the Brussels region. Bordered in the south by the beautiful Forêt de Soignes, dotted with grand old houses, and surrounded by lush woodland, it's no surprise the area is a popular place to live, particularly with British and Irish Eurocrats, although strangely enough it remains firmly off the tourist track.

Connected to the city by the ten-kilometre-long avenue de Tervuren, a route most easily covered by tram #44 from Métro Montgomery, its centrepiece is the impressive **Musée Royal de l'Afrique Centrale** situated in the **Parc de Tervuren** – an attractive park of ancient trees, manicured lawns, lakes and flower-beds. Once here, a few other sights also merit a visit, particularly the church of St Jean l'Evangéliste, on Tervuren's main square, and the Arboretum, which lies half a kilometre to the south.

The Town

From the museum, backtrack for a few minutes along Leuvensestweg until you reach Kerkstraat, where you'll find the prettily cobbled town square and a few sights worth investigating. The square itself is dominated by the imposing church of **St Jean l'Evangéliste**, a thirteenth-century Gothic edifice which contains the tomb of the Duke of Brabant, Antoine of Burgundy, who was killed at Agincourt in 1415. Close by, the **Schaakboard art gallery**, at Kerkstraat 33 (Sat & Sun 2–5pm; free), exhibits a modest but palatable collection of paintings (mainly landscapes) from the nineteenth-century Tervuren school. The square is also home to *Glacerie Mont Blanc*, where you can pause for one of the delicious homemade ice creams.

From here, continue on Kerkstraat which turns into Pardenmaktstraat, after which take the first left down Pauwstraat, which runs into Arboretumlaan; this will bring you to Tervuren's **Arboretum Géographique**. Originally part of the Forêt de Soignes, this was converted into an arboretum in 1905 on the instructions of Léopold II, and was used to train European officers for the African and Asian colonies. Today it's home to hundreds of different species of trees

– redwoods, maples, Scots pines and larches, to name but a few – and is a great place for an afternoon stroll.

Musée Royal de l'Afrique Centrale

Without a doubt Tervuren's main attraction is the **Musée Royal de l'Afrique Centrale**, Leuvensesteeweg 13 (Tues–Fri 10am–5pm, Sat & Sun 10am–6pm; €4; ⓦwww.africamuseum.be). Only a short walk along Leuvensesteeweg from the Tervuren tram terminal, it's housed in a pompous, custom-built pile constructed on the orders of King Léopold II around 1900. Personally presented with the vast Congo River basin by a conference of the European powers in 1885, Léopold became one of the country's richest men as a result. His initial attempts to secure control of the area were abetted by the explorer and ex-Confederate soldier Henry Stanley, who went to the Congo on a five-year fact-finding mission in 1879, just a few years after he had famously found the missionary David Livingstone. Even by the standards of the colonial powers, Léopold's regime was too chaotic and too extraordinarily cruel to stomach, and in 1908, one year before the museum opened, the Belgian government took over the territory, installing a marginally more liberal state bureaucracy. The country gained independence as Zaire in 1960, and its subsequent history has been one of the most bloodstained in Africa.

The museum was Léopold's own idea, a blatantly colonialist and racist enterprise which treated the Africans as a naive and primitive people and the Belgians as their paternalistic benefactors. However, the collection is undeniably rich, and its old-fashioned attitudes and presentation are currently under review, with a top-to-bottom renovation project underway that has already been going on for a couple of years and won't be complete until 2010. As such, it's hard to say what you might see for the moment; what's certain is that the museum is keen to reinvent itself as a modern ethnographical collection that takes a self-critical approach to Belgium's history – and colonialism in general. Currently you're most likely to catch temporary exhibitions from the museum's collection, of which the most interesting parts cover many aspects of Congolese life, from masks, idols and musical instruments to weapons and an impressive array

△ The Musée Royal de l'Afrique Centrale

of dope pipes; and there's a superb 22-metre-long dugout canoe. The museum's grounds are also well worth a stroll, with the formal gardens set around a series of geometric lakes, flanked by wanderable woods.

Uccle

The leafy suburb of **UCCLE** was originally a string of out-of-town hamlets which only became part of the city in the mid-nineteenth century when the aristocracy, attracted by the lush greenery, took up residence here. There's not much to bring you here, although it's pleasant enough, and is a nice way to wind up after spending time in Ixelles or St Gilles, especially to see the excellent **David and Alice van Buuren museum** (see below). To get here, take tram #92 from rue de la Régence or Gare Centrale.

Among other sights, the **Chapelle Notre Dame des Afflingés** at rue de Stalle 50, just off avenue Brugmann, is a lovely little church which dates back to the fifteenth century. Its centrepiece is the beautiful stucco ceiling which was added in the seventeenth century. From here, a ten-minute walk along avenue Vanderaey will bring you to the tranquil **Cimetière Dieweg**, unused for burials since 1958, though a waiver was granted allowing Hergé, the creator of Tintin, to be interred here in 1983. From the cemetery continue east up Diewag, crossing avenue de Wolvendael, and on the left you'll find the entrance to **Parc de Wolvendael**, a historic 45-acre estate, which is mentioned in documents dating back to 1209. It makes a lovely place for a picnic and afterwards you can view (from outside only) the small white stone **castle** built in 1753. Close by is the beautiful Louis XV summerhouse, a lovely building which, sadly, has been converted into an unimpressive restaurant. From the park, head north to avenue de Fré, where on the corner of chemin du Crabbegat you'll find **Le Cornet**, a one-time tavern much frequented by artists and writers throughout the nineteenth and early twentieth centuries. It is here that famous Belgian writer Charles de Coster sets a delightful scene in his epic novel *Till Ulenspiegel* (1867), where the hero, Till, meets women archers from Uccle.

Musée David et Alice van Buuren

A few minutes' stroll north of avenue de Fré, at avenue Léo Errera 41, the **Musée David et Alice van Buuren** (Sun & Mon 2–6pm & Sun 1–6pm, Wed 2–6pm; €7.50) is a wonderful little gallery housed in a glorious Art Deco house. Once the home of Dutch banker David van Buuren and his wife Alice, who bought the property in 1928, the house served as a live-in museum for their collection of furniture, carpets and art until 1970, a global salon of sorts, with great names like Satie, Magritte, Chanel, Ben Gurion and Lalique passing through – Van Buuren was a very well-connected banker. During World War II, David (who was Jewish) and Alice were forced to leave their home for five long years, but on their return – much to their surprise – the house and the works of art within it remained intact. The house became a museum in 1973, on the death of Alice van Buuren.

The interior is fantastic, utterly stylish yet extremely comfortable, the creation of a team of Dutch, Belgian and French master craftsmen, and a perfect reflection of the Art Deco style of the late-1920s. There are Cubist carpets and tapestries by Gidding, woodwork and furniture by the fashionable Dominique studio of Paris, including van Buuren's enormous desk, and a piano in the music room that once belonged to Erik Satie. As for the art, it's an incredibly diverse small collection, spanning five centuries and including Flemish and Italian masters, as well as many twentieth-century artists. The earlier works include

△ The Musée David et Alice van Buuren

still lifes by Fantin-Latour, several landscapes by the sixteenth-century painter Joachim Patenier, a Guardi view of Venice, a Saenredam church interior, and sketches by van Gogh – not to mention a version of *The Fall of Icarus* by Bruegel the Elder on wood, a work David acquired shortly before his death in 1955 (it's the same as the one in the Brussels' Royal Museum, though the provenance of this one is now considered dubious). Later canvases take in a couple of lovely paintings by Gustave van de Woestyne and James Ensor (a still life of shrimps and shells), Max Ernst, Rik Wouters and Constant Permeke. The picturesque garden, designed by Belgian landscape architect René Pechère, contains many rare species of rose, as well as 300 yew trees and a genuinely complex maze, in which it's fairly easy to get lost. If you go nowhere else in Uccle, this museum alone is worth the tram-ride.

7

Excursions from Brussels

Almost all of Belgium is within easy striking distance of Brussels, making the list of possible excursions almost endless. In this chapter we've picked out seven of the most appealing destinations, all within an hour's travelling time by train from the capital. To the south of Brussels lies **Waterloo**, site of Napoleon's final defeat at the hands of the Duke of Wellington in 1815. The battlefield has long been a popular tourist attraction and was once part of the "grand tour". Also to the south of Brussels, deep in the wilds of French-speaking Brabant, lies the Cistercian abbey of **Villers-la-Ville**, perhaps the most beautiful medieval ruins in the country and a popular "romantic" spot with newlyweds, who go there to have their photo snapped. To the north of the capital, in Flemish Belgium, lies **Mechelen**, with its amiable small-town airs and superb cathedral, and it's north again for the big city and port of **Antwerp**, which possesses a flourishing nightlife, medieval churches and first-rate museums, as well as an unrivalled collection of the work of its most celebrated son, Pieter Paul Rubens. There's also **Leuven**, just to the east of Brussels, the epitome of the lively university town with student cafés and bars galore plus a pair of especially handsome medieval buildings.

The flatlands of Flanders stretch west of Brussels as far as the North Sea. In medieval times, this region was the most prosperous and urbanized part of Europe and its merchants grew rich from the profits of the cloth industry. Those heady days are recalled by the superb architecture and excellent art museums of **Ghent** and especially **Bruges**, one of the most perfectly preserved medieval cities in Europe.

Waterloo

WATERLOO, now a run-of-the-mill suburb about 18km south of the centre of Brussels, has a resonance far beyond its size. On June 18, 1815, at this small crossroads town on what was once the main route into Brussels from France, Wellington masterminded the battle that put an end to the imperial ambitions of Napoleon. The battle turned out to have far more significance than even its generals realized, for not only was this the last throw of the dice for the

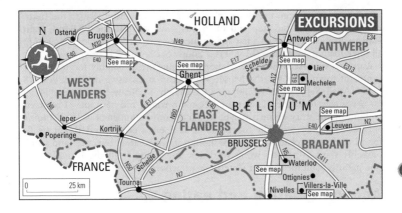

formidable army born of the French Revolution, but it also marked the end of France's prolonged attempts to dominate Europe militarily. Subsequently, however, popular memory refused to vilify Napoleon as the aggressor – and not just in France, but right across Europe, where the Emperor's bust was a common feature of the nineteenth-century drawing room. In part, this was to do with Napoleon's obvious all-round brilliance, but more crucially, he soon became a symbol of opportunity: in him the emergent middle classes of western Europe saw a common man becoming greater than the crowned heads of Europe, an almost unique event at the time.

Nevertheless, the historic importance of Waterloo has not saved the **battle-field** from interference – a motorway cuts right across it – and if you do visit you'll need a lively imagination to picture what happened and where, unless, that is, you're around to see the large-scale re-enactment which takes place every five years in June; the next one is scheduled for 2010. Scattered round the **battlefield** are several monuments and memorials, the most satisfying of which is the **Butte de Lion**, a huge earth mound that's part viewpoint and part commemoration. The battlefield is 3km north of the centre of Waterloo, where the **Musée Wellington** is the pick of the district's museums.

Arrival and information

There are several ways of getting to Waterloo and its scattering of sights, but the most effective is to make a circular loop by train, bus and train. From any of Brussels' three main stations, **trains** take you direct to Waterloo (Mon–Fri 2 hourly, Sat & Sun 1 hourly; 25min). From Waterloo train station, it's an easy fifteen-minute **walk** – turn right outside the station building and then first left along rue de la Station – to Waterloo tourist office and the Musée Wellington (see below). After you've finished at the museum, you can take **bus** #W (every 30min) from across the street – the chaussée de Bruxelles – to the Butte de Lion (see below). The bus

Getting there by train

Trains to all seven destinations described in this chapter leave from all three of the city's three main train stations – that is Bruxelles-Nord, Bruxelles-Centrale and Bruxelles-Midi (see p.28).

stops about 600m from the Butte, which you can't miss. After visiting the Butte, return to the same bus stop and catch bus #W onto **Braine-l'Alleud train station**, from where there's a fast and frequent service back to Brussels – again to all three main train stations (Mon–Fri 3 hourly, Sat & Sun 2 hourly; 15min).

Waterloo **tourist office**, the Maison du Tourisme, is handily located in the centre of town, opposite the Musée Wellington at chaussée de Bruxelles 218 (daily: April–Sept 9.30am–6.30pm; Oct–March 10.30am–5pm; ☎02 354 99 10, ⊛www.waterloo.be). They issue free town **maps** and have lots of booklets recounting the story of the battle, of which the most competent is *The Battlefield of Waterloo Step by Step*. The tourist office also sells a **combined ticket** (€12) for all the battle-related attractions, though if you're at all selective (and you'll probably want to be) this won't work out as a saving at all; the Brussels Card (see p.25) is valid for most of Waterloo's attractions, too.

Accommodation and eating

There's no compelling reason to stay the night, but Waterloo tourist office does have the details of several **hotels**, amongst which the comfortable *Hotel Le 1815* (☎02 387 01 60, ⊛www.hotelrestaurant1815.com; doubles from €125) has the advantage of being near the Butte de Lion at route du Lion 367; the rooms are decorated in smart, modern style. For **food**, *La Brioche* is a pleasant, modern café serving up a reasonably good line in sandwiches, pancakes and pastries; it's located just up along and across the street from the tourist office at chaussée de Bruxelles 161.

The Musée Wellington

Across the street from the tourist office, at chaussée de Bruxelles 147, is the **Musée Wellington** (daily: April–Sept 9.30am–6.30pm; Oct–March 10.30am–5pm; €5), which occupies the old inn where Wellington slept the nights before and after the battle. It's an enjoyable museum, whose displays detail the build-up to – and the course of – the battle with plans and models, all displayed alongside an engaging hotchpotch of personal effects. Room 4 holds the bed where Alexander Gordon, Wellington's aide-de-camp, was brought to die, and here also is the artificial leg of Lord Uxbridge, another British commander. Uxbridge is reported to have said during the battle, "I say, I've lost my leg," to which Wellington replied, "By God, sir, so you have!" After the battle, Uxbridge's leg was buried here in Waterloo, but it was returned to London when he died to join the rest of his body; in exchange, his artificial leg was donated to the museum. Neither were the bits and pieces of dead soldiers considered sacrosanct: tooth dealers roamed the battlefields of the Napoleonic Wars pulling out teeth which were then stuck on two pieces of board with a spring at the back – primitive dentures known in England as "Waterloos".

In Wellington's bedroom, Room 6, there are copies of the messages Wellington sent to his commanders during the course of the battle, curiously formal epistles laced with phrases like "Could you be so kind as to..." and "We ought to...". Wellington had a real knack for the nonchalant turn of phrase: famously, he was at the Duchess of Richmond's ball in Brussels when he heard of Napoleon's rapid advance, prompting the duke to declare "Napoleon has humbugged me". The museum's last room – Room 14 – occupies a new extension out at the back. This reprises, albeit on a slightly larger scale, what has gone before with more models and plans and military paraphernalia, plus a lucid outline of the historical background.

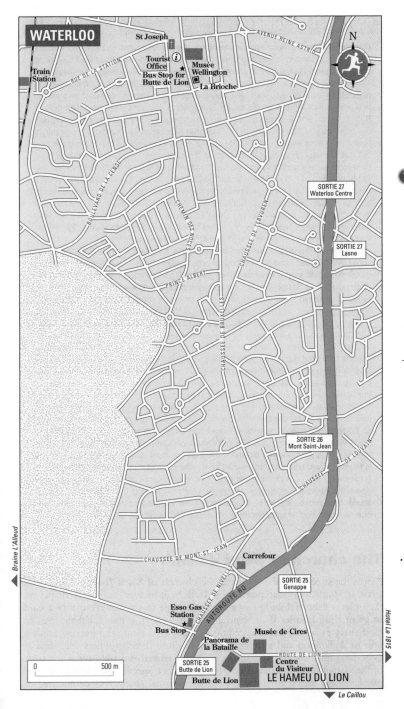

The Battle of Waterloo

Napoleon escaped from imprisonment on the Italian island of Elba on February 26, 1815. He landed in Cannes three days later and moved swiftly north, entering Paris on March 20 just as his unpopular replacement – the slothful King Louis XVIII – high-tailed it to Ghent in present-day Belgium. Thousands of Frenchmen rallied to Napoleon's colours and, with little delay, Napoleon marched northeast to fight the two armies that threatened his future. Both were in Belgium. One, an assortment of British, Dutch and German soldiers, was commanded by the **Duke of Wellington**, the other was a Prussian army led by **Marshal Blücher**. At the start of the campaign, Napoleon's army was about 130,000 strong, larger than each of the opposing armies but not big enough to fight them both at the same time. Napoleon's strategy was, therefore, quite straightforward: he had to stop Wellington and Blücher from joining together – and to this end he crossed the Belgian frontier near Charleroi to launch a quick attack. On June 16, the French hit the Prussians hard, forcing them to retreat and giving Napoleon the opportunity he was looking for. Napoleon detached a force of 30,000 soldiers to harry the retreating Prussians, while he concentrated his main army against Wellington, hoping to deliver a knock-out blow. Meanwhile, Wellington had assembled his troops at Waterloo, on the main road to Brussels.

At **dawn on Sunday June 18**, the two armies faced each other. Wellington had some 68,000 men, about one third of whom were British, and Napoleon around 5,000 more. The armies were deployed just 1500 metres apart with Wellington on the ridge north of – and uphill from – the enemy. It had rained heavily during the night, so Napoleon delayed his first attack to give the ground a chance to dry. At **11.30am**, the battle began when the French assaulted the fortified farm of Hougoumont, which was crucial for the defence of Wellington's right. The assault failed and at approximately **1pm** there was more bad news for Napoleon when he heard that the Prussians had eluded their pursuers and were closing fast. To gain time he sent 14,000 troops off to impede their progress and at **2pm** he tried to regain the initiative by launching a large-scale infantry attack against Wellington's left. This second French attack also proved inconclusive and so at **4pm** Napoleon's cavalry charged Wellington's centre, where the British infantry formed into squares and just managed to keep the French at bay – a desperate engagement that cost hundreds of lives. By **5.30pm**, the Prussians had begun to reach the battlefield in numbers to the right of the French lines and, at **7.30pm**, with the odds getting longer and longer, Napoleon made a final bid to break Wellington's centre, sending in his Imperial Guard. These were the best soldiers Napoleon had, but, slowed down by the mud churned up by their own cavalry, the veterans proved easy targets for the British infantry, and they were beaten back with great loss of life. At **8.15pm**, Wellington, who knew victory was within his grasp, rode down the ranks to encourage his soldiers before ordering the large-scale counter attack that proved decisive. The French were vanquished and Napoleon subsequently abdicated, ending his days in exile on St Helena. He died there in 1821.

The church of Saint Joseph

Across the street from the museum, the **church of Saint Joseph** is a curious affair, its domed, circular **portico** of 1689 built as part of a larger chapel on the orders of the Habsburg governor in the hope that it would encourage God to grant King Charles II of Spain an heir (see p.47). It didn't, but the plea to God survives in the Latin inscription on the pediment. The portico holds a bust of Wellington and a monument to all those British soldiers who died at Waterloo and there's an assortment of British **memorial plaques** at the back of the chapel beyond. They are, however, a rather jumbled bunch as they were plonked here unceremoniously when the original chapel was demolished in the nineteenth century to be replaced by the substantial building of today. Most of the plaques were paid for by voluntary contributions from the soldiers who survived – in the days when the British state rarely coughed up anything for all but the most aristocratic of its veterans.

The battlefield – the Butte de Lion

From outside the church of Saint Joseph, pick up bus #W for the quick (4km) journey to the **battlefield** – a landscape of rolling farmland interrupted by a couple of main roads and more pleasingly punctuated by the odd copse and whitewashed farmstead. Today, the ridge where Wellington once marshalled his army holds a motley assortment of attractions collectively known as **Le Hameau du Lion** (Lion's Hamlet). This comprises four separate sites, beginning with the **Centre du Visiteur** (daily: March 10am–5pm; April–Sept 9.30am–6.30pm; Oct 9.30am–5.30pm; Nov–Feb 10.30am–4pm), which issues entry tickets for all four attractions – though this may change – with a combined ticket costing €8.50; it's also possible to buy individual tickets at each attraction. The Centre itself (€4.50) features an absolutely dire audiovisual display on the battle and you're much better off heading straight to the adjacent hundred-metre-high **Butte de Lion** (same hours; €2.50). Built by local women with soil from the battlefield, the Butte marks the spot where Holland's Prince William of Orange – one of Wellington's commanders and later King William II of the Netherlands – was wounded. It was only a nick, so goodness knows how high they would

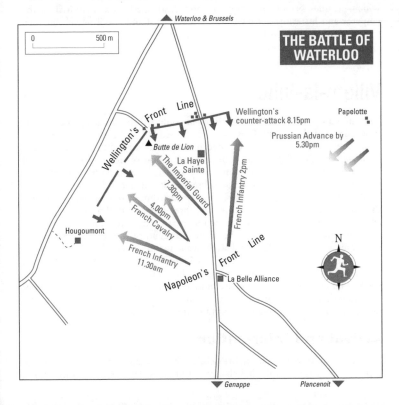

THE BATTLE OF WATERLOO

0   500 m

Waterloo & Brussels

Front Line
Wellington's
Butte de Lion
La Haye Sainte
The Imperial Guard 7.30pm
4.00pm
French Cavalry
Hougoumont
French Infantry 11.30am
Napoleon's Front Line
La Belle Alliance
Wellington's counter-attack 8.15pm
Papelotte
Prussian Advance by 5.30pm
French Infantry 2pm
N

Genappe   Plancenoit

have built it if William had been seriously wounded, but even as it is, the mound is a commanding monument, surmounted by a regal 28-tonne lion atop a stout column. From the viewing platform, there's a panoramic view over the battle-field, and a plan identifies which army was where.

A few metres from the base of the Butte is the **Panorama de la Bataille** (daily: March 10am–5pm; April–Sept 9.30am–6.30pm; Oct 9.30am–5.30pm; Nov–Feb 10.30am–4pm; €5), where a circular naturalistic painting of the battle, on a canvas no less than 110m in circumference, is displayed in a purpose-built, rotunda-like gallery – all to a thundering soundtrack of bugles, snorting horses and cannon fire. Panorama painting was extremely difficult – controlling perspective was always a real problem – but it was very much in vogue when the Parisian artist Louis Dumoulin began the painting in 1912. Precious few panoramas have survived, and unfortunately much of this one is poorly executed and showing signs of decay; even worse, small sections of it appear to have been clumsily amended.

Back across the street is the final site, the **Musée de Cires** (April–Sept daily 9.30am–7pm, Oct daily 10am–6pm; Nov–March Sat & Sun 10am–5pm; €4.50), an uninspiring wax museum kitted out with models of the soldiers of the various Waterloo regiments and their commanders.

Le Caillou

Napoleon spent the eve of the battle at **Le Caillou** (daily: April–Oct 10am–6.30pm; Nov–March 1–5pm; €2.) a two-storey brick farmhouse about 4km south from the Butte de Lion on the chaussée de Bruxelles. The museum, which includes Napoleon's army cot and death mask, is a memorial to the emperor and his army, but it's hardly riveting stuff and you'll need your own transport to get there, as there aren't any buses.

Villers-la-Ville

The ruined Cistercian abbey of **Villers-la-Ville** (April–Oct daily 10am–6pm; Nov–March daily except Tues 10am–5pm; €3.80; ☎071/88 09 80, ⊛www .villers.be) nestles in a lovely wooded dell about 30km south of Brussels, and is altogether one of the most haunting and evocative sights in the whole of Belgium. The first monastic community settled here in 1146, consisting of just one abbot and twelve monks. Subsequently the abbey became a wealthy local landowner, managing a domain of several thousand acres, with numbers that rose to about a hundred monks and three hundred lay brothers. A healthy annual income funded the construction of an extensive monastic complex, most of which was erected in the thirteenth century, though the less austere structures, such as the Abbot's Palace, went up in a second spurt of activity some four hundred years later. In 1794 French revolutionaries ransacked the monastery and later on a railway was ploughed through the grounds. Today the site is wild and overgrown and the buildings are all in varying states of decay, but more than enough survives to pick out Romanesque, Gothic and Renais-sance features and to make some kind of mental reconstruction possible.

Arrival and information

To get to Villers-la-Ville from Brussels, catch a Namur **train** from any of the capital's three main stations and change at Ottignies; depending on connections,

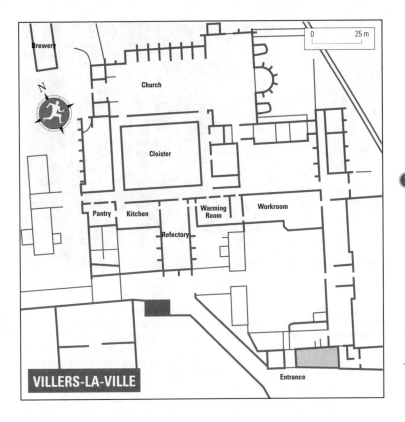

VILLERS-LA-VILLE

the whole train journey takes between an hour and an hour and a half. The abbey is 1.6km (about a fifteen-minute walk), from Villers-la-Ville train station which consists of just two platforms. Near the platforms – back towards Ottignies – you'll spot a small, faded sign to Monticelli; follow the sign and you'll head up and over a little slope until, after about 100m, you reach a T-junction; turn right and follow the road round, and you'll see the ruins ahead. The abbey sells both an in-depth English **guide to the ruins** and a booklet (in French) detailing local walks.

The ruins

From the entrance a path crosses the courtyard in front of the Abbot's Palace to reach the **warming room** (*chauffoir*), the only place in the monastery where a fire would have been kept going all winter, and which still has its original chimney. The fire provided a little heat to the adjacent rooms: on one side the monks' **workroom** (*salle des moines*), used for reading and studying; on the other the large Romanesque-Gothic **refectory** (*réfectoire*), lit by ribbed twin windows topped with chunky rose windows. Next door is the **kitchen** (*cuisine*), which contains a few remnants of the drainage system, which once piped waste to the river, and of a central hearth, whose chimney helped air the room. Just behind this lies the **pantry** (*salle des convers*), where a segment of the original vaulting has survived, supported

△ Villers-la-Ville

by a single column, and beyond, on the northwestern edge of the complex, is the **brewery** (*brasserie*), one of the biggest and oldest buildings in the abbey.

The most spectacular building, however, is the **church** (*église*), which fills out the north corner of the complex. It has the dimensions of a cathedral, with pure lines and elegant proportions, and displays the change from Romanesque to Gothic – the transept and choir are the first known examples of Gothic in Brabant. The church is 90m long and 40m wide with a majestic nave whose roof was supported on strong cylindrical columns. An unusual feature is the series of bull's-eye windows which light the transepts. Of the original twelfth-century **cloister** (*cloître*) adjoining the church, a pair of twin windows is pretty much all that remains, though it is flanked by a two-storey section of the old monks' quarters. Around the edge of the cloister are tombstones and the solitary sarcophagus of the Crusader Gobert d'Aspremont.

Mechelen

MECHELEN, midway between Brussels and Antwerp and just twenty minutes by train from the capital, is a lovely little Flemish town with a surprisingly grand history. Now the country's ecclesiastical capital and home of the Primate of Belgium, its Christian past dates back to **St Rombout**, an Irish evangelist who converted the locals in the seventh century. Martyred for his faith, Rombout proved a popular saint and pilgrims flocked here, ensuring Mechelen a steady revenue. The town went on to become one of the most powerful in medieval Flanders and entered a brief golden age when, in the 1470s, the dukes of Burgundy moved their court here. The good times lasted just sixty years until, with the Burgundians gone, Mechelen slipped into obscurity, becoming the low-key, laidback medium-sized town of today. The town's pride and joy is its magnificent Gothic **cathedral**, St Rombouts, the foremost

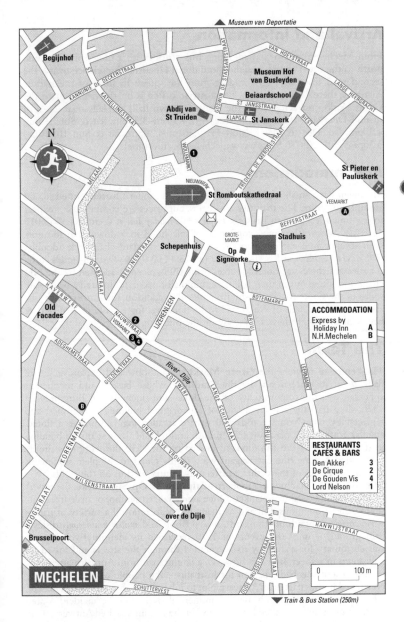

▲ *Museum van Deportatie*

Begijnhof

KANNUNIE DE DECKERSTRAAT

KATHELIJNESTRAAT

GOSWIN DE STASSARTSTRAAT

VAN HOEYSTRAAT

Museum Hof van Busleyden

Beiaardschool

LANGE HEERGRACHT

ST JANSSTRAAT

Abdij van St Truiden

KLAPGAT

St Janskerk

MELAAN

WOLLEMARKT

❶

FREDERIK DE MERODESTRAAT

BIEST

NIEUWWERK

St Romboutskathedraal

St Pieter en Pauluskerk

VEEMARKT

Ⓐ

BEFFERSTRAAT

GROTE-MARKT

Stadhuis

Schepenhuis

Op Signoorke

ⓘ

BEGIJNENSTRAAT

DRABSTRAAT

HAVERWERF

BOTERMARKT

BRUUL

Old Facades

NAUWSTRAAT

VISMARKT

❷

IJZERENLEEN

ACCOMMODATION
Express by
  Holiday Inn   **A**
N.H.Mechelen   **B**

ADEGHEMSTRAAT

❸❹

GULDENSTRAAT

River Dijle

ZOUTWERF

LEERMARKT

KORENMARKT

Ⓑ

ONZE LIEVE VROUWSTRAAT

LANGE SCHIPSTRAAT

BRUUL

MILSENSTRAAT

HOOGSTRAAT

OLV over de Dijle

GR. VON EGMONTSTRAAT

HANWIJSTRAAT

RESTAURANTS CAFÉS & BARS
Den Akker   **3**
De Cirque   **2**
De Gouden Vis **4**
Lord Nelson   **1**

Brusselpoort

OUDE BRUSSELSESTRAAT

0   100 m

MECHELEN

SCHUTTERVEST

▼ *Train & Bus Station (250m)*

of the town's several medieval churches. There's also a sombre **Jewish Deportation Museum** (Joods Museum van Deportatie), recalling the terrible days when the Germans used the town as a transit camp for Jews on their way to the concentration camps. Mechelen is easily explored on a day-trip from Brussels, but spending a night here will give you the time to give the place the attention it really deserves.

Arrival and information

From Mechelen's **train** and adjoining **bus station**, it's a fifteen-minute walk north to the town centre, straight ahead down Hendrik Consciencestraat – the second road from the right leading from the square in front of the station; currently, there's no street sign. The **tourist office** is on the main square, the Grote Markt, just across from the Stadhuis (town hall) at Hallestraat 2 (April to mid–Dec Mon 9.30am–7pm, Tues–Fri 9.30am–5.30pm, Sat & Sun 10am–4.30pm, late Dec to March Mon–Fri 9.30am–4.30pm, Sat & Sun 10.30am–3.30pm; ☎015/29 76 55; ⍟www.mechelen.be/toerisme).

Accommodation

Mechelen has a small supply of comfortable and modern **hotels** dotted in and around the centre. The majority are chains, but prices are competitive – expect to pay much less than in Brussels. *Express by Holiday Inn* at Veemarkt 37 (☎015 44 84 20, ⍟www.hiexpress.com) is a reliable hotel in a downtown location, with seventy well-equipped rooms decorated in standard chain style (doubles €95). *NH Mechelen*, at Korenmarkt 22 (☎015 42 03 03, ⍟www.nh-hotels.com), is a pleasant three-star hotel (doubles from €95), recently adopted by the NH chain, and kitted out in their hallmark minimalist decor; it's located a brief walk south of the Grote Markt via the Ijzerenleen. In addition, the tourist office (see above) has the details of – and will make bookings for – a number of **bed & breakfasts**, though these are mostly on the outskirts of town.

The Town

The centre of town is the **Grote Markt**, a handsome and expansive square flanked on its eastern side by the **Stadhuis**, whose bizarre and incoherent appearance is the responsibility of the dukes and duchesses of Burgundy. In 1526, they had the left-hand side of the original building demolished and replaced by what you see today, an ornate arcaded loggia fronting a fluted, angular edifice. The plan was to demolish and rebuild the rest of the building in stages, but after the Burgundians moved out in 1530 the work was simply abandoned, leaving one extravagant wing firmly glued to the plain stonework and simple gables of the earlier, fourteenth-century section on the right.

In front of the Stadhuis is a modern **sculpture of Op Signoorke**, the town's mascot, being tossed in a blanket. Once a generalized symbol of male irresponsibility, the eponymous doll and its many forebears enjoyed a variety of names – *vuilen bras* (unfaithful drunkard), *sotscop* (fool) and *vuilen bruidegom* (disloyal bridegroom) – until the events of 1775 redefined its identity. Every year it was customary for a dummy to be paraded through the streets and tossed up and down in a sheet. In 1775, however, a young man from Antwerp attempted to steal it and was badly beaten for his pains – the people of Mechelen were convinced he was part of an Antwerp plot to rob them of their cherished mascot. The two cities were already fierce commercial rivals, and the incident soured relations even further. Indeed, when news of the beating reached Antwerp, there was sporadic rioting and calls for the city burghers to take some sort of revenge. Refusing to be intimidated, the people of Mechelen derisively renamed the doll after their old nickname for the people of Antwerp – "Op Signoorke", from "Signor", a reference to that city's favoured status under earlier Spanish kings. It was sweet revenge for an incident of 1687 that had made Mechelen a laughing stock: staggering home, a drunk had roused the town when he thought he saw a fire in the cathedral. In fact, the "fire" was moonlight, earning the Mechelaars the insulting soubriquet "Maneblussers" (Moondousers).

St Romboutskathedraal

A little way west of the Grote Markt, **St Romboutskathedraal** (Mon–Sat 8.30am–4.30pm & Sun 2–4.30pm; free) dominates the town centre just as it was

△ St Romboutskathedraal, Mechelen

supposed to. In particular, it's the cathedral's mighty square tower that takes the breath away, a wonderful, almost imperial Gothic structure with soaring, canopied pinnacles and extraordinarily long and slender windows that are matched down below with the pointed windows encircling the nave and the choir. The church's main entrance is on the Grote Markt and leads straight into the **south transept**, where the cathedral's most distinguished painting, **Anthony van Dyck**'s dramatic *Crucifixion*, portrays the writhing, muscular bodies of the two thieves in the shadows to either side of Christ, who is bathed in a white light of wonderful clarity. The painting now forms part of a heavy, marble Baroque altarpiece carved for the Guild of Masons, but it was only installed here after the French revolutionary army razed the church where it was originally displayed. Across the church, the chapel next to the **north transept** contains the tomb of Mechelen's **Cardinal Mercier** as well as a plaque presented by the Church of England, commemorating the Cardinal's part in co-ordinating the Mechelen Conversations. These ran from 1921 up to the time of Mercier's death in 1926, investigating the possibility of reuniting the two churches.

The transepts are, however, overshadowed by the thirteenth-century **nave**, which has all the cloistered elegance of the Brabantine Gothic style, though the original lines are somewhat spoiled by an unfortunate series of later statues of the apostles. Between the arches lurks an extraordinary Baroque **pulpit**, a playful mass of twisted and curled oak dotted with carefully camouflaged animal carvings – squirrels, frogs and snails, a salamander and a pelican. The main scene shows **St Norbert** being thrown from his horse, a narrow escape which convinced this twelfth-century German prince to give his possessions to the poor and dedicate his life to the church.

Exhibited in the **aisle of the ambulatory** are twenty-five **panel paintings** relating the legend of St Rombout. Such devotional series were comparatively common in medieval Flanders, but this is one of the few to have survived, painted by several unknown artists between 1480 and 1510. As individual works of art, the paintings are not perhaps of the highest order, but the cumulative attention to detail - in the true Flemish tradition - is quite remarkable, with all manner of folksy minutiae illuminating what would otherwise be a predictable tale of sacrifice and sanctity. Legend asserts that Rombout was the son of a powerful chieftain, who gave up his worldly possessions to preach to the heathen, but met an untimely end when a stone mason he had criticized for adultery chopped Rombout up with his axe and chucked the body into the river. In the way of such things, Rombout's remains were retrieved and showed no signs of decay, ample justification for the construction of a shrine in his honour. The panels retell the legend in chronological order, though their meaning is not always obvious. Many of the panels carry a sombre-looking kneeling man and woman – these were the donors. As for the ambulatory itself, it's not quite all that it seems: many of the columns are made of wood painted as marble, a trompe l'oeil technique for which Mechelen was once famous.

The cathedral tower contains Belgium's finest **carillon**, a fifteenth-century affair of 49 bells, which resounds over the town on high days and holidays. There are also regular, hour-long performances on Saturdays (11.30am), Sundays (3pm), and from June through to mid-September on Monday evenings (8.30pm).

To St Janskerk

From the north side of the cathedral, Wollemarkt wends its way past the refuge of the **Abdij van St Truiden** (Abbey of St Trudo; no public access), which sits prettily beside an old weed-choked canal, its picturesque gables once home to the destitute. Almost opposite, now on Goswin de Stassartstraat, an alley called **Klapgat** leads through to **St Janskerk** (theoretically Tues–Sun 1.30–5.30pm, Nov–March till 4.30pm; free), a largely medieval church whose decaying sandstone exterior belies its richly decorated, immaculately maintained interior. Almost everything is on the grand scale here, from the massive pulpit and the whopping organ through to two large and unusual canons' pews, but it's the Baroque high altarpiece that grabs the attention, a suitably flashy setting for a flashy but wonderful painting – Rubens' *Adoration of the Magi*. Painted in 1619, the central panel, after which the triptych is named, is a fine example of the artist's use of variegated lighting – and also has his first wife portrayed as the Virgin. The side panels are occasionally rotated, so on the left-hand side you'll see either Jesus baptised by John the Baptist or John the Baptist's head on a platter; to the right it's St John on Patmos or the same saint being dipped in boiling oil.

The Beiaardschool (Carillon School) and Museum Hof van Busleyden

A few metres further east, at the far end of St Jansstraat, Mechelen's **Beiaardschool** (Carillon School; no public access) has become one of the most prestigious institutions of its sort in the world, attracting students from as far away as Japan. Playing the carillon is, by all accounts, extremely difficult and the diploma course offered here takes all of six years to complete. Next door to the school, the **Museum Hof van Busleyden** (Tues–Sun 10am–5pm; €2) occupies a splendid early sixteenth-century mansion, built in high Gothic style with Renaissance touches. Highlights of its rambling collection include an interesting assortment of mostly unattributed paintings, a display of miscellaneous bells, a variety of guild knick-knacks and a collection of Gallo-Roman artefacts – hardly enough to set the pulse racing, but an agreeable way to spend an hour or so.

Museum van Deportatie en Verzet (Museum of Deportation and Resistance)

Doubling back to Goswin de Stassartstraat, turn right for the five-minute walk to the **Joods Museum van Deportatie en Verzet**, at no.153 (Sun–Thurs 10am–5pm, Fri 10am–1pm; closed Sat & for 2 weeks in the middle of Aug; free). During the German occupation, Nazi officials chose Mechelen as a staging point for Belgian Jews destined for the concentration camps of Eastern Europe. Their reasoning was quite straightforward: most of Belgium's Jews were in either Antwerp or Brussels and Mechelen was halfway between the two. Today's Museum of Deportation occupies the old barracks that were adapted by the Gestapo for use as the principal internment centre. Between 1942 and 1944 over 25,000 Jews passed through its doors; most ended up in Auschwitz and only 1,200 survived the war. In a series of well-conceived, multilingual displays, the museum explores this dreadful episode, beginning with Jewish life in Belgium before the war and continuing with sections on the rise of anti-Semitism, the occupation, the deportations, the concentration camps and liberation. It's designed with older Belgian school children in mind, so you may share the museum with one or more school parties, but it's still harrowing stuff and some of the photographs are deeply disturbing. The final section, entitled "Personal Testimonies," is particularly affecting – one of its exhibits is a postcard thrown from a deportation train.

From the Deportation Museum, it is a ten-minute walk back to the Grote Markt.

Eating and drinking

Mechelen is a tad short on good – or at least distinctive – **cafés** and **restaurants**, though there's lots of choice amongst the workaday cafés that fringe the Grote Markt. Otherwise, head off to Nauwstraat, a short sidestreet by the river at the south end of Ijzerenleen, where *De Cirque* is an appealing café-bar-cum-restaurant with modish decor and a wide-ranging menu; it's closed on Sundays

As for **bars**, the laid-back *De Gouden Vis*, also on Nauwstraat, has more than a little of the New-Age-meets-hippy about it, and the adjacent *Den Akker* is much the same. As well as these, there's a cluster of bars beside the cathedral on Wollemarkt – nothing special, though the *Lord Nelson* does a good line in ersatz nautical decoration and sells several fine beers – the dark and malty Corsendonk Pater is especially recommended. Amongst local ales, be sure to try Gouden Carolus (Golden Charles), a delicious dark-brown brew once tippled by – or so they say – the Emperor Charles V.

Antwerp

About 50km north of Brussels – and forty minutes by train – **ANTWERP**, Belgium's second city, is an animated cultural centre that lays fair claim to be the effective capital of Flemish Belgium. The city fans out carelessly from the east bank of the River Scheldt, its centre a rough polygon formed and framed by its enclosing boulevards and the river. It's not an especially handsome city – the terrain is too flat and industry too prevalent for that – but its centre is sprinkled with some lovely old churches and excellent museums, reminders of its auspicious past as the centre of a large trading empire. In particular, there's the enormous legacy of **Rubens**, whose works adorn Antwerp's galleries and churches, and the presence of a veritable raft of local fashion designers, who gather at exhibitions held in the **MoMu** fashion museum. Add to this a spirited nightlife and a first-rate bar and restaurant scene and you have a city that's well worth an overnight stay.

Arrival and information

Antwerp has two main **train stations**, Berchem and Centraal. The latter is the one you want for the city centre; if your train terminates at Berchem, catch the next train to Centraal Station – it only takes a couple of minutes and services are very frequent. **Centraal Station** is located about 2km east of the main square, the Grote Markt; **trams** #2 or #15 (to Groenplaats) connect the two. A standard single fare on any part of the city's transport system costs €1; **tickets** are available at underground stations, authorized newsagents, and on board buses and trams.

Antwerp's **tourist office** is at Grote Markt 13 (Mon–Sat 9am–5.45pm, Sun 9am–4.45pm; ☎03 232 01 03, ⊛www.visitantwerpen.be). It operates a free hotel reservation service.

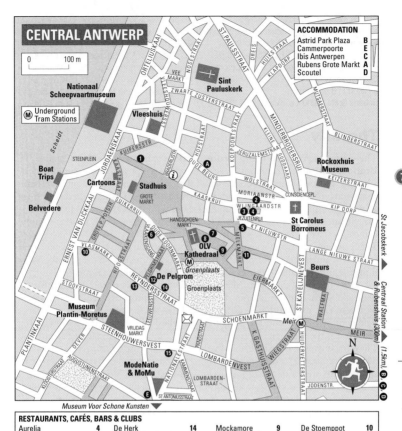

CENTRAL ANTWERP

0 — 100 m

ACCOMMODATION
Astrid Park Plaza **B**
Cammerpoorte **E**
Ibis Antwerpen **C**
Rubens Grote Markt **A**
Scoutel **D**

Nationaal Scheepvaartmuseum

Sint Pauluskerk

M Underground Tram Stations

Vleeshuis

Boat Trips

Cartoons
Stadhuis

GROTE MARKT

Belvedere

Rockoxhuis Museum

St Carolus Borromeus

OLV Kathedraal

De Pelgrom
Groenplaats

Beurs

Museum Plantin-Moretus

VRIJDAG MARKT

Meir M

MEIR

ModeNatie & MoMu

N

Museum Voor Schone Kunsten ▼

EXCURSIONS FROM BRUSSELS | Antwerp

St Jacobskerk ▶

Centraal Station & Rubenshuis (300m) ▶

(1.5km) B C D

7

RESTAURANTS, CAFÉS, BARS & CLUBS

Aurelia	4	De Herk	14	Mockamore	9	De Stoemppot	10
Café Pelikaan	11	Het Dagelijks Brood	15	De Peerdestal	3	De Vagant	12
Den Engel	1	Het Elfde Gebod	7	Paters' Vaetje	8	't Zolderke	2
De Groote Witte Arend	13	Hoorn des Overloeds	5	Popoff	6		

Accommodation

Astrid Park Plaza Koningin Astridplein 7 ☏03 203 12 34, ⓦ www.parkplazaeurope.com. Part of an imaginative plan to revamp Koningin Astridplein, this whopping four-star hotel, with over 200 very comfortable rooms, has a bold modern design with retro flourishes. The bright exterior paintwork – ochre and yellow – is certainly striking. Doubles from €130.

Cammerpoorte Nationalestraat 38 ☏03 231 97 36, ℻03 226 29 68. Modern two-star hotel with 39 frugal en-suite rooms in a building that looks a bit like a car park. The hotel has a mildly forlorn air, but is reasonably priced and has a handy location, just five minutes'

walk south of Groenplaats. Doubles from €75.

Ibis Antwerpen Centrum Meirstraat 39 ☏03 231 88 30, ⓦ www.ibishotel.com. Competitively priced chain hotel with routine modern rooms hidden away behind a particularly ghastly concrete exterior but compensated by a decent location, close to the Rubenshuis. Doubles from €102.

Scoutel Stoomstraat 3 ☏03 226 46 06, ⓦ www .scoutel.be. Neat and trim hostel-cum-hotel offering plain but perfectly adequate singles (€25), doubles (€20 per person), triples (€17) and quadruples (€15) with breakfast. It's about five minutes' walk from Centraal

Station: head south down Pelikaanstraat, turn left along Lange Kievitstraat, go through the tunnel and it's the first road on the right. There's no curfew (guests have their own keys), but be sure to check in before 6pm when reception closes. Reservations advised in the summer.

Rubens Grote Markt Oude Beurs ☎ 03 226

95 82, ⓦ www.hotelrubensantwerp.be. Arguably the most agreeable hotel in town, the *Rubens* occupies attractive old premises in a handy downtown location just a couple of minutes' walk north of the Grote Markt. It's a small hotel (36 rooms) with a relaxing air; the modern rooms are both comfortable and attractively furnished. Doubles from €130.

The City

The centre of Antwerp is the **Grote Markt**, at the heart of which stands the **Brabo Fountain**, a haphazard pile of roughly sculpted rocks surmounted by a bronze of one Silvius Brabo, depicted flinging the hand of the prostate giant Antigonus into the Scheldt. Legend asserts that Antigonus extracted tolls from all passing ships, cutting off the hands of those who refused to pay. He was eventually beaten by the valiant Brabo, a local brave who tore off his hand and threw it into the river, giving the city its name, which literally means "hand-throw". There are more plausible explanations of the city's name, but this is the most colourful, and it certainly reflects Antwerp's early success at freeing the river from the innumerable taxes levied on shipping by local landowners.

The north side of the Grote Markt is lined with daintily restored **guildhouses**, their sixteenth-century facades decorated with appropriate reliefs and topped by finely cast gilded figures. No. 7, the House of the Crossbowmen, with its figures of St George and the dragon, is the tallest and most distinctive; standing next to it is the Coopers' House, with its barrel motifs and statue of St Matthew. They are, however, overshadowed by the town hall – the **Stadhuis** (tours Mon–Thurs at 2pm; €1), completed in 1566, and in the striking symmetries of its architecture one of the most important buildings of the Northern Renaissance. Among rooms you can visit are the Leys Room, named after Baron Hendrik Leys, who painted the frescoes in the 1860s, and the Wedding Room, which has a chimneypiece decorated with two caryatids carved by Cornelius Floris, the architect of the building.

The Onze Lieve Vrouwekathedraal

Just to the southeast of the Grote Markt, the **Onze Lieve Vrouwekathedraal** (Cathedral of Our Lady; Mon–Fri 10am–5pm, Sat 10am–3pm, Sun 1–4pm; €2) is one of the finest Gothic churches in Belgium, a forceful and self-confident structure that mostly dates from the middle of the fifteenth century. Its graceful spire dominated the skyline of the medieval city and was long a favourite with British travellers. Inside, the seven-aisled **nave** is breathtaking, if only because of its sense of space, an impression reinforced by the bright, light stonework. The religious troubles of the sixteenth century – primarily the Iconoclastic Fury of 1566 – polished off the cathedral's early furnishings and fittings, so what you see today are largely Baroque embellishments, most notably four early paintings by Pieter Paul **Rubens** (1577–1640). Of these, the *Descent from the Cross*, just to the right of the central crossing, is without doubt the most beautiful, a triptych painted after the artist's return from Italy in 1612 that displays an uncharacteristically moving realism, derived from Caravaggio.

The Plantin-Moretus and Nationaal Scheepvaart museums

It takes about five minutes to walk southwest from the cathedral to the **Plantin-Moretus Museum**, on Vrijdagmarkt (Tues–Sun 10am–5pm; €4),

△ The Brabo Fountain and Stadhuis, Antwerp

which occupies the grand old mansion of Rubens' father-in-law, the printer Christopher Plantin. One of Antwerp's most interesting museums, it provides a marvellous insight into how Plantin and his family conducted their business, its rabbit-warren rooms holding all sorts of antique books, printers' woodcuts and copper plates plus several ancient printing presses.

From here it's a brief stroll to the riverfront **Nationaal Scheepvaartmuseum** (National Maritime Museum; Tues–Sun 10am–5pm; €4), which is located at the end of Suikerrui and inhabits the Steen, the remaining gatehouse of what was once an impressive medieval fortress. Inside, the cramped rooms feature exhibits on inland navigation, shipbuilding and waterfront life, while the open-air section has a long line of tugs and barges under a rickety corrugated roof.

Vleeshuis and Sint Pauluskerk

Footsteps from the Maritime Museum is the impressively gabled **Vleeshuis** (Tues–Sun 10am–5pm; €2), built for the guild of butchers in 1503 and now used for temporary exhibitions, mostly of applied art. From here, it's a couple of minutes' walk north to the **Veemarkt** (Cattle Market), where an extravagant Baroque portal leads through to **Sint Pauluskerk** (early March to early Oct daily 2–5pm; free), one of the city's most delightful churches, an airy, dignified late Gothic structure dating from 1517. The Dominicans, for whom the church was built, commissioned a series of paintings to line the wall of the nave's north aisle depicting the "Fifteen Mysteries of the Rosary". Dating from 1617, the series has survived intact, a remarkable snapshot of Antwerp's artistic talent, with works by the likes of Cornelis De Vos, David Teniers the Elder and van Dyck, but it is **Rubens**' contribution – the *Scourging at the Pillar* – which stands out, a brilliant, brutal canvas showing Jesus clad in a blood-spattered loin cloth. There's more Rubens close by – at the far end of the *Mysteries* series - in the *Adoration of the Shepherds* and another, the *Disputation on the Nature of the Holy Sacrament*, in the south transept; both are early works dating back to 1609.

Back outside, in between the Baroque portal and the church lurks another curiosity in the form of the **Calvarieberg**, an artificial **grotto** of 1697–1747. The grotto clings to the buttresses of the south transept, eerily adorned with statues of Christ and other figures of angels, prophets and saints in a tawdry representation of the Crucifixion and Entombment. Writing in the nineteenth century, the traveller Charles Tennant described it as "exhibiting a more striking instance of religious fanaticism than good taste".

The Rockoxhuis Museum

The **Rockoxhuis Museum**, a five- to ten-minute walk southeast of Sint Pauluskerk at Keizerstraat 12 (Tues–Sun 10am–5pm; €2.50), occupies the attractively restored seventeenth-century town house of Nicolaas Rockox, friend and patron of Rubens. Inside, a sequence of rooms has been crammed with period furnishings and art work, based on an inventory taken after the owner's death in 1640. Nevertheless, it's far from a recreation of Rockox's old home, but rather a museum with a small but highly prized collection. Particular highlights include, in **Room 1**, a gentle *Holy Virgin and Child* by Quentin Matsys, and a *St Christopher Bearing the Christ Child*, a typical work by Quentin's collaborator Joachim Patenier. Moving on, **Room 2** displays two pictures by Rubens, beginning with the small and romantic *Virgin in Adoration before the sleeping Christ Child*, which depicts the Virgin with the features of Rubens' first wife and has Jesus modelled on his son. The second work is his *Christ on the Cross*, a fascinating oil sketch made in preparation for an altarpiece he never had time to paint. **Room 3** is distinguished by a flashy and fleshy genre painting, *Woman Selling Vegetables* by Joachim Beuckelaer, while **Room 6** holds Pieter Bruegel the Younger's (1564–1638) *Proverbs*, an intriguing folksy work, one of several he did in direct imitation of his father, a frenetic mixture of the observed and imagined set in a Flemish village. The meaning of many of the pictured proverbs has been the subject of long debate, but there's little doubt about the meaning of the central image depicting an old man dressed in the blue-hooded cape of the cuckold at the behest of his young wife.

The Rubenshuis and St Jacobskerk

From either the Grote Markt or the Rockoxhuis, it's a five- to ten-minute walk to the city's most popular tourist attraction, the **Rubenshuis** at Wapper 9 (Tues–Sun 10am–5pm; €5). Rubens lived here for most of his adult life, though it's not so much a house as a mansion, splitting into two parts: on the right the classical studio, where Rubens worked and taught, and on the left the traditional, gabled Flemish house. Attached to the latter is the art gallery, an Italianate chamber where Rubens entertained the artistic and cultural elite of Europe. Unfortunately, only a handful of his paintings are here, and there's very little to represent the works of those other artists he collected so avidly throughout his life, but the restoration of Rubens' rooms is pleasant and convincing in equal measure.

Rubens died in 1640 and was buried in **St Jacobskerk**, north of the Rubenshuis at Lange Nieuwstraat 73 (April–Oct daily except Tues 2–5pm; €2). Rubens and his immediate family are buried in the chapel behind the high altar, where in one of his last works, *Our Lady Surrounded by Saints*, he painted himself as St George, his two wives as Martha and Mary, and his father as St Jerome.

South of the centre – MoMu and the Museum voor Schone Kunsten

Heading south from Groenplaats along Nationalestraat, it takes about five minutes to reach **ModeNatie** (@www.modenatie.com), a lavish and ambitious fashion complex. Spread over several floors, it showcases the work of local fashion designers and incorporates both the fashion department of the Royal Academy of Fine Arts and the Flanders Fashion Institute. As such, it reflects the international success of local designers, beginning in the 1980s with the so-called "Antwerp Six" – including Dries van Noten, Dirk Bikkembergs, Marina Yee and Martin Margiela – and continuing with younger designers like Raf Simons and Veronique Branquinho; all are graduates of the Academy. Part of the building contains a fashion museum, **MoMu** (Tues–Sun 10am–6pm; €6), which has an extensive historical textile collection, though the contemporary

---

Fashion shopping in Antwerp

The success of Antwerp's **fashion designers** has left the city with dozens of excellent designer shops. These can be found all over the city centre, but there's a particular concentration of cutting-edge **fashion shops** around the ModeNatie complex. Notable places include the chic and colourful men and women's clothes of Dries van Noten's Modepaleis, at Nationalestraat 16, on the corner of Kammenstraat; the imported designer clothes of Alamode, Nationalestraat 27; the contemporary jewellery of Anne Zellien, Kammenstraat 47; and the secondhand clothes of Naughty-I, at Kammenstraat 65. Nearby, Sint-Antoniusstraat has *Walter*, at no.12, which features the clothes of several domestic designers in its delightful premises in what was formerly a car showroom, and the comparable *Louis*, Lombardenstraat 2 and Chris Janssens, Lombardenstraat 10.

fashion displays are of more immediate interest to the non-specialist, featuring everything from the widest of flairs to the glitziest jewellery.

From ModeNatie, it's a good fifteen-minute walk south – or a quick trip on tram #8 from Groenplaats along Nationalestraat – to the **Museum voor Schone Kunsten**, Leopold de Waelplaats (Fine Art Museum; Tues–Sat 10am–5pm, Sun 10am–6pm; €5), the possessor of one of the country's better fine art collections. Its early Flemish section features paintings by Jan van Eyck, Memling, Rogier van der Weyden and Quentin Matsys, and Rubens has two large rooms to himself. The museum also displays a comprehensive collection of modern Belgian art with Paul Delvaux and James Ensor being particularly well represented.

Eating and drinking

Antwerp is an enjoyable and inexpensive place to eat, its busy centre liberally sprinkled with informal **cafés** and **restaurants**, which excel at combining traditional Flemish dishes with Mediterranean, French and vegetarian cuisines. Antwerp is also a great place to drink, its centre dotted with lots of tiny, darkly lit **bars** that exude a cheerful vitality.

Restaurants and cafés

Aurelia Wijngaardstraat 22 ☎ 03 233 62 59. Smart little restaurant, metres from Hendrik Conscienceplein, in an immaculately restored old merchant's house. Delicious seafood and meat dishes with main courses hovering between €15 and €25. Closed Tues & Wed.

Het Dagelijks Brood Steenhouwersvest 48. Enjoyable and distinctive café where the variety of breads is the main event, served with delicious, wholesome soups and light meals at one long wooden table. No smoking. Daily 7am–7pm.

Hoorn des Overloeds Melkmarkt 1 ☎ 03 232 83 99. Excellent and very unpretentious fish restaurant, good for lunch and dinner; look out for the daily specials. Just east of the cathedral. Daily noon–10pm.

Mockamore Groenplaats 30. Appealing little café with modern furnishings and a rickety old staircase that somehow manages to climb three floors. Great coffees, plus good cakes and snacks. On the northeast corner

of the Groenplaats. Mon–Sat 8.30am–6.30pm, Sun 11am–6pm.

De Peerdestal Wijngaardstraat 8 ☎ 03 231 95 03. Medium-range restaurant with an uninspiring menu – and an older clientele – but *the* place to try horsemeat. Just west of Hendrik Conscienceplein. Daily 11.30am–3pm & 5–10pm.

Popoff Oude Koornmarkt 18. The best pies, desserts and gateaux in town served from noon till 10pm. Closed Mon.

De Stoempot Vlasmarkt 12 ☎ 03 231 36 86. *Stoemp* is a traditional Flemish dish consisting of puréed meat and vegetables – and this cosy little restaurant is the best place to eat it. Closed Wed.

't Zolderke Hoofdkerkstraat 7 ☎ 03 233 84 27. In an attractively converted old mansion a few steps from Hendrik Conscienceplein, this appealing restaurant offers a mix of tasty Belgian and Mediterranean dishes. Main courses average out at about €15–20. Mon–Fri 6–11pm, Sat & Sun noon–midnight.

Bars

Het Elfde Gebod Torfbrug 10. On one of the tiny squares fronting the north side of the cathedral, this long-established bar has become something of a tourist trap, but it's still worth visiting for the kitsch, nineteenth-century religious statues which cram the interior; don't bother with the food.

Den Engel Grote Markt 3. Handily located, traditional bar with an easy-going atmosphere in a guildhouse on the north-west corner of the main square; attracts a mixture of businesspeople and locals from the residential enclave round the Vleeshuis.

De Groote Witte Arend Reyndersstraat 18.
Attractive café-bar set around a courtyard
in an old mansion; classical music sets
the tone. A good range of beers – including authentic Gueuze and Kriek – plus
pancakes, waffles and ice cream.

De Herk Reyndersstraat 33. Tiny bar in ancient
premises – down an alley and set around a
courtyard. Twentysomething, modish clientele. Good range of beers and ales – including an excellent Lindemans Gueuze.

Paters' Vaetje Blauwmoezelstraat 1. Popular
bar ("the Priests' Casket") in the shadow

of the cathedral offering the widest range
of beers and ales in this little area – over a
hundred at the last count. Old-fashioned
main bar downstairs, gallery bar upstairs.

Café Pelikaan Melkmarkt 14. There's nothing
touristy about the *Pelikaan*, a packed and
smoky bar where locals get down to some
serious drinking. On the east side of the
cathedral. Closed Sun.

De Vagant Reyndersstraat 21. Specialist gin
bar serving an extravagant range of Belgian
and Dutch *jenevers* in comfortable, laidback
surroundings.

Leuven

Less than half an hour by train from Brussels, **LEUVEN** makes for an easy and
enjoyable day-trip. The town is home to Belgium's oldest university, nowadays a
bastion of Flemish thinking and the wielder of considerable influence over the
region's political and economic elite. Leuven's many students give the place a
lively, informal air – and sustain lots of inexpensive bars and cafés, especially on
and around one of the city's most appealing squares, the **Oude Markt**. What's
more, Leuven also boasts a pair of notable medieval buildings, the splendid
Stadhuis (City Hall) and **St Pieterskerk**, a late Gothic church that's home to
two wonderful early Flemish paintings by Dieric Bouts. Otherwise, the centre
is not much more than an undistinguished tangle of streets with a lot of the
new and few remnants of the old. Then again, it's something of a miracle that
any of Leuven's ancient buildings have survived at all, since the town suffered
badly in both world wars. Some 1500 houses were destroyed in World War I,
and the university library and main church were gutted, only to suffer further
damage in World War II.

Arrival and information

It's a gentle ten- to fifteen-minute walk west along Bondgenotenlaan from the
train station to the main sqaure, the Grote Markt, where you'll find Leuven's
tourist office in the Stadhuis (April–Oct daily 10am–5pm; Nov–March same
hours but closed Sun; ☎016 21 15 39, ⦿www.leuven.be).

The Town

The town centre is marked by two adjacent squares, the more easterly of
which is the **Fochplein**, basically just a road junction whose one noteworthy
feature is the modern **Font Sapienza**, a wittily cynical fountain depicting a
student being literally brainwashed by the book he's reading. Next door, the
wedge-shaped main square, the **Grote Markt** is Leuven's architectural high
spot, dominated by two notable late Gothic buildings – St Pieterskerk and the
Stadhuis. The **Stadhuis** is the more flamboyant of the two, an extraordinarily
light and lacy confection, crowned by soaring pinnacles and a dainty, high-
pitched roof studded with dormer windows. It's a beautiful building, though
slightly spoiled by the clumsiness of its statues, which were inserted in the
nineteenth century and represent everything from important citizens, artists

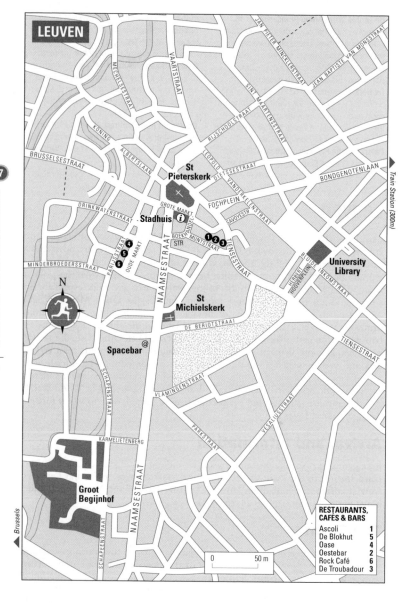

**RESTAURANTS,
CAFÉS & BARS**

Ascoli	**1**
De Blokhut	**5**
Oase	**4**
Oestebar	**2**
Rock Café	**6**
De Troubadour	**3**

and nobles to virtues, vices and municipal institutions. Until then, the lavishly carved niches stood empty for lack of money. In contrast, the niche bases are exuberantly medieval, depicting biblical subjects in a free, colloquial style and adorned by a panoply of grotesques. By comparison, the **inside** of the Stadhuis is something of an anticlimax; **guided tours** (April–Sept Mon–Fri at 11am & 3pm, Sat & Sun at 3pm; Oct–March daily at 3pm; €2) amble through just a handful of rooms, including overblown salons in the high French style and a neo-Gothic council chamber.

St Pieterskerk

Across from the Stadhuis, **St Pieterskerk** (Mid-March to mid-Oct Mon–Fri 10am–5pm, Sat 10am–4.30pm & Sun 2–5pm; mid-Oct to mid-March closed Mon; free, but treasury €5) is a rambling, heavily buttressed late Gothic pile whose stumpy western facade defeated its architects. Work began on the present church in the 1420s and continued until the start of the sixteenth century when the Romanesque towers of the west facade, the last remaining part of its predecessor, were pulled down to make way for a grand design by Joos Matsys, the brother of the painter Quentin. It didn't work out – the foundations proved too weak – and finally, another hundred years on, the unfinished second-attempt towers were capped, creating the truncated, asymmetrical versions that rise above the entrance today.

Inside, the church is distinguished by its soaring nave whose enormous pillars frame a fabulous **rood screen**, an intricately carved piece of stonework surmounted by a wooden Christ. The nave's Baroque **pulpit** is also striking – a weighty wooden extravagance which shows **St Norbert** being thrown off his horse by lightning, a dramatic scene set beneath spiky palm trees. It was this brush with death that persuaded Norbert, a twelfth-century German noble, to abandon his worldly ways and dedicate himself to the church, on whose behalf he founded a devout religious order, the Premonstratensian Canons, in 1120.

The Schatkamer (Treasury) of St Pieterskerk

The ambulatory of St Pieterskerk accommodates the church's **Schatkamer** (Treasury; same times as church; €5), whose three key paintings date from the fifteenth century. There's a copy of Rogier van der Weyden's marvellous triptych, the *Descent from the Cross*, the original of which is now at the Prado in Madrid,

△ The University, Leuven

and two of the few surviving paintings by Weyden's apprentice **Dieric Bouts** (c1415–75), who worked for most of his life in Leuven, ultimately becoming the city's official painter. An influential artist in his own right, Bouts' carefully contrived paintings are inhabited by stiff and slender figures in religious scenes that are almost totally devoid of action – a frozen narrative designed to induce contemplation rather than stir strong emotion. His use of colour and attention to detail are quite superb, especially in the exquisite landscapes that act as a backdrop to much of his work. Of the two triptychs on display here, first up is the *Last Supper*, showing Christ and his disciples in a Flemish dining room, with the (half-built) Stadhuis just visible through the left-hand window; the two men standing up and the couple peeping through the service hatch are the rectors of the fraternity who commissioned the work. Dressed in a purple robe, the colour reserved for royalty, Jesus is depicted as taller than his disciples. It was customary for Judas to be portrayed in a yellow robe, the colour of hatred and cowardice, but Bouts broke with tradition and made him almost indistinguishable from the others – he's the one with his face in shadow and his hand on his left hip. The change of emphasis, away from the betrayal to the mystery of the Eucharist, is continued on the side panels: to the left Abraham is offered bread and wine above a Jewish Passover; to the right the Israelites gather manna; and below the Prophet Elijah receives angelic succour. In the next chapel along you'll find the second Bouts' triptych, the gruesome *Martyrdom of St Erasmus*, which depicts the executioner extracting the saint's entrails with a winch watched by seemingly regretful court officials.

From the Grote Markt to the Groot Begijnhof

South of the Grote Markt is the boisterous core of Leuven's student scene, the **Oude Markt**, a large cobblestoned square surrounded by a fetching ensemble of tall gabled houses that are now home to one of the liveliest collections of bars in the region. To the immediate east of Oude Markt, Naamsestraat leads south past the florid Baroque facade of the Jesuit **St Michielskerk**, restored after wartime damage, towards the wonderfully preserved **Groot Begijnhof**, a labyrinthine sixteenth-century enclave of tall and austere red-brick houses, which was once home to around three hundred *begijns* – women living as nuns but without taking vows. The Begijnhof was bought by the university in 1962, since when its buildings have been painstakingly restored as student residences. To get there from Naamsestraat, turn right down the little lane called Karmelietenberg and then take Schapenstraat, the first on the left.

Eating and drinking

Leuven takes its **eating and drinking** very seriously, with a wide range of establishments in which to exercise your stomach and strain your liver. For **cafés** and **restaurants**, the first place to head for is Muntstraat, just southeast of the Grote Markt. Among the choices here you'll find *Ascoli* at Muntstraat 17 (☎016 23 93 64; closed Wed in July and Aug), a competitively priced Franco-Italian restaurant with a large and ambitious menu (mains from as little as €12). Also on this street, at no. 23, is *Oesterbar* (☎016 20 28 38; closed Sun & Mon), a gourmet restaurant offering what many consider to be the best seafood in town, the house speciality being – no surprises given the name – oysters. Mains here cost €20–26. Just southeast of the Grote Markt, at Tiensestraat 32, smart and well-appointed *De Troubadour* (☎016 22 50 65; closed Tues all day & Wed lunch time) is especially good for grilled meat and fish dishes; main courses average around €18.

As a university town, Leuven is chock-a-block with lively student **bars**. The best selection – and setting – is down on the Oude Markt, where almost all of the old gabled houses have been turned into drinking holes. The best tactic is to wander around until you find somewhere whose decor or music takes your fancy, though in warm weather you'll probably want to join the sea of people sitting out in the square itself. Things change fast, but three good options at the moment are *Oase*, at Oude Markt 53, *De Blokhut*, at no. 49, and the *Rock Café*, at no. 32.

Ghent

Just 56km from Brussels, Flemish-speaking **GHENT** is Belgium's third-largest city: a thriving, busy metropolis with an amiable atmosphere, a smashing restaurant and bar scene, and an outstanding assortment of medieval buildings. The pick of them is **St Baafskathedraal**, a handsome Gothic structure which holds one of Europe's most remarkable paintings, the *Adoration of the Mystic Lamb* by Jan van Eyck. Close rivals include an especially dour and surly castle, **Het Gravensteen**, and the late medieval guildhouses of the **Graslei** quay, not to mention **S.M.A.K.** one of the country's finest contemporary art museums, and the **Museum voor Schone Kunsten** (Fine Art Museum), though this is closed for a revamp until at least 2006. Nonetheless, it is, perhaps, the general appearance of the city centre that appeals rather than any specific sight, its web of cobbled lanes and alleys overlooked by an enchanting medley of antique terraces and grand mansions, all woven round a tangle of canals.

Arrival and information

Trains from Brussels (3 or 4 hourly; 40min) pull into **St Pieters train station**, about 2km south of the city centre. From the covered stops beside St Pieters, **trams** run up to the Korenmarkt, plumb in the centre of town, every few minutes. All trams have destination signs and numbers at the front, but if in doubt check with the driver. The flat-rate fare per journey is €1; tickets can be bought from the driver.

Ghent's **tourist office** (daily: April–Oct 9.30am–6.30pm; Nov–March 9.30am–4.30pm; ☎09 266 52 32, ⊛www.visitgent.be) is right in the centre of the city, in the crypt of the old cloth hall, the Lakenhalle, on the Botermarkt.

Accommodation

Ghent has several especially enticing **places to stay**, all of them detailed in the free and comprehensive brochure published by the tourist office. The latter also offers a **hotel accommodation service**, which is especially useful in July and August, when vacant rooms are thin on the ground.

Arguably the most distinctive of Ghent's **hotels**, the two-star *Boatel* at Voorhoutkaai 44 (☎09 267 10 30, ⊛www.theboatel.com) is, as its name implies, a converted boat, an immaculately refurbished canal barge to be precise, moored in one of the city's outer canals, a ten- to fifteen-minute walk east from the centre. The seven bedrooms are decked out in crisp, modern style – five standard at €105 and two deluxe at €130 – and breakfasts, taken on the deck, are first rate. Another unusual offering is the *Monasterium Poortackere* at Oude

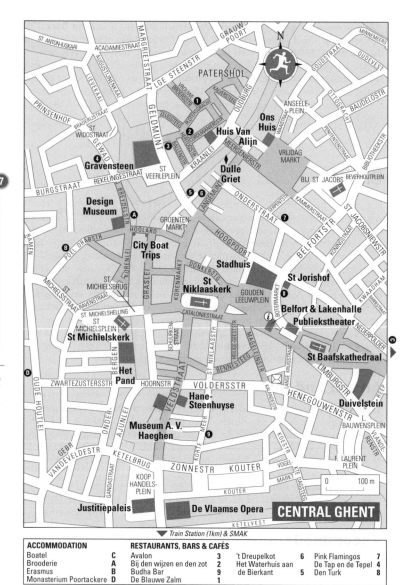

CENTRAL GHENT

ACCOMMODATION		RESTAURANTS, BARS & CAFÉS				
Boatel	**C**	Avalon	**3**	't Dreupelkot	**6**	Pink Flamingos	**7**
Brooderie	**A**	Bij den wijzen en den zot	**2**	Het Waterhuis aan		De Tap en de Tepel	**4**
Erasmus	**B**	Budha Bar	**9**	de Bierkant	**5**	Den Turk	**8**
Monasterium Poortackere	**D**	De Blauwe Zalm	**1**				

Houtlei 56 (☎09 269 22 10, ⒲www.monasterium.be), a one-star hotel-cum-guesthouse occupying a rambling and rather spartan former monastery dating from the nineteenth century. Guests choose between spick and span en-suite rooms in the hotel section (€125), or the more authentic monastic-cell experience in the guesthouse, either en suite or with shared facilities (both €100). *Brooderie*, Jan Breydelstraat 8 (☎09 225 06 23), has three neat and trim little rooms above an appealing café, handily located in the city centre, near the Korenmarkt. Rooms cost €60/65 for a double, €40 for a single, including an excellent breakfast. Small, friendly *Erasmus*, meanwhile, at Poel 25 (☎09 224 21 95, ✉hotel.erasmus@proximedia.be), is a family-run establishment in an old and commodious town house a few yards from the Korenlei, with thoughtfully decorated – if slightly twee – rooms (from €100) furnished with antiques. Reservations are advised in summer, and it's closed mid-Dec to mid-Jan.

The City

The shape and structure of Ghent's **city centre** reflects ancient class and linguistic divides. The streets to the south of the **Korenmarkt**, the former Corn Market, tend to be straight and wide, lined with elegant old mansions, the former habitations of the wealthier, French-speaking classes, while, to the north, Flemish Ghent is all narrow alleys and low brick houses. They meet at the somewhat confusing sequence of large squares that surrounds the town's principal buildings, spreading out to the immediate east of the Korenmarkt. Most of Ghent's leading attractions are within easy walking distance of the Korenmarkt.

St Baafskathedraal

The best place to start an exploration of the city is **St Baafskathedraal** (St Bavo's Cathedral; April–Oct Mon–Sat 8.30am–6pm, Sun 1–5pm; Nov–March Mon–Sat 8.30am–5pm, Sun 1–5pm; free), squeezed into the eastern corner of a tapering square, St Baafsplein. The third church to be built on this site, and 250 years in the making, the cathedral is a tad lopsided, but there's no gainsaying the imposing beauty of its west tower with its long, elegant windows and perky corner turrets. Some 82m high, the tower was the last major part of the church to be completed, topped off in 1554 – just before the outbreak of the religious wars which were to wrack the country for the next hundred years.

△ Ghent city centre

Inside, the mighty fifteenth-century **nave** is supported by tall, slender columns, which give the whole interior a cheerful sense of lightness, though the Baroque marble screen spoils the effect by darkening the choir.

In a small **side chapel** (April–Oct Mon–Sat 9.30am–4.45pm, Sun 1–4.30pm; Nov–March Mon–Sat 10.30am–3.45pm, Sun 1–3.30pm; €3) to the left of the cathedral entrance is Ghent's greatest treasure, **Jan van Eyck**'s **Adoration of the Mystic Lamb**. The altarpiece's cover screens display a beautiful Annunciation scene with the archangel Gabriel's wings reaching up to the timbered ceiling of a Flemish house, while below the donor and his wife kneel piously alongside statues of the saints. The restrained exterior painting is, however, merely a foretaste of what's within – a striking, visionary work of art that would have been revealed only when the shutters were opened on Sundays and feast days. On the upper level sit God the Father, the Virgin and John the Baptist in gleaming clarity; to the right are musician-angels and a nude, pregnant Eve; and on the left is Adam plus a group of singing angels, who strain to read their music. In the lower panel, the Lamb, the symbol of Christ's sacrifice, is approached by bishops, saintly virgins and Old and New Testament figures in a heavenly paradise seen as a sort of idealized Low Countries. There's more exquisite medieval art in the cathedral's Romanesque **crypt** (same hours as church), which holds all sorts of religious bric-a-brac as well as a handful of early Flemish paintings moved here from the city's Museum voor Schone Kunsten (Fine Art Museum), which is closed for refurbishment until at least 2006. Amongst the paintings are two superb works by Hieronymus Bosch (1450–1516), the *Bearing of the Cross* and *St Jerome at Prayer*.

The Lakenhalle and Belfort

Across from the cathedral lurks the **Lakenhalle** (cloth hall), a sturdy hunk of a building with an unhappy history. Work began on the hall in the early fifteenth century, but the cloth trade slumped before it was finished and it was only grudgingly completed in 1903. No one has ever quite worked out what to do with the building, and today it's little more than an empty stone shell with the city's tourist office (see p.159) tucked away in the basement on the north side. On the west side of the Lakenhalle is the entrance to the adjoining **Belfort** (Belfry; mid-March to mid-Nov daily 10am–12.30pm & 2–5.30pm; €3), a much-amended medieval edifice whose soaring spire is topped by a comically corpulent, gilded copper dragon. Once a watchtower-cum-storehouse for civic documents, the interior is now dusty and bare and holds little of interest, mainly a few old bells and statues. The belfry is equipped with a glass-sided lift that climbs up to the roof, where consolation is provided in the form of excellent views over the city centre.

The Stadhuis and St Niklaaskerk

Across from the Lakenhalle is the **Stadhuis** (town hall; guided tours bookable at the tourist office, May–Oct Mon–Thurs; €3), whose main facade comprises two contrasting sections. Dating from the 1580s, the later section offers a good example of Italian Renaissance architecture, its crisp symmetries faced by a multitude of black-painted columns, whilst immediately to the north are the wild, curling patterns of the earlier section, carved in Flamboyant Gothic style at the turn of the sixteenth century. It should all have been completed in the earlier style, but the money ran out when the wool trade collapsed and the city couldn't afford to finish it off until much later.

Back down the slope from the Stadhuis, the last of this central cluster of buildings is **St Niklaaskerk** (Mon 2–5pm, Tues–Sun 10am–5pm; free), whose arching buttresses and pencil-thin turrets represent a classic example of the early Scheldt Gothic style. Inside, many of the Baroque furnishings and fittings have been removed, thus returning the church to its early appearance, though unfortunately this does not apply to a clumsy and clichéd set of statues of the apostles. Much better is the giant-sized Baroque high altar with its mammoth representation of God glowering down its back, blowing the hot wind of the Last Judgment from his mouth and surrounded by a flock of cherubic angels.

The Korenmarkt and St Michielsbrug

St Niklaaskerk marks the southern end of the **Korenmarkt** (Corn Market), a long and wide cobbled area where the grain which once kept the city fed was traded after it was unloaded from the boats that anchored on the Graslei dock (see below). The one noteworthy building here is the former post office, whose combination of Gothic Revival and neo-Renaissance styles illustrates the eclecticism popular in Belgium at the beginning of the twentieth century.

Behind the old post office, the neo-Gothic **St Michielsbrug** (St Michael's bridge) offers fine views back over the towers and turrets that pierce the Ghent skyline. The bridge also overlooks the city's oldest harbour, the **Tussen Bruggen** (Between the Bridges), from whose quays – the Korenlei and the Graslei – boats leave for trips around the city's canals (see box below).

The guildhouses of the Graslei

Ghent's boatmen and grainweighers were crucial to the functioning of the medieval city, and they built a row of splendid guildhouses along the **Graslei** quayside, each gable decorated with an appropriate sign or symbol. At no. 14 stands the **Gildehuis van de Vrije Schippers** (Guildhouse of the Free Boatmen), whose badly weathered sandstone is decorated with scenes of boatmen weighing anchor, plus a delicate carving of a caravel – the type of Mediterranean sailing ship used by Columbus – above the door. Next door, at Graslei 12–13, the seventeenth-century **Coorenmetershuis** (Corn Measurers' House) was where city officials weighed and graded corn behind a facade graced by cartouches and garlands of fruit. Next to this, at no. 11, stands the quaint **Tolhuisje**, built to house the customs officers in 1698, while the adjacent limestone **Spijker** (Staple House), at no. 10, boasts a surly Romanesque facade dating from around 1200. It was here that the city stored its grain supply for over five hundred years until a fire gutted the interior. Close by, the dainty **Coorenmetershuis**, at no. 9, was the original home of the city's Corn Measurers until the construction of their second, larger premises at Graslei 12–13 (see above). Finally, the splendid **Den Enghel**, at no. 8, takes its name from the angel bearing a banner that decorates the facade; the building was originally the stone masons' guildhouse, as evidenced by the effigies of the four Roman martyrs who were the guild's patron saints.

Boat trips

Throughout the year, **boat trips** explore Ghent's inner waterways, departing from the Korenlei and Graslei quays, near the Korenmarkt (April–Oct daily 10am–6pm, Nov–March Sat & Sun 11am–4pm). Trips last forty minutes, cost €5, and leave roughly once every fifteen minutes, though the wait can be longer as boats often only depart when reasonably full. The trip serves as a good introduction to the older parts of Ghent, its architecture and history, though the multilingual commentary can be a tad irksome.

Het Gravensteen

From the north end of the Graslei, it's a couple of minutes' walk to **Het Gravensteen** (daily: April–Sept 9am–6pm; Oct–March 9am–5pm; €6), the former castle of the Counts of Flanders, which looks sinister enough to have been lifted from a Bosch painting, its cold, dark walls and unyielding turrets first raised in 1180 as much to intimidate the town's unruly citizens as to protect them. Entry is through a long and heavily fortified gateway, which leads to the main courtyard, framed by protective battlements complete with ancient arrow slits and holes through which boiling oil and water were poured onto attackers. Overlooking the courtyard stand the castle's two main buildings: the keep is on the right and to the left is the count's residence, riddled with narrow, interconnected staircases set within the thickness of the walls. A self-guided tour takes you (in approximately half an hour) through this labyrinth; highlights include the count's cavernous state rooms, a gruesome collection of instruments of torture, and a particularly dank, underground dungeon. It's also possible to walk along most of the castle's encircling wall, from where there are pleasing views over the city centre.

The Patershol

East of the castle, the narrow cobbled lanes and alleys of the **Patershol** are restrained by a tight web of brick terraced houses dating back to the seventeenth century. Once the heart of the Flemish working-class city, this thriving residential quarter had, by the 1970s, become a slum threatened with demolition. After much to-ing and fro-ing, the area was saved from the developers and a process of gentrification began, the result being today's gaggle of good bars and first-class restaurants. Here also, at Kraanlei 65, is the **Het Huis van Alijn** (Tues–Sun 11am–5pm; €2.50), a folklore museum that occupies a series of exceptionally pretty little almshouses set around a central courtyard and dinky chapel.

Vrijdagmarkt and Bij St Jacobs

From the Patershol, it's the briefest of strolls to the **Vrijdagmarkt**, a wide and open square that was long the political centre of Ghent, the site of both public meetings and executions – and sometimes both at the same time. Of the buildings flanking the Vrijdagmarkt, the most appealing is the old headquarters of the trade unions, the whopping **Ons Huis** (Our House), a sterling edifice built in eclectic style at the turn of the twentieth century. Adjoining the Vrijdagmarkt is busy **Bij St Jacobs**, a sprawling square sprinkled with antique shops and set around a sulky medieval church. The square hosts the city's biggest and best **flea market** (*prondelmarkt*) on Fridays, Saturdays and Sundays from 8am to 1pm.

From Bij St Jacobs, it takes a little less than ten minutes to get back to the Korenmarkt.

S.M.A.K. and the Museum voor Schone Kunsten

From the city centre, it's a quick tram ride or twenty-minute walk south to **S.M.A.K.** – the Stedelijk Museum voor Actuele Kunst (Contemporary Art Museum; Tues–Sun 10am–6pm; €5; ⑩www.smak.be). Housed in one part of a sprawling 1940s building that previously served as the city's casino, S.M.A.K. is one of Belgium's most adventurous contemporary art galleries. The ground floor is given over to temporary displays of international standing and upstairs features a regularly rotated selection of sculptures, paintings and installations distilled from the museum's wide-ranging permanent collection. S.M.A.K.

possesses examples of all the major artistic movements since World War II as well as their forerunners, most notably René Magritte and Paul Delvaux. Facing S.M.A.K. is the heavy-duty stonework of the **Museum voor Schone Kunsten** (Fine Art Museum), which possesses a distinguished collection of medieval Flemish and later Dutch and Flemish paintings. It is, however, closed for refurbishment until 2006, if not later.

Eating and drinking

Ghent's numerous **restaurants** and **cafés** offer the very best of Flemish and French cuisines with a sprinkling of Italian, Chinese and Arab places for variety. There is a concentration of deluxe restaurants in and around the narrow lanes of the Patershol and another, of less expensive options, on and around the Korenmarkt. Ghent also has a first-rate range of **bars**, from antique drinking dens with nicotine-stained ceilings through to slick, modern places with hi-tech furnishings and fittings.

Cafés and restaurants

Avalon Geldmunt 32 ☏ 09 224 37 24. This spick and span café and tearoom offers a wide range of well-prepared vegetarian food, from salads through to nut roasts, all served in a calm and tranquil environment. The daily lunchtime specials, at about €8, are particularly popular. Choose from one of the many different rooms or the terrace at the back in the summer. Café: Mon–Sat noon–2pm; tearoom: Mon–Fri 2–6pm.

Bij den wijzen en den zot Hertogstraat 42 ☏ 09 223 42 30. One of the best restaurants in the Patershol, serving up delicious Flemish cuisine with more than a dash of French flair – house specialities include eel, cooked in several different ways, and *waterzooi*, a filling and especially delicious broth of fish or chicken. Soft lighting and classical music set the tone, and the premises are charming too – an old brick house of tiny rooms and narrow stairs with dining on two floors. Mains around €20. Tues–Sat noon–2pm & 7–10pm.

De Blauwe Zalm Vrouwebroersstraat 2 ☏ 09 224 08 52. Brilliant seafood restaurant – the best in town – serving up a superb range

of dishes ranging from cod, salmon, monkfish and haddock through to the likes of seawolf, turbot and John Dory. Fish tanks keep the crustacea alive and biting, and the decor has a distinctly maritime feel – though it's all done in impeccable, ultra-cool style. Mains from €20. Reservations advised. Mon & Sat 7–9.30pm, Tues–Fri noon–1.30pm & 7–9.30pm.

Brooderie Jan Breydelstraat 8 ☏ 09 225 06 23. Pleasant and informal café with a healthfood slant, offering wholesome breakfasts, lunches, sandwiches and salads (from around €9), plus cakes and coffee. Also does bed-and-breakfast (see p.160). Tues–Sun 8am–6pm.

Budha Bar Korte Meer 27 ☏ 09 223 23 32, ⊛ www.budhabar.be. Concept food and lounge bar offering everything from tapas and dim sum through to pepper steak. Sit either up at the tapas bar and choose dishes from the conveyor belt or order at one of the tables on the mezzanine floor. Downstairs is a lounge area complete with beanbags. Takeaway too. Mon–Sat noon–2.30pm & 6–10.30pm.

Bars

't Dreupelkot Groentenmarkt 12. Cosy bar specializing in *jenever* (Dutch gin), of which it stocks more than 215 brands, all kept at icy temperatures. Down a little alley off the Groentenmarkt. Daily: July & Aug from 6pm until late; Sept–June from 4pm until late.

Pink Flamingos Onderstraat 55. Weird and wacky little place stuffed with everything kitsch, from plastic statues to awful religious icons. Attracts a groovy crowd, and is a great place for an aperitif or cocktails. Mon–Wed noon–midnight, Thurs & Fri noon–3am, Sat 2pm–3am, Sun 2pm–midnight.

De Tap en de Tepel Gewad 7. This charming candlelit bar ("The Tap and Nipple") has an open fire and a clutter of antique furnishings. Wine is the main deal, served with a good selection of cheeses. Wed–Sat 6pm until late; closed most of Aug.
Den Turk Botermarkt 3. The oldest bar in the city, this tiny rabbit-warren of a place offers a very good range of beers and whiskies.

There's also occasional live music, mainly jazz and blues. Daily from 11am until late.
Het Waterhuis aan de Bierkant Groentenmarkt 9. More than a hundred types of beer are available in this engaging, canalside bar, which is popular with tourists and locals alike. Be sure to try a delicious local brew called *Stropken* (literally "noose"). Daily from 11am until late.

Bruges

BRUGES is one of the most beautifully preserved medieval – or, in parts at least, ersatz medieval – cities in western Europe and it draws visitors in their thousands. Inevitably, the crowds tend to overwhelm the town's charms, but as a day-trip destination from Brussels – it's just an hour away by train – Bruges is hard to resist: its museums hold some of the country's finest collections of Flemish art and its intimate streets, woven around a pattern of narrow canals, live up to even the most inflated tourist hype. Indeed, many visitors choose to spend several days here rather than day-tripping in from Brussels – if you plan to do the same, you may want to take a look at Rough Guides' *Bruges DIRECTIONS* before you go.

Bruges came to prominence in the thirteenth century when it shared effective control of the **cloth trade** with its great rival, Ghent (see pp.159–160), turning high-quality English wool into clothing that was exported all over the known world. It was an immensely profitable business, and it made the city a centre of international trade. By the end of the fifteenth century, however, Bruges was in decline, principally because the River Zwin – the city's vital link to the North Sea – was silting up. By the 1530s, the town's sea trade had collapsed completely, and Bruges simply withered away. Frozen in time, Bruges escaped damage in both world wars to emerge the perfect tourist attraction.

Arrival and information

Bruges' **train station** adjoins the **bus station**, about 2km southwest of the town centre. If the twenty-minute walk into the centre doesn't appeal, you can get a local **bus** from outside the train station: most head off either to the Biekorf or the neighbouring Markt, bang in the centre of town; the single fare costs €1.

There are two tourist offices. The first – and smaller – office is at the train station (April–Sept Tues–Sat 10am–1pm & 2–6pm; Oct–March Tues–Sat 9.30am–12.30pm & 1–5pm; ☎050 44 86 86); it offers a limited range of tourist information, concentrating on making hotel reservations for visitors – the service is free, though you do have to pay a small deposit, which is deducted from the final bill. The **main tourist office**, which also operates an accommodation service, has recently been moved to the main concert hall, the Concertgebouw, a ten-minute walk west of the Markt at 't Zand 34 (April–Sept Mon–Fri 9.30am–6.30pm, Sat & Sun 9.30am–12.30pm & 2–6.30pm; Oct–March Mon–Fri 9.30am–5pm, Sat & Sun 9.30am–1pm & 2–5.30pm; ☎050 44 86 86, ⓦwww.brugge.be); buses from the train station usually pause here on their way to the Markt.

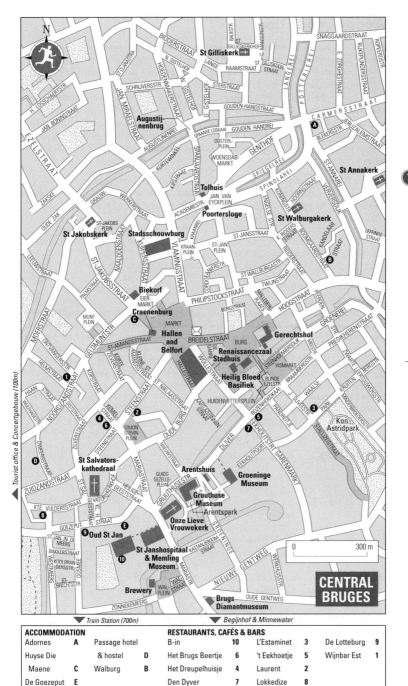

CENTRAL BRUGES

0   300 m

ACCOMMODATION				RESTAURANTS, CAFÉS & BARS					
Adornes	**A**	Passage hotel		B-in	**10**	L'Estaminet	**3**	De Lotteburg	**9**
Huyse Die		& hostel	**D**	Het Brugs Beertje	**6**	't Eekhoetje	**5**	Wijnbar Est	**1**
Maene	**C**	Walburg	**B**	Het Dreupelhuisje	**4**	Laurent	**2**		
De Goezeput	**E**			Den Dyver	**7**	Lokkedize	**8**		

Accommodation

Bruges has over one hundred hotels, dozens of bed-and-breakfasts and several unofficial youth hostels, but still can't accommodate all its visitors at the height of the season. If you're arriving in July or August, be sure to **book ahead** or, at a pinch, make sure you get here in the morning before all the rooms have gone. Given the crush, many visitors use the hotel and B&B **accommodation service** provided by the tourist office (see p.166) – it's efficient and can save you endless hassle. At other times of the year, things are usually much less pressing, though it's still a good idea to reserve ahead, especially if you are picky. The tourist office issues a free **accommodation booklet** providing comprehensive listings including hotel photographs, websites and a city map.

Adornes St Annarei 26 ☎ 050 34 13 36, ⓦ www .adornes.be. Three-star hotel in a tastefully converted old Flemish town house, with a plain, high-gabled facade. Both the public areas and the comfortable bedrooms are decorated in bright whites and creams, which emphasize the antique charm of the place. Great location, too, at the junction of two canals near the east end of Spiegelrei, and delicious breakfasts. Doubles from €95.

De Goezeput Goezeputstraat 29 ☎ 050 34 26 94, Ⓕ 050 34 20 13. Set in a charming location on a quiet street near the cathedral, this outstanding two-star hotel occupies an immaculately refurbished eighteenth-century convent complete with wooden beams and oodles of antiques. A snip, with en-suite doubles from €70.

Huyze Die Maene Markt 17 ☎ 050 33 39 59, ⓦ www.huyzediemaene.be. This B&B is above a brasserie plumb in the centre of town overlooking the Markt; it has two cosy deluxe rooms and one spacious top-floor suite, each decorated in grand style. Closed Feb. Doubles €115.

Passage Hostel Dweersstraat 26 ☎ 050 34 02 32, ⓦ www.passagebruges.com. The most agreeable hostel in Bruges, accommodating fifty people in ten comparatively comfortable dormitories (all with shared bathrooms). Located in an old and interesting part of town, about ten minutes' walk west of the Markt. Meals are available at the bar, and guests get a free beer with food. Rates from €14 for a dorm bed, €3 extra for breakfast.

Walburg Boomgaardstraat 13 ☎ 050 34 94 14, ⓦ www.hotels-belgium.com. Engaging hotel in an elegant nineteenth-century mansion (with splendidly large doors), a short walk east of the Burg along Hoogstraat. The rooms are smart and comfortable, and there are also capacious suites. Doubles from €175.

The City

The oldest part of Bruges fans out from two central squares, the Markt and the Burg. The larger of the two is the **Markt**, an expansive open area edged on three sides by nineteenth-century gabled buildings and on the south side by the city's most famous edifice, the **Belfort** (Belfry; Tues–Sun 9.30am–5pm; €5), which was built in the thirteenth century when the town was at its richest. Inside, the belfry staircase passes the room where the town charters were locked for safekeeping, and an eighteenth-century carillon, before emerging onto the roof, from where there are wondrous views over the city centre. At the foot of the belfry, the quadrangular **Hallen** is a much-restored edifice dating from the thirteenth century, its arcaded galleries built to facilitate the cloth trade.

Boat trips in Bruges

Half-hour **boat trips** around the central canals leave every few minutes from a number of jetties south of the Burg; March–Nov daily 10am–6pm; €5.70. For the rest of the year there's a sporadic service on the weekend only.

The Burg

From the Markt, Breidelstraat leads through to the **Burg**, whose southern half is fringed by the city's finest group of buildings. One of the best of these is the **Heilig Bloed Basiliek** (Basilica of the Holy Blood; daily: April–Sept 9.30–11.50am & 2–5.50pm; Oct–March Mon, Tues & Thurs–Sun 10–11.50am & 2–3.50pm, Wed 10–11.50am; free), named after the holy relic that found its way here in 1150. The basilica divides into two parts. Tucked away in the corner, the **lower chapel** is a shadowy, crypt-like affair, originally built at the beginning of the twelfth century to shelter another relic, that of St Basil, one of the great figures of the early Greek Church. Next door, approached up a wide staircase, the **upper chapel** was built at the same time, but it's impossible to make out the original structure behind the excessive nineteenth-century decoration. The phial containing the Holy Blood is stored here, within a magnificent silver **tabernacle**, the gift of the Habsburg governors Albert and Isabella of Spain in 1611. One of the holiest relics in medieval Europe, the phial supposedly contains a few drops of blood and water washed from the body of Christ by Joseph of Arimathea. The Holy Blood is still venerated in the upper chapel on Fridays, and reverence for it remains strong, not least on Ascension Day when it is carried through the town in a colourful but solemn procession.

To the left of the basilica, the **Stadhuis** (town hall) is graced by a beautiful, turreted sandstone facade from 1376, though its statues of the counts and countesses of Flanders are much more recent. Inside, the magnificent **Gothic Hall** (Tues–Sun 9.30am–5pm; €2.50) boasts fancy vault-keys depicting New Testament scenes and romantic paintings commissioned in 1895 to illustrate the history of the town.

△ Bruges

The Groeninge Museum

From the arch beside the Stadhuis, Blinde Ezelstraat ("Blind Donkey Street") leads south across the canal to the huddle of picturesque houses crimping the **Huidenvettersplein**, the old tanners' quarter that now holds some of the busiest drinking and eating places in town. Nearby, Dijver follows the canal to the **Groeninge Museum**, Dijver 12 (Tues–Sun 9.30am–5pm; €8), which boasts an outstanding collection of early Flemish paintings. Among them are several works by **Jan van Eyck**, who lived and worked in Bruges from 1430 until his death eleven years later. Featured also are works by Rogier van der Weyden, Hugo van der Goes, Hans Memling, Gerard David and **Hieronymus Bosch**, whose paintings are crammed with mysterious beasts, microscopic mutants and scenes of awful cruelty. The museum's selection of late sixteenth- and seventeenth-century paintings is far more modest, though highlights here include canvases by Pieter Bruegel the Younger and Pieter Pourbus. The modern paintings are distinguished by the spooky surrealism of Paul Delvaux and by Constant Permeke, noted for his dark and earthy representations of Belgian peasant life.

The Arentshuis and Gruuthuse museums

Also on the Dijver, in a big old mansion just west of the Groeninge, is the **Arentshuis Museum** (Tues–Sun 9.30am–5pm; €2.50), whose ground floor is given over to temporary exhibitions, usually of fine art. The floor up above displays the moody etchings, lithographs, studies and paintings of the much-travelled artist **Frank Brangwyn** (1867–1956). Born in Bruges, of Welsh parents, Brangwyn donated this sample of his work to his native town in 1936. Apprenticed to William Morris in the early 1880s and an official UK war artist in World War I, Brangwyn was a versatile artist who turned his hand to several different media, though his drawings are much more appealing than his paintings, which often slide into sentimentality.

Close by, at Dijver 17, the **Gruuthuse Museum** (Tues–Sun 9.30am–5pm; €6) occupies a rambling mansion that dates from the fifteenth century. Distributed amongst the mansion's many rooms is a hotchpotch of Flemish fine, applied and decorative arts, mostly dating from the medieval and early modern period, plus paintings and sculptures, silverware, lace, ceramics and musical instruments, while antique furniture crops up just about everywhere. The museum's strongest suite is its superb collection of **tapestries**, mostly woven in Brussels or Bruges and dating from the sixteenth and seventeenth centuries. Most intriguing of all, however, is the 1472 oak-panelled **oratory**, which, very unusually, juts out from the first floor of the museum to overlook the high altar of the adjacent Onze Lieve Vrouwekerk (see below).

The Onze Lieve Vrouwekerk

Beyond the Gruuthuse, the **Onze Lieve Vrouwekerk** (Mon–Fri 9.30am–12.30pm & 1.30–5pm, Sat 9.30am–12.30pm & 1.30–4pm, Sun 1.30–5pm; free) is a rambling shambles of a church, a clamour of different dates and different styles, whose brick spire is – at 122m – one of the tallest in Belgium. Entered from the south, the **nave** was three hundred years in the making, an architecturally discordant affair, whose thirteenth-century, grey-stone central aisle, with its precise blind arcading, is the oldest part of the church. At the east end of the south aisle is the church's most celebrated *objet d'art*, a delicate marble *Madonna and Child* by Michelangelo. Otherwise, the most interesting of the church's accumulated treasures are situated in the **chancel**

(€2.50), where the **mausoleums** of Charles the Bold and his daughter Mary of Burgundy are exquisite examples of Renaissance carving, their side panels decorated with coats of arms connected by the most intricate of floral designs. In the 1970s archeologists dug beneath the mausoleums. The hole was never filled in and today mirrors allow you to see Mary's coffin along with the brick **burial vaults** of several unknown medieval dignitaries. In total, seventeen of these vaults were unearthed and three have been placed in the **Lanchals Chapel**, just across the ambulatory. Plastered with lime mortar, the inside walls of all the vaults sport brightly coloured **grave frescoes**, a specific art that flourished hereabouts from the late thirteenth to the middle of the fifteenth century.

St Janshospitaal and the Hans Memling Museum

Opposite the entrance to the Onze Lieve Vrouwekerk is **St Janshospitaal** (Tues–Sun 9.30am–5pm; €8), a sprawling complex that was used as an infirmary until the nineteenth century. The oldest part of the hospital is at the front behind two church-like gable ends. It dates from the twelfth century and has recently been turned into a sleek and slick **museum** with one large section – in the former ward – exploring the hospital's historical background by means of documents, paintings and religious *objets d'art*. A second, smaller but much more alluring section, sited in the old hospital chapel, is dedicated to the paintings of **Hans Memling** (1433–94). Born near Frankfurt, Memling spent most of his working life in Bruges, where he stuck to the detailed symbolism of his contemporaries, but suffused his figures with a velvet-like gracefulness that greatly appealed to the city's burghers. Indeed, their enthusiasm made Memling a rich man – in 1480 he was listed among the town's major moneylenders. Of the six works on display in the chapel, Memling's *Reliquary of St Ursula* of 1489 is the most unusual, a lovely piece of craftsmanship comprising a miniature wooden Gothic church painted with the story of St Ursula.

St Salvatorskathedraal

From St Janshospitaal, it's a couple of minutes' walk north to **St Salvators kathedraal** (Holy Saviour's Cathedral; Mon 2–5.45pm, Tues–Fri 8.30-11.45am & 2–5.45pm, Sat 8.30–11.45am & 2–3.30pm, Sun 9–10.15am & 2–5.45pm; free), a bulky Gothic edifice that mostly dates from the late thirteenth century, though the Flamboyant Gothic ambulatory was added some two centuries later. At the end of a long-term refurbishment, the cathedral's **nave** has recently emerged from centuries of accumulated grime, its soaring columns and arches home to a splendid set of tapestries hanging in the choir and transepts, showing biblical scenes. The **cathedral treasury** (Sun–Fri 2–5pm; €2.50), ranged around the neo-Gothic chapter house, is packed with ecclesiastical tackle, from religious paintings and statues through to an assortment of reliquaries, vestments and croziers.

South to the Begijnhof and the Minnewater

Heading south from St Janshospitaal, it's a brief stroll to the much-visited **Begijnhof** (daily 9am–6pm or sunset if earlier; free), where a rough circle of old and infinitely pretty whitewashed houses surrounds a central green. There were once *begijnhofs* all over Belgium and this is one of the few to have survived in good nick. They were built to encourage widows and unmarried women to live in communities, the better to do pious acts, especially caring for the sick. The occupants – the **beguines** (*begijns*) – were different from nuns in so far as they did not have to take convential vows and had the right to return to the secular world if they wished. Margaret, Countess of Flanders, founded Bruges' *begijnhof* in 1245 and, although most of the houses now standing date from the eighteenth century, the medieval lay-out has survived intact, retaining the impression of the *begijnhof* as a self-contained village with access controlled through two large gates. The houses are still in private hands, but, with the beguines long gone, they are now occupied by Benedictine nuns. Only one is open to the public – the **Begijnenhuisje** (Mon–Sat 10am–noon & 1.45–5pm, Sun 10.45am–noon & 1.45–5pm; €2), a pint-sized celebration of the simple life of the beguines.

It's a short walk from the begijnhof to the **Minnewater**, billed in much publicity hype as the "Lake of Love". The tag certainly gets the canoodlers going, but in fact the lake – more a large pond – started life as a city harbour. The distinctive stone lock house at the head of the Minnewater recalls its earlier function, though it's actually a very fanciful nineteenth-century reconstruction of the medieval original.

Eating and drinking

In Bruges, most of the **restaurants** and **cafés** – and there are scores of them – are geared up for the tourist industry. Standards are very variable, with a whole slew of places churning out some pretty mediocre stuff to cater for the enormous number of day-trippers, though there are, of course, lots of exceptions – including the places we recommend below. Few would say Bruges' **bars** are cutting edge, but neither are they staid and dull – far from it if you know where to go. Indeed, drinking in the city can be a real pleasure and one of the potential highlights of any visit.

Cafés and restaurants

Den Dyver Dijver 5 ℡050 33 60 69. Top-flight restaurant specializing in traditional Flemish dishes cooked in beer – the quail and rabbit are magnificent, though the seafood runs them close. The decor is plush and antique, with tapestries on the wall beneath an ancient wood-beam ceiling. The service is attentive, but not unduly so, and the only real drawback is the muzak, which can be tiresome. Popular with an older clientele. Reservations advised. Mains around €25. Daily noon–2pm & 6.30–9pm, but closed Wed & Thurs lunch.

't Eekhoetje Eekhoutstraat 3 ℡050 34 89 79. Bright and airy tearoom, with a small courtyard, just a short walk from the crowds of Huidenvettersplein. The efficient and friendly staff serve a good selection of tasty snacks and light meals such as omelettes, pasta and toasties. Takeaway available too. Daily except Wed 7.30am–7.30pm.

Laurent Steenstraat 79c. Cheap and cheerful café-restaurant metres from the cathedral. No points for decor or atmosphere, but the snacks are filling and fresh and the pancakes first rate. Very popular with locals. Daily 9am–5.30pm.

Lokkedize Korte Vuldersstraat 33 ℡050 33 44 50. Attracting a youthful crowd, this sympathetic café-bar – all subdued lighting, fresh flowers and jazz music – serves up a good line in Mediterranean food, with main courses averaging around €9 and bar snacks from €4. Wed & Thurs 7pm–midnight, Fri & Sat 6pm–1am, Sun 6pm–midnight.

De Lotteburg Goezeputstraat 43 ℡050 33 75 35, ⊛www.lotteburg.com. Arguably the town's best fish restaurant, this smart and formal little place has a superb menu, with imaginative, carefully prepared dishes – don't miss the fish soup. The set menus cost an arm and a leg, but main courses average €30–35 – expensive, but well worth it. Lunches cost in the region of €30. Reservations essential. Wed–Fri & Sun noon–2pm & 7–9.30pm, Sat 7–9.30pm; last orders 30min before closing. Usually closed for holidays for two weeks in Jan and again in late July.

Bars

B-in Mariastraat 38 ⓦ www.b-in.be. The coolest place in town, this recently opened bar-club is kitted out in attractive modern style with low, comfy seating and an eye-grabbing mix of coloured fluorescent tubes and soft ceiling lights. Guest DJs play funky, uplifting house, and there are reasonably priced drinks and cocktails plus a relaxed and friendly crowd. Gets going about 11pm. Free entry. Daily except Tues 10am–3am, Fri & Sat until 5am.

Het Brugs Beertje Kemelstraat 5. This small and friendly speciality beer bar claims a stock of three hundred beers, which aficionados reckon is one of the best selections in Belgium, and there are tasty snacks too, such as cheeses and salad. Popular with backpackers. Daily except Wed 4pm–1am.

Het Dreupelhuisje Kemelstraat 9. Tiny, laid-back and eminently agreeable bar specializing in *jenever* (gin) and advocaat, of which it has an outstanding range. Two doors down

from *Het Brugs Beertje* (see opposite). Daily except Tues 6pm–2am.

L'Estaminet Park 5. Groovy neighbourhood café-bar with a relaxed feel and a diverse and cosmopolitan clientele. Rickety furniture both inside and on the large outside terrace adds to the flavour of the place, as does the world music backtrack, while the first-rate beer menu skilfully picks its way through Belgium's myriad beers. Daily except Thurs 11.30am–1am or later.

Wijnbar Est Noordzandstraat 34 ☎ 050/33 38 39. The best wine bar in town, with a friendly and relaxed atmosphere, an extensive cellar and over 25 different wines available by the glass every day – it's especially strong on New World vintages, and also serves a selection of cheeses in the evening. There's live jazz, blues and folk music every Sunday from 8pm to 10.30pm. Mon, Thurs & Sun 5pm till late, Fri & Sat 3pm–1am.

Listings

Listings

8

Accommodation

With over seventy hotels and several hostels dotted within its central ring of boulevards, Brussels has no shortage of **places to stay**. Some of the most opulent – as well as some of the most basic – are scattered amongst the cobbled lanes on and around the **Grand–Place** and there's another equally convenient cluster round the **Bourse**. Nearby, the groovy **Ste–Catherine** district weighs in with a good selection of low- to mid-range hotels, or you can venture out of the Lower Town, south to the smart chain hotels of **avenue Louise**. Nevertheless, despite the number and variety of hotels and hostels, finding accommodation can still prove difficult, particularly in the **spring** and **autumn** when the capital enjoys what amounts to its **high seasons** – July and August are much slacker as the business trade dips when the EU (pretty much) closes down for its summer recess.

We have selected nearly forty hotels and hostels in this chapter, and given their prices and contact details, but if you want to view all of the city's (registered) accommodation, consult the BIT (Brussels tourist office) website on ⓦ www .brusselsinternational.be. BIT also publishes a free and comprehensive **Hôtel booklet**, which can be ordered via their website or picked up in person at any of their offices in Brussels (see p.25). All the accommodation we describe is marked on the **colour maps** at the end of the book.

Hotels

The capital's **hotels** are ranked according to a **five–star system** common across the whole of Belgium, though note that stars are allocated on amenities – 24hr reception, en-suite rooms, etc – and never on aesthetics and therefore tend to favour chain (as distinct from family) hotels. Generally speaking, standards in Belgian hotels are fairly high and you can usually be sure that a wide range of facilities and services – bar, restaurant, TV, air conditioning – is available.

Prices in the capital's hotels vary hugely. Many have both deluxe and more standard rooms, with charges adjusted accordingly, and **special and weekend discounts** are legion with the average discount being about fifteen percent, though some places (sometimes) knock down prices by up to fifty percent. Almost everywhere, **breakfast is included** in the overnight rate; where this isn't the case, reckon on paying an extra €10. An increasing number of hotels will accommodate children for free if they stay in their parents' room; others require you to pay the cost of an extra bed.

Whatever the time of the year, it's prudent to **reserve a room ahead of time**, most simply by contacting the hotel or hostel direct – language is rarely a problem as almost all receptionists speak at least some English. Alternatively, contact Belgium's central reservation agency, **Resotel** (☎0032 2 779 39 39 Ⓦwww.belgium-hospitality.com), who operate an efficient hotel reservation service, seeking out the best deals and discounts. If you arrive in the city with nowhere to stay, the BIT tourist office on the Grand-Place (May–Sept daily 9am–6pm; Oct–Dec & Easter to end April Mon–Sat 9am–6pm, Sun 10am–2pm; Jan till Easter Mon–Sat 9am–6pm; ☎02 513 89 40, Ⓕ02 513 83 20), operates a **same-night hotel booking service** – they don't make advance reservations. The service is provided free – you just pay a percentage of the room rate as a deposit and this is then subtracted from your final hotel bill.

The Grand-Place and around

Amigo rue de l'Amigo 1-3 ☎02 547 47 47, Ⓦwww.hotelamigo.com. This lavish hotel is one of Brussels' oldest, and boasts impeccable service, a central location, just around the corner from the Grand-Place, and elegant furnishings, including Flemish tapestries, paintings and Oriental rugs. It has, however, fallen into the hands of Rocco Forte and a refit has robbed it of much of its former individuality – where it was once plush with character, now it's just plush. Curiously, the building itself started out as a prison. Prémétro Bourse or Métro Gare Centrale. Doubles listed at €550, but significant discounts are commonplace.

Aris Grand-Place rue du Marché-aux-Herbes 78 ☎02 514 43 00, Ⓦwww.arishotel.be. Aesthetically not the most pleasing of buildings, despite the nineteenth-century stone facade – but the 55 modern rooms are clean and functional and you're just 20m or so from the Grand-Place. Prices are slightly inflated during the week. Facilities include TV, air conditioning and wheelchair access. Prémétro Bourse or Métro Gare Centrale. Doubles €75–180.

Le Dixseptième rue de la Madeleine 25 ☎02 517 17 17, Ⓦwww.ledixseptieme.be. Arguably the most charming hotel in Brussels, *Le Dixseptième* has just 24 deluxe rooms and suites, half of which are in the tastefully renovated seventeenth-century mansion at the front, the remainder in the contemporary extension at the back. Parquet flooring, crystal chandeliers and pastel-painted woodwork all add to the flavour. Facilities

include a sauna, a dinky interior patio, a Louis XVI-style lounge and a bar. The hotel is just a couple of minutes' walk from the Grand-Place on the way to Gare Centrale. Doubles from €200 to a wallet-shattering €430, but discounts of up to fifty percent are commonplace, especially at the weekend. Métro Gare Centrale.

Floris Grand Place rue des Harengs 6 ☎02 514 07 60, Ⓔfloris.grandplace@grouptours.com. Unusual chain hotel in a pair of adjoining old terrace houses down a narrow side-street off the Grand-Place. The interior has been kitted out in a modern version of antique style – all stained wood and pastel-painted walls – and there are eleven comfortable, en-suite rooms of varying size; rooms at the back are much quieter than those at the front. One disadvantage is that the hotel is short of natural light. Métro Gare Centrale. Weekend discounts; rack rate for a double room is €112.

La Légende rue du Lombard 35 ☎02 512 82 90, Ⓦwww.hotellalegende.com. Pleasant, if frugal, accommodation in an old building along a busy road (back rooms are quieter) in the heart of the city centre, not far from the Grand-Place. All of the hotel's 26 bedrooms are fairly large and en suite, but the decor is bland and mundane. A central location and special discounts, mostly at the weekend, make this a popular choice. Prémétro Bourse. Minimum two nights' stay. Doubles €90–120.

La Madeleine rue de la Montagne 22 ☎02 513 29 73, Ⓦwww.hotel-la-madeleine.be. Small, competent chain hotel with 52 routine, modern rooms, most of which are en suite. Handy location – just down the hill from Gare Centrale and metres from the

Grand-Place. Métro Gare Centrale. Doubles €110–125.

Le Méridien carrefour de l'Europe 3 ☎02 548 42 11, ⓦ www.brussels.lemeridien.com. Modern and expansive 224-room, five-star chain hotel in a convenient location, a couple of minutes' walk down from Gare Centrale. Not overloaded with character, but the rooms are large and pleasant with all mod cons and the building itself is in an attractive retro style that blends well with its surroundings. Discounts of around fifty percent are routine at the weekend. Métro Gare Centrale. Rack-rate doubles €175 and up.

Mozart rue Marché aux Fromages 23 ☎02 502 66 61, ⓦ www.hotel-mozart.be. Gem of a hotel housed in a seventeenth-century building nestled amongst the fast-food joints along "Pitta Street". Grand lobby dripping with fine art, painted tiles and rich ormolu furnishings, and an ornate staircase leading to 47 characterful rooms, some with exposed beams, and all with shower. Drawing room-style breakfast area and a small terrace. Métro Gare Centrale. A snip at doubles for €95.

Novotel Brussels off Grand-Place, rue du Marché aux Herbes 120 ☎02 514 33 33, ⓦ www.novotel.com. This well-presented chain hotel occupies a modern block that has been tastefully designed to blend in with its surroundings just down the hill from the Gare Centrale. The 136 rooms are decorated in brisk modern style and a programme of refurbishment is quickly bringing all of them up to the latest standards. Métro Gare Centrale. The rack rate for a double is €190, but discounts at the weekend or for advance booking usually bring the price down to around €110–120.

Saint-Michel Grand-Place 15 ☎02 511 09 56, ⒻP 02 511 46 00. The only hotel to look out over the Grand-Place, this small, friendly place occupies an old guildhouse on the east side of the square. The hotel's prime location and handsome facade do, however, belie a rather humble interior with fifteen rooms offering a sort of faded elegance, complete with chintz bedspreads and cushioned headboards. All the rooms have either en-suite bath or shower and seven are at the front, overlooking the square, though note that for these you will certainly need to make an advance booking, and neither will they suit light sleepers – revellers on

the Grand-Place can make a real echoing racket. Breakfast is taken in your room or at the café across from the hotel. Prémétro Bourse. Doubles €98.

La Vieille Lanterne rue des Grands Carmes 29 ☎02 512 74 94, Ⓔ lavieillelanterne@hotmail .com. Tiny, family-run pension tucked away above a souvenir shop overlooking the Manneken Pis, the briefest of strolls from the Grand-Place. Six boxy but perfectly adequate rooms simply furnished and each with shower. Breakfast is brought up to your room. Advance bookings advisable. Prémétro Bourse. Doubles €65.

The Lower Town

Arlequin rue de la Fourche 17–19 ☎02 514 16 15, ⓦ www.arlequin.be. Large, slick-looking lobby and efficient staff reveal little about the hotel's ninety or so small, functional bedrooms, but this hotel is right in the thick of the downtown action and the seventh-floor breakfast room offers amazing views of the Hôtel de Ville. Don't be too deterred by the grotty approach to the hotel. Prémétro Bourse. Doubles €130.

Astrid Centre place du Samedi 11 ☎02 219 31 19, ⓦ www.astridhotel.be. Built in 1994, the *Astrid* isn't as atmospheric as some of the other hotels in the Ste-Catherine district, with each of its hundred rooms decorated in crisp, modern, chain-hotel style. The hotel is popular with visiting business folk and has wheelchair access. Métro Ste-Catherine. Rates for doubles can soar to €220, but €75–130 is the listed tariff.

Atlas rue du Vieux Marché-aux-Grains 30 ☎02 502 60 06, ⓦ www.atlas.be. Modern, four-star hotel behind the handsome stone facade of a nineteenth-century mansion in the heart of the Ste-Catherine district, a five-minute walk or so from the Grand-Place. The 88 rooms are a (slight) cut above the average chain offering and the hotel is wheelchair accessible. Métro Ste Catherine. Doubles €90–200.

Brussels Welcome Hotel quai au Bois à Brûler 23 ☎02 219 95 46, ⓦ www.hotelwelcome .com. Friendly, family-run three-star hotel well positioned in the heart of the Ste-Catherine district. Each of the seventeen themed rooms is decorated in the style of a particular country or region, for instance Bali, Japan and Tibet. The Silk Road suite is a particularly sumptuous affair, and there's an attractive wood-panelled breakfast room too. Glowing recommendations from several of our readers. Métro Ste Catherine. Doubles €95–160.

Comfort Art Hotel Siru place Rogier 1 ☏ 02 203 35 80, ⓦ www.comforthotelsiru.com. It may not look like much from the outside – just another skyrise overlooking place Rogier – but the interior of this 101-room hotel is encouragingly original. In the late 1980s, a team of Belgian art students was given carte blanche to decorate the hotel's corridors and bedrooms. They opted for a broadly modernist style with all manner of figurines, mini-polystyrene effigies, murals and cartoon strips – everything from Tintin to Marilyn Monroe – popping up just about everywhere. It's all good fun, and hopefully the hotel chain which now owns the place will keep to the same arty message. Métro Rogier. Doubles from as little as €62.

Ibis Brussels Centre Ste Catherine rue Joseph Plateau 2 ☏ 02 513 76 20, ⓦ www.ibishotel .com. The giant Ibis chain hardly lights the fires of the imagination, but it does provide perfectly adequate accommodation at affordable prices. Ibis have five hotels in and around Brussels and this has the best location, at the heart of the enjoyable Ste-Catherine district, the briefest of walks from Métro Ste Catherine. Over 230 briskly decorated modern rooms with doubles from €85 to €150.

Métropole place de Brouckère 31 ☏ 02 217 23 00, ⓦ www.metropolehotel.com. Dating from 1895, this grand hotel, one of Brussels' finest, boasts exquisite Empire and Art Nouveau decor in its public areas, and although some of the rooms beyond are comparatively routine, albeit very spacious, others retain their original fittings. The rack rate for a double starts at €350, but substantial discounts are commonplace. The classic Art Nouveau bar remains a popular meeting point for tourists and locals alike. Métro De Brouckère. Doubles €350–450.

Mirabeau place Fontainas 18 ☏ 02 511 19 72, ⓦ www.hotelmirabeau.be. This friendly, medium-sized hotel has thirty small en-suite rooms, plainly decorated with uniform grey furnishings. Surrounded by office blocks, it occupies the corner of an early twentieth-century, seven-storey block, complete with long slender windows and wrought-iron grilles, but overlooks an uninspiring square

edging onto boulevard Anspach. Windows are not sound-proofed, so interior rooms are quieter than those on the square. Large, modern breakfast room at the front with a small bar. Prémétro Anneessens. Doubles €80–85.

NH Atlanta blvd Adolphe Max 7 ☏ 02 217 01 20, ⓦ www.nh-hotels.com. The NH chain has moved in on Brussels with gusto and it now operates four hotels in and around the city centre. This is the pick of the bunch, deco-rated in the chain's trademark style of sleek modern furnishings and fittings matched by pastel-painted walls – the epitome of IKEA. All the *Atlanta's* 241 rooms are pleasantly comfortable and similarly well appointed, though those on the front, overlooking the boulevard, can be a tad noisy. Otherwise, it's a good location, immediately to the north of place de Brouckère – and Métro De Brouckère. Special deals and discounts are commonplace, but the rack rate for doubles begins at €150.

Noga rue du Béguinage 38 ☏ 02 218 67 63, ⓦ www.nogahotel.com. Not the grandest of the city's hotels by a long chalk, but this pleasant two-star offers nineteen comfort-able rooms decorated in clean modern style. Competitive rates and a handy loca-tion close to Métro Ste Catherine. Doubles €80–100.

Radisson SAS rue Fosse-aux-Loups 47 ☏ 02 219 28 28, ⓦ www.radissonsas.com. Large, expense-account chain hotel centred around an enormous glass-roofed atrium. Handy location, about five minutes' walk north of the Grand-Place, and rooms with every mod con. Métro Gare Centrale. Doubles start at €210.

The Upper Town

Du Congrès rue du Congrès 38–44 ☏ 02 217 18 90, ⓦ www.hotelducongres.be. Pleasant, three-star hotel occupying a set of attrac-tive late nineteenth-century town houses in an especially good-looking corner of the Lower Town, a survivor from the 1890s with a network of mini-boulevards inter-rupted by leafy little squares. Each of the hotel's seventy-odd en-suite rooms is spacious and airy and decorated in plain, modern style. Métro Madou. Doubles €90–140.

Jolly Hotel du Grand Sablon rue Bodenbroeck 2–4 ☏ 02 518 11 00, ⓦ www.jollyhotels.com.

Pretty expensive for what you get, but this plush, 200-room hotel, with its spick and span modern bedrooms, does overlook the appealing place du Grand Sablon with its terraced cafés and designer shops. The excellent restaurant and convivial bar rate as the other main attractions. A five- to ten-minute walk from Métro Louise. Doubles begin at a steep €270.

Sabina rue du Nord 78 ☎ 02 218 26 37, ⓦ www .hotelsabina.be. Basic pension in an attractive late nineteenth-century town house with 24 workaday, en-suite rooms. In an appealing residential area that was once a favourite haunt of the city's Victorian bourgeoisie. Triples and quads available. Discounts and cheaper weekend rates. A five- to ten-minute walk from Métro Madou. Doubles €90.

Le Sablon rue de la Paille 2–8 ☎ 02 513 60 40, ⓦ www.hotellessablon.be. Smartly turned out, if otherwise unexceptional, medium-sized, modern hotel situated right next to place du Grand Sablon, one of the city's most appealing squares, lying at the heart of a chichi neighbourhood known for its antiques shops and open-air market. Wheelchair access. A five- to ten-minute walk from Métro Louise. Slightly cheaper than other hotels in the vicinity, but doubles still begin at a substantial €150.

Sofitel Astoria Brussels rue Royale 103 ☎ 02 227 05 05, ⓦ www.sofitel.com. Winston Churchill once stayed at this grand 118-room hotel, whose public areas feature turn-of-the-century fixtures and fittings, including a spectacular Orient Express-style "Pullman Bar". The bedrooms beyond are spacious and extremely comfortable, but only in a lavish chain-hotel sort of way. Métro Botanique is a brief walk away. Expect to pay an arm, leg and torso with doubles kicking off at €300, though special offers do abound.

St Gilles, avenue Louise and Ixelles

Argus rue Capitaine Crespel 6 ☎ 02 514 07 70, ⓦ www.hotel-argus.be. Not in the city centre, but a good location nonetheless, just to the south of the boulevards of the petit ring, a five-minute walk from place Louise. The hotel's forty modern and modest rooms are a bit on the small side, but they're cosy enough and the service is impeccable. A nice alternative to the gargantuan – and expensive – hotels that pepper this district. Métro Louise. Doubles €65–120.

Les Bluets rue Berckmans 124 ☎ 02 534 39 83, ⓔ bluets@swing.be. Charming, family-run hotel with just ten en-suite rooms in a large, handsome old stone terrace house. Immaculate decor in rich fin-de-siècle style. No lift at present. One block south of the petit ring – and métro station Hôtel des Monnaies. Doubles €75.

Conrad Brussels ave Louise 71 ☎ 02 542 42 42, ⓦ www.conradhotels.com. One of the capital's top hotels, the *Conrad* was former US president Clinton's top choice when in town. Housed in an immaculate tower block, with all sorts of retro flourishes, the hotel boasts over 250 large and lavish rooms, comprehensive facilities and impeccable service. It's situated near the north end of the avenue, a five-minute walk from Métro Louise. Doubles €200–600.

Four Points rue Paul Spaak 15 ☎ 02 645 61 11, ⓦ www.fourpoints.com/brussels. Smart and efficient Sheraton hotel in a rather ungainly modern building just off – and about halfway down – avenue Louise. Has over 120 ample-sized rooms decked out in fresh, contemporary style plus a so-called Wellness Centre with sauna, steam bath and Jacuzzi. Trams #93 and #94 run along avenue Louise. Doubles €125–220.

Hyatt Regency Brussels-Barsey ave Louise 381–383 ☎ 02 649 98 00, ⓦ www.brussels .regency.hyatt.com. Chic, recently redesigned chain hotel whose public areas are decorated in an eclectic version of Victorian style down to (or up as far as) the ersatz Greek friezes. The hotel's 99 bedrooms eschew uniformity, but many of them continue with the neo-Victoriana, a star feature being the fancily-tiled bathrooms. Popular with a business clientele. The hotel is located at the south end of avenue Louise, near the Musée Constantin Meunier; to get there by public transport, take tram #93 or #94 along avenue Louise. Doubles from €120–350 with the cheapest rates at the weekend.

Rembrandt rue de la Concorde 42 ☎ 02 512 71 39, ⓦ www.hotel-rembrandt.be. Quiet, pension-style hotel with thirteen clean and comfortable rooms situated on a dispiriting side-street just off avenue Louise. Half the rooms are en suite, half are not; popular with an older clientele. To get there under your own steam, take tram #93 or #94 along avenue Louise. En-suite doubles €95, shared facilities €85.

Leopold rue du Luxembourg 35 ⊕ **02 511 18 28,** ⓦ **www.hotel-leopold.be.** Staying in the EU Quarter, it's easy to get stuck beside a thundering boulevard. This smart, four-star hotel has over 110 rooms, all kitted out in modern chain-hotel style, and a first-rate location – on a quiet(ish) side-street, a brief walk from the terrace cafés of the place du Luxembourg. Métro Trône. Doubles begin at €180.

Monty blvd Brand Whitlock 101 ⊕ **02 734 56 36,** ⓦ **www.monty-hotel.be.** New, pocket-sized boutique hotel, where every fixture and fitting has been carefully designed in crisp, modernist style. Each of the eighteen guest rooms is imaginatively designed too – no bland, chain hotel colours here. Métro Georges-Henri. Doubles (and singles) €150.

B&Bs

For those on a tight budget, staying at a **B&B** can prove a cheaper alternative to a hotel, and the standard of accommodation can be just as good. The tourist office on the Grand-Place can make reservations for free; alternatively, contact one of the budget accommodation agencies listed below. Rooms are often comfortable although location is sometimes a problem – don't expect to be in the centre of things.

Bed & Brussels rue Kindermans 9 ⊕ **02 646 07 37,** ⓦ **www.BnB-Brussels.be.** Agency with a good reputation and English website: the standard of rooms is usually high and they can generally obtain a double in the city centre for around €75, or further out for less. Reduced rates available for longer stays. **Taxistop Bed & Breakfast rue du Fossé-aux-Loups 28** ⊕ **02 223 22 31 (closed Sat & Sun),**

ⓦ **www.taxistop.be.** One of the best-known B&B agencies, with a wide range of budget accommodation. It now has a comprehensive website where you can see what's on offer, but to make a booking you need to call a premium line, ⊕ 070 222 292. In the Lower Town. Doubles anywhere between €40 and €80.

Self-catering

Brussels' hotels are undeniably expensive, and it can be cheaper to rent a furnished **apartment** for a few days, especially if you're travelling as a family, when **self-catering** might be preferable. There are a number of agencies who rent out apartments on short-term lets, one of the best of which is *Rue Souveraine*, rue Souveraine 40 (⊕ 02 513 4164, ⓦ www.ruesouveraine.com), who rent furnished apartments for anything from a few nights to six months in Ixelles, mostly in several buildings on rue Souveraine itself, which runs between place Fernand Cocq and avenue Louise. Prices range from about €125 to €150 per night for a one- or two-bedroom place (for a month you can expect to pay around €1500–2000), plus a deposit for the telephone. The apartments are clean and excellently serviced, with phone, Internet access and even a nearby gym.

Another option is the 169-room *Citadines Ste Catherine* apartment-hotel in the lively Ste-Catherine district, a short stroll northwest of the Grand-Place **at quai au Bois à Brûler 51** (⊕ 02 221 14 11, ⓦ www.citadines.com; **métro Ste Catherine**). Its cheerfully decorated apartments (1–4 persons, with one double and one sofa bed) and studios (1–2 persons, with a sofa bed) all come with a fridge, hob, microwave and toaster. Rates are cheaper the longer you stay, but initially studios cost €120–145.

Hostels

If you don't like communal living or the idea of a complete stranger snoring in your ear all night, don't panic – Brussels has its fair share of **hostels** offering cheap, modern and private accommodation. Practically all the hostels in the capital eschew large dorms in favour of singles, doubles and rooms for four. **Prices** vary slightly, but generally speaking a **single** costs around €26, a **double** €20 and a **quad** €17 per person. Most hostels are located either within the petit ring or just outside it and are close to the métro – Métro Botanique in particular has two good hostels within easy striking distance. The majority provide disabled access and are well worth contacting for special offers for groups or for longer stays. Official IYHF hostels will cost an extra €3 per night if you don't have a membership card. You can buy a card from any IYHF hostel for €15 – worth it if you're staying for longer than five days.

Bruegel rue du Saint-Esprit 2 ☎ **02 511 04 36, ⓦ www.vjh.be.** This official IYHF hostel, housed in a pleasantly designed modern building, has 135 beds and a basic breakfast – as well as the hire of sheets – is included in the overnight fee: singles cost €26, doubles €20 and quads €17.30 per person. Dinner costs an extra €8.50 and you can request a packed lunch for €5.25. You're paying a little extra for the central location, by the church of Notre-Dame de la Chapelle close to the Upper Town, but you have to be back by 1am or you may find yourself locked out. Check-in 10am–1pm & 2-4pm. In the Lower Town. Métro Gare Centrale.

Le Centre Vincent Van Gogh rue Traversière 8 ☎ **02 217 01 58, ⓦ www.chab.be.** A rambling, spacious, 210-bed hostel with a good reputation and friendly staff, though it can all seem a bit chaotic. Prices are fairly standard – singles €27, doubles €20.50 and quads €16 per person – but its main advantage is that there's no curfew. Breakfast is included and there are sinks in all rooms, but sheets will cost you an extra €3.80. Launderette and kitchen facilities available. In the Lower Town. Métro Botanique.

Génération Europe rue de l'Eléphant 4 ☎ **02 410 38 58, ⓦ www.laj.be.** This brand-new IYHF hostel is located in a modern barracks-like building in Molenbeek, an inner-city industrial district that is slowly being revived. Molenbeek lies just to the west of the

centre, across the canal de Charleroi, a 15-minute walk from the Grand Place, and the hostel is 500m from the Compte de Flandres métro station. Prices, including breakfast and sheets, are €26 for singles, €20.50 for doubles, and €17.30 for quads per person. Check-in is from 7.45am to 11.30pm and there's no curfew. Métro Compte de Flandres.

Jacques Brel rue de la Sablonnière 30 ☎ **02 218 01 87, ⓦ www.laj.be.** This official IYHF hostel is modern and comfortable, and has a hotel-like atmosphere. Breakfast is included in the price: €26 for singles, €20.50 for doubles and €17.30 for quads per person. There's no curfew (you get a key), and cheap meals can be bought on the premises. Very close in comfort to some of the capital's cheaper hotels. Check-in 7.30am–1am. In the Lower Town, close to both Métro Madou and Métro Botanique.

Sleep Well rue du Damier 23 ☎ **02 218 50 50, ⓦ www.sleepwell.be.** Bright and breezy hostel close to the city centre and only a five-minute walk from place Rogier. Hotel-style facilities include a bar-cum-restaurant, which serves traditional Belgian beers and well-priced local dishes. There's also an excellent information point for tourists and no curfew. Prices, including breakfast, are €27 for singles, €24.35 for doubles, and €19.85 for quads, a little less if you stay more than one night. In the Lower Town. Métro Rogier.

9

Eating and drinking

Brussels has a deserved reputation for the quality of its food. Even at the dowdiest snack bar, you'll almost always find that the food is well prepared, and the city's **restaurants** are the equal of anywhere in Europe. Traditional Bruxellois dishes feature on many restaurant menus, canny amalgamations of Walloon and Flemish ingredients and cooking styles – whether it be rabbit cooked in beer, steamed pigs' feet or *waterzooi* (see box opposite for more on Belgian specialities). In the Lower Town, you can consume magnificent fish and seafood, especially in and around the appealing Ste-Catherine quarter, enjoy the fashionable restaurants dotted along rue Antoine Dansaert, or venture south to the burgeoning restaurant scene in the Marolles. Elsewhere, there are slim but occasionally exquisite gastronomic pickings in the Upper Town and a raft of great places in both St Gilles and Ixelles, where you will rarely see a tourist. The only negatives apply to the Lower Town's well-known rue des Bouchers, where a gaggle of restaurants attracts tourists in their hundreds, despite the excessive prices and – for the most part at least – uninspired food. Brussels is also among Europe's best for sampling a wide range of different cuisines – from ubiquitous Italian places and the Turkish restaurants of St Josse, through to Spanish, Vietnamese, Japanese, and vegetarian restaurants.

Opening times are pretty standard but restaurants only tend to open for relatively short hours – a couple of hours at lunch, usually noon to 2pm or 2.30pm, and again in the evening from 7pm to around 10pm. Each of our restaurant listings details opening hours along with phone numbers: advance reservations are rarely essential, but they are usually a good idea in more popular spots, especially at the weekend. For the most part, eating out is rarely inexpensive, but the **prices** are almost universally justified by the quality. As a general rule, the less formal the restaurant, the less expensive the meal, although foodwise price is no guide; indeed it's sometimes hard to distinguish between the less expensive restaurants and the city's **cafés**, which provide some of the tastiest food in town. In addition, many bars also serve

---

For convenience, the listings below are divided as follows: **restaurants**: Grand-Place and around (p.185); Lower Town and St Josse (p.186); Upper Town (p.190); St Gilles, avenue Louise and Ixelles (p.190); EU Quarter and around (p.194); **cafés**: Grand-Place and around (p.194); Lower Town and St Josse (p.195); Upper Town (p.190); St Gilles, avenue Louise and Ixelles (p.196); EU Quarter and around (p.197); **bars**: Grand-Place and around (p.198); Lower Town and St Josse (p.199); Upper Town (p.203); St Gilles, avenue Louise and Ixelles (p.204); EU Quarter and around (p.205).

Some Belgian specialities

anguilles au vert	eels in green sauce.
faisan à la brabançonne	pheasant in butter, white wine and chicory.
carbonnade flamande	beef braised with beer, onions, carrots and some times prunes.
crevettes roses/grises	red/grey shrimps – used in salads.
croque monsieur	toasted cheese and ham sandwich.
dame blanche	ice cream with melted chocolate.
gaufres au chocolat	chocolate waffles.
kip-kap	jellied meat (often sold in bars).
lammekezoet	fresh herring croquettes.
lapin à la Kriek	rabbit in cherry beer.
poulet à la Bruxelles	chicken stuffed with cheese and basted in beer.
poulet à la framboise	chicken in raspberry beer.
salade à l'ardennaise	salad with strips of Ardennes ham.
steak américaine	raw minced steak.
stoemp	mashed potatoes and mashed seasonal vegetables with sausages and/or bacon
waterzooi	stew with eels, fish, or chicken, cooked in a broth that is often enriched with cream.

food, often just spaghetti, sandwiches and *croque monsieurs*, though some offer a much more ambitious spread. A **service charge** is often included in the bill, but otherwise a ten to fifteen percent tip is the norm. A basic **menu reader** is provided on pp.270–272.

Drinking in Brussels, as in the rest of the country, is a joy. The city has an enormous variety of **bars** and café-bars from swanky, Parisian-style, terrace cafés and Art Nouveau extravagances to traditional drinking dens with ceilings stained by a century's smoke. Many of the city's most enjoyable bars are concentrated in the Lower Town around the Grand-Place, Bourse and the place St-Géry, though some of the most fashionable and arty are located in St Gilles and Ixelles. There are slimmer pickings in the Upper Town, where the drinking scene is more restrained, and the EU Quarter only musters up a handful of good expat places, all within comfortable walking distance of Métro Schuman. **Bar opening hours** are fairly elastic, but in practice the majority close around 2am, sometimes later on the weekend. **Prices** for drinks can vary hugely depending on where you are. As for **prices**, as a general rule you pay over the odds for the privilege of drinking on the Grand-Place, though not necessarily in the streets around it. Beer is cheap: a glass of draught Belgian beer costs around €2; spirits are relatively expensive, and a gin and tonic can cost you between €4 and €5, though the measures are often generous. There's a good selection of reasonably priced wines (especially white and red Burgundy) available by the bottle or glass. But the main event is the **beer**, as it is everywhere in Belgium: almost every bar has a choice of at least a dozen brews and the more specialized places have beer menus that can list several hundred. To get you started, we've recommended Belgium's Top Twenty beers on p.200.

All of the establishments we've listed are marked on the **colour maps** at the back of the book.

Restaurants

The Grand-Place and around

Katya's Kitchen rue Marché au Charbon 87
℡0497 473 337. A short walk from the
Grand-Place, in the vibrant St-Jacques area
of the city, Tuscany meets Asia meets good
old Belgian cuisine here at this appealing
restaurant. The menu changes regularly and
there are always vegetarian options amongst
the main dishes, which range from €10–16.
The owner has an impressive collection of
vinyl and will treat you to some great jazz
moments while you sit back and enjoy.
Wed–Sun 6–11pm. Prémétro Anneessens.

't Kelderke Grand-Place 15 ℡02 513 73 44.
You can't get more Belgian than this well-
known restaurant, housed in an ancient
cellar right on the Grand-Place. Dishes
include all the old Belgian favourites (see
box on p.185) such as *moules*, *stoemp*,
carbonnade flamande à la bière, and
waterzooi; prices range from €9 to €15 for
a main dish, with mussels between €17
and €20. The waiters can be a little stuffy,
but the house beer – the 't Kelderke – will
smooth things over nicely. Daily noon–2am.
Métro Gare Centrale.

**La Roue d'Or rue des Chapeliers 26 ℡02
514 25 54.** This old and eminently appealing brasserie, with Art Nouveau panelling,
stained glass and brass fittings, serves

▽ Brasserie *La Roue d'Or*

generous portions of Belgian regional
specialities, such as *poulet à la Bruxelles*,
and a good selection of seafood. Also
recommended are the endive salad with
salmon and the (mountainous) leg of lamb
with mustard. Main courses average around
€19. Daily noon–midnight, but closed for
one month in the summer, usually July.
Métro Gare Centrale.

Tapas Locas rue du Marché au Charbon, 74
℡02 502 12 68. This light, informal Spanish
restaurant in a trendy area attracts a mainly
youthful clientele, and serves a wide range
of excellent cheap tapas at €3 a portion.
Standard tapas such as tortilla, calamares
or chorizo are listed in the menu and there's
a changing selection of more unusual
dishes chalked up on the blackboards.
Spanish wine and sangria available by the
jug. No credit cards. Wed, Thurs & Sun
6pm–midnight, Fri & Sat 6pm–1am.

▽ *Taverne du Passage*

Taverne du Passage Galerie de la Reine 30
℡02.512.37.31. Brussels has changed
hugely in the past seventy or so years, but
this place hardly at all – and with its Art
Deco interior and all-day opening hours,
it's a worthwhile stop at any time of day.
Reasonably priced (with set menus from
€30) and popular with families, if you want
classic Belgian (and French) cuisine in a
classic setting right in the heart of Brussels, there's no better place – though these
days the service can be a bit hit and miss.
Open every day noon–midnight. Métro Gare
Centrale.

The Lower Town and St Josse

**L'Achepot place Ste-Catherine 1 ℡02 511 62
21.** A welcoming, family-run restaurant in

the appealing Ste-Catherine district that specializes – unlike most of its neighbours – in meat rather than fish. The menu is traditional Belgian and French at €10–16 a main dish; try the *boulettes à la sauce tomates* – meatballs in tomato sauce. Mon–Sat noon–3pm, 6–10.30pm. Métro Ste Catherine.

Agastache & Tonka rue Royale 290 ☎02 217 58 02. Agastache is a rare but robust plant with a slight taste of aniseed, Tonka is a sweet-smelling Venezuelan bean. Put them together and you get the highly original 'happy cooking!' restaurant of Claude Pohlig. Tastes are subtle and unusual, combining fine ingredients with a creative flair, and served up in a brightly coloured, rather chic setting. Main courses and starters all around €20. Mon–Wed noon–2.30pm, Thurs & Fri noon–2.30pm & 7–10.30pm, Sat 7–10.30pm. Métro Botanique.

Ateliers de la Grande Ile rue de la Grande Ile 33 ☎02 512 81 90. Only a couple of minutes' walk from place St-Géry, located in a converted nineteenth-century foundry, this winding, candlelit, Russian restaurant serves large and hearty meat dishes, and a delicious array of flavoured vodkas. Specialist dishes from all over Eastern Europe at €10–16, although a plate of top-notch caviar could set you back a whopping €87. With occasional live gypsy violin music, it's worth paying a visit simply for the joyous, if a tad eccentric, atmosphere. Tues–Sun 8pm–1am. Prémétro Bourse.

Belga Queen rue Fossé aux Loups 32 ☎02 217 21 87. There's no grander setting for a restaurant in the whole of Brussels: the deluxe Belga Queen occupies the former headquarters of the Crédit du Nord, a nineteenth-century building which comes

▽ *Belga Queen*

complete with a high and mighty, curved and vaulted stained-glass ceiling, an army of Greek columns and stucco griffins and coats of arms. What's more, the revamp has added a clutch of modern sculptures and sleek modern furnishings, and the waiters are styled up in slick tabards, gently jigging to a housey backtrack. All this attracts a young and fashionable crowd and although the food doesn't quite live up to the setting (how could it?), it's certainly very good and is especially strong on seafood. Main courses mostly cost in the region of €25, though the Iranian caviar will rush you €93; lunches are cheaper with the *plat du jour* costing just €10. Daily noon–2.30pm & 7pm–midnight. Métro De Brouckère.

La Belle Maraichère place Ste-Catherine 11 ☎02 512 97 59. Smart, bistro-style restaurant with oodles of wood panelling and waiters hovering as you tuck into the excellent seafood – with main courses averaging €20–25. Lobster is a house speciality. Pulls in an older crowd. Daily noon–2.30pm & 6–9.30pm; closed most of July. Métro Ste Catherine.

Bij den Boer quai aux Briques 60 ☎02 512 61 22. There's nothing pretentious here in this good old neighbourhood café-restaurant with its tiled floor and bygones on the wall. They serve up a wide range of tasty seafood with main courses averaging around €20–30 plus a first-class range of daily specials that cost much less. A great place for either a drink or a meal. Mon–Sat noon–3pm, 6–11pm. Métro Ste Catherine.

Bleu de Toi rue des Alexiens 73 ☎02 502 43 71. The name means "Crazy about you", but this charming restaurant near place de la Chapelle is just crazy about spuds. Never has a baked potato been offered with so many exotic fillings. There are two floors, two atmospheres and two specialities, the second being lobster. Lunch from €12 and main dishes vary from €10 to €30. Mon–Fri noon–2pm & 7–11pm, Sat 7–11pm. Prémétro Anneessens.

Bonsoir Clara rue Antoine Dansaert 22 ☎02 502 09 90. Moody, atmospheric lighting, geometrically mirrored walls and smooth jazz-meets-house background music make this one of the city's chicest restaurants, attracting a well-heeled twenty-to-forty-something crew. The wine list is particularly well chosen, and the menu full of Mediterranean, French and Belgian classics rendered in full nouvelle style. Main courses average €20. Reservations recommended. Mon–Fri noon–2.30pm & 7–11.30pm, Sat 7–11.30pm. Prémétro Bourse.

Les Brigittines aux Marchés de la Chapelle place de la Chapelle 5 ☎02 512 68 91. This large and well-established restaurant is popular with a mixed clientele, who enjoy the Art Nouveau furnishings and fittings, from the fancy lighting to the dark-green walls. It's true that the place lacks intimacy, but the quality of the food more than compensates with a choice selection of meat and seafood dishes prepared in the French style, but without an over-reliance on creams for the sauces. The *cabillaud danois poché aux poireaux* (Danish cod poached with pears) is particularly tasty. Main courses €15–25. Located behind the church of Notre-Dame de la Chapelle. Mon–Fri noon–2.30pm & 7–10.30pm, Sat 7–10.30pm; closes for two weeks in the summer. Prémétro Anneessens.

Au Chat Perché rue de la Samaritaine 20 ☎02 513 52 13. Just west of place du Grand Sablon, this excellent French restaurant serves up very tasty and copious salads, pastas and quiches in pleasant surroundings. It's a good spot for lunch, and ideal in the evenings for an intimate candlelit dinner. Impressive vegetarian selection, and cheaper than most neighbouring restaurants. Occasional live jazz. Wed–Sun noon–3pm & 7–11pm. Métro Louise or Prémétro Anneessens.

Chez Vincent rue des Dominicains 8–10 ☎02 511 26 07. The entrance to this lively restaurant is through the kitchen, which gives customers a good view of the culinary action. Keep going for the restaurant beyond, which specializes in Belgo-French cuisine with meat and seafood dishes both prominent. The dashing waiters in their long aprons will do a flambée at your table, an entertainment itself. Well worth the extra minute walk to get off the depressingly touristy rue des Bouchers. Main dishes €12–25. Daily noon–3pm, 6.30–11pm. Métro De Brouckère.

Comme Chez Soi place Rouppe 23 ☎02 512 29 21. Tucked away in the corner of place Rouppe, *Comme Chez Soi* is something of a gastronomic legend. The restaurant's successful blending of new and more traditional French cuisine has cemented the loyalty of an extremely varied clientele, who come to have their taste buds massaged

by dishes such as spring chicken with crayfish béarnaise sauce. The three fixed menus on offer are the most "cost-effective" ways to dine, with the three-course lunch, for example, costing €64. Exquisite and discreet service. Reservations are necessary weeks in advance. Wed–Sun noon–1.30pm & 7–9.30pm, but closed throughout July. Prémétro Anneessens.

Domaine de Lintillac rue de Flandre 25 ☎02 511 51 23. Delicious cuisine from the southwest of France at this warm, easy-going restaurant. The prices are ridiculously cheap for what might just be some of the best *foie d'oie* and *foie gras* in Brussels (€8–10). Down to earth and full of character, the relaxed ambience and clientele make it perfect for family outings. Mon 7.30–10.30pm, Tues–Sat noon–2pm & 7.30–10.30pm. Métro Ste Catherine.

François quai aux Briques 2 ☎02 511 60 89. Smart, long-established bistro-style seafood restaurant with softly glistening cutlery, bright white tablecloths and a tasteful mishmash of nautical bygones sprinkled here and there. Lobster and oysters are the house speciality, but there's always a catch of the day and the fish soup is simply stunning. Fish main courses range from €20 to €35. Recommended. Tues–Sat noon–2.30pm & 6.30–10.30pm. Métro Ste Catherine.

Le Gourmandin rue Haute 152 ☎02 512 98 92. Situated in a tiny town house just below the Palais de Justice, this intimate restaurant, with only twenty places, serves up outstanding French cuisine. Fine dishes such as succulent garlic-roasted breast of Bresse chicken are delicately prepared in the open kitchen with diners able to look on. A choice of good-value set menus at either €25 or €50, and main dishes between €20 and €23. Be sure to reserve. Sun & Mon noon–2.30pm, Tues–Fri noon–2.30pm & 7–10.30pm, Sat 7–10.30pm. Métro Louise or Porte de Hal.

La Grande Porte rue Notre Seigneur 9 ☎02 512 89 98. On the northern edge of the Marolles near Notre-Dame de la Chapelle, and some distance from the métro, this is a long, narrow and cosy old café-restaurant, whose walls are plastered with ancient posters and photos. The food is good and hearty – *stoemp*, mussels, *carbonnade flamande*, for €10–15 – and you're quite free to just go for a drink. Be warned, though, that it can get very crowded. Mon–Fri noon–3pm & 6pm–2am, Sat 6pm–2am. Prémétro Anneessens.

La Iberica rue de Flandre 8 ☎02 511 79 36. A Spanish restaurant much favoured by Spanish expats at the place Ste-Catherine end of rue de Flandre. The decor verges on the tacky – red velvet-like wallpaper and mock Tudor beams – but the paella is second to none. It's also reasonably good value for money, with most tapas costing around €7 and main dishes €10–17. Thurs–Tues 11.30am–2.30pm & 6.30–10pm. Closed Wed. Métro Ste Catherine.

Kasbah rue Antoine Dansaert 20 ☎02 502 40 26. Popular with a youthful, groovy crowd, this Moroccan eatery is famous for its (enormous portions of) couscous and other North African specialities. It's run by the same people as *Bonsoir Clara* next door (see p.187), and although equally hip, the lantern-lit decor makes it seem slightly less fashion-conscious and perhaps far more welcoming. Main dishes (€12–18) are on the expensive side for this type of food, but there's no gainsaying the quality. Reservations necessary at the weekend. Daily noon–3pm & 6.30pm–midnight. Prémétro Bourse.

La Manufacture rue Notre-Dame du Sommeil 12–20 ☎02 502 25 25. A good ten-minute walk from the Bourse down rue du Chartreux, this converted factory makes an impressive setting for an evening out. High ceilings and industrial architecture inside and a grassy courtyard with tables outside for those balmier evenings. Food is fusion with variations on some Belgian staples and prices range from €9 for the daily special to €12–22 for a main course. Especially good for large groups. Mon–Fri noon–2pm & 7–11pm, Sat 7–11pm. Prémétro Bourse.

La Marée rue de Flandre 99 ☎02 511 00 40. There's another *La Marée* on rue au Beurre, so don't get confused – this one (the better of the two) is a pocket-sized bistro specializing in fish and mussels and is located in the agreeable Ste-Catherine district. The decor is pretty basic, but the restaurant still musters up a cosy feel and the food is creatively made and reasonably priced. The menu includes eight different types of mussels dishes from €12. Wed–Sat noon–2pm & 6.30–10pm. Métro Ste Catherine.

Orphyse Chaussette rue Charles Hanssens 5 ☎02 502 75 81. The chef and owner Philippe

Renoux prides himself on his simple dishes and excellent ingredients, and although the menu is very French, there's always at least one imaginative vegetarian option. The setting is candle lit and cosy, and the staff willing to help you navigate your way around the extensive Tour de France wine menu. Main dishes €12–25. Tues–Sat noon–2.30pm, 7–10pm. Métro Louise.

La Papaye Verte rue Antoine Dansaert 53 ☎02 502 70 82. Tasty and inexpensive Thai and Vietnamese food served up in smart, authentically Southeast Asian surroundings. Good range of vegetarian options. Handy location near the Bourse. Main courses from as little as €5. Mon–Sat noon–2.30pm & 6.30–11.30pm, Sun 6.30–11.30pm; closed for one month in summer. Prémétro Bourse.

Pasta Basta rue de la Grande Ile 34 ☎0477/202 090. Situated in the heart of the St-Géry area, this pasta-lovers' haven is popular with a young crowd. They serve up a constantly changing, zesty menu, as well as staples such as cannelloni with spinach and ricotta at around €11 a dish. A DJ spins tunes every Friday and Saturday night, when the cosy interior struggles to contain the jumping crowd and slamming beats. Tues–Sun 7pm–midnight. Prémétro Bourse.

▽ *Le Pré Sale*

Le Pré Sale rue de Flandre 20 ☎02 513 65 45. Great Belgian food, especially mussels, in this atmospheric old dairy in the heart of Ste-Catherine. Decent prices too, but it's fairly small and gets very crowded. Wed–Sun noon–2.30pm & 6.30–10.30pm. Métro Ste Catherine.

Resource rue du Midi 164 ☎02 514 32 23. This creative restaurant signs up to the slow food movement, and a four-course set menu, guaranteed to last a few hours, will set you back a very competitive €38. Portions are on the small side, very nouvelle, but the quality of the ingredients, all prepared in the French manner, is second to none. Be willing to relax and enjoy – it's a restaurant to spend some time in. Lunch menu also available for €15. Tues–Sat noon–2.30pm & 7–10pm. Prémétro Anneessens.

Sahbaz chaussée de Haecht 102 ☎02 217 02 77. This is undoubtedly one of the best Turkish restaurants in the capital. The food is cheap and delicious, the staff friendly and attentive, and there's a cheerful atmosphere almost every night of the week. Favourites include Turkish pizzas (€4–7) and lamb *kofte* (under €10) helped down with a glass of *ayran*, a delicious yoghurt drink. Daily except Wed 11.30am–3pm & 6pm–midnight. Tram #92, #93.

▽ Turkish restaurants on chaussée de Haecht

Vert de Gris rue des Alexiens 63 ☎02 514 21 68. A varied crowd gathers here to dine at this large restaurant, which offers French cuisine with a strong Mediterranean slant, including a few vegetarian starters. The interior is a little dark, but there's a pleasant outdoor terrace at the back, with views of the pretty Eglise de la Chapelle. Main dishes €10–23. Mon–Fri noon–2pm & 7–11pm, Sat & Sun 7pm–midnight. Prémétro Anneessens.

Aux Bons Enfants place du Grand Sablon 49 ☎02 512 40 95. A well-established, cosy old Italian place, housed in a seventeenth-century building on the attractive place du Grand Sablon. Expect to find rustic-style decor, classical music and a menu of simple but tasty Italian dishes – steaks, pasta, hearty soups, pizza – at very reasonable prices (€6–9 for pasta, €8 for pizza, meat dishes €11–14). Daily except Wed noon–3pm & 6.30–10.30pm. Métro Louise.

L'Ecailler du Palais Royal rue Bodenbroeck ☎02 521 87 51. This ultra smart and formal restaurant – there's even a dress code – is probably the finest seafood restaurant in Brussels, and certainly one of the most expensive, with main courses kicking off at around €30. The classically elegant decor attracts an older clientele and the deep carpets mean that you eat to the hushed swish of all that jewellery. Wonderful lobster; immaculate service. At the back of place du Grand Sablon. Mon–Sat noon–2.30pm & 7–10.30pm; closed Aug. Métro Louise.

Pablo's rue de Namur 51 ☎02 502 41 35. Lively Tex-Mex joint, which is a great place to go with a bunch of loud and frolicking friends. The starters and main courses – spare ribs, steaks, tacos, and tasty burritos – are straightforward enough, if a little pricey, but the desserts, especially the cheesecake, are delicious, and there's a long bar serving interesting (and lethal) cocktails. Mon–Sat noon–3pm & 6pm–midnight, Sun 6–11.30pm. Métro Porte de Namur.

▽ Au Stekerlapatte

Au Stekerlapatte rue des Prêtres 4 ☎02 512 86 81. A famous old brasserie in an obscure and somewhat scruffy side-street behind the Palais de Justice, frequented by a crowd who come for the typical Belgian cuisine

– beef casseroles, grilled pork, poulet à la Bruxelles – and friendly atmosphere. Main course average around €18 and are simply delicious with the early twentieth-century bistro decor an attractive bonus. Tues–Sun 7pm–1am. Métro Hôtel des Monnaies.

St Gilles, avenue Louise and Ixelles

Chez Marie rue Alphonse de Witte 40 ☎02 644 30 31. This well-known and long-established Ixelles haunt serves impressive, mostly French, cuisine in lavish but never snobbish surroundings. There's also an extensive wine list. You can get a lovely two-course lunch for a very reasonable €16.50, but in the evenings prices are considerably inflated (main dish €24–30). You'll need to reserve in advance. Tues–Fri noon–2pm & 7.30–10.30pm, Sat 7.30–10.30pm. Tram #81, bus #71.

Citizen place St-Boniface 4 ☎02 502 00 08. How hot can you go? The handy guide of one, two or three chillies on the menu gives you a good idea of what to expect. This is the new kid on the St-Boniface block with Thai and Vietnamese food served by friendly staff. Decor is black and black, but with a rather distracting big screen, running a classic film throughout the evening – okay if your conversation is not up to much. Main dishes €9–14. Mon–Fri noon–2.30pm & 7–11pm. Métro Porte de Namur.

La Danse des Paysans chaussée de Boondael 441 ☎02 649 85 05. Up near the university, at the south end of Ixelles, this Belgian brasserie serves up a variety of mainly meat dishes cooked in typical beers such as Duvel, Chimay and Kriek, costing €12–15. The interior is very *moderne* with bare brick walls and dim lighting. Mon–Sat noon–3pm & 6.30pm–midnight. Bus #71, #95, #96.

Dolma chaussée d'Ixelles 331 ☎02 649 89 81. Excellent, new-agey veggie joint that serves a €12 buffet lunch and €15 buffet dinner, has a great and friendly atmosphere, and a veg/organic/wholefood shop next door. Popular with locals. Mon–Sat noon–2pm & 7–9.30pm. Bus #71.

L'Elément Terre chaussée de Waterloo 465 ☎02 649 37 27. One of the few entirely vegetarian restaurants left in Brussels, serving imaginative food from a creative menu. Combines local vegetables with sauces and spices from around the world – enough to seduce the most determined carnivore. Great

garden open as weather allows and friendly staff will help you distinguish tofu from tempeh, and a mung bean from a chickpea. Tues–Fri noon–2.30pm & 7–10.30pm, Sat 7–10.30pm. Bus #60.

Le Fils de Jules rue du Page 37 ☎02 534 00 57. Basque chefs serve up first-class cuisine from southwestern France at this small and chicly decorated restaurant. The setting, in the swankiest part of Ixelles, is a perfect backdrop to the delightful food. Meat and fish main dishes €14–24. Reservations usually necessary, particularly at weekends. Mon–Thurs noon–2pm & 7–11pm, Fri & Sat 7–11pm. Tram #81, bus #54.

La Gioconda Store Convivio rue de l'Aqueduc 76 ☎02 539 32 99. This bright, wedge-shaped wine and pasta shop doubles up as a restaurant and is a great place for a spot of lunch or an evening meal. The prices are pretty reasonable, and the food – mainly Italian pasta dishes – is nice and tasty. There's usually an upbeat, chatty atmosphere, and the place is both good for vegetarians and is child-friendly. Mon–Sat noon–2.30pm & 6.30–10.30pm. Tram #81, bus #54.

Le Grain de Sel chaussée de Vleurgat 9 ☎02 648 18 58. Mainly French cuisine here at this amenable restaurant, but other influences nose their way onto the menu. Ingredients are fresh and seasonal, limiting choice but maximizing quality. Set menu for a very affordable €20 with five choices of starter and main course (meat and fish) – €5 less for pretty much the same at lunchtime. A good place to try a snail or two. Tues–Fri noon–2pm & 7.30–10pm, Sat 7.30–10pm. Bus #38, #60.

Le Hasard des Choses rue du Page 31 ☎02 538 18 63. Extremely popular Mediterranean restaurant serving generous portions of pasta and salads at reasonable prices. Decor is a tasteful combination of iron and wood and the atmosphere is warm if perhaps a little too self-consciously cool. Terrace at the back for summer evenings. Main dishes €8–16; reservations advised. Mon–Fri noon–2.30pm & 7–10.30pm, Sat & Sun 7–11pm. Tram #81, bus #54.

L'Horloge du Sud rue du Trône 141 ☎02 512 18 64. Senegalese and Congolese restaurant offering many African specialities at highly affordable prices. Plantain, yucca and spices form a major part of the daily specials and there's always a vegetarian dish of the day.

Taste the zingy *jus sauvage* ("wild juice"), a mix of ginger and baobab. At lunch time, the special plus coffee costs €8.50 and in the evening a main dish is around €12. Mon–Fri 11am–midnight, Sat 5pm–2am, Sun 5pm–midnight. Métro Trône.

Leonor ave de la Porte de Hal 19 ☎02 537 51 56. This well-established tapas restaurant, with a pleasant view out onto the old Porte de Hal gateway, has been going strong for thirty years. The ground floor doubles up as a bar while upstairs the wooden tables and warm lighting make for a more intimate experience. Tapas are mainly fish-based and include plenty of octopus and Coquilles Saint-Jacques (€5–15). No visa cards accepted. Mon–Sat noon–3pm & 6.30–10pm, Sun noon–3pm. Métro Porte de Hal.

Le Macaron rue de Mail 1 ☎02 537 89 43. Charming French-Italian tavern just off place du Châtelain. The convivial ambience, homely surroundings and cheap fish, meat and pasta dishes – main meals around €10 – mean the place is often packed to the gunnels, even on weekdays. The spaghetti bolognese is superlative. Tues–Sun 6.30pm–1am. Tram #81, bus #54.

La Maison Berbere ave Brugmann 1 ☎02 534 50 50. Located in a former theatre and full of North African flavour, with dozens of overhead lanterns, ceramic-tile tables and earthen colours, this restaurant serves up an excellent couscous (€11–18) and veggies can be confident that the *couscous végétarien* has no hidden surprises. Good wine list and special deals at lunch time, Monday through Friday. Daily noon–3pm & 6–10.30pm. Tram #91, #92.

La Medina ave de la Couronne 2 ☎02 640 43 28. Popular Moroccan restaurant kitted out in traditional/predictable North African style, though there's a tasteful combination of mosaics and lighting. The *tajines* and couscous both have an excellent reputation for the freshness of their ingredients and the delicacy of their spices, and cost €12–16. Belly dancers on the weekend. Daily 10.30am–3pm & 6–11pm. Bus #38, #60, #95, #96.

La Meilleure Jeunesse rue de l'Aurore 58 ☎02 640 23 94. Hidden away near the Abbaye de la Cambre (see p.103), this chic and polished restaurant is decorated in an idiosyncratic version of the Baroque. The food is a real exotic mix – African, Asian and

European – though service can be tardy, perhaps a trick to lure you into drinking the fruity house cocktails. Main dishes – meat and fish only – cost €16–26. Daily noon–3pm & 7pm–midnight. Tram #93, #94.

Mille et une nuits rue Mouscou 7 ☎02 537 41 27. There's a host of Moroccan restaurants on rue Mouscou, just off the Parvis de St Gilles, and the competition keeps prices low and standards high. The luxuriant decor of this particular restaurant – the "1001 Nights" – is a perfect setting to dive into your couscous (€10.50–16) and devour your tajine (€14.50–15.50). Second helpings of couscous available on request. Mon–Sat noon–2.30pm & 6–11pm. Métro Porte de Hal.

Mont Liban rue de Livourne 30–32 ☎02 537 71 31. Combination Lebanese restaurant and café, where the food is excellent at both – it's the same kitchen – but prices at the café are noticeably cheaper. The hummus is particularly heavenly and there's a big choice of mezzes. The restaurant gets lively at the weekend when the belly dancers turn up. Café: daily 11am–11pm; restaurant daily noon–3pm & 7–11pm. Tram #91, #92, #93, #94.

Notos rue de Livourne 154 ☎02 513 29 59. Airy and well-lit Greek restaurant just off avenue Louise that serves up refined and flavourful cuisine at €16–23 a main course – much better than the usual mezzes and sirtakis. Reservations recommended. Tues–Sat 7–11pm. Tram #81, #93, #94.

O-Chinoise-Riz rue de l'Aqueduc 94 ☎02 534 91 08. This small restaurant, just round the corner from place du Châtelain, is where the Chinese come to eat Chinese food. The food is excellent and you get the spectacle of seeing the cooks boiling and sizzling your meal in the open-plan kitchen. It's also remarkably cheap by Brussels standards – for example, a three-course lunch for €8 – but there again the service is usually curt and offhand. Mon–Fri noon–2.30pm & 6–11pm, Sat & Sun 6–11pm. Tram #81, bus #54.

Ouzerie Mezedopolio chaussée d'Ixelles 235 ☎02 646 44 49. This is the Greek island in Ixelles, lacking the sunshine perhaps, but the wine and the *mezzes* are the genuine article. Wide choice of all the old Greek favourites and some original variations too; try the stuffed peppers with three cheeses. Dishes range from €3 to €10. Mon–Sat 7pm–midnight. Bus #54, #71.

Un Peu Beaucoup rue de la Paix 22 ☎ **02 503 22 36.** Brisk, modern restaurant, where the decor has a 1960s look and the mismatching crockery appears to be straight from the flea market (praise not condemnation). A daily choice of a fish, meat or vegetarian main dish is combined with the "starter plate" for €20 – add the "dessert plate" and it's €27. These plates aim to give you a taste of just about everything – for starters a small soup, a dip, a bruschetta, for dessert a combination of lots of sweet delights. The most original place around place St-Boniface. Mon & Tues 9.30am–6.30pm, Wed–Fri 9.30am–6.30pm & 7.15–11pm. Métro Porte de Namur.

Premier Comptoir Noi chaussée de Charleroi 39 ☎ **02 537 44 47.** Don't be put off by the bright-yellow facade as behind it is a simple and welcoming Thai restaurant where the service is exemplary. Amongst many inexpensive dishes, there are incredibly spicy raw scampis and red pepper/bamboo chicken. Vegetarian menu is available on request. Dishes average out at €12. Mon–Fri noon–2pm & 7–10.30pm, Sat 7–10.30pm. Tram #91 and #92.

La Quincaillerie rue du Page 45 ☎ **02 533 98 33.** The chic, stylish and downright loaded make their way to this delightful restaurant, occupying an imaginatively revamped old hardware shop, a couple of streets away from the Musée Horta. Well-known for its mouthwatering Belgian and French cuisine, specialities include fish and fowl, often cooked up in imaginative ways. A three-course set meal at lunchtimes costs as little as €15, but at night the à la carte is pricey with main courses weighing in at €25 and up. Mon–Fri noon–2.30pm & 7pm–midnight, Sat & Sun 7pm–midnight. Tram #81, bus #54.

Shanti ave Adolphe Buyl 68 ☎ **02 649 40 96.** Vegetarian and fish restaurant boasting a neo-Baroque oriental interior filled with plants. Dishes are elaborately presented and include tofu tandoori and fish and crab combinations at between €15–18. A bio and natural products store shares the same name and occupies the ground floor next door. Tues–Sat noon–2pm & 6.30–10pm. Tram #93, #94, bus #71.

Tom Yam chaussée de Boondael 341 ☎ **02 646 64 04.** Out by the university, this popular Thai restaurant has a warm and welcoming feel. The menu is large, but still based on a handful of key ingredients and sauces; plenty of vegetarian options. Lunch menu on offer for €10 and evening main dishes range from €9 to €15. Mon–Fri noon–2pm & 6.30–10.30pm, Sat 6.30–10.30pm. Tram #93, #94.

Toucan ave Louis Lepoutre 1 ☎ **02 345 30 17.** The name of this brasserie may come from the tropical bird, but the decorative theme is more about clocks – with a massive clockwork sculpture on the wall and a projected image of a clock behind the bar. The food is excellent with a varied menu featuring meat, fish and vegetarian dishes, and there's an excellent wine list. Main dishes range from €10 to €33, but save some space for the delicious desserts, including the crème brûlée with acacia honey and saffron. Reservations advised. Daily noon–2.30pm, 7–11pm. Bus #60.

La Vallée du Kashmir rue du Page 49 ☎ **02 538 33 53.** Brussels is not renowned for its Indian and Pakistani cuisine, and there's often a "blanding-down" to suit the local palate, but this small restaurant leads the pack. It offers tasty and spicy Pakistani and Indian food, all served in a charming setting with an original Kashmiri door as its decorative centrepiece. Set menu €12–24 and daily specials for €9. Mon–Fri noon–2pm & 7–11pm, Sat & Sun 7–11pm. Tram #81, bus #54, #60.

▽ *La Quincaillerie*

⑨

EATING AND DRINKING | Restaurants

Volle Gas place Fernand Cocq 21 ☎02 502 89 17. This traditional, wood-panelled bar-brasserie serves classic Belgian cuisine in a friendly, family atmosphere. The Brussels specialities on offer include the delicious *carbonnades de boeuf à la Gueuze* and lapin *à la Kriek* – beef or rabbit cooked in beer, but there's also pasta and salads. Main dishes €12–20. Non-smoking area available. Mon–Sat 11am–midnight. Bus #54, #71.

Yamato rue Francart 11 ☎02 502 28 93. A tiny and busy Japanese noodle bar with minimalist decor just round the corner from rue St-Boniface. Authentic Japanese food at affordable prices, with mains for as little as €8. Vegetarians must not be fooled by the noodles with vegetables – there's a big bone simmering in the pot. Not the place for a leisurely lunch – it's eat and go. Tues–Sat noon–2pm & 7–10pm. Closed Thurs lunchtime. Métro Porte de Namur.

Yamayu Santatsu chaussée d'Ixelles 141 ☎02 513 53 12. This well-established sushi and sashimi restaurant is one of the finest in Brussels and is justifiably popular with Belgians and Japanese alike. Ask to sit downstairs, where the sushi bar is the centre of the action. Usually packed, you should be snappy with your orders and settle down with some cold *sake* for what can be a considerable wait. Reservations essential. Sushi €13–25. Tues–Sat noon–2pm & 7–10pm, Sun 7–10pm. Bus #54, #71.

EU Quarter and around

L'Ancienne Poissonerie rue du Trône 65 ☎02 502 75 05. Small and flashy Italian restaurant in a cleverly reworked old fish shop – the Art Nouveau trimmings on the outside have been kept, but everything within is stylishly modern (and in full view from the street). The food is very nouvelle, so if you're really

hungry you're probably better off elsewhere. Main courses €17–23. Mon–Thurs noon–3pm, Fri noon–3pm & 7–11pm, Sat 7–11pm. Métro Trône.

L'Atelier rue Franklin 28 ☎02.734 91 40. Set back behind a peaceful courtyard, this French-Belgian restaurant has a light, airy feel, and serves good food at reasonable prices – steak, lamb, *waterzooi* feature, either at €15–20 for a main course, or from a €23.50 *prix-fixe* three-course menu. Outside seating in summer. Mon–Fri noon–2.30pm & 7–10pm. Métro Schuman.

La Bodeguilla rue Archimède 65–67 ☎02 736 34 49. A simple Spanish basement tapas bar popular with legions of Spanish expats, who are attracted by the home cooking and inexpensive prices. Good place for a quick snack before hitting the town. Mon–Sat noon–midnight. Métro Schuman.

Il Cappuccino ave d'Auderghem ☎02 733 61 85. Italian/Belgian chef Philippe Josse only closes his restaurant on Sundays and national holidays if they fall on a Monday – so if you need a Christmas Day or May Day bite to eat, then this is a good bet. Fresh pasta caters for the Italians and mussels for the Brussels. Main dishes €15–20 and a nice garden at the back. Mon–Fri noon–3pm & 6pm–midnight, Sat 6pm–midnight. Métro Schuman.

L'Esprit du Sel place Jourdan 52–54 ☎02 230 60 40. Long, thin, busy brasserie serving a good menu of Belgian specialities on workaday place Jourdan. Brisk service, good food and atmosphere. Mon–Sat noon–midnight. Métro Schuman.

Le Rocher Fleuri rue Franklin 19 ☎02 735 00 21. Simple yet cosy Vietnamese in the heart of the EU Quarter whose colourful owner is responsible for some great yet reasonably priced food and a fine, unpretentious atmosphere. Quite a find in this part of town. Mon–Thurs noon–3pm, Fri noon–3pm & 6.30–10pm. Métro Schuman

Cafés

The Grand-Place and around

L'Express Quality rue des Chapeliers 8 ☎02 512 88 83. Lebanese specialities, which you can either eat in, downstairs in the cushion-filled cellar, or take away. Pitta with meat or falafel, delicious hummus and halloumi. Mon–Fri noon–3pm & 6pm–1am, Sat & Sun

1pm–1am. Prémétro Bourse.

Le Falstaff rue Henri Maus 17–23 ☎02 511 87 89. Across the street from the Bourse, this long-established café-cum-restaurant is much lauded for its charming Art Nouveau decoration. Attracts a mixed bag of tourists, Eurocrats and bourgeois Bruxellois, and is a great place to sit back and soak up some

▽ Le Falstaff

atmosphere. There's a predictable choice of Belgian fare on offer and a mouthwatering selection of cakes and tarts. The waiters can be disarmingly brusque, apparently thinking you are privileged to be there. Daily 10am–1am. Prémétro Bourse.

Senne rue du Bon Secours 4 ☎02 502 24 26. Named after the river that used to run through Brussels, but was covered over in the middle of the nineteenth century, this modern snack-bar provides simple, fresh and healthy food at reasonable prices. It's both a shop that tempts you with its Italian delicacies and a café serving homemade quiches, pastas, soups and cakes (€6.50 – 11.50). You can take away, but the funky music and lively atmosphere make it an ideal place to eat in. Just off boulevard Anspach. Tues–Sat 10am–6pm. Prémétro Anneessens.

The Lower Town

Arcadi rue d'Arenberg 18 ☎02 511 33 43. At the north end of the Galeries St-Hubert, this hard-to-beat café is a perfect spot for lunch, afternoon tea or a bite before the cinema. Decorated in brisk, functional style, it's something of a rabbit warren with three small areas: two on the ground floor and one mezzanine up above. The menu offers lots and lots of choices, but the salads, quiches and fruit tarts are particularly delicious and only cost a few euros. Can get a little too crowded for comfort at lunchtimes. Daily 7/8am–11pm. Métro De Brouckère or Gare Centrale.

Arteaspoon rue des Chartreux 32 ☎02 513 51 17. An art gallery and café rolled into one. The decor is minimalist, with sleek oak furniture, and there's a lovely little mezzanine. They do a variety of delicious quiches,

omelettes and salads for €6–7. The art on display is mostly local. Mon–Fri 10.30am–4pm, Sat noon–5pm. Prémétro Bourse.

Eetcafé de Markten place du Vieux Marché aux Grains 5 ☎02 514 66 04. Flemish café buzzing with chatter and activity. Offers no-nonsense, good quality food at very reasonable prices. Long wooden tables and friendly staff add a zip. Just off rue Dansaert. Mon–Sat 11am–11pm, Sun 11am–6pm. Métro Ste Catherine.

Het Warm Water rue des Renards 25 ☎02 513 91 59. At the top of this cobbled street, lined with galleries and shops, *Warm Water* is a very typical Marolles café. One evening a week there's also a political debate when you're bound to hear a spot of Brusselse Sproek, the local lingo. Food is simple and it's one of the few Belgian originals that's great for veggies. Mon, Tues and Sun 8am–7pm, Thurs–Sat 8am–10pm. Métro Louise or Porte de Hal.

De Skieven Architek place du Jeu de Balle 50 ☎02 514 43 69. The smartest place on the square, this high-ceilinged, airy café-bar has an impressive beer menu, newspapers to browse, and serves a wide range of cheap but tasty meals and snacks. "The Slanted Architect" is named after Joseph Poelaert, the architect responsible for the Palais de Justice (see p.93): the construction of the Palais involved the demolition of a large slice of the Marolles, making Poelaert one of the most hated men in the city – and allegedly the victim of all sorts of witches' spells. Whatever the truth, he did indeed go bonkers. The café is at its busiest on Sunday afternoons during and after the Jeu de Balle flea market. Daily 6am–7pm. Métro Porte de Hal.

Den Teepot rue des Chartreux 66 ☎02 511 94 02. There's much more than a cup of tea on offer here – take the stairs up from the entrance of the health food shop and you find yourself in a small and simple café offering one inexpensive vegetarian soup and a daily special. All the ingredients are guaranteed organic. Health shop: Mon–Sat 8.30am–7pm; café: Mon–Sat noon–2pm. Prémétro Bourse.

The Upper Town

Artipasta place de la Liberté 1 ☎02 217 07 37. Real Italian homemade pasta – much, much more than the usual suspects – served in this corner café that, as the name suggests, doubles up as an art gallery. Great variety of antipasti on offer too. Both the menu and the art change regularly. Salads and pasta are €11–13 and you can eat in or take away. Note the restricted opening hours. Mon–Fri 11am–4pm, Fri 7–11pm. Métro Madou.

MIM Café rue Montagne de la Cour 2 ☎ 02 502 95 08. On the top floor of the Musical Instrument Museum in the stunning Art Nouveau Old England building (see p.78), this café boasts a breathtaking view over the Lower Town. Just mention at the museum entrance that you are going to the café and then take the lift up to the sixth floor. Not always the friendliest of service or the tastiest of food, but the view more than compensates. Tues–Sun 9.30am–5pm. Métro Gare Centrale.

L'Orangerie du Parc d'Egmont parc d'Egmont ☎ 02 513 99 48. Hidden away near the Palais de Justice, the parc d'Egmont features on few itineraries, but it's a pleasant slice of greenery and an enjoyable setting for the Orangerie, which makes the most of its location with a large terrace. Soups and quiches, as well as more substantial main dishes (€11–15) are available, but also ideal for just tea and cakes on a sunny afternoon. Sun–Fri 10.30am–6pm. Closed Saturday. Métro Louise.

Le Pain Quotidien rue des Sablons 11 ☎ 02 513 51 54. One of an extremely successful chain of bakery-cafés serving simple but delicious home-baked food such as bread, croissants, quiches and pastries. Expect to find plain wooden decor, ochre colours and a whole range of goodies on sale – chocolate cookies, homemade jams and great coffee. Excellent food and a relaxing atmosphere. Mon–Fri 7.30am–7pm, Sat & Sun 8am–7pm. Métro Louise. Also at rue Antoine Dansaert 22 (Métro Ste Catherine).

▽ Le Pain Quotidien

Le Perroquet rue Watteau 31 ☎ 02 512 99 22. This small, semicircular café-bar, a two-minute walk from place du Grand Sablon, has stained-glass windows and original Art Nouveau decor. Young and old rub shoulders over cheap salads and pittas (€5–10), whilst those of a more dipsomaniacal disposition work their way through the long list of speciality beers. Although it's often difficult to get a seat no matter when you turn up, it's worth the hassle. Daily noon–1am. Métro Louise.

Vieux Saint Martin place du Grand Sablon 38 ☎ 02 512 64 76. Kitted out in slick modern style, this family-owned café-restaurant serves all the Belgian favourites – *waterzoois*, *witloof*, rabbit and so on – all washed down with a good range of local beers. Main courses €20–25. Daily noon–midnight. Métro Louise.

St Gilles, avenue Louise and Ixelles

Alias ave Paul Dejaer 20 ☎ 02 537 77 07. In the shadow of the Maison Communale in St Gilles, *Alias* is a pleasant café/tea room serving a soup and sandwich lunch during the day, and something a bit more substantial – fish, meat and pasta dishes for €15 – a couple of evenings a week. A welcome addition to the neighbourhood. Tues–Thurs 8am–4pm, Fri 8am–10pm, Sat 2pm–10pm. Prémétro Horta.

Café Belga place Flagey 18 ☎ 02 640 35 08. With its terrace overlooking the top end of the etangs d'Ixelles, this big, modern café-bar is an ideal spot for breakfast, lunch or dinner – or just a drink or two. Good for after visiting the place Flagey market, or a bite to eat in the evening before a film or concert next door, though sadly the square is a building site and has been for some time. Another Nicolay classic (see *Zebra*, p.203). Sun–Thurs 8am–2am, Fri & Sat 8am–3am. Tram #81 or bus #71.

Le Châtelain place du Châtelain 17 ☎ 02 538 67 94. A cheerful café with a well-worn decor serving all the Belgian classics, including *chicons au gratin* and the delicious *stoemp saucisse et lard* – mashed potatoes, carrots and bacon. Combine with a visit to the market on the square on Wednesday evenings and you can mingle with the locals to your heart's content. Mon–Sat 10.30am–2am. Tram #81.

The Coffee Shop rue de Stassart 131 ☏ 02 503 07 75. Open during the week for breakfast and lunch, but one of the main attractions of this bright café is the Sunday brunch with a full English breakfast for just €9.50. Just off Place Stéphanie. Mon–Fri 7.30am–3.30pm, Sat & Sun 10am–6pm. Métro Louise.

La Cuisine rue Francart 9 ☏ 0498 841 470. Only one item on the menu here, the *piadina,* but the range of Mediterranean fillings is enormous (€4–6). There's plenty of history behind this bread-cum-pancake, which dates back to 1200BC, but you can chat about that sitting at the long table in the kitchen of this one-room café. Mon–Fri noon–2.30pm. Métro Porte de Namur.

Mundo Pain rue Jean Stas 20 ☏ 02 537 97 00. Down-to-earth good quality food at this well-turned-out modern café with terrace. Specialists in bread and all things associated plus a great line in cakes, homemade ice cream and fresh fruit juices. Mon–Fri 7.30am–3.30pm, Sat & Sun 10am–6pm. Métro Louise.

Passiflore rue du Bailli 97 ☏ 02 538 42 10. Overlooking the church of Ste-Trinité, this trendy but relaxing café serves light lunches, including homemade salmon and spinach quiche, crêpes, and a variety of salads, all for under €12. It's usually packed on Sunday mornings, when hordes of pasty-faced late-twenty-something revellers attempt to cure their hangovers with one of the good-value continental breakfasts. The *croque monsieurs* are the finest in the capital. Mon–Fri 8am–7pm, Sat & Sun 9am–7.30pm. Tram #81, bus #54.

SiSiSi chaussée de Charleroi 174 ☏ 02 534 14 00. Popular and well-established late-opening café, which enjoys a loyal, local following of hip, vaguely New Age young things. Large windows so they (and you) can watch the world drift by. It's a particularly good spot for lunch – the delicious panini and baked potatoes (*bintjes*) come recommended. Mon–Fri 10am–2am, Sat & Sun noon–1am. Tram #91, #92.

Tartisan rue de la Paix 27 ☏ 02 503 36 00. Well-established café and takeaway that's famous for its quiches – with fillings such as goats' cheese and spinach or *provencale*, served with a large salad for €8. Leave room for dessert – the chocolate log just melts in the mouth. Mon–Sat 10am–11pm. Métro Porte de Namur.

L'Ultime Atome rue St-Boniface 14 ☏ 02 513 48 84. A large selection of beers and wines, simple but tasty cuisine (open till 12.30am), and late opening hours, make this funky café-bar a hit with the trendy Ixelles crowd weekdays and weekends alike. Its location, on the laidback place St-Boniface, also makes it a great place to sit outside with a newspaper in the summer. Sun–Thurs 8.30am–12.30am, Fri 8.30am–1.30am, Sat 9am–1.30am, Sun 10am–12.30am. Métro Porte de Namur.

EU Quarter and around

Kafeneio rue Stevin 134 ☏ 02 231 55 55. Greek-themed café and ouzeri behind the Berlaymont that does good coffee and Greek cakes, ouzo and retsina and cold mezze to go with it – dips, grilled vegetables, etc – as well as more substantial fare. Daily 8am–1am. Métro Schuman.

Maison Antoine place Jourdan. Not a café at all, but generally regarded as the best *frites* stand in the city. Lots of toppings, and not just *frites* either, but lots of other fast food options – all of which can be consumed without complaint in any one of the bars around the square as long as you buy a drink. The antithesis of the Eurocrat lunch. Daily 11.30am–2pm. Métro Schuman.

Le Midi Cinquante parc du Cinquantenaire 10 ☏ 02 735 87 54. On the right of the arc de triomphe as you enter Le Cinquantenaire park from Métro Schuman, the café of the Royal Museum of Art and History (see p.118) is worth a visit in its own right. It's airy and light and in the summer there's a smashing terrace overlooking the park. Tues–Sun 9.30am–5pm. Métro Schuman.

Mi Figue-Mi Raisin rue Archimede 71 ☏ 02 734 24 84. Organic breakfasts and lunches in the tiled café or served in the garden when the elements permit. Also a pleasant spot for afternoon tea. Lunch €10–15. Mon–Fri 8am–7pm. Métro Schuman.

Le Thé au Harem d'Archi Ahmed chaussée de Louvain 52–54 ☏ 02 219 80 19. Belgians like to play with words and the name of this Art Nouveau café is a great example – "Archi Ahmed's Harem" or "Archimedes's Theorem" – whichever way you want to read it, though it's probably the former judging by the fancy decoration. Great for a fresh mint tea break during a shopping trip and simple food is also served until 4.30pm. Mon–Sat 11.30am–7pm. Métro Madou.

Bars

The Grand-Place and around

La Bécasse rue de Tabora 11 ☎ **02 511 00 06.**
Down a short and inconsequential-looking
alley, this old-fashioned bar, with its long
wooden benches, stained panelling and
draped curtains, has an excellent beer
menu and a sort of community hall atmosphere. It's one of the few places in Belgium
where you can drink authentic Lambic (see
p.201) and Gueuze (see p.200), served
in earthenware jugs. Avoid the food; no
smoking. Located just to the northwest
of the Grand-Place, and metres from
St-Nicolas. Mon–Thurs 2pm–midnight,
Fri–Sun 2pm–2am. Métro De Brouckère or
Prémétro Bourse.

▽ *La Bécasse*

**Au Bon Vieux Temps rue du Marché-aux-Herbes
12** ☎ **02 217 26 26.** Tucked away down an
alley and only a minute's walk from the
Grand-Place, this is a small, intimate and
wonderfully cosy place, with tile-inlaid tables
and a big old wooden bar. The building
dates back to 1695 and the stained-glass
window depicting the Virgin Mary and St
Michael was originally in a local parish
church. Popular with British servicemen just
after the end of World War II, the bar still
has ancient signs advertising Mackenzie's
Port and Bass pale ale. It's occupied by a
convivial, older (and often very loaded) crew.
Mon–Thurs & Sun 1pm–12.30am, Fri & Sat
1pm–2am. Métro De Brouckère or Prémétro
Bourse.

La Brouette Grand-Place 2–3 ☎ **02 511 54
94.** Arguably the pick of the many café-
bars lining the Grand-Place, *La Brouette*
has reassuringly comfortable furniture and
fittings, including a splendid open fireplace,
and an upstairs section whose window
seats offer a charming view over the main
square. Provides a tasty range of snacks,
salads, cakes and pancakes, and the service is usually rapid, which cannot be said for
many of its neighbours. Daily 8.30am–1am.
Prémétro Bourse.

**Le Cercle des Voyagers rue des Grandes Carmes
18** ☎ **02 514 39 49.** This colonial-style lounge
bar with deep leather chairs and atmospheric lighting is a perfect place to begin
any journey. Browse through the brochures
on the tables or pop next door to the travel
bookshop (Wed–Sun 1pm–7pm). Daily
11am–midnight. Prémétro Bourse.

Goupil Le Fol rue de la Violette 22 ☎ **02 511 13
96.** This unusual bar, between the Grand-
Place and the Manneken Pis, should not be
missed, especially if you're keen on traditional French singing from the likes of Edith
Piaf or Belgium's own Jacques Brel (see
p.68). Every surface is covered with *chan-
son française* memorabilia and there are
reminders of the building's previous incarna-
tion as a brothel in the decor, with three
floors of cosy corners, sink-into sofas, and
dimmed red lights. A house speciality is the
delicious and extremely potent fruit wines
which come in all manner of combinations.
Daily 8pm–5am. Métro Gare Centrale.

**A l'Imaige de Nostre-Dame rue du Marché aux
Herbes 6** ☎ **02 219 42 49.** A quirky little bar
of two small rooms and rough plaster walls
situated at the end of a long, narrow alley.
Wooden benches propel strangers into
conversation as do the bar staff, at least
one of whom loves letting rip with his *chansons*. Good range of speciality beers. Daily
noon–midnight. Prémétro Bourse.

El Metteko blvd Anspach 88 ☎ **02 512 46 48.**
The noise of the traffic on the main road
does nothing to dissuade an eclectic,
youthful clientele from gathering here on
the terrace. Frequent live music at the
weekends with anything from *klezmer* to
salsa. Some food on offer – mainly pastas,
salads and tapas. Next door to the Bourse.
Mon–Thurs 9am–1am, Fri 9am–3am, Sat

EATING AND DRINKING | Bars

⑨

10am–3am, Sun noon–1am. Prémétro Bourse.

Ommegang rue Charles Buls 2 ☏ 02 511 82 44. Surprisingly enough, this venerable establishment, attached to the posh *Maison du Cygne* restaurant just off the Grand-Place, was once Karl Marx's local. Marx knew it as the *Cygne Café* and it was here that he polished and buffed the *Communist Manifesto* at meetings of exiled German socialists. There's nothing to commemorate Marx's visits, but there is a plaque on the wall celebrating the founding of the Belgian Socialist Party here in April 1885. The café serves capital food and is nice for a quiet drink, though poor old Karl would doubtless find it a bit bourgeois these days. Mon–Fri noon–2pm & 7pm–1am, Sat 7pm–1am. Prémétro Bourse.

O'Reilly's place de la Bourse 1 ☏ 02 552 04 80. This large Irish theme bar directly opposite the Bourse is the unofficial venue for Irish supporters when there's a rugby or football game. It's also the only bar in the centre which screens live English premiership football. Although nothing to write home about, it's a handy enough meeting place, except on Friday and Saturday nights when the bar is mobbed with drunken revellers. Food (fries, baked potatoes, Irish stew, chicken) is available from 11am–10pm. Sun–Thurs 11am–1am, Fri & Sat 11am–4am. Prémétro Bourse.

Le Roi d'Espagne Grand-Place 1 ☏ 02 513 08 07. Well-known, supremely touristy café-bar housed in one of the Grand-Place's handsome guildhouses. Inside, a collection of marionettes and inflated animal bladders is suspended from the ceiling and there are naff imitation pikes in the boys' toilet. To its credit, you do get a fine view of the Grand-Place from the room upstairs, as well as from the pavement-terrace, but frankly *La Brouette* (see oppsite), just along the square, is a much better bet. Daily 10am–1am. Prémétro Bourse.

Au Soleil rue du Marché au Charbon 86 ☏ 02 512 34 30. Formerly a men's clothing shop, this cramped and popular bar attracts a mixed arty-verging-on-the-simply-down-at-heel crew. Bar snacks plus a good range of beers at very competitive prices. Appealingly laidback atmosphere, but it's often difficult to get a seat come nightfall. A brief walk southwest of the Grand-Place, at the corner of rue des Grands Carmes. Sun–Thurs

10am–1am, Fri & Sat 10am–2am. Prémétro Bourse.

▽ *Au Soleil*

Théâtre de Toone Impasse Schuddeveld 6 ☏ 02 513 54 86. Ancient bar belonging to the Toone puppet theatre (see p.233) that comprises two small rooms with old posters on rough plaster walls, plus a small (and really rather uninviting) outside terrace. Has a reasonably priced beer list, a modest selection of snacks, and a soundtrack of classical and jazz, making it one of the centre's more congenial watering holes. There are two alley-entrances, one on Petite rue des Bouchers, the other on rue du Marché aux Herbes, opposite rue des Harengs. Daily noon–11pm. Métro Gare Centrale.

The Lower Town and St Josse

Ane Fou rue Royale Ste-Marie 19 ☏ 02 218 86 62. Bistro-bar just opposite the Halles de Schaarbeek – a perfect spot for a pre-concert drink or to sit in the curved Art Deco windows and watch St Josse stroll by. Pasta available by the cone to take away – beats the late-night chip shop by a long chalk. Daily 10am–midnight. Tram #92, #93, #94.

Café Métropole place de Brouckère 31 ☏ 02 219 23 84. This ritzy café, belonging to an equally opulent hotel (see p.180), boasts sumptuous fin-de-siècle decoration, altogether an appealing blast of frilly mirrors, gilded woodwork, stained-glass windows and ornate candelabras. Astonishingly, many people prefer to sit outside, presumably for a view of the flashing ads and zipping traffic of place de Brouckère, rather than enjoying the unhurried charms inside. If you've got cash to spare, indulge in a brunch of smoked salmon or caviar. Daily 9am–1am. Métro De Brouckère.

A Top Twenty of Belgian beers

Belgium's beer-making history goes back centuries and official estimates suggest that there are now more than 700 **beers** to choose from, with the rarest and most precious given all the reverence of a fine wine. Every half-decent bar in Brussels has a beer menu and although it's unlikely that any one establishment will have all those listed below, all of them should have at least a couple.

Bush Beer
A Wallonian speciality, it's claimed that the original version is – at 12% – the strongest beer in Belgium. Resembles a barley wine with a lovely golden colour, and an earthy aroma. The 7.5% Bush is a tasty pale ale with a zip of coriander.

Brugse Straffe Hendrik
Straffe Hendrik, a smart little brewery located in the centre of Bruges, produces zippy, refreshing ales. Their Blond (6.5%) is a light and tangy pale ale, whereas the Bruin (8.5%) is a classic brown ale with a full body.

Chimay
Made by the Trappist monks of Forges-les-Chimay in southern Belgium, Chimay beers are widely regarded as being amongst the best in the world. Of the several brews they produce, red top (7%) and blue top (9%) are the most readily available: fruity and strong, deep in body, and somewhat spicy with a hint of nutmeg and thyme.

La Chouffe
Produced in the Ardennes, La Chouffe (8%) is a distinctive beer, instantly recognizable by the red-hooded gnome (or *chouffe*) which adorns its label. It's a refreshing pale ale with a hint of coriander and it leaves a peachy aftertaste.

Corsendonk Pater Noster
Created by Jef Keersmaekers, the bottled Pater Noster (5.6%), known for its Burgundy-brown colour and smoky bouquet, is easily the pick of the many Corsendonk brews.

Delirium Tremens
Great name for this spicy amber ale (9%) that is the leading product of Ghent's Huyghe brewery.

Gouden Carolus
Named after – and allegedly the favourite tipple of – the Habsburg emperor Charles V, Gouden Carolus (8%) is a full-bodied dark brown ale with a sour and slightly fruity aftertaste. Brewed in the Flemish town of Mechelen.

Gueuze
A type of beer rather than an individual brew, Gueuze is made by blending old and new lambic (see below) to fuel re-fermentation, with the end result being bottled. This process makes Gueuze a little sweeter and fuller bodied than lambic. Traditional Gueuze – like Cantillon Gueze Lambic (5%) – can, however, be hard to track down and you may have to settle for the sweeter, more commercial brands, notably Belle Vue Gueuze (5.2%), Timmermans Gueuze (5.5%) and the exemplary Lindemans Gueuze (5.2%).

Hoegaarden
The role model of all Belgian wheat beers (once something of a rarity, now drunk with relish all over western Europe), Hoegaarden (5%) – named after a small town east of Leuven – is light and extremely refreshing, despite its cloudy appearance. It's brewed from equal parts of wheat and malted barley and is the ideal drink for a hot summer's day.

De Koninck
Antwerp's leading brewery, De Koninck, is something of a Flemish institution – for some a way of life. Its standard beer, De Koninck (5%), is a smooth, yellowish pale ale that is better on draft than in the bottle. Very drinkable and with a sharp aftertaste.

Kriek
A type of beer rather than a particular brew, Kriek is made from a base beer to which

cherries are added or, in the case of the more commercial brands, cherry juice and perhaps even sugar. It's decanted from a bottle with a cork, as with sparkling wine. The better examples – including Cantillon Kriek Lambic (5%), Belle Vue Kriek (5.2%) and Mort Subite (4.3%) – are not too sweet and taste simply wonderful.

Kwak

A Flemish beer, the main product of the family-run Bosteels brewery, Kwak (8%) is not all that special – it's an amber ale sweetened by a little sugar – but it's served in dramatic style with its distinctive hourglass placed in a wooden stand.

Lambic

Specific to the Brussels area and representing one of the world's oldest styles of beer manufacture, lambic beers are tart because they're brewed with at least thirty percent raw wheat as well as the more usual malted barley. The key feature is, however, the use of wild yeast in their production, a process of spontaneous fermentation in which the yeasts of the atmosphere gravitate down into open wooden casks over a period of between two and three years. Draught lambic is extremely rare, but is served in central Brussels at *A la Bécasse* (see p.198). The bottled varieties are often modified, but Cantillon Lambik (5%) is an authentic, excellent drink with a lemony zip. It's produced at the Cantillon brewery, in Anderlecht, which is home to the Gueuze Museum (see p.124). Lindemans Lambik (4%) is similar and a tad more commonplace.

Leffe

Brewed in Leuven, east of Brussels, strong and malty Leffe comes in two main varieties: Blond (6.6%), which is bright, fragrant, with a slight orangey flavour, and Brune (6.5%), which is dark, aromatic and full of body. Very popular, if a little gassy for some tastes.

Orval

A particularly distinctive malt beer, Orval (6.2%) is made in the Ardennes at the Abbaye d'Orval, which was founded in the twelfth century by Benedictine monks from Calabria. The beer is a lovely amber colour, refreshingly bitter and makes a great aperitif.

Rochefort

Produced at a Trappist monastery in the Ardennes, Rochefort beers are typically dark and sweet and come in three main versions: Rochefort 6 (7.5%), Rochefort 8 (9.2%), and the extremely popular Rochefort 10 (11.3%), which has a deep reddish-brown colour and a delicious fruity palate.

Rodenbach

Located in the Flemish town of Roeselare, the Rodenbach brewery produces a reddish-brown ale in several different formats, with the best brews aged in oak containers. Their widely available Rodenbach (5%) is a tangy brown ale with a hint of sourness. The much fuller – and sourer – Rodenbach Grand Cru (6.5%) is far more difficult to get hold of, but is particularly delicious – quite enough to be one of the authors' favourite drinks.

Verboden Vrucht, or Forbidden Fruit

Hoegaarden's Forbidden Fruit (9%) is worth buying just for the label, sporting a fig-leaf-clad Adam offering a strategically covered Eve a beer in the Garden of Eden. Dark, strong and with a spicy aroma, the brew has something of a cult following in Belgium.

Westmalle

The Trappist monks of Westmalle, just north of Antwerp, claim their beers not only cure loss of appetite and insomnia, but reduce stress by half. Whatever the truth, they certainly taste good: Westmalle Tripel (9%) is deliciously creamy and aromatic, while the popular Westmalle Dubbel (7%) is dark and supremely malty.

Westvleteren

Made at the abbey of St Sixtus in West Flanders, Westvleteren beers come in several varieties. Special 6° (6.2%) and Extra 8° (8%) are the most common – dark and full-bodied, sour with an almost chocolate-like taste.

Chaff place du Jeu de Balle 21 ⊕ **02 502 58 48.**
There's no better place to take in the hustle
and bustle of the city's biggest and best
flea market (see p.222) than this amenable
café-bar-restaurant, where the food is delicious and very French. There are some real
bargains at lunchtime – fresh tuna and coriander costs, for example, just €9 – and the
menu is posted on a board. In the evening,
you can pop in just for a drink or have a
full meal. Tues–Sun 8.30am–midnight, Mon
8.30am–7pm. Métro Porte de Hal.

Le Cirio rue de la Bourse 18 ⊕ **02 512 13 95.**
Established in 1886, this is one of Brussels'
oldest café-bars and although the elaborate
Art Nouveau decor is now somewhat frayed
round the edges, it remains one of the most
attractive. Once frequented, they say, by
Jacques Brel it appeals, for the most part,
to an older clientele, many of whom come
here specially for their "half-and-half", made
up of champagne and white wine – a drink
the house claims to have invented. On
the north side of the Bourse. Daily 10am–
midnight. Prémétro Bourse.

La Fleur en Papier Doré rue des Alexiens 53
⊕ **02 511 16 59.** Cosy locals' bar cluttered
with antique bygones, its walls covered with
oodles of doodles. This was once (one of)
the chosen drinking holes of René Magritte
and the novelist Hugo Claus (see p.264)

▽ *La Fleur en Papier Doré*

apparently held his second wedding reception here. Things are much more restrained
(and much less arty) today, but it's still a
perfect spot for a quiet drink – it's rather like
sitting in a great aunt's living room. Small
but eclectic selection of beers, including
Gueuze and Kriek. Only five minutes from
the Grand-Place, though it can be a little
hard to locate (there's no sign). Sun–Thurs
11am–2am, Fri & Sat 11am–4am. Métro
Gare Centrale or Prémétro Anneessens.

Le Greenwich rue des Chartreux 7 ⊕ **02 511 41
67.** An oasis of calm in a commercial storm,
this smoky, traditional chess bar has long
been patronized by chess and backgam-
mon enthusiasts, including, according to the
locals, Magritte. Although a little down-at-
heel, the cheap beer and get-away-from-
it-all atmosphere easily make up for it. The
crowd varies from ancient pipe-smokers to
suave twenty-somethings. Daily 11am–1am.
Prémétro Bourse.

Le Java rue St-Géry 31 ⊕ **02 512 37 16.** Close
to the attractive place St-Géry, this small
triangular bar seems perpetually thronged
with city slickers and funksters living it up on
schnapps and cocktails. If you like Gaudí-
inspired decor, groovy music, and a kicking atmosphere, go no further. Sun–Thurs
5.30pm–1am, Fri & Sat 5.30pm–4am.
Prémétro Bourse.

Kafka rue de la Vierge Noire 6 ⊕ **02 513 54 89.**
No prizes for guessing the theme of this
place – though it's certainly not as surreal
as its Czech namesake. Dark and smoky,
even on the sunniest of days, but the place
does have its own particular charm. Daily
4pm–2am. Métro De Brouckère

Mappa Mundo rue du Pont de la Carpe 2 ⊕ **02
514 35 55.** An oak-lined pub where people
come for some serious drinking. To soak
it all up, try one of their copious all-morn-
ing breakfasts or the Sunday brunch (for
which reservations are essential). The rest of
the food consists of bagels, pittas, salads,
soups and is served from 11am to 3pm and
from 6pm to 1am. Another Frédéric Nicolay
adventure (see *Zebra* below). Mon–Fri 8am–
2am, Sat & Sun 10–2am. Prémétro Bourse.

Monk rue Ste-Catherine 42 ⊕ **02 503 08 80.**
With its high ceilings and dark wooden
panelling, this large and popular, mostly
Flemish bar is named after the jazz musi-
cian Thelonious Monk – and appropriately
a grand piano takes pride of place here.
Unusually for Brussels, the service is at the

bar. Located just off place Ste-Catherine. Mon–Sat 11am–1am, Sunday and bank holidays 4pm–1am. Métro Ste Catherine.

A la Mort Subite rue Montagne aux Herbes Potagères 7 ☎02 513 13 18. Famous/notorious 1920s bar that loaned its name to a popular bottled beer. Occupies a long, narrow room with nicotine-stained walls, long tables and lots of mirrors. On a good night it's inhabited by a dissolute-arty clientele, but on others by large groups of young, college-aged tourists. Snacks served, or just order a plate of cheese cubes to accompany your beer. Just northeast of the Grand-Place opposite the far end of the Galeries St-Hubert. Mon–Fri 10am–1am, Sat 11am–1am, Sun 1pm–1am. Métro Gare Centrale.

▽ A la Mort Subite

De Ultieme Hallucinatie rue Royale 316 ☎02 217 06 14. This well-known and fancifully ornate Art Nouveau bar is done up like an old 1920s train car. It offers a good choice of beers and reasonably priced food – omelettes, lasagne, etc – and there's a lavishly decorated restaurant here too, serving up Franco-Belgian cuisine with main dishes costing €25–36.

▽ De Ultieme Hallucinatie

Restaurant: Mon–Fri 12.30pm–2.30pm & 7.30–10.30pm, Sat 7.30–10.30pm; bar: Mon–Fri 11am–2am, Sat & Sun 5pm–3am. Tram #92, #93, #94.

Walvis rue Dansaert 209 ☎02 219 95 32. Frédéric Nicolay (see *Zebra* below) strikes again, attracting a young canalside café-bar, a ten-minute walk from place Ste-Catherine at the far end of rue Danseart. DJs at the weekends. Sun–Thurs 11am–2am, Fri & Sat 11am–4am. Métro Ste Catherine.

Zebra place St-Géry 33–35 ☎02 511 19 01. This small but trendy bar on the corner of place St-Géry was the first venture of Frédéric Nicolay, the Belgian entrepreneur who went on to reinvigorate the city's nightlife with *Bonsoir Clara* (see p.187), *Belga* (see p.196), *Mappo Mundo* (see p.202) and *Walvis* (see above). It remains the chicest of locations – anyone who's anyone has been here at some point – and attracts a young, fashionable crowd who come for the upbeat atmosphere and groovy music. It's also terrifically popular in summer when people come here in their droves to read their newspapers on the large terrace. Sun–Thurs noon–1am, Fri & Sat noon–3am. Prémétro Bourse.

The Upper Town

Vogue rue de la Louvain 2–4 ☎02 513 13 56. During the week, this is where Belgian politicians rub shoulders with thirsty journalists and there are lots of "off the record" briefings, but in the evening and on the weekend the place comes to life with visiting DJs. Prices higher than elsewhere in the area – but that's the kind of crowd it is. Has wi-fi connection if you want to surf the net. Mon–Sat 11am–3am. Métro Parc.

St Gilles, avenue Louise and Ixelles

L'Amour Fou chaussée d'Ixelles 185 ☎02 514 27 09. An upbeat café-bar off place Fernand Cocq, where you can drink a delicious selection of vodkas, mescal and tequila while checking your emails (now with wi-fi connection) and taking in the contemporary art that decorates the walls. The spacious central room has a cool, modern feel and there's also a back room filled with immense couches and lit by soft lighting. The food is quite good and includes such snack staples as *croque monsieurs*, as well as more substantial offerings; the kitchen is open from 11am till 1am, but note that service can be erratic. Sun–Thurs 9am–2am, Fri & Sat 9am–3am. Bus #54, #71.

▽ L' Amour Fou

▽ L' Amour Fou

The Bank rue du Bailli 79 ℡**02 537 52 65.** Champions league and international football on Saturday afternoon, live music in the evening, and Rugby Sunday afternoon, all intermittently aided by bowls of Irish stew and pints of Guinness – hell for some, heaven for others, but it's all here. Sun–Thurs noon–1am, Fri & Sat noon–2am. Tram #81 or bus #54.

Bar Parallèle place Fernand Cocq 27 ℡**02 512 30 41.** Next to the Maison Communale of Ixelles, this simple café gets the balance of good-value food, relaxed atmosphere and cool music just right. It even offers a few no-smoking tables. Also has nifty outdoor terrace to enjoy those sunny afternoons with a chilled beer. Mon–Sat 10am–1am, Sun 5pm–1am. Bus #54, #71.

Belladone rue Moris 17a ℡**0479 48 46 63.** Eastern European bar, whose menu sports all sorts of interesting information – "Belladone" is, for instance, the plant used by women to bring about success in love or business, or bad luck to an enemy. Pilsner Urquell on tap and available by the litre, flavoured vodkas, specialist teas, including Hot Attila – tea with schnapps – and many tasty sweet and savoury bites. Mon–Fri 2pm–midnight, Sat 6pm–1am. Tram #81, #91, #92.

Brasserie Verschueren Parvis de Saint Gilles 11–13 ℡**02 539 40 68.** Vaguely Art Deco neighbourhood bar with a laidback atmosphere and old wooden panels with the football league results on the wall – essential in the days before television. You can

buy your croissant in the bakery opposite and just come in for a coffee to dip it in. A good range of Belgian beers too. Daily 8am–1am. Prémétro Parvis de St Gilles.

Café des Spores chaussée d'Alsemberg 103 ℡**02 534 13 03.** A wine bar dedicated to mushrooms of all shapes and sizes. Great for an aperitif but they also serve some more substantial dishes – all with mushrooms of course. If you want to eat, it's best to phone in advance. Wine ranges from €5 a glass to €250 for the best bottle in the cellar. Mon 7.30–10.30pm, Tues–Fri noon–3pm & 7.30–10.30pm, Sat 7.30–10.30pm. Prémétro Horta. Tram #81.

Chez Moeder Lambic rue de Savoie 68 ℡**02 535 14 19.** A small bar in upper St Gilles, just behind the commune's Hôtel de Ville. Has over a thousand beers available, including five hundred Belgian varieties. Often very busy (and smoky). Daily 4pm–3am. Prémétro Horta.

Le Pantin chaussée d'Ixelles 355 ℡**02 502 42 76.** Laid-back café-bar, where you can lose yourself in a game of chess or join the others rolling a cigarette and putting the world to rights. Candlelit – daylight is always excluded. Mon–Sat 11am–1am, Sun 5pm–2am. Bus #71, tram #81.

La Porteuse d'Eau ave Jean Volders 48a ℡**02 537 66 46.** In the heart of St Gilles, on the corner of rue Vanderschrick, this Art Nouveau café has a delightfully ornate interior – well worth the price of a beer. Daily 10am–1am. Métro Porte de Hal.

Roxi rue du Bailli 82 ℡**02 646 17 92.** Trendy corner café-bar with large windows that open out to the street and a vibrant crowd spilling out over the sidewalk at weekends. There's more space – and a terrace – on the upper floor. Non-stop kitchen from noon to midnight with cheese and ham boards, pastas and salads – all for €8–12. Also serves breakfast earlier on for €3–8. Daily 8am–1am. Tram #81, bus #54.

Les Salons de l'Atalaïde chaussée de Charleroi 89 ℡**02 537 21 54.** There are mixed reports about the restaurant here, but the bar is good fun and its terrace is used for a variety of events, the current craze being the afternoon tea dance held on the last Sunday of each month from 2–10pm, with brunch included until 4pm. Otherwise, daily 11am–3am. Métro Porte de Hal.

Le Tavernier chaussée de Boendael 445 ℡**02 640 71 91.** A cool, happening bar, filled with students and other bouncing bunnies, so who else could be behind it but Fred Nicolay (see *Zebra*, p.203). It's all here: a great outdoor terrace, exposed brick and slightly scruffy furnishings, DJs, concerts and movies projected onto giant screens. Located on the southern periphery of Ixelles. Sun–Thurs 10am–2am, Fri & Sat 10am–4am. Tram #95, #96 and bus #71.

EU Quarter and around

Chez Bernard place Jourdan 47 ☏ **02 230 22 38.** Pleasant and very authentically Belgian bar that like most of the places around here lets you sit and eat your *frites* from Maison Antoine right opposite. Like the rest of the square, it's a breath of fresh air just a few minutes from rue de la Loi. Daily 6am–midnight. Métro Schuman.

Fat Boy's place Luxembourg 5 ☏ **02 511 32 66.** A fairly ordinary bar mainly aimed at ex pats who flock here for the numerous TVs showing a regular diet of football and rugby from home. Daily 11am–2am. Métro Trône.

La Galia rue Jacques Lalaing 22 ☏ **02 230 24 27.** Quite a rarity in this part of town, this is an unpretentious neighbourhood bar full of locals who aren't Eurocrats, and provides the perfect place to escape this most de-humanised bit of the EU Quarter. Sandwiches and other snacks at lunchtime make it an option for lunch too. Mon–Fri 9am–11pm. Métro Belliard.

Hairy Canary rue Archimède 12. Victorian pub in the heart of the EU area. Happy hour every day 5–7pm and on Sunday mornings they offer the full heart-stopping English/Irish breakfast for €12.50. Daily noon–1am. Métro Schuman.

Kitty O'Shea's blvd Charlemagne 42 ☏ **02 230 78 75.** This large Irish bar, part of an international chain, is *the* place to come for Irish food and draught Guinness, and is handily situated behind the Berlaymont building. Although it gets a bit rowdy when there's a football or rugby international, it's one of the more palatable bars in the area. Mon–Sat noon–3am, Sun noon–3pm. Métro Schuman.

Le Pullman place Luxembourg 12 ☏ **02 230 15 82.** A very basic bar a stone's throw from the glass wall of the European Parliament that serves a mixed clientele, and does cheap lunches from around €10 – steak-*frites*, pasta, omlettes and the like. Open 24 hours too. Métro Trône.

La Terrasse ave Des Celtes 1 ☏ **02 732 28 51.** Hidden away behind a holly and ivy hedge, this cosy bar of wood and red leather makes a nice retreat form the Cinquantenaire museums, five minutes' walk away. It also serves good, reasonably priced food – around €12 for a main dish – and a wide range of beers, including all the Trappist specials. Outside seating in summer. Sun–Thurs 11am–midnight, Fri & Sat 11pm–1am. Métro Merode.

Clubs and live music

B russels boasts a number of established **clubs**, playing anything from acid and techno beats to deep house, including the throbbing *Fuse* (see p.207) with its regular line-up of big-name DJs, including Monika Kruse, Carl Cox and Dave Clarke. All the best clubs are located in the Lower Town, with particular concentrations in the Marolles quarter and around place St-Géry, whereas **club-bars** are almost entirely confined to the vicinity of place St-Géry. Clubs and club-bars often **open** Thursday to Saturday from 11pm until dawn, but it's possible to go clubbing every night of the week. **Entry prices** are fairly low: club-bars are usually free and you rarely have to pay more than €10 for any club – and many have no cover charge at all, although in both cases men may be asked to tip the bouncer a nominal fee (€1 or so) on the way out. The **cost of drinks** varies depending on where you are, although shorts and cocktails are expensive across the board. If you're on a limited budget it's worth remembering that the bars which morph into clubs on a weekend, such as *Beursschouwburg* (see p.209) and *Café Central* (see p.208), tend to have cheaper drinks than ordinary clubs.

As for **live music**, Brussels has a vibrant **jazz** scene, with many bars, both in the centre and on the outskirts, playing host to local and international acts. Jazz buffs will be pleased to learn that live jazz has been popular in Brussels since the 1920s – a tradition kept alive today by small atmospheric venues such as *Sounds* (see p.210) and *L'Archiduc* (see p.209), and by the annual *Audi Jazz Festival* (see p.240) – widely regarded as being one of the best in Europe. The same cannot be said of the local **rock** and **indie** scene, though the annual *Les Nuits Botanique* festival in May (see p.238) is a great time to catch new bands of all genres. The good news for mainstream **gig-goers** is that Brussels is a regular stop on the European tours of major artists. The biggest gigs are held in *Forest National*, although many medium-sized gigs are held in *Le Botanique* (see p.210), *Cirque Royal* (see p.210) and *Ancienne Belgique* (see p.209). It's also worth considering going to one of the **music festivals** (see "Festivals", p.237) held regularly in and around Brussels; these usually attract a good line-up of rock bands mixed with dance DJs. The *Werchter Festival* (see p.239), held in early July, is the biggest. Note also that the **public transport** system winds up around 12.30am and starts again about 5.30am. Night buses partly fill the gap, but they are fairly infrequent and only operate on the #N71 bus route (De Brouckère to Delta every 30min; €3).

For **listings** of concerts and events, check the *What's On* section of the weekly English-language *Bulletin* or the Wednesday pull-out section of *Le Soir*. **Flyers** for most clubs and raves can be picked up in many of the city's trendier bars and cafés, particularly in the *Zebra* (see p.203) and the *Beursschouwburg*, which also has its own events list. Tickets for most concerts are available from *Caroline*

Music (see p.222), *Fnac* in the City 2 complex, on rue Neuve (see p.223), or directly from the Internet sites of the venues.

All of the clubs and club-bars listed are marked on the **colour maps** at the back of the book.

Clubs

Grand-Place and around

Montecristo rue Henri Maus 25. Just next door to the *Falstaff* (see p.194), the *Montecristo* is well known as a salsa venue. Wednesday night is pure salsa night, while on the weekend there's a mix of Latin beats and mainstream music. Mixed crowd and lots of hip gyrating a-going on. Entrance up to €5. Wed 10.30pm–2am, Thurs–Sat 10.30pm–5am. Prémétro Bourse.

You rue du Duquesnoy 18 🌐 www.leyou.be. *You*'s interior design is by Miguel Cancio Martins, the man behind the *Buddha Bar* in Paris. Not surprisingly then, this establishment claims to be much more than just a club, but rather a design concept – and they're looking for the punters to match it. On two levels, with comfy couches in the bar-lounge. Visiting DJs and a wide musical repertoire from funk and disco to electro and house. Check out the website for programme details. Also organizes gay tea dances on Sundays. Entry price varies: normally up to €6. Thurs–Sun 11pm–late. Métro Gare Centrale.

The Lower Town

Le Bazaar rue des Capucins 63 ☏ 02 511 26 00, 🌐 www.bazaarresto.be. Try out the delicious international cuisine in the upstairs bar-restaurant before picking up your drinks and descending to the cellar-like club below for a mixture of funk, soul, rock and indie. Not far from rue Haute, down from the Palais de Justice. Tues–Thurs & Sun 7.30pm–midnight, Fri & Sat 7.30pm–4am. Métro Porte de Hal or Louise.

La Bodega rue de Birmingham 30 ☏ 02 410 04 49, 🌐 www.la-bodega.be or www.cremaegusto .be. Impressive venue showcasing various club nights, located in Molenbeek, a gritty inner-city suburb immediately to the west of – and across the Charleroi canal from – the Lower Town. Downstairs is a tapas bar while the rooms upstairs and at the back are where the dancing takes place. One of the highlights is the second Saturday in the month when the popular club night organizers "Crema e Gusto" arrive with an eclectic funk, disco, electro night. Entry €5. Opening times vary – check website. Métro Gare de l'Ouest.

The Fuse rue Blaes 208 🌐 www.fuse.be. Widely recognized as the finest techno club in Belgium, this pulsating dance club has played host to some of the best DJs in Europe, including The Orb, Daft Punk, Carl Cox, Stacey Pullen and Dave Angel. Three floors of techno, house, jungle and occasional hip-hop, as well as the usual staple of chill-out rooms and visuals. The acts are slightly oriented towards Belgian DJs, but big international guest DJs are still a regular feature. Entrance is €3 before midnight, €8 after. The price goes up if there's a big name spinning the discs. On other evenings, when *The Fuse* is closed, the venue hosts other parties and dos. Sat 11pm–7am. Métro Porte de Hal.

Havana rue de l'Epée 4 🌐 www.havana -brussels.com. A Latino club very popular with the thirty-something, expat crowd. Punters mostly start early with a bite to eat, then smooze the night away on mojitos and magaritas before dancing till dawn to hot Latin beats. Free entry. Tues–Thurs 7pm–4am, Fri & Sat 7pm–7am. Métro Porte de Hal.

Recyclart rue des Ursulines 25 🌐 www.recyclart .be. Based in the old station building of Gare de la Chapelle, *Recyclart* puts on a wide range of underground parties and happenings. The bar is the old ticket booth and there's also the station café. It's a hub of urban art and social activity bringing together young creative minds to put on some of the most memorable nights in Brussels. Usually free. Opening times vary – check website. Prémétro Anneessens.

Ric's Art Boat quai des Péniches 44. Dance the night away on a one-time canal barge. *Ric's* is hired for numerous club nights and (private) parties. Regular fixtures include techno night,

Nemo Underground Adventures, Pop 0 and Movida. Entry varies from free to around €6. Fri & Sat 10pm–5am. Métro Yser.

Studio Athanor rue de la Fourche 17–19 Ⓦ www.studio-athanor.be. Venue inside *Hotel Arlequin* with red and black decor and low couches and tables. It's a cross between a jazz venue and a place for soul, funk and hip-hop club nights. Entry prices (sometimes free) and opening times/programme vary – check the website. Prémétro Bourse.

Milk Club rue de Livourne 40 Ⓦ www.milkclub.be. Carefully selected programme of DJs playing house, electro and rock in an impressive setting that's, well… white. Free before midnight, after which it's €5. Tues–Sun 11pm–6am. Tram #93 or #94.

Club-bars

Grand-Place and around

Canoa Quebrada rue du Marché au Charbon 53. This lively Latin American bar, close to *Au Soleil* (see p.199), mutates into a club at weekends. It's popular with the post-party crowd and other drunken revellers who come to salsa and samba the night away on the (compact) dance floor. If it gets too hectic, head for the small bar at the back where you can down a few delicious *Caipirinhas* – typical Brazilian cocktails of *cachaça* (white rum), lemon and sugar. No cover charge, but all the cocktails cost around €8. Thurs–Sat 10pm–late. Prémétro Bourse.

Dalí's Bar petite rue des Bouchers 35 Ⓦ www.dalisbar.com. As the name suggests, this bar's decor is suitably surreal, with Dalí prints, weird and wonderful-looking furniture and bright colours. Impromptu percussion and didgeridoo concerts can trade off with trip-hop, house and funk DJs on Wednesday, Friday and Saturday nights. The comfortable space and equally relaxed crowd ensure this is a chill-out rather than heat-up session. Tues–Sat 10pm–late. Prémétro Bourse.

Soixante rue du Marché au Charbon 60 ☎0477 704 156. As well as a lively programme of DJs playing everything from retro-house to electro from Wednesday through to Saturday evenings, there's a Saturday morning "party continuation" groove from 8am. Wed–Sun 5pm–6am. Prémétro Bourse.

The Lower Town

Café Central rue Borgval 14 ☎0486 72 26 24, Ⓦ www.lecafecentral.com. Cool bar just off Place St-Géry with D-Geranium (yes, named after the flower) as the

excellent DJ in residence. English-style battle at the bar for a drink but great atmosphere and clientele. Regular film shows – see website for details. Sun–Thurs 4pm–1am, Fri & Sat 4pm–4am. Prémétro Bourse.

Coasters rue des Riches Claires 28. This cosy, two-roomed bar around the corner from *Java* is where students come to play table football and take advantage of the very generous happy hour (8–11pm). In the early hours, however, especially on weekends, the place becomes a pulsating mass of gyrating bodies. Daily 8pm–6am. Prémétro Bourse.

Disque Au Bar place du Nouveau Marché au Grains 5. Five minutes' walk from the Grand-Place, this colourful, five-room bar used to double as a shop for well-known Brussels DJ Miss Elorak. Her Stress Da Bass store is now at Plattesteen 3, and her leaving Disque au Bar has left it a bit lost in space, but no doubt they'll get over it soon enough. Smashing atmosphere. Tues–Sat 10pm–late. Prémétro Bourse.

PP Café rue van Praet 28 Ⓦ www.ppcafe.be. Versatile café-bar-club serving food and drinks, but probably best on one of its regular music sessions. Fridays are resident DJ nights; on Sundays at 5pm there's apero-jazz with pianist and vocals; and once a month there's a more exclusive jazz concert with an entrance fee of €5. Daily 11am–2am, Fri & Sat till 3am. Prémétro Bourse.

Living Room chaussée de Charleroi 50. A perfect spot for pre-partying, the *Living*

Room has settled down from its early, jam-packed days to a nice, pleasant roar. The very comfortable surroundings – velour walls, soft chairs – live up to the name. A beaming crowd shows up for hot tunes on the weekends and a variety of top-notch house DJs keep your feet tapping. You can also grab a bite to eat, although the food isn't great. Daily 9pm–3am. Tram #91 or #92.

Live music venues

The Lower Town

Ancienne Belgique blvd Anspach 110 ☎ 02 548 24 24, 🌐 www.abconcerts.be. The capital's premier rock and indie venue with a seating capacity of 2000 (plus 750 standing) and a reputation for showcasing local bands and international acts who perform either in the main auditorium or the smaller space on the first floor (capacity around 400). There are usually around four gigs a week; visiting artists to the AB, as it's known, have included the Buena Vista Social Club, Guru, Roni Size and Roger Hodgson of Supertramp fame. Concert tickets cost around €20. The ticket shop is nearby at rue des Pierres 23 (Mon–Fri 11am–6pm). Closed July & Aug. Prémétro Bourse.

L'Archiduc rue Antoine Dansaert 6 ☎ 02 512 06 52. A famous Art Deco jazz café, close to place St-Géry, full of thirty-something media types tapping their fingers and wiggling their toes to Blue Note and post-1960s modern sounds. Legend has it that Nat King Cole once played here, and jazz fans will be pleased to hear the quality of the acts is still very high. Live jazz can be heard every Saturday 1–5pm for free and most Sunday evenings from October to April at 5pm with an entrance fee of around €15. Mon–Fri 4pm–2am, Sat 1pm–2am. Prémétro Bourse.

Beursschouwburg rue Auguste Orts 22 ☎ 02 550 03 50, 🌐 www.beursschouwburg.be. Occupying a handsomely restored building dating from 1885, this is a fine venue that makes the most of its several different spaces, from the cellar to the stairs, the theatre to the café. Great place to go in the evening to listen to DJs of all genres, plus an eclectic programme catering for a wide range of musical tastes. Free. Thurs–Sat 7pm–late. Prémétro Bourse.

Halles de Schaerbeek rue Royale Ste-Marie 22a ☎ 02 218 21 07, 🌐 www.halles.be. In the Schaerbeek neighbourhood, just to the north of the Lower Town, this magnificent wrought-iron building dates from 1865 and started its life as an indoor market. Now it's a venue for an eclectic programme of contemporary and international productions. The concert programme is not extensive but features some excellent, if lesser-known, artists of many types. Tram #91, #92, #93, #94.

Magasin 4 rue du Magasin 4 ☎ 02 223 34 74, 🌐 www.magasin4.be. This small converted warehouse is a good place to catch the latest punk, indie or rap/hip-hop band – indeed it has something of a reputation for featuring "the next big thing". A five- to ten-minute walk from Métro Yser – head south from the station and turn left along rue des Commerçants. Entrance usually sets you back around €8. Check their website for the programme. Métro Yser.

The Music Village rue des Pierres 50 ☎ 02 513 13 45, 🌐 www.themusicvillage.com. Jazz venue showcasing live music on most Wednesdays, Thursdays, Fridays and Saturdays. Line up includes swing jazz, jam sessions, Cuban jazz and plenty of jazz singers. Reservations are highly recommended and can be made via the website, which also gives opening times and performance schedule. Entry usually €10 Fri & Sat, other days €5. Prémétro Bourse.

La Tentation rue de Laeken 28 ☎ 02 223 22 75, 🌐 www.latentation.org. Galician cultural centre in an impressive building. Most of the week is taken up with Flamenco and Galician dance lessons, but if there's a folk concert in Brussels it's likely to be here. They usually put on a good St Patrick's Day event – a bit less rowdy than the Irish pubs nearby. Métro De Brouckère.

De Vaartkapoen (VK) rue de l'Ecole 76 ☎ 02 414 29 07, 🌐 www.vaartkapoen.be. One of the best cutting-edge "alternative" venues in the capital, VK regularly features top-class hip-hop, ragga, rock and indie acts and occasionally puts on the odd punk band.

One word of caution: it's not the best area to hang around after the gig, so try to clear off quickly. In the inner-city suburb of Molenbeek, to the west of the Lower Town, across the Charleroi canal. Tickets normally around €5–10. Métro Ribaucourt or Compte de Flandre.

The Upper Town

Botanique rue Royale 236 ☎02 218 37 32, Ⓦwww.botanique.be. Housed in the nineteenth-century conservatory of the Parc du Jardin Botanique and including an art gallery, two theatres, and a small cinema. Frequent rock and pop concerts, and some good, mostly contemporary, theatre. *Les Nuits Botanique* (see p.238) have become one of the highlights of the Brussels musical calendar. Tickets €7.50–15. Métro Botanique.

Cirque Royal rue de l'Enseignement 81 ☎02 218 20 15, Ⓦwww.cirque-royal.org. Formerly an indoor circus, this impressive venue has been host to the likes of David Byrne and Lou Reed and more recently The Divine Comedy and even Kool & the Gang. Gigs are fairly frequent and it's also the venue for the larger bands that come for *Les Nuits Botanique* (see p.238). Métro Madou.

Palais des Beaux Arts rue Ravenstein 23 ☎02 507 82 00, Ⓦwww.bozar.be. With a concert hall holding around 2000, as well as some smaller theatres, the Palais is used for anything from contemporary dance to Tom Jones, though the major-

ity of performances are of classical music – the place is the home of the Orchestre National de Belgique (see p.213). Métro Gare Centrale.

Ixelles

Le Grain d'Orge chaussée de Wavre 142 ☎02 511 26 47. Belgian brown café that hosts regular (and free) rock and blues concerts, normally on a Friday or Saturday night. It also has pinball-style machines and a happy hour with beer for just €0.90 between 7pm and 8pm. Open Mon–Fri 11am–3am, Sat & Sun 6pm–3am. Métro Porte de Namur.

Sounds rue de la Tulipe 28 ☎02 512 92 50. Atmospheric jazz café that has showcased both local and internationally-renowned jazz acts every night for the last twenty years or so. The bigger names mostly appear at the weekend. Concerts usually start at 10pm and admission costs €3–10. Close to place Fernand Cocq. Mon–Sat 8pm–1am. Bus #54 or #71.

Forest

Forest National ave du Globe 36 ☎0900 00 991, Ⓦwww.forestnational.be. Brussels' main arena for big-name international concerts, holding around 11,000. Recent names have included Michael Jackson, B.B. King, Jon Bon Jovi and MC Solaar. Tram #18, bus #54.

The performing arts and cinema

The more time you spend in Brussels, the more you discover the quality and diversity of its **cultural scene**, which is characteristically discrete and hardly ever brazen. Domestic talent flourishes, particularly in the **theatre**, which has nurtured a new generation of young playwrights, including Philippe Blasand and Jean-Marie Piemme, and the same applies to **modern dance**. The city also scores well when it comes to **opera** and **classical music** with the Orchestre National de Belgique continuing to thrive. By comparison, home-grown film-makers are thin on the ground, but the Belgians are avid cinema-goers – how could it be otherwise with the city that produced Jean-Claude van Damme, aka the "Muscles from Brussels"? – so there's no problem when it comes to going to the **cinema**, both for mainstream and art-house films.

Listings of theatre and dance performances, concert recitals and film showings are published in the "What's On" section of the weekly English-language *Bulletin* magazine. They also appear in the Wednesday pull-out section of *Le Soir*. For tickets and information, either go to the appropriate website or visit the tourist office on the Grand-Place (see p.25). **Last-minute tickets** (taking in theatre, dance and other performances in a wide range of venues) are available at discount prices at *Arsène50*, in the **Théâtre du Vaudeville,** Galerie de la Reine 13–15, Galeries St-Hubert, near the Grand-Place (Ⓦ www.arsene50.be; Tues–Sat 12.30–5.30pm).

Theatre and dance

Despite some underfunding, the Brussels **theatre** scene remains strong. The city currently has more than thirty theatres staging a variety of productions, ranging from Shakespeare to Stoppard. Most theatre is performed in French or Flemish, but there are also a number of high-quality, amateur theatre groups of American, Irish and British extraction. Being at the centre of Europe, Brussels is also a **tour stop-off point** for many international dance and theatre groups – including the RSC, the Comédie Française and the Israeli dance group Badsheva – and it's quite common for the capital's theatres to stage joint productions with other European theatre companies.

Brussels' **dance** tradition has been impressing visitors ever since Maurice Béjart brought his classical Twentieth Century Ballet here in 1959. However, the city still lacks a proper dance venue, and unfortunately companies have to make do with stages better suited to plays and concert recitals. Commonly used venues are the Palais des Beaux Arts, the Théâtre de la Monnaie and the Cirque Royal. The innovative legacy of Béjart lives on, however, with his old company (now called Rosas and led by Anne Theresa de Keersmaeker) regularly performing at La Monnaie.

Ticket prices for dance and theatre vary with the venue, but a good seat at most places costs around €18–25.

Cirque Royal rue de l'Enseignement 81 ⊕ **02 218 20 15,** Ⓦ **www.cirque-royal.org.** This former indoor circus offers one of the city's most eclectic performing arts programmes. It's best known for dance, classical music, musicals and operettas, but has also staged acts ranging from David Byrne to the Chippendales. Métro Madou.

Kaai Theater place Sainctelette 20 ⊕ **02 201 59 59,** Ⓦ **www.kaaitheater.be.** Beautiful Art Deco theatre on the banks of the Charleroi canal run by the Flemish community. Programme includes plenty of dance and music as well as theatre from local and visiting companies with occasional performances in English. Tickets cost around €12.50 per performance. Métro Yser.

Koninklijke Vlaamse Schouwberg quai aux Pierres de Taille 7 ⊕ **02 210 11 00,** Ⓦ **www .kvs.be.** This Flemish-language theatre has a good reputation for showcasing the works of up-and-coming young playwrights, as well as staging modern classics by the likes of Chekhov, Pinget and Beckett. It's also an excellent place to catch some innovative dance. Métro Yser.

Palais des Beaux Arts rue Ravenstein 23 ⊕ **02 507 82 00,** Ⓦ **www.bozar.be and www .rideaudebruxelles.be.** The Palais des Beaux Arts' resident theatre company – Rideau de Bruxelles – has been putting on modern theatre productions since its inception in 1943. Performances are in French, and playwrights to have had their work performed include David Hare, Paul Willems and Jean Sigrid. It's also an excellent venue for modern dance and classical ballet, and is often one of the first ports of call for touring dance companies, though tickets can rise to €50 for these performances. Métro Parc.

Théâtre 140 ave Eugène Plasky 140, EU Quarter ⊕ **02 733 97 08,** Ⓦ **www.theatre140.be.** Théâtre 140, or "Le 140", has been offering an international outlook on the world of performing arts through music, variety theatre, dance

and visual theatre for the past 39 years. It's also the venue for regular English-language comedy nights ("Stand Up World") featuring some talented comedians from the UK and USA. Tickets for the comedy nights are €21, but allow an extra €9 to tuck into the Indian buffet before the show. For dates see Ⓦ www.standupworld.com. Tram #23, #90.

Théâtre National blvd Emile Jacqmain 111–115 ⊕ **02 203 41 55,** Ⓦ **www.theatrenational.be.** Opened in 2004, this plush venue was built to accommodate the national theatre. Performances, invariably in French, are highly-polished productions of everything from the classics – Molière and so forth – to cabaret. Métro Rogier.

Théâtre de Poche chemin du Gymnase 1A ⊕ **02 649 17 27,** Ⓦ **www.poche.be.** Politically engaged Francophone theatre well to the south of the city centre in the middle of the Bois de la Cambre (see p.104). The programme here covers a variety of social issues, for example immigration and religion, and reveals many international influences. The performances often combine movement and music, making them enjoyable even if you're not fluent in French. The bar attached is a fun place to hang around with lots of activity and artists presenting their work. Tram #23, #90; bus #38.

Théâtre Royal du Parc rue de la Loi 3 ⊕ **02 512 23 39.** Stage productions are in French only, but even if you don't fancy a performance it's worth visiting this glorious theatre for the beautiful architecture alone – the building dates back to 1782. The programme consists mainly of French burlesques and twentieth-century classics – Ionesco, Brecht, Camus – but they also stage more modern pieces, and have been known to put on the odd bit of Shakespeare. Métro Parc.

The Warehouse rue Waelham 73, Schaerbeek ⊕ **02 203 53 03,** Ⓦ **www.atc-brussels.com.** In 1994 the American Theatre Company, the

English Comedy Club and the Irish Theatre Group clubbed together to purchase a performance complex now known as The Warehouse. If you want English-language theatre, this is where you'll find it, but unfortunately it's a fair old trek north from the centre in the suburb of Schaerbeek. Tram #92, #93.

Classical music and opera

The **classical music** concert scene in Brussels is impressive. The main venue is the Palais des Beaux Arts, while the Conservatoire Royal de Musique has an excellent reputation for its programme of chamber music and song recitals. **Annual events** include the recently established Ars Musica (see p.237), held in March, and the prestigious Concours International Musical Reine Elisabeth de Belgique (see p.238), a competition for piano, violin or voice held in May and numbering among its prize-winners Vladimir Ashkenazy, David Oistrakh and Gidon Kremer.

Opera–lovers need go no further than the beautiful and historic Théâtre de la Monnaie, which has enjoyed something of a renaissance of late, first under the direction of Bernard Foccroule, but more recently with the inspired conductor Kazushi Ono.

Tickets for concerts and the opera start from as little as €7.40–12.40, but can zoom up to as much as €154 for a first night at La Monnaie.

Conservatoire Royal de Musique rue de la Régence 30 ☎ 02 511 04 27, ⓦ www .conservatoire.be. Although the Orchestre National de Belgique sometimes plays here, it's more suited to chamber music and song recitals. The acoustics are second to none and there is an impressive, at times highly innovative, programme interspersed with the early rounds of the Concours Musical International Reine Elisabeth de Belgique competition. Métro Louise.

Palais des Beaux Arts rue Ravenstein 23 ☎ 02 507 82 00, ⓦ www.pskpba.be. The pick of the capital's classical music scene, the Palais des Beaux Arts is not only the home of Belgium's national orchestra, but also the Philharmonic Society, which organizes classical music performances throughout the city. Visiting orchestras have included the Los Angeles Philharmonic and the Chicago Symphony Orchestra. The season runs from September to June, and the Palais hosts in excess of 350 concerts each year. Métro Parc.

Théâtre de la Monnaie place de la Monnaie ☎ 02 229 12 11, ⓦ www.lamonnaie.be. This is Belgium's premier opera house. Renowned for its adventurous repertoire and production style, it has earned itself glowing reviews over the years, whilst its policy of nurturing promising singers – rather than casting the more established stars – makes it a great place to spot newcomers. Book well in advance: tickets are always difficult to obtain as the house contains only 1200 seats. The building itself is also of considerable significance: during a performance of Auber's *The Mute Girl of Portici* in 1830, a nationalistic libretto sent the audience charging out into the street, where they promptly started a rebellion that was soon to lead to the establishment of an independent Belgium (see p.249). Métro De Brouckère.

Cinema

Belgium's contribution to world **cinema** may be modest – *The Sexual Life of the Belgians*, *Man Bites Dog* spring to mind – but nonetheless Brussels is still very good for cinema-goers. As you might expect, the city has several large commercial cinemas showing Hollywood blockbusters, notably UGC De Brouckère and Heysel's Kinepolis, but more encouragingly the city also has a decent flush of art-house cinemas as well as a couple of places devoted to classic films. Look out also for a couple of highly recommended, annual **film festivals**, the Brussels Festival of European Film (see p.239) and the bizarre, but wonderful, Brussels Festival of Fantasy Film, Science Fiction and Thrillers (see p.237).

About half the films shown in Brussels' cinemas are in English (coded "VO" or "version originale"); **subtitles** for non-French and/or non-Flemish films are in French and/or Flemish as appropriate. *The Bulletin* and *The Agenda* (free magazine available in bars and cafes) are the best sources for **listings** of the week's movies, as is the internet site ⓦ www.cinebel.be. Cinemas usually change their programmes on Wednesdays. **Ticket prices** depend on the venue: at the large commercial cinemas they are €8.20, while in the smaller art-house venues expect to pay between €5.50 and €7. In the cheaper independent cinemas also expect to be asked to tip the person who takes your ticket; €0.50 will do fine.

Actors' Studio petite rue des Bouchers 16 ⓣ **02 512 16 96.** This small cinema is probably the best place in the centre to catch art-house or independent films. It's also cheaper than its more commercial rivals with the added advantage that you can buy a beer and take it with you. Prémétro Bourse.

Arenberg Galleries Galerie de la Reine 26, Galeries St-Hubert ⓣ **02 512 80 63.** Set in a good-looking Art Deco building converted from a theatre, the Arenberg Galleries is best known for its "Ecran Total", a programme of classic and art-house films shown over the summer months. Occasionally they take a poll to gauge audience reaction to the film. An adventurous variety of world films is also screened. Métro Gare Centrale.

Flagey Studio place Sainte-Croix 5, Ixelles ⓣ **02 641 10 20.** Part of the Art Deco cultural centre situated on place Eugene Flagey, this studio cinema showcases an impressive range of films, usually focusing on a particular genre or director. The whole building becomes a haven for film-lovers once a year when it plays host to the Brussels Festival of European Film (see p.239). Bus #71 from Métro Porte de Namur.

Kinepolis blvd du Centenaire 20 ⓣ **0900 00 555.** A hi-tech cinema complex with 27 auditoriums and one of the largest IMAX screens in Europe. The line-up is purely commercial but the choice of mainstream films is unrivalled. Métro Heysel.

Musée du Cinéma rue Baron Horta 8 ⓣ **02 507 83 70.** This small museum-cum-cinema is popular with film buffs, who come to watch an excellent selection of films including old

silent movies with piano accompaniment. The museum is pretty interesting as well, especially the early attempts at moving pictures such as the "mutoscope" and "kinetoscope". Children under 16 not admitted. Not many seats, so you need to get there early. Métro Gare Centrale.

Nova rue d'Arenberg 3 ⓣ **02 511 27 74,** ⓦ **www.nova-cinema.com.** There's no regular programme at the Nova, so you need to check their website. A young crowd of film fanatics keep this venue going and it is indeed a great place to catch new and local cinematic talent. In the summer, they organize an outdoor film festival, PleinOpenAir, on disused sites around the city. Métro De Brouckère.

Styx rue de l'Arbre Bénit 72, Ixelles ⓣ **0900 27 854.** A tiny, recently renovated, two-screen repertory cinema showing a selection of old and new films, always in the original language, as well as midnight screenings. A ten-minute walk from Métro Porte de Namur.

UGC De Brouckère place de Brouckère 38 ⓣ **0900 10 440.** A ten-screen cinema showing mainstream and blockbuster Hollywood fare. By the by, make sure you go into the right room, as they often show two versions of the same film, one in the original version and one dubbed. Métro De Brouckère.

Vendôm chaussée de Wavre 18 ⓣ **02 502 37 00.** A trendy, five-screen cinema well known for showing a wide selection of arty films plus more mainstream stuff. They also offer a multiple ticket – six for €30 – which is very good value. A stone's throw from Métro Porte de Namur.

Shopping

A s you might expect of a capital city and EU mainstay, Brussels has a wide range and variety of **shops and stores**. The city centre's main shopping street is pedestrianized **rue Neuve**, and this is where you'll find City 2, the ultimate inner-city shopping mall, but this is all pretty standard stuff – a long string of multinational outlets – and there are much more distinctive offerings elsewhere. Behind the Bourse, **rue Antoine Dansaert** is dotted with quality fashion shops of both established and up-and-coming designers and there are a couple of smashing secondhand clothes shops here too. The narrow streets around **place St-Géry** hold a clutch of inventive street-wear shops, whereas wallet-crunching designer shops – Armani, Versace and so forth – are concentrated in the vicinity of **place Louise**. The city's most expensive antique shops are to be found around **place du Grand Sablon**, with another, slightly less pricey, group strung along the more northerly part of **rue Blaes**. Central Brussels is also liberally sprinkled with **galeries** and **passages** – sheltered shopping arcades ranging from the illustrious **Galeries St-Hubert**, near the Grand-Place, and the attractive old bookstores of the **Galerie Bortier**, close to Gare Centrale, to the **Galerie Agora**, whose shops peddle cheap leather jackets, incense, piercing jewellery and ethnic goods. Another of the city's strengths is its open-air **markets**, two key targets being the weekend **antiques market** held on the place du Grand Sablon and the sprawling **flea market** that takes place daily on the place du Jeu de Balle in the Marolles district. Otherwise, specialist shops are spread across much of the city, though you should never have to walk far to hunt down Belgium's shopping trinity – beer, chocolate and the comic strip, "bande dessinée", or just BD.

The **shops** recommended in this chapter have been divided into the following **categories**: art, antiques and design p.216; books and comics p.217; chocolate p.218; department stores and *galeries* p.219; fashion and secondhand clothes p.219; food and drink p.220; lace p.221; markets p.221; music p.222; and toys and games p.223.

Opening hours

Shops are generally **open** from Monday to Saturday, 10am to 6pm or 7pm, though the more tourist-orientated places, especially on and around the Grand-Place, are usually open on Sundays too. On Fridays, department stores typically stay open until 8pm. In most districts there are also **night shops** – mainly selling booze, cigarettes and food – and these stay open till 1am or 2am, sometimes later in the city centre. Sundays, when most shops are closed, see many of the city's open-air markets at their busiest and best.

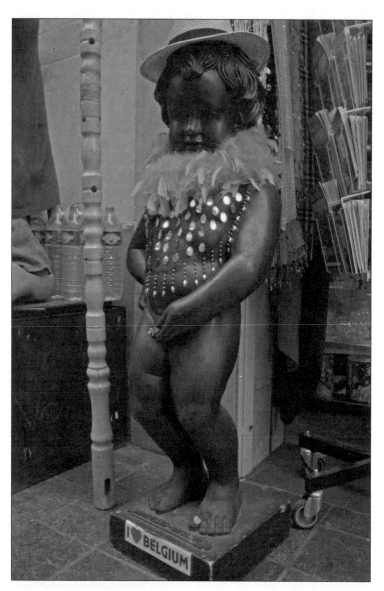

△ Kitsch souvenirs

Art, antiques and design

**Art Deco 1920-1940 ave Adolphe Demeur 16,
St Gilles** ☎ 02 534 70 25. As you might guess
from the name, Anne Bastin's shop is a shrine
to Art Deco. Walk by in the evening to see the

beautifully lit windows, or pass during the day
to explore her collection of lamps, furniture
and jewellery. Wed–Sat 11am–6.30pm, Sun
11.30am–6.30pm. Prémétro Horta.
La Caravane Passe rue de Tamines 2, St Gilles
☎ 02 538 05 90. Wondering where those

elaborate Moroccan restaurants get their furnishings? Look no further than this beautiful shop filled with teapots, lamps, plates and carpets direct from North Africa. There's also a branch in Anderlecht at rue Gheude 45. Wed–Sat noon–6.30pm. Tram #18, #81.

Costermans place du Grand Sablon 5 (Upper Town) ☎ 02 512 21 33. Famous Grand Sablon antiques shop, established in 1839 and now run by Marc-Henri Jaspar-Costermans. Its speciality is eighteenth-century furniture and *objets d'art* as well as old paintings and beautifully crafted clocks. There's also an impressive range of antique fireplaces and wrought ironwork too. Prices are mostly prohibitive, but it's a lovely place to look around nonetheless. Mon–Fri 9am–6pm, Sat 10am–noon & 2–6pm. Métro Louise.

D Plus Design rue Blaes 83–87, Marolles (Lower Town) ☎ 02 512 44 04. D Plus specializes in twentieth-century design and decorative arts, with collections of items designed by the great Italian designers like Ettore Sottsass, Gio Ponti, Ico Parisi and Castiglioni. You can also find modern designs from Scandinavia (somewhat classier and pricier than their Ikea equivalents). Mon–Sat 11am–6pm, Sun 10am–4pm. Closed Wednesday. Métro Porte de Hal.

L'Instant Présent rue Blaes 136, Marolles (Lower Town) ☎ 02 513 28 91. Photographer Nicolas Springael opens his shop at weekends to sell his stunning black and white photos of Brussels, including unusual shots capturing some back streets of the Marolles district as well as more classic takes of the Musical Instrument Museum and the Grand-Place. You can buy the photos alone or in a simple frame. A keen traveller, he also has selections from trips to India and Africa. Fri & Sun 10.30am–4pm, Sat 10.30am–6pm. Métro Porte de Hal.

De Leye rue Lebeau 16 (Upper Town) ☎ 02 514 34 77. Bruxellois Bernard De Leye's shop specializes in high-quality seventeenth- and eighteenth-century silverware with everything from silver candlesticks to serving ladles, mirrors, statuettes, teapots and gravy boats. Excellent selection and competitive prices. Just off place du Grand Sablon. Tues–Sat 10.30am–12.30pm & 2.30–6.30pm. Métro Louise.

Passage 125 Blaes rue Blaes 125, Marolles (Lower Town) ☎ 02 503 10 27, ⊛ www .passage125.be. Thirty antique dealers occupy the four floors and 1200 square metres of this shop in the Marolles district. Retro, Art Deco, lamps, jewellery and piles of other stuff – what they don't have hanging from some ceiling or other in this labyrinth is really not worth having. If you prefer less stairs and dust, check out their website. Mon, Wed & Fri 10am–5pm, Tues, Thurs and Sat 10am–6pm, Sun 10am–5.30pm. Métro Porte de Hal.

Sabine Wachters ave de Stalingrad 26 (Lower Town) ☎ 02 502 39 93. Modern and contemporary gallery specializing in upcoming artists, as well as big names such as Andy Warhol, Donald Judd and Daniel Spoerri. Tues–Sat 11am–7pm. Prémétro Lemonnier.

Books and comics

Brüsel blvd Anspach 100 (near Grand-Place) ☎ 02 511 08 09. This well-known comic shop stocks more than eight thousand new issues and specializes in French underground editions – Association, Amok and Bill to name but a few. You'll also find the complete works of the famous Belgian comic-book artist Schuiten, most popularly known for his controversial comic *Brüsel*, which depicts the architectural destruction of a city (guess which one) in the 1960s. Calvin and Hobbes make an appearance, as does Tintin in a babel of language versions. The shop is particularly worth visiting when it hosts a pop-art or comic-book exhibition. Mon–Sat 10am–6.30pm, Sun noon–6.30pm. Prémétro Bourse.

Centre Belge de la Bande Dessinée rue des Sables 20 (Lower Town) ☎ 02 219 19 80. This museum bookstore (see p.65) is definitely worth a visit even if you haven't been to the museum as it contains a wide range of new comics. Tues–Sun 10am–6pm. Métro Botanique or Rogier.

Le Dépôt/Le Dépôt Jonas chaussée d'Ixelles 120 & 142, Ixelles ☎ 02 511 75 04. Le Dépôt has the latest comics and Le Dépôt Jonas is a rather more dingy but vast space containing several thousand secondhand comics, videos, gaming software, music and collectable prints. Mon–Sat 10am–6pm. Bus #71, #54.

Espace BD place Fernand Coq 2, Ixelles. ☎ 02 512 68 69. Selling principally adult-themed comics, Espace BD features a beautiful gallery displaying a host of prints and sketches from all sorts of artists, including Dany, Gimenez, Berthet and Alice. Immaculately organized and a pleasant place to spend an afternoon browsing. Mon 1.30–6.30pm, Tues–Sat 10.30am–6.30pm. Bus #71, #54.

Espace Tintin rue de la Colline 13 (near Grand-Place) ☏02 514 51 52. Set up, no doubt, by someone with an unhealthy obsession with Hergé's quiffed hero. Expect to find anything and everything to do with Tintin – comic books, postcards, stationery, figurines, T-shirts and sweaters – and all Hergé's other cartoon creations, such as Quick & Flupke. Just off the Grand-Place. Mon–Sat 10am–6pm, Sun 11am–5pm. Prémétro Bourse.

Filigranes ave des Arts (Upper Town) ☏02 511 90 15. Open 365 days a year for anyone who is desperate to get their hands on a particular book. Novels are mainly French-language, but there's a good range of travel and art books in English as well as magazines. Excellent café right in the middle of the shop too. Regular events and readings. Mon–Fri 7am–7pm, Sat 9.30am–7pm, Sun and public holidays 10am–6pm. Métro Arts–Loi.

Librairie Européene rue de la Loi 244 ☏02 231 04 35. Small shop stocking EU publications, dictionaries and phrasebooks, books on Brussels and a sprinkling of fiction in different languages. Mon–Fri 9am–6pm. Métro Schuman.

Nicola's Bookshop rue de Stassart 106, Ixelles ☏02 513 94 00, ⓦwww.nicolasbookshop .com. Located just off Place Stéphanie, this independent English-language bookshop offers an excellent selection of books from around the world and a relaxed and friendly atmosphere. Occasional events too – check the website for details. Mon–Thurs & Sat 11am–7pm, Fri 11am–8pm. Métro Louise.

Pêle-Mêle blvd Maurice Lemonnier 55–59 (Lower Town) ☏ 02 548 78 00. A maze-like shop with a jumble of secondhand books stacked up against the walls. Thrillers, classics, comics, magazines and even CDs retail at some of the lowest prices in Brussels: a Balzac or a Camus will cost around €0.50. The whole wall devoted to English-language titles houses novels selling at €1–1.50. A good place to unload any unwanted books as they also buy. Mon–Sat 10am–6.30pm. Prémétro Anneessens.

Sterling Books rue du Fossé aux Loups 38 (Lower Town) ☏02 223 78 35. This large English-language bookshop has more than 50,000 UK and US titles, including a large selection of magazines, and is much cheaper than Waterstone's – they sell books at the cover price, converted at the day's exchange rate, plus six percent VAT. You can also pay directly in pounds sterling. Has a children's corner with a small play area. Mon–Sat 10am–7pm, Sun noon–6.30pm. Métro De Brouckère.

Waterstones blvd Adolphe Max 71–75 (Lower Town) ☏02 219 27 08. The Brussels branch of the British parent company, selling over 70,000 English-language titles. The premises are a bit cramped, making it far from ideal for browsing, but there's an excellent selection of books and magazines and a good ordering service. Mon–Sat 9am–7pm, Sun 10.30am–6pm. Métro De Brouckère or Rogier.

Chocolate

Galler rue au Beurre 44 (Grand-Place) ☏02 502 02 66. Chocolatier to the King as the holder of the Royal Warrant. Less well-known than many of its rivals, unless you're Belgian royalty of course. Not often seen outside Belgium, so a good choice for those who want to take home something you can't buy at any airport. Excellent dark chocolate; 250g will set you back €11. Daily 10am– 9.30pm. Prémétro Bourse.

Godiva place du Grand Sablon 47/48 (Upper Town) ☏02 502 99 06. The popular chain chocolatier Godiva definitely holds its own against the best of the rest. Jealously-guarded recipes and seasonal, handcrafted packaging ensure customers keep coming back for more; in the upper price range of €11 for 250g. Daily 9am–7pm. Métro Louise.

Léonidas blvd Anspach 46 (Lower Town) ☏02 218 03 63. Léonidas is one of the largest and most popular chain chocolatiers in Brussels with branches all over the city and, for that matter, Belgium and much of the rest of the

▽ Neuhaus chocolate shop

world. One reason for the company's popularity is the competitive price of its chocolates and pralines (€4 for 250g), though this is production-line stuff and they tend to be rather sugary and sickly-sweet, especially in comparison with those of their (more expensive) rivals. Mon–Fri 9am–6.30pm, Sun 10am–6pm. Prémétro Bourse.

Mary's rue Royale 73 (Upper Town) ☎02 217 45 00. A very exclusive and expensive shop, with beautiful antique decor, specializing in pricey handmade chocolates. The extra expense is, however, well worth it: the difference between the chocolates here and those of the chains is palpable. Mon–Sat 9.30am–6pm. Tram #92, #93, #94.

Neuhaus Grand-Place 27 ☎02 514 28 50. Belgium's best chocolate chain sells superb and beautifully presented chocolates. Check out their specialities such as the handmade Caprices – pralines stuffed with crispy nougat, fresh cream and soft-centred chocolate – and the delicious Manons – stuffed white chocolates, which come with fresh cream, vanilla and coffee fillings. Prices are € 9.75 for 250g, €19.50 for 500g or €39 for a 1kg box. Also has other branches across the city, including especially attractive premises in the Galeries St-Hubert, near the Grand-Place. Daily 9am–10.15pm. Métro Gare Centrale.

Pierre Marcolini place du Grand Sablon 39 (Upper Town) ☎02 514 12 06. Considered by many to be the best chocolatier in the world, Pierre Marcolini sells simply wonderful chocolates – try his spice- and tea-filled chocs to get you started. Classy service and beautiful packaging plus chocolate cakes to die for. At the weekend you can have a glass of his mouthwatering hot chocolate at the small bar in the shop. Expect to pay for the quality with 250g costing €13.50. Wed–Sun 10am–7pm, Sat 10am–7pm. Also has a branch at ave Louise 75 (☎02 538 42 24). Métro Louise for both branches.

Wittamer place du Grand Sablon 6 (Upper Town) ☎02 512 37 42. Brussels' most famous patisserie and chocolate shop, established in 1910 and still run by the Wittamer family, who sell gorgeous if expensive light pastries, cakes, mousses, and chocolates. Also serve speciality teas and coffees in their tearoom along the street at no. 12. Mon 8am–6pm, Tues–Sat 7am–7pm, Sun 7am–6pm. Métro Louise.

Department stores and galeries

City 2 rue Neuve 123 (Lower Town) ☎02 219 18 76. Whopping shopping mall, easily the biggest in the city centre, with a superabundance of multinational shops plus the INNO department store (see below) and the massive Fnac music store (see p.223). Mon–Sat 10am–7pm, Fri until 7.30pm. Métro Rogier.

Galerie Agora off rue des Eperonniers (near Grand-Place). Large and central *galerie* where the emphasis is on the cheap and quasi-exotic, from ethnic clothes and incense through to tattooists and ear-piercers. Mon–Sat 10am–7pm. Métro Gare Centrale.

Galerie Bortier off rue de la Madeleine (near Grand-Place). This cloistered shopping arcade, with its glass roof and wood-panelled shops, dates back to the middle of the nineteenth century. It's known for its new and secondhand bookshops. Métro Gare Centrale.

Galeries St-Hubert between place Espagne and rue de l'Ecuyer (near Grand-Place). Dating back to the 1840s, this splendid glass-roofed *galerie* divides up into three subsections – the Galerie de la Reine, the Galerie du Roi and, at right angles to the other two, the Galerie des Princes. It holds several bookshops, a cinema, a couple of exclusive clothes shops, cafés, a restaurant and the smartest outlet of the Neuhaus chocolate chain (see opposite). Métro Gare Centrale.

Inno rue Neuve 111–123 (Lower Town) ☎02 211 21 11. Brussels' largest department store has five floors peddling goods ranging from perfume and lingerie to home furnishings, clothing and shoes. Prices vary from the high-rise to the bargain basement. Mon–Thurs 9.30am–7pm, Fri 9.30am–8pm & Sat 9.30am–7pm. Métro De Brouckère or Rogier.

Fashion and secondhand clothes

Cora Kemperman rue du Marché aux Herbes 16 (near Grand-Place) ☎02 223 68 74. This well-known Dutch designer is popular amongst Belgian women for her unique but accessible designs and natural colours and fabrics. Mon–Sat 10am–6pm. Prémétro Bourse.

Emporio Armani place du Grand Sablon 37 (Upper Town) ☎02 551 04 04. Sleek and smart casual suits, jeans, underwear and accessories for both men and women in the mainstream Armani vein. The store is spacious and the staff welcoming. Mon & Wed–Sat 10.30am–7pm, Sun 11am–6pm. Métro Louise.

Ethic Wear rue des Chartreux 25 (Lower Town) ☎02 514 78 08. The clothes here are made of organic cotton, their production respects the environment and they are fair trade. You can't get much better than that. In addition, shop owner and designer of the collection Marie Cabanac has found a conveniently central spot to promote her clothes and values. Not cheap – but this kind of quality isn't. Mon–Sat 11am–7pm. Prémétro Bourse.

Gabriele Vintage rue des Chartreux 27 (Lower Town) ☎02 512 67 43. Well-presented and stylish secondhand clothes of several periods and many styles, from bowler hats to ball gowns, flairs to platform shoes. Wed–Sat 11am–6.30pm, Mon 2–6.30pm. Prémétro Bourse.

Gianni Versace blvd de Waterloo 64, Ixelles ☎02 511 85 59. Everything you'd expect from a Versace outlet – swish marble decor, stylish clothing and enormous prices. Caters for both men and women. Mon–Sat 10am–6.30pm. Métro Louise.

Idiz Bogam Antoine Dansaert 76 (Lower Town) ☎02 512 10 32. Pricey vintage clothing featuring a real treasure trove of one-off pieces, including newer designs from Idiz's own collection such as well-cut dresses in colourful prints. Excellent range of new vintage-look shoes and leather boots as well as a wide selection of leather handbags. In-store displays are well presented and often have an imaginative theme. Mon–Sat 11am–7pm. Métro Ste Catherine.

Mr Ego rue des Pierres 29 (near Grand-Place) ☎02 502 47 87. Large, airy store with top hip labels such as Carhartt, Kangol and Boxfresh for men and women. Watch out for the signs in the changing rooms. Mon, Tue, Thurs 11am–6.30pm, Wed & Fri 11am–7pm, Sat 10.30am–7pm. Métro De Brouckère or Prémétro Bourse.

Olivier Strelli ave Louise 72, Ixelles ☎02 512 56 07. One of Belgium's most established designers, Olivier Strelli has been creating simple, classic and very modern clothes for many years, often with a splash of colour – the rainbow scarves for women are very popular. Prices are, however, on the high side. Mon–Sat 10am–6.30pm. Métro Louise.

Pax rue de la Paix 8, Ixelles ☎02 502 52 31. One of several new street-wear shops on rue de la Paix, this one just that little bit different, stocking shoes to undies, as well as coats and a good selection of T-shirts. Brands include Camper and Hardcore Session. Mon–Sat 10.30am–7pm. Métro Porte de Namur.

Sambalou chaussée de Waterloo 203, St Gilles ☎02 534 90 74. Distinctive designs on colourful T-shirts, hippy-style trousers, African jewellery and a few musical instruments to boot. If you go to any of the music festivals in Belgium you're bound to see a few Sambalou fans hanging around. Tues–Sat 10am–7pm. Prémétro Horta.

Stijl rue Antoine Dansaert 74 (Lower Town) ☎02 512 03 13. Capacious men and womenswear emporium focusing on cutting-edge Belgian designers such as Ann Demeulemeester, Martin Margiela, Dries Van Noten, Dirk Bikkembergs and Raf Simons. They also sell Helmut Lang, John Smedley and Romeo Gigli. Their children's clothing shop, Kat en Muis, is at no. 32. Mon–Sat 10.30am–6.30pm. Métro Ste Catherine.

Underwear rue Antoine Dansaert 47 (Lower Town) ☎02 514 27 31. For those who want to take fashion right down to the bare essentials, this place is worth a visit. Designer undies at designer prices. A La Fille d'O set for women can ring in at an incredible €107. Mon–Sat 10.30am–6.30pm. Métro Ste Catherine.

Food and drink

Beer Mania chaussée de Wavre 174–176, Ixelles ☎02 512 17 88, ⊛www.beermania.be. Perhaps the city's best beer shop, stocking more than 400 different types of beer, with a good selection of both the well-known and more obscure brands. Prices are competitive and you can even buy the correct glass in which to serve your favourite tipple. There are also a few tables at the back of the shop where you can take the weight off your feet and enjoy your purchases on the premises. There's a website for home delivery, and they have regular classes (some given in English) and tasting sessions. Mon–Sat 11am–9pm. Métro Porte de Namur.

Le Caprice des Lieux rue du Bois de Linthout 3 (EU Quarter) ☎02 773 17 99. A cheese lover's heaven, with hundreds of immaculately-presented cheeses set amid tasteful decor. You can also purchase entire cheese platters. Tues–Sat 9am–7pm, Sun 9am–12.30pm. Métro Georges Henri.

Dandoy rue au Beurre 31 (near Grand-Place) ☏02 511 03 26. This famous shop has been making biscuits since 1829, so it's no surprise that they have it down to a fine art. Their main speciality is known locally as "speculoos", a kind of hard gingerbread biscuit, which is something of an acquired taste. They also sell some extremely large biscuits, the size of small children and costing as much as €50; they arrive in a weird variety of shapes – the most unappetizing being a life-size Manneken Pis. Dandoy also operates a tearoom just off the Grand-Place at rue Charles Buls 14. Mon–Sun 10am–7pm. Prémétro Bourse.

▽ Window-shopping at Dandoy

Delitraiteur Ixelles rue du Page 10–12, Ixelles ☏02 539 41 27. Just off place du Châtelain, deep in the heart of Ixelles, this supermarket-cum-café-cum-delicatessen is an entirely new concept in Brussels. Those with more money than time can pick up freshly made meals and either heat and eat in or take them home. Pick up a bottle of wine and dessert at the same time and you're rolling. Daily 7.30am–10pm. Tram #81 or #82.

La Maison du Miel rue du Midi 121 (Lower Town) ☏02 512 32 50. As the name suggests, this tiny family-run shop is all about honey, and has been trading from these premises since the late nineteenth century. Stacked high with jar upon jar of the sticky stuff and its by-products, from soap and candles to sweets and face creams plus a number of curious honey pots and receptacles. Also has a branch at rue du Marché aux Herbes 11. Mon–Sat 9.30am–6pm. Prémétro Anneessens.

Menus Propos rue Ernest Solvay 22, Ixelles ☏02 502 79 29. A deli with a difference, owned by Valerie Janssens who recently gave up making hats and re-opened her shop to sell all kinds of gastronomic delights. Each Friday evening she hosts a tasting session giving different culinary ideas around the themes of mushrooms, cheeses, or special occasions. Tues–Sat 11am–6.30pm, Fri 11am–8.30pm. Métro Porte de Namur.

La Miche de Pain ave Brugmann 2A, Ixelles ☏02 345 87 60. Brussels *boulangerie* at its best – breads of varying shapes and sizes to cater for all tastes, mouthwatering cakes and pastries – all hidden away in this unassuming shop on the border between St Gilles and Ixelles. Mon–Fri 7am–7.30pm, Sat 7am–7pm, Sun 7am–3pm. Tram #91 and #92.

Le Palais des Thés place de la Vieille Halles aux Blés (Lower Town) ☏02 502 50 95. A shop dedicated to the good ol' cuppa tea, but not your average English brew, rather the whole world of teas – smell them, read about them, taste them. Pots, cups, strainers and all other tea paraphernalia on sale too. Daily 11am–6.30pm. Prémétro Bourse.

Lace

Manufacture Belge de Dentelle Galerie de la Reine 6–8, in the Galeries St-Hubert, near the Grand-Place ☏02 511 44 77. The city's largest lace merchant, in business since 1810. Sells a wide variety of modern and antique lace at fairly reasonable prices. The service is helpfully old fashioned. Mon–Sat 9.30am–6pm, Sun 10am–4pm. Métro Gare Centrale.

Louise Verschueren rue Watteeu 16 (Upper Town) ☏02 511 04 44. Four generations of lace-making in the Verschueren family and the shop aims to keep the spirit of that long standing tradition alive. No cheap imitations here – they guarantee craftsmanship and authenticity and contribute to the survival of this most traditional of Belgian industries. Daily 9am–6pm. Métro Louise.

Markets

Among the city's plethora of **open-air markets**, the Grand-Place's **flower and plant market** wins the prize for the most picturesque (March–Oct

Lace

Renowned for the fineness of its thread and beautiful motifs, **Belgian lace** is famous the world over. **Flanders lace**, as it was formerly known, was once worn in the courts of Brussels, Paris, Madrid and London – Queen Elizabeth I of England is said to have had no fewer than three thousand lace dresses – and across Europe the ruffs of the royal courtiers were made in Flanders and Brussels too. Indeed, the Bruxellois helped their own commercial cause by first using starch to keep the ruffs stiff. Lace reached the peak of its popularity in the late nineteenth century, when an estimated ten thousand women and girls worked as lacemakers in the capital, though by then much of it was produced by machine. The industry collapsed after World War I when lace, a symbol of an old and discredited order, suddenly had no place in the wardrobe of most women. An excellent sample of old lace, both hand- and machine-made, is displayed at Brussels' Musée du Costume et de la Dentelle (see p.53), but if you're keen to buy, be warned that most of the lace on sale in the capital today is actually made in China. Furthermore, the authentic handmade stuff can be very pricey, particularly in the much-hyped lace shops in and around the Grand-Place. Your best bet is to head for the flea market at place du Jeu de Balle, in the Marolles district (see p.70), where you can usually pick up far nicer pieces for much less money or try the (more expensive) lace shops listed on p.221.

Tues–Sun 8am–6pm). The swankiest **antiques and collectibles** market is held at the **place du Grand Sablon** (Sat 9am–6pm, Sun 9am–2pm), but the real bargains (if there are any left in the city) can be found at the flea market on the **place du Jeu de Balle** in the Marolles quarter. It's held every morning from 7am to 2pm, but it's at its biggest – and most expensive – at weekends, where the eccentric muddle of colonial spoils, quirky odds and ends and domestic and ecclesiastical bric-a-brac give the flavour of a century's bourgeois fads and fashions. The largest and most colourful **food** market is held every Sunday (6am–1pm) at **Gare du Midi**, a bazaar-like affair, with traders crammed under the railway bridge and spilling out into the surrounding streets. Stands sell pitta, olives, North African raï tapes, spices, herbs and pulses, among vegetables and cheap clothes. There's also a picturesque food market at **place du Châtelain** every Wednesday (2–7pm), jam-packed with tiny stalls selling fresh vegetables, cheeses, cakes and pastries, as well as plants and flowers, and homemade wines.

Music

Arlequin rue de L'Athenée 7 & 8, Ixelles ☎02 514 54 28. Small, beat-up secondhand record and CD shop offering decent collections of almost every type of music you can imagine and then some. The vinyl is in good shape – with some sealed copies around – and the service amiable. The store at no. 8 sells classical and jazz, while no. 7 offers everything else. Mon–Sat 10.30am–6.30pm. Métro Porte de Namur.

Le Bonheur rue Antoine Dansaert 196 (Lower Town) ☎02 511 64 14. At the top end of rue Dansaert, this record shop-cum-épicerie offers a great range including lounge, electro and funk as well as some tasty treats. Mon–Sat 11am–7pm, Sun 1.30–7pm. Métro Ste Catherine.

La Boîte à Musique Coudenberg 74 (Upper Town) ☎02 513 09 65. Supplier to the Belgian court, owner Bertrand de Wauters is a veritable encyclopaedia of classical music. Not only can he describe differing interpretations of classical works, he can also advise you on the quality of the recordings. Highly recommended. Mon–Sat 9am–6.30pm. Métro Gare Centrale.

Caroline Music Passage St-Honoré 20, off rue du Marché aux Poulets (Lower Town) ☎02 217 07 31. One of the best shops in the city for general rock and new releases.

Also sells concert tickets for many of the city's venues. Mon 10am–6pm, Tue–Sat 10.30am–6.30pm. Métro De Brouckère.

Fnac City 2, rue Neuve 123 (Lower Town) ☎02 275 11 11. A large, mainstream store with a fairly wide selection of French and English CDs, along with DVDs, books, newspapers and CD players. It's also the place to come to buy tickets for mainstream gigs and concerts. Mon–Thurs & Sat 10am–7pm, Fri 10am–8pm. Métro Rogier.

Music Man rue Plattesteen 6 (near Grand-Place) ☎02 502 09 72. If you've come to Belgium to explore the techno scene, this is where to find your vinyl. They also stock lots of drum 'n' bass, speed-garage, and house. Mon–Sat 11am–6.30pm. Prémétro Bourse.

Music Mania rue de la Fourche 4 (Lower Town)

☎02 217 53 69. The place to come for the latest release or that elusive vinyl or CD. This independent music store is frequented by rappers, straight-edge skaters and house or drum 'n' bass DJs alike, and sells tickets before general sale to large and smaller gigs and parties. It's also a good source for flyers. Mon–Sat 11am–6pm. Métro De Brouckère.

Toys and games

Serneels ave Louise 69 ☎02 538 30 66, ⓦ www.serneels.be. A beautiful and quite traditional toy shop, with lots of great if pricey stuff for kids – cuddly toys, wooden toys, puppets, puzzles and more. A lovely shop, worth visiting just to look at. Mon–Sat 9.30am–6.30pm.

Sports

Cycling and football are the nation's top sports, though Belgians also have an ongoing love affair with motorsports, be it motorcross (in which the country has had a number of successes on the international scene), hill climbing or amateur rallying.

Perhaps the most common sports in Brussels itself, however, are the extremely strenuous "baby-foot" (table football), as well as the many versions of bar billiards. Pétanque is also making a comeback with the young and sunny days can be whiled away with your set of boules on the Vieux Marché aux Grains or les étangs d'Ixelles. More surreally, there's the traditional sport of tir à l'arc found in big parks like the Parc Josaphat, in which contestants shoot down feathers from the top of a very tall pole with a bow and arrow.

Athletics

Two major events dominate the city's athletics calendar. The Ivo van Damme Memorial IAHF Grand Prix is one of the International Athletic Federation meetings that's held yearly (last fortnight in August) in the Stade Roi Baudouin and attracts many of the stars of the sport. It's named after the Belgian 800m silver-medallist of the 1976 Olympics in Montréal. Call ☏02 479 36 54 for tickets and details.

There's also the popular Brussels 20km Race, which takes place the last weekend in May, and usually attracts a field of twenty thousand runners and more than fifty thousand spectators. Although it consists of mostly serious runners, there are lots of festivities along the way and some people semi-walk it. The course takes participants halfway round the city near the EU Quarter, the Palais Royale, avenue Louise, the Bois de la Cambre and through the tunnels of the Brussels inner ring road. It starts and finishes at the Esplanade du Cinquantenaire, and participants are charged €12 for the privilege of running their socks off for three hours. Call ☏02 511 90 00 for details.

Cycling

Cycling is immensely popular in Belgium, both as a sport and as a hobby with the sheer flatness of much of the country being to cycling's advantage. Brussels plays host to many national cycling meets, having also been a stop-off point for the Tour de France. In honour of the great Belgian cyclist, the Eddy Merckx Grand Prix, held on the last Sunday of August, is a timed event attracting top

Just five cyclists have achieved the extraordinary distinction of winning the Tour de France five times: Jacques Anquetil, Bernard Hinault, Miguel Indurain, Lance Armstrong and – arguably the best of the lot – Belgium's Eddy Merckx.

In his very first Tour, in 1969, Eddy finished eighteen minutes in front of the runner-up (this in a race in which five minutes is a big gap), destroying the field in a style that was to earn him the nickname "The Cannibal". As strong on mountain climbs as in races against the clock (he set a world record for the greatest distance covered in an hour), and as able in one-day events as in the huge multi-stage tours, Merckx amassed a tally of titles that no rider is ever likely to equal: five victories in the Giro d'Italia (Tour of Italy); three-times winner of the Paris–Nice race; three-times World Road Champion; five-times winner of the Liège–Bastogne–Liège race; three-times winner of the Paris–Roubaix (the so-called "Hell of the North"); seven-times winner of the Milan–San Remo . . . the list goes on. In the 1974 season he managed to win the tours of Italy and France, then the World Championship, a Grand Slam that only Stephen Roche has matched. Indeed, so complete was his dominance that a disconsolate rival once observed: "If Merckx has decided he wants to win today, then he will."

Merckx retired in 1978, having totalled 525 victories, and has since divided his time between punditry, running his own bike factory (ⓦ www.eddymerckx.be), and nurturing the talent of his son Axel, who is now following hot in his father's wheeltracks.

⑬

SPORTS | Football

professionals. Other cycling highlights in Brussels are the **European Car-Free Day** (September 22), when cyclists take over the entire city centre, the **May 1 Dring Dring bike festival** in the Cinquantenaire park and summer Sundays in the **Bois de la Cambre**, when Provélo (see below) offer bike rental and the city is out cycling, jogging and rollerblading around the park.

For **bike rental**, go to Provélo at rue de Londres 15 (Mon–Fri 10am–6pm, Sat 1–7pm and open Sun in July and Aug; ☏ 02 217 01 58, ⓦ www.provelo .org; métro Trône). English is spoken and guided bike tours of Brussels and the outskirts in English are possible – themes include Art Nouveau Brussels and Comic Strips and Cafés. Bike hire itself costs from €3 for an hour to €60 for a week. Alternatively, check out the Train-plus-Vélo schemes offered at most railway stations – a bike is thrown in with the price of a train ticket to fifteen destinations in Belgium (☏ 02 555 25 25 for details). Those who already have their own bike can take it on the train for €4.30 per single journey. You can also contact the Fédération Belge du Cyclotourisme, who organize some six hundred cycle rides every year throughout Belgium (ave du Limbourg 34 ☏ 02 521 86 40, ⓦ www.cyclo.be).

Football

Brussels' standing in European **football** went down several notches following the 1985 Heysel disaster. Not only was the city's reputation in tatters, but Heysel was banned from staging European matches. Even the home club who played in the stadium complex, Racing Jet Brussels, moved out to Wavre, 30km away. However, after being rebuilt and renamed the Stade Roi Baudouin, the new ground was used for several matches in the 2000 European Championship. Despite occasional outbreaks of violence, the championship – hosted jointly by Belgium and Holland – helped restore the country's place as an international football host.

The Heysel disaster is synonymous with football violence. The stadium, built in 1930 in the Parc des Expositions in northwest Brussels, was the site for the 1985 European Cup Final between Liverpool FC and Juventus. Liverpool fans had started drinking early in the day, and were probably joined by neo-Nazi elements in the stands, as seems manifest from the pamphlets later found near the seats. Local policing was disorganized and parts of the stadium were in need of renovation. Shortly before kick-off, a group of Liverpool fans charged through the supposedly neutral block Z and 39 supporters (mainly Italian) were crushed to death when the sector wall collapsed. The match was played out to avoid further pandemonium, resulting in a win for Juventus. English clubs were banned from Europe for five years.

The stadium obviously had to be refurbished, and after various arguments, the Belgian FA agreed to foot the bill. The Stade du Roi Baudouin was built in its place, although some of the original Heysel infrastructure remains. The stadium, with a capacity of fifty thousand, all seated, boasts its own new métro station at the end of the 1A line. The stadium ticket office, marked Kartenverkoop/Vente Tickets, is along avenue du Marathon by Tribune no. 1 and sells tickets in four different colour-coded price brackets. Call ☏ 02 477 12 11 for ticket details.

In terms of **league football**, Brussels has been dominated by one club – **Anderlecht**. Most of the city's other clubs have either folded, migrated or merged to help form the city's poor relation, **FC Brussels** (formerly Racing White Daring Molenbeek, or RWDM). Anderlecht's facilities and resources put other Belgian clubs in the shade, but this difference is all the more marked in Brussels, as FC Brussels attracts only a few thousand fans. A third city club, **Union Saint-Gilloise**, was a significant Brussels club until its relegation in 1973. It has an identifiable neighbourhood feel and its sardonic Bruxellois humour can still be heard in the club bar. In 2004 it managed to get back into division two, giving its few fans, who still shuffle up religiously to the rue du Stade, a ray of hope.

Royal Sporting Club Anderlecht

Stade Constant Vanden Stock, ave Théo Verbeeck 2 ☏ **02 529 40 67,** ⓦ **www.rsca.be. Métro St-Guidon.** Founded in 1908, Anderlecht won its first title only in 1947. Two years afterwards, an England ex-goalie by the name of Bill Gormlie was appointed first team coach, ushering in a decade of seven titles that established Anderlecht as the country's biggest club.

In the early 1960s Real Madrid, CDNA Sofia and Bologna were all beaten by Anderlecht, while at home it won five titles in a row. In 1964, the Belgian team that beat Holland 1–0 was composed entirely of Anderlecht players. All of Anderlecht's three European successes came during the late 1970s and early 1980s, the club's golden period. Its greatest triumph was its Cup Winners' Cup victory in 1976, with a 4–2 victory over West Ham in the final. Other successes included victory over Liverpool in the European Super Cup in 1978 and an impressive win over Benfica in the UEFA Cup Final in 1983.

After that, the money needed to convert the stadium meant that there was less to spend on players. The Mauves (because of their strip) have thus under-achieved in Europe for most of the 1990s and into the next century – the only highlight being an appearance in the 1990 Cup Winners' Cup Final, which it went on to lose to Sampdoria. Various corruption sagas have also haunted the club. In 1983 the club president Vanden Stock admitted that he had paid a Spanish referee a million francs (€25,000) after a UEFA semi-final with Nottingham Forest.

The only comfort remaining to fans is that the club now has a classy stadium with over 26,000 seats – it's where the Belgian team practised and played during the Heysel refurbishment.

FC Brussels (former RWD Molenbeek)

Stade Edmond Machtens, rue Charles Malis 61 ☎02 411 69 86, ⓦwww.fcmbs.be. Métro Beekkant. FC Brussels started life as RWDM, which itself was formed by the merging of two Brussels football clubs, Daring and Racing White, in 1973. Only two years later, a goal from international Jacques Teugels against Anderlecht won the club its first and only title. Key player Johan Boskamp became a local hero – until, that is, he moved to – you guessed it – Anderlecht. Though it was unable to keep its title, the team remained in the top six, and in 1977 it was only one goal away from a UEFA Cup Final against Juventus. The club has done little since, but in 2004 it was rebranded, adopting its present name, FC Brussels.

To get there, go to Métro Beekkant, then take bus #85 or a ten-minute walk down rue Jules Vieujant, followed by a left down rue Osseghem.

Union Saint-Gilloise

Stade Joseph Marien, chaussée de Bruxelles 223 ☎02 344 16 56, ⓦwww.rusg.be. Prémétro Horta. A more romantic ground would be difficult to imagine. The Stade Joseph Marien, named after a former club president, is bordered by the forest of Parc Duden on one side and by a wonderful old club bar on the other. People banked up the hillside in their thousands to see Union in its golden prewar days, when it was the biggest club in Belgium. The last decent Union side, that of the late 1950s and early 1960s, made occasional forays into the Fairs' Cup, even beating Roma and Olympique Marseille.

Union was too proud to agree to any of the mergers that swallowed up the lesser Brussels clubs in the 1970s. The result was that the club celebrated its centenary in 1997 by being relegated to the third division, though a return to division two in 2004 means that there's hope left for this very local side.

To get there, take the tram to Horta and then tram #18, getting off at Van Haelen. From there the stadium is a five-minute walk up rue des Glands.

Go-karting

Given the Belgians' infatuation with motorsports, it comes as no surprise that **go-karting** is a popular pastime. There's a track at City Kart, square des Grées du Loû 5A, in Forest (€12 per hour; ☎02 332 36 96, ⓦwww.citykart .com), or you can head for the Brussels Formula One indoor carting, petite rue de Cerf 45 in Anderlecht (€26 per 30min; ☎02 332 37 37, ⓦwww .brusselsformula1.be).

Golf

Most **golf** courses are outside Brussels and the Fédération Royale Belge de Golf, Chausée de la Hulpe 110 (☎02 672 23 89, ⓦwww.golfbelgium.be) can provide information on proper, full-size golf courses in Belgium. The best 18-hole course in Brussels itself is the Royal Amicale Anderlecht Golf Club, rue Scholle 1 (☎02 521 16 87), which has training and driving ranges and is well-laid-out in wooded surroundings with lakes. The Brabantse Golf at Steenwagenstraat 11, Melsbroek (☎02 751 82 05), is near the airport and is a pleasant and not too challenging full practice course, just 5km long. The Golf de l'Empereur near Waterloo (☎067 77 15 71) is both challenging and beautiful, with the clubhouse in an old farmhouse. It has both nine- and eighteen-hole courses.

Skating

Ice-skaters will be delighted at the whimsical faerie-atmosphere surrounding the rink on place Ste-Catherine in December and January. Other public rinks include the Patinoire de Forest, avenue du Globe 36 (☏02 345 16 11), which is open all year round, and Poséidon, avenue des Vaillants 4 (☏02 762 16 33). **Skateboarders** meet at various spots around the city including Mont des Arts near Gare Centrale and rue des Ursulines, near the old Gare de la Chapelle, where a skate park is being constructed – for information see ⓦwww.brusk.be. **Rollerbladers** are in seventh heaven on Fridays between June and September when the roller parade begins (ⓦwww.belgiumrollers.com). Take off is from the Palais de Justice and roads are closed to give the rollers right of way. On a smaller scale there is also rollerblading in the Bois de la Cambre on Sundays, when the roads are closed to traffic.

Sports centres and gyms

Brussels offers a good choice of **sports centres** and **gyms**. Winner's, at rue Bonneel 13 (☏02 280 02 70), has an inside climbing wall, as well as squash courts and a gym. The Golden Club at place du Châtelain 33 (Mon–Fri noon–10pm, Sat & Sun 10am–4pm; ☏02 538 19 06) is a beefcake haven/heaven since the rise in popularity of that great Belgian export Jean-Claude van Damme, who started off here. It has two thousand square metres of muscle-building machines, plus saunas and sunbeds, and runs aerobics, step and fitness classes, as well as popular martial arts classes. The American Gym at boulevard Général Jacques 144 (Mon–Fri 10am–10pm, Sat 10am–3pm, Sun 10am–2pm; ☏02 640 59 92) has similar facilities. The boxing and kick-boxing on offer here are top notch, given the gym's several champions in both categories, and the kung-fu classes are well known across the city. For more martial action, contact the Centre de la Culture Japonaise, rue des Augustines 44 (☏02 426 50 00), which offers English-speaking classes in judo and karate, among others.

Sport City at Woluwe St Pierre, at avenue Salomé 2 (☏02 773 18 20), has a full range of sporting facilities including a multi-sports hall and squash and tennis courts (the latter are open till 11pm). The Complexe Sportif du Palais du Midi at rue Rogier van der Weyden 3–9 (☏02 279 59 56) is a bit more centrally located and has a sports hall which it rents out to teams including the first-division Brussels basketball team.

There's **skiing** and **snowboarding** available on the artificial slopes of the Parc de Neerpede's Yeti Ski and Snowboard venue, dreve Olympique 11 (☏02 520 77 57, ⓦwww.yetiski.be). Lessons are available, and you can rent all the equipment you need; note that wearing gloves is obligatory.

Swimming pools

The city has a number of **swimming pools** in local sports centres, including an Olympic-sized one at Sport City in Woluwe St Pierre (Mon–Thurs 8am–7pm, Fri 8am–8pm, Sat 8am–7pm; ☏02 773 18 20). The St Gilles pool at rue de la Perche 38 (Mon, Tues, Thurs & Fri 8am–7pm, Wed 2–7pm and Sat 9am–6pm) also has a **Turkish steam room** available for €18 a session (☏02 539 06 15), while Poséidon, avenue des Vaillants 2, has a **sauna** and a separate **children's pool**, but can get crowded at weekends. Alternatively, both Aqualibi and the

Océade water park (see "Kids' Brussels") are great places to go for water slides, wave-making machines and other aquatic havoc.

Tenpin bowling

The city has a number of **bowling alleys**, the biggest, and most centrally located, being Crosly Super Bowling at boulevard de l'Empereur 36 (Mon–Sat 2pm–1am, Sun 2pm–midnight; ℡02 512 08 74). It has twenty lanes and a late bar.

14

Kids' Brussels

I nevitably, many of the main monuments and museums in Brussels hold little of interest for all but the most studious of children, but worry not – the city can be very child-friendly. In the centre, the comic strips of the **Centre Belge de la Bande Dessiné** and the puppets of the **Théâtre de Toone** are the main attractions for younger and older children alike. Elsewhere, the **Musée des Sciences Naturelles** is host to an impressive display of dinosaur skeletons and is ideal for pre-teens, whereas the **Musée du Jouet**, with its huge collection of toys throughout the ages, seems to be a hit with everybody regardless of age.

Out of town, Heysel sometimes gives the impression it was specifically designed for the under-12s, and is home to both **Mini-Europe** and **Océade**, as well as the excellent **Planétarium**, which holds regular exhibitions, and the landmark **Atomium** (due to reopen early 2005 following major renovations; see p.127). Further afield, the **Walibi** amusement park and attached **Aqualibi** water park (see p.231) offer enough roller-coasters, amusement rides and water slides to make a day of it.

Most of the city's **parks** have playgrounds – the most popular one is at the lovely Bois de la Cambre. The city also has a summer funfair – **Foire du Midi** – which is held near the Gare du Midi from mid-July to mid-August. Here you'll find the usual riot of candy floss, amusement arcades and rides, including a large Ferris wheel.

Full listings of children's exhibitions, shows and fairs can be found in the "Jeunes Publics" section of Wednesday's *Le Soir* supplement.

Activities

City Kart square des Grées du Loû 59 ⊕02 332 36 96, ⊛www.citykart.com. Kids will have a great time tearing around the track at these children-only sessions under adult supervision; lessons are available on Wednesdays. Karts can reach speeds of up to 60kph, so you'd better make sure your nerves are up to it first. Reservations not necessary. Children's sessions (ages 4–16) are on Sat & Sun 9.30am–2pm, and cost €15 per 15min plus €3 for an obligatory membership card valid for a year. Tram #52.

Océade Brupark, blvd du Centenaire 20

⊕02 478 43 20. Year-round water park with a number of attractions including high-speed slides, wavepools, whirlpools, solariums and saunas. Four hours of splashing costs €13.80 for adults and €11.20 for children under 1.30m; children under 1.15m go free. Call for times. A special combination ticket for Mini-Europe (see p.231), Océade and the Atomium (see p.127) costs €18.40 for adults and €15.90 for children; it's available from all three venues. Métro Heysel.

The Picky Club rue de Neerpede 805–807, Anderlecht ⊕02 522 20 84, ⊛www.pickyclub.be.

This is a clever solution for parents who want a day to themselves in the city, laying on a number of wildly divergent activities for children aged 2–10. There are inflatable castles, a swimming pool, a go-kart track and even a rock-climbing wall, and the helpful staff can also introduce kids to model building, archery and mini-golf. The Picky Club can also organize special theme days for birthdays, and has its very own hotel open at weekends. Sessions take place on Sat & Sun 9.30am–7pm and school holidays. Prices vary but approximately €4 for 1hr, €14 half-day, €28 for a full day including meal. Bus #47.

Walibi & Aqualibi 20km from Brussels on autoroute E411 ☎010 42 15 00, ⓦwww.walibi.be. Recently-overhauled theme park sporting twenty new attractions – thrill seekers will especially like the Dalton Terror tower, which takes you up to a height of 77m before letting you drop at speeds reaching up to 110kph. The attached water park, Aqualibi, has two 140-metre-long water slides amongst the usual water park offerings. Call for times. Costs €28.50 for adults and €24.50 for children age 3–11; free for under-3s. Can be reached by train via Leuven or Ottignies – the station (Walibi-Bierges) is just 150m from the park entrance.

Museums and sights

Centre Belge de la Bande Dessinée rue des Sables 20 ☎02 219 19 80, ⓦwww .comicscenter.net. As popular with adults as it is with children, the comic museum documents the illustrious history of the Belgian comic book with numerous displays ranging from Tintin and the Smurfs to comic-book production. There's a comprehensive bookshop attached, as well as a restaurant and brasserie. Open Tues–Sun 10am–6pm. Adults €6.20, under-12s €2.50. Métro Botanique or Rogier.
Mini-Europe blvd du Centenaire 20 ☎02 478 05 50, ⓦwww.minieurope.com. Mini-Europe is pure tack, but children love it. All the historic European sights are reproduced in miniature – there are three hundred in all – and you can even re-enact the eruption of Vesuvius and the fall of the Berlin wall. Firework displays are held regularly throughout July and August. Open daily 9.30am–6pm, but check for seasonal variations. Adults €11.80, under-12s €8.80, children under 1.20m free. A special combination ticket for Mini-Europe, Océade (see p.230) and the Atomium (see p.127) costs €18.40 for adults, and €15.90 for under-12s; it's available from all three venues. Métro Heysel.
Musée des Enfants rue du Bourgmestre 15 ☎02 640 01 07, ⓦwww.museedesenfants.be. Like Scientastic (see p.232), this museum's strong point is that it's interactive, with lots of buttons to press and knobs to turn. It's aimed mostly at under-12s. As well as looking at the many exhibits, children can paint, engage in basic woodwork or even participate in a play. Open Wed, Sat & Sun 2.30–5pm; closed Aug. Adults and children €6.70. Bus #71; tram #90, #23.

▽ Musée des Enfants

Other sights and museums that may be of particular interest to – but are not specifically geared up for – children include the Atomium p.127; Autoworld p.119; and the Musée des Instruments de Musique p.78.

Musée du Jouet rue de l'Association 24 ☏ 02
219 61 68, ⓦ www.museedujouet.be.
Three floors of toys, ancient and modern,
stacked up in every corner and filling dusty
cabinets to overflowing. There's virtually no
labelling, and the attitude of the museum is
deliberately inclusive, encouraging kids to
hurtle around from one battered object to
the next. Kids and their parents will enjoy
the jumbled-up nature of the collection, and
even if you don't have children, it's a chance
to see the chipped and faded interior of one
of these large central Brussels nineteenth-
century town houses. Most suitable for 5- to
12-year-olds. Daily 10am–noon and 2–6pm.
Adults €4.50, children €3.50. Métro Botanique or Madou.

Musée des Sciences Naturelles rue Vautier 29
☏ 02 627 42 38, ⓦ www.sciencesnaturelles.be.
The centrepiece of this collection is the 35-
metre-high Iguanadon skeletons, which were
found in southern Belgium in 1878, when
prospectors were digging for gold. They
date back some 65 million years. If Jurassic
monsters aren't your thing, there are four
more floors covering mammals (stuffed lions,
tigers and bears), sea creatures (including
a gigantic whale skeleton), and sections
on how people live in the Arctic. They also
have entertaining temporary exhibitions.
Open Tues–Fri 9.30am–4.45pm, Sat & Sun
10am–6pm. Adults €4, children aged 6–17
€3, under-6s free. Métro Trône.

National Planetarium ave de Bouchout 10 ☏ 02
474 70 50, ⓦ www.planetarium.be. A great
place for children to take time out and look
skyward. Apart from the regular shows such
as a "voyage through the cosmos" and "the
movement of the stars", there are a number
of permanent exhibits on the ground floor
including displays on rockets, satellites and
astronomical instruments. Temporary exhibitions are held in the entrance hall. Mon–Fri
& Sun 9am–4.30pm. Adults €4, children
€3. Métro Heysel.

Scientastic Level –1, Prémétro Bourse station
☏ 02 732 13 36, ⓦ www.scientastic.be. Both
younger and older children seem to love
the hands-on nature of this small science
museum, which has over seventy interactive
exhibits including visual illusions such as
an impossible box, and sensory games like
smelling your way out of a maze, or changing your voice and fusing your image with
that of a friend. Weekends and school holidays 2–5.30pm. Admissions costs €6 for
adults, or €4.30 if you're under 26 or over
65. Prémétro Bourse.

△ Théâtre de Toone

Parks

Bois de la Cambre At the intersection of ave Louise and blvd de la Cambre. The capital's largest and most popular inner-city park, including lakes and woods. There's plenty of room for the kids to go crazy, and when they get bored of that, you can take them to the Halle du Bois – a giant playground in the middle of the park equipped with a bouncy castle and toboggan run. It's open on school holidays and weekends 2–6pm and only costs €2.50 per child. Tram #93, #94.

> For a full overview of the city's parks and gardens, see ⓦwww.ibgebim.be

Theatre

Théâtre de Toone impasse de Schuddeveld 6, off petite rue des Bouchers ☎02 511 71 37, ⓦwww.toone.be. World-famous puppet theatre housed in a seventeenth-century building a few steps from the Grand-Place. Performances are in several languages and range from *The Three Musketeers* and *the Hunchback of Notre Dame* to *Faust* and *Hamlet*. There's also a puppet museum which can be visited free of charge during the intermission. Suitable for children, who love the puppets, and adults, who appreciate the sly references to recent news, politicians and other salacious titbits.

Call or check website for times and shows; reservations advised. Adults €10, children €7. Métro Gare Centrale.

Gay and lesbian
Brussels

russels often seems to lag behind the times when it comes to **gay politics** – the city's first gay and lesbian pride event, for example, wasn't held until 1996. Nevertheless, though Brussels could hardly be described as a gay capital like Amsterdam, the **gay scene** is itself reasonably well developed, with a decent selection of gay bars, clubs and restaurants. The area just south of the Bourse remains the centre of the action, particularly in the triangle between rue des Pierres, rue du Marché au Charbon, and rue St-Géry, which is the closest the capital has to a designated **gay quarter**, though even here few of the bars are specifically gay as such. The **lesbian scene**, on the other hand, continues to remain cloistered. A few venues welcome both gays and lesbians equally, but there are very few lesbian-only nightspots.

The city's gay and lesbian scene changes fast and the first port of call for anyone visiting Brussels should be the **listings** provided by the gay and lesbian associations mentioned below.

Gay and lesbian associations

Among the city's many **gay associations**, Infor Homo (℡02 733 10 24, Ⓦwww.infor-homo.be) and the student equivalent Cercle Homosexuel Etudi-ant (℡02 650 47 27) organize regular nights out and gay activities, while the EGG (Ⓦwww.geocities.com/eggbrussels), the main English-speaking gay group in Brussels, operates an informative website with events and listings and organizes a couple of parties a month on Sunday afternoons. There's also BGS (Brussels Gay Sports; Ⓦwww.bgs.org), which arranges events and tournaments, and Egalité (Ⓦwww.egalite.be), a political association that lobbies for equal rights for gays and lesbians. The Rainbow House, at rue Marché au Charbon 42 (℡02 503 59 90), is a good initial port of call for gays and lesbians and hosts regular events, but the main provider of information is Tels Quels (see "Information Services" below), which caters for both gays and lesbians and coordinates a number of leading events, notably the Gay and Lesbian Film Festival held every January at Le Botanique (Ⓦwww.fglb.org). For something a little unusual, there are Sunday "Gay & friendly tea dances" at *You* (see p. 207) from 4pm to 11pm. As regards **lesbian associations**, there are actually more of them than lesbian venues, the most popular being the excellent and very reliable Attirent d'Elles (T 02 512 45 87, W www.attirentdelles.org).

Inevitably, many of the city's gay associations focus on **HIV and AIDS**, supporting its victims and providing sexual health education. The most high-profile organizations are Aide Info Sida (T 02 514 29 65, W www.aideinfosida .be) and Act Up (T 02 512 02 02), which also aims to inform government policy. Act Together, at rue d'Artois 5 (T 02 512 05 05), provides support for the families of AIDS sufferers, and has an English-speaking helpline.

The **age of consent** for gay men and women is 16.

Tels Quels rue Marché au Charbon 81 T **02 512 45 87,** W **www.telsquels.be.** Gay and lesbian meeting place just round the corner from *Chez Maman* (see below). Although there's a small café, it's best known for its documentation centre, which has information on gay and lesbian rights and forthcoming events. It also hosts occasional art exhibitions and group discussions. Its monthly French-language publication includes political reports and a full gay and lesbian listings section for bars, clubs and restaurants, as well as hairdressers, saunas and sex shops. Sun–Tues & Thurs 5pm–2am, Wed 2pm–2am, Fri & Sat 5pm–4am. Métro Bourse.

Gay restaurants

Le Comptoir place de la Vieille Halle-aux-Blés 24 T **02 514 05 00.** Well-known gay restaurant and bar, just off rue du Chêne, popular with a chic and stylish crowd, who are attracted by the excellent food and candlelit ambience. Tasty nouvelle cuisine in the upstairs restaurant and a lively dance floor below, featuring dance, house and techno. Riotous transvestite shows every Sunday. Daily 7pm–midnight. Métro Bourse.

El Papagayo place Rouppe 6 T **02 514 50 83.** Busy gay restaurant, which gets packed out at weekends when you'll have to wait for a table. The decor is a flush of colour, there's a small dancefloor (salsa music nightly) and the Latin American food is spicy and inexpensive. A healthy blend of people and styles ensures the place is never dull. Mon–Thurs & Sun 4pm–2am, Fri & Sat 6pm–2am. Métro Anneessens.

H2O rue du Marché au Charbon 27 T **02 512 38 43.** A fashionable gay restaurant, close to the Bourse and popular with late-twenty-something couples, who come to sample the simple but tasty world cuisine. Some may find the fantasy-theme decor – Tolkien-style sculptures and pictures, and aquamarine-coloured walls – to their liking, others not. The service is friendly (gay or straight) and the food well priced. Reservations are not always necessary. Daily 7pm–midnight. Métro Bourse.

Gay bars and clubs

Le Belgica rue du Marché au Charbon 32 W **www.lebelgica.be.** A respected fixture of the Brussels gay scene, *Le Belgica* is arguably the capital's most popular gay bar and pick-up joint. Admittedly it's a tad rundown, with formica tables and dilapidated chairs that have seen better days, but if you're out for a lively, friendly atmosphere, you could hardly do better. Come at the weekend when the place is heaving – all are welcome, whether male, female, gay or straight – and be sure to sample the house speciality, lemon-vodka "Belgica" shots. Thurs–Sat 10pm–3am. Métro Bourse.

Chez Maman rue des Grands Carmes 7. This tiny bar has achieved an almost cult-like status in Brussels – mainly because of the supremely flamboyant proprietor, "Maman", and his hugely popular half-hour transvestite shows. People flock from all corners of the city to see him strut up and down the bar – which serves as an impromptu stage – singing his heart out, Marlene Dietrich-style. Not for those who can't deal with crowds. Fri & Sat midnight till dawn. Métro Bourse.

La Démence The Fuse, rue Blaes 208 ☏ 02 538 99 31, Ⓦ www.lademence.com. The city's most popular gay club, held on two floors in *The Fuse* (see p.207) and playing cutting edge techno. The crowd is a bit difficult to pigeonhole – expect to find a hybrid mix of muscle men, transsexuals, the chic and fashionable, and out-and-out ravers. Back rooms available. Entrance €18. Sun 11pm–7am only. Métro Porte de Hal.

Le Duquesnoy rue Duquesnoy 12. Known simply as *Le Duq* to its regulars, this bar-cum-club is open every night and on Sunday afternoons from 3pm, when there's a themed party. Dress code is leather, rubber, latex, uniform or naked – no suits or ties. Mon–Thurs 9pm–3am, Fri & Sat 9pm–5am, Sun 3pm–3am. Free

except Sundays, when it's €5. Métro Bourse.

L'Homo Erectus rue des Pierres 57 ☏ 02 514 74 93. It's a tight squeeze in this brazenly named gay bar, but the atmosphere is cosy and personal and there's an intimate dance-floor, complete with obligatory disco balls. Music ranges from house to disco. Daily 11am–late. Métro Bourse.

L'Incognito rue des Pierres 36. A popular gay bar, with a lively atmosphere, camp music – Madonna, Celine Dion, disco, and French pop – and a photo gallery of beefy studs and pert behinds lining the walls. It's well situated, not far from the Grand-Place, but can be a bit cliquey. Daily 11pm–late. Métro Bourse.

Why Not rue des Riches Claires 7 ☏ 02 512 63 43. Brussels nightclub that's open every night of the week, the three-level *Why Not* is absolutely heaving on the weekends with mostly young men dancing to house and dance tracks. Daily 11pm–6am, free admission. Métro Bourse.

Lesbian bars and clubs

Biche Party Le Cercle, rue Ste-Anne 20–22 Ⓦ www.mega-top-biches.org. Lesbian parties organized by the mega top *biches*. Electro, pop, rock and world music. Entry costs €7; check the website for dates and times. Métro Louise.

Girly Mondays Les Salons de l'Atalaïde, chaussée de Charleroi 89 Ⓦ www.moonday.org. Great setting in the first-floor bar of the *Salons de l'Atalaïde* for this regular lesbian night. Open-air terrace too. DJ and girly performances throughout the evening. Mondays 8pm–2am; no entry charge. Métro Louise.

Next Party La Raffinerie, rue de Manchester 21 Ⓦ www.next-party.be. Self-proclaimed "queer

party for lesbians and gays". A little way out of town, but a free party bus will take you to (and from) the venue every half-hour from rue du Lombard 11 (the White Night shop). First bus at 11pm, last bus 5am. Every second Saturday of the month.

Soixante rue du Marché au Charbon 60 ☏ 0477 704 156. Not an exclusively lesbian bar, but very lesbian-friendly. Offers an evening programme of DJs (Wed–Sat) playing everything from retro-house to electro, plus special Saturday parties beginning at 8am for second-winders. Sunday evening is almost exclusively lesbian. Wed–Sun 5pm–6am. Métro Bourse.

Festivals and special events

M usic and film feature most prominently in the Brussels calendar of annual **festivals**, although flower lovers and those who appreciate dance and fine art will not be disappointed. The more traditional festivals – the medieval-style **Ommegang** and the **Planting of the Meiboom** (maypole) – centre on the Grand-Place, while most of the modern ones like the **jazz** or **film** festivals take place in various venues around the city and bring the whole of the capital to life. The main annual events are listed below; for information on the dozens of mini-festivals held in Brussels during the year, check the widely available English-language city magazine, *The Bulletin*, or ask for a programme of upcoming events at the tourist office (see p.25). Alternatively, it's well worth catching a train to one of the many festivals held in the towns outside the capital, primarily Bruges, Ghent or Leuven.

January

Antiques fair (last two weeks; ☎02 513 48 31) This annual event is a meeting point for all dedicated antique dealers, international as well as Belgian, who display their choicest pieces at the Tours and Taxis exhibition centre, on rue Picard, to the northwest of the city centre, about twenty minutes' walk from Métro Yser. There's everything here from blunderbusses to African and Oriental art, silverware, jewellery, furniture, *objets d'art*, paintings, sculptures, carpets, tapestries, books and so forth – the list is endless.

February

Animation and Cartoon Festival (beginning Feb; ☎02 534 41 25, ⓦwww.awn.com/folioscope) A little-known animation festival, which screens as many as 120 new and old cartoons from around the world over the course of the event. Held at Auditorium du Passage 44, just off boulevard du Jardin Botanique, near place Rogier. Métro Botanique or Place Rogier.

March

Ars Musica (first two weeks; ☎02 219 26 60, ⓦwww.arsmusica.be) This contemporary classical music festival regularly features internationally renowned composers such as Argentina's Mauricio Kagel and France's Pascal Dusapin. The festival organizers are keen to promote interaction between the audience and the musicians, and it's often possible to meet the musicians before the concert. The festival has built up an impressive international reputation. Performances are held in numerous venues around the city.

Festival of Fantasy Film, Science Fiction and Thrillers (last two weeks; ☎02 208 03 42, ⓦwww.bifff.org) This well-established festival is a favourite with cult-film lovers, and has become the place to see all those entertainingly dreadful B-movies, as well as more modern sci-fi classics, thrillers and fantasy epics. It's held at Auditorium du Passage 44, off boulevard du Jardin Botanique; the last day features a vampires' ball – admission by suitable costume only. Métro Botanique or Place Rogier.

April

The Royal Glasshouses in Laeken (ten days late April to early May; ☎02 513 89 40) For ten days every year, the Royal Glasshouses, or *Serres Royales*, at Laeken (see p.129) are open to the public. The handsome glass and iron greenhouses shelter numerous palm trees and tropical plants, altogether a popular attraction that draws thousands of visitors; expect long queues at the entrance.

May

Bruges: Heilig Bloedprocessie (Procession of the Holy Blood; Ascension Day, forty days after Easter; ☎05 044 86 86, ⓦwww.holyblood .org) One of Christendom's holiest relics, the phial of the Holy Blood, believed to contain a few drops of the blood of Christ, is carried through the centre of Bruges once every year on Ascension Day. For safe-keeping, the phial is protected by – and held within – an ornate reliquary. Nowadays, the procession is as much a tourist attraction as a religious ceremony, but it remains a prominent event for many Bruggelingen (citizens of Bruges). The procession starts on 't Zand in front of the new Concertge-bouw (the Concert Hall, see p.166) at 3pm and wends its way round the centre taking in Steenstraat, Simon Stevinplein, Dyver, Wollestraat, the Markt, Geldmunstraat and Noordzandstraat before regaining 't Zand at about 5.30pm. Grandstand tickets (€5–11) are sold at the Concertgebouw ticket office on 't Zand (☎070 22 33 02, ⓦwww .concertgebouw.be) from March 1.

Kunsten Festival des Arts (all May; ☎02 219 07 07, ⓦwww.kfda.be) Contemporary and interdisciplinary festival that puts together over 130 performances in twenty venues all over the city – from the Théâtre Nationale to the Beurschouwberg. Performances are in different languages and the festival's forte is the showcasing of new theatrical talent. A festival pass to see everything costs €125,

and this also provides a reduced price ticket for the person accompanying the holder.

Concours Musical International Reine Elisabeth de Belgique (beginning to late May; ☎02 213 40 50, ⓦwww.concours-reine-elisabeth.be) A world-famous classical music competition founded fifty years ago by Belgium's violin-playing Queen Elisabeth. The categories change annually, rotating piano, voice and violin and the winners perform live in the Grand-Place in July. Tickets for the competition can be difficult to get hold of and can cost as much as €50, but the venues do include the splendid Palais des Beaux Arts and the Conservatoire Royal de Musique.

Jazz Marathon (three days in May; ☎02 456 04 94, ⓦwww.brusselsjazzmarathon.be) Hip jazz cats can listen to non-stop groove around the city for three whole days (which change each year – check the website), and although most of the sixty-plus bands are perhaps less familiar names, the quality of the vibe is usually very high. Entrance fees vary depending on the venue, but you can buy a three-day pass from the tourist office for around €15. Alternatively head for one of the free jazz concerts on the Grand-Place, place Ste-Catherine or place de la Monnaie.

Les Nuits Botanique (mid-May; ☎02 218 37 32, ⓦwww.botanique.be) For one week during May the auditorium at the Le Botanique (the Botanical gardens, see p.66) opens its doors to four to six bands a night – lots of new stuff to be discovered with a real international cross section covering all genres. Prices are around €8–25 a ticket. Food and drink stalls in the park help to provide a festival atmosphere.

Zinneke Parade (one Sat in May every two years; ☎02 214 20 04, ⓦwww.zinneke .org) Municipal tinkering at its very best, the Zinneke is an ambitious and inventive attempt to boost local neighbourhoods by encouraging them into a veritable frenzy of artistic activity. The end result is a remarkably lively and extraordinarily diverse parade-cum-carnival, which literally overwhelms the city centre for one day every two years – 2006 is the next. Anything goes, except for the combustion engine and amplified music, both of which are banned.

June

Festival van Vlaanderen (Flanders Festival; June to Oct across Flanders; ☎070 70 00 00,

Ⓦ www.festival-van-vlaanderen.be) Begun in 1958, the year of the World Expo in Brussels, the Flanders Festival has provided over four decades of classical music in churches, castles and other impressive venues in over sixty Flemish towns. The festival comprises more than 120 concerts and features international symphony and philharmonic orchestras. Each of the big Flemish-speaking towns – including Antwerp, Ghent and Bruges – gets a fair crack of the cultural whip with the festival celebrated for about two weeks in each city before it moves on to the next. Most of the festival's international symphony orchestras can be seen in Brussels: in the past these have included the London Symphony Orchestra, the Los Angeles Philharmonic, the Chicago Symphony Orchestra and the Vienna Philharmonic to name but four.

Couleur Café Festival (last weekend of June; ☎ 0900 26025, Ⓦ www.couleurcafe.be) A fashionable, three-day live music festival held in a big tent on the site of the Tour & Taxi exhibition centre, on rue Picard, to the northwest of the city centre, about twenty minutes' walk from Métro Yser. The festival announces the arrival of summer and you can expect a fair share of African rhythms, acid-jazz and world music, as well as ragga and hip-hop. There are plenty of stands with food from around the world, clothes and ornaments as well as a fair bit of political activity.

July

Ommegang (first Tues and Thurs of July; ☎ 02 513 89 40, Ⓦ www.ommegang-brussels.be) One of the capital's best-known annual events, the Ommegang is essentially a grand procession that cuts a colourful course from place du Grand Sablon to the Grand-Place. It began in the fourteenth century as a religious event, celebrating the arrival of a miracle-working statue of the Virgin from Antwerp, but nowadays it's almost entirely secular with a whole gaggle of locals dressed up in period costume. It all finishes up with a traditional dance on the Grand-Place and has proved so popular that it's now held twice a year, when originally it was just once. If you want a ticket for a seat on the Grand-Place for the finale, you'll need to reserve at the tourist office (see p.25) at least six months ahead.

Brussels Festival of European Film (first two weeks of July; ☎ 02 533 34 20, Ⓦ www.fffb.be) In 2004 this event was held at the end of April, in 2005 it was in July, but there's no guaranteeing when it will be held in 2006. Whatever the date, the festival promotes young film directors from the 45 countries of the Council of Europe. Admittedly, this is not one of Europe's better-known film festivals, but the organizers have worked hard to establish a solid reputation and it's a great opportunity to catch up on some of the latest European (and Belgian) films. The festival takes place at the Flagey arts centre (see p.214).

Brosella Folk and Jazz Festival (second weekend of July; ☎ 02 270 98 56, Ⓦ www.brosella .be) A small, long-established jazz and folk festival held at the Théâtre de Verdure, Parc d'Osseghem, near Métro Heysel. The surrounding chaos (things rarely start on time) somehow adds to the attraction and the bands, mostly Belgian, but occasionally international, offer quality entertainment.

Bruges: Cactusfestival (three days over the second weekend of July; ☎ 050 33 20 14, Ⓦ www.cactusmusic.be) Going strong for over twenty years, the Cactusfestival is something of a classic. Known for its amiable atmosphere, it proudly pushes against the musical mainstream with rock, reggae, rap, roots and R&B all rolling along together. The festival features both domestic and foreign artists – recent show-stoppers have included Elvis Costello, Patti Smith and Richard Thompson. It's held in Bruges' city centre, in the park beside the Minnewater.

Ghent: Gentse Feesten (Ghent Festival; mid- to late July, but always including July 21; Ⓦ www .gentsefeesten.be) For ten days every July, Ghent gets stuck into partying in a big way, pretty much round the clock. Local bands perform free open-air gigs throughout the city and street performers turn up all over the place – fire-eaters, buskers, comedians, actors, puppeteers and so forth. There's also an outdoor market selling everything from *jenever* (gin) to handmade crafts.

Rock Werchter Festival (last weekend of July; ☎ 01 660 04 06, Ⓦ www.rockwerchter.be) Belgium's premier rock and pop festival and one of the largest open-air music festivals in Europe. In recent years the all-star line-up has included Massive Attack, Nick Cave and the Bad Seeds, Pulp, Björk, as well as the Beastie Boys, Garbage, Sonic Youth and

FESTIVALS AND SPECIAL EVENTS

Tricky. To reach Werchter from Brussels, take the train to Leuven (25min), after which a special festival bus will take you to the site. **Bruges: Klinkers (two and a half weeks, usually from the last weekend of July; ☏050 33 20 14, ⓦwww.cactusmusic.be)** Bruges' biggest annual knees-up, and the chance for city folk to really let their hair down. There are big-time concerts on the Markt and the Burg, the city's two main squares, more intimate performances in various bars and cafés, and film screenings in Astrid Park, plus all sorts of other entertainments. It's Bruges at its best – and most of the events are free.

Bruxelles Les Bains (end July to end Aug; ⓦwww.bruxelleslesbain.be) Inspired by the artificial urban beach created in Paris, Brussels took its first sandy steps in 2003 – and it proved to be a great success with beach volleyball, pétanque, seafood stalls, and plain and simple sunbathing by the Charleroi canal. To get there, go to Métro Yser and follow the buckets and spades. Opening hours are Tues–Thurs 11am–8pm & Fri–Sun 11am–10pm; closed Mon.

August

Planting of the Meiboom (Aug 9) An annual event in which a *meiboom* (maypole) is planted at the corner of rue des Sables and rue du Marais, involving a procession accompanied by much boozing, food and general partying. The story goes that in 1213 a wedding party was celebrating outside the city's gates when it was attacked by a street gang from Leuven. They were beaten off (with the help of a group of archers who happened to be passing by) and, in thanks, the duke gave them permission to plant a maypole on the eve of their patron saint's feast day.

Tapis des Fleurs (mid-Aug weekend every two years) If you like flowers and floral designs, head down to the Grand-Place in mid-August, where the old cobblestones are covered with a lovely floral carpet made up of over 700,000 begonias from Ghent. This event takes place every two years (2006 is next).

Leuven: Marktrock (three days in the middle of Aug; ⓦwww.marktrock.be) Leuven's lively Marktrock ("Market Square Rock") is an extremely popular city-centre event showcasing local rock groups and solo artists with a handful of foreign acts thrown in for good measure.

October

Ghent: Ghent Film Festival (twelve days in Oct; ☏09 242 80 60, ⓦwww.filmfestival.be) The Ghent Film Festival in Ghent has developed into one of Europe's foremost cinematic events. Every year, the city's art-house cinemas combine to present a total of around two hundred feature films and a hundred shorts from all over the world, screening Belgian films and the best of world cinema well before it hits the international circuit. There's also a special focus on music in film.

Audi Jazz Festival (mid-Oct to Nov; ☏02 456 04 85, ⓦwww.audijazz.be) A month-long jazz extravaganza, featuring a wide range of local and international acts which in the past have included Courtney Pine, Steve Coleman and Ray Charles. Like the Jazz Marathon, concerts are held in many live music venues around the city.

Europalia (mid-Oct to mid-Jan; ☏02 507 85 95, ⓦwww.europalia.be) Started in 1969, the Europalia festival focuses on a different country each year – in 2005 it was Russia, while the UK took its turn in back in 1973. The festival comprises paintings and exhibitions, as well as theatre, dance and live music from the country concerned. The Palais des Beaux Arts is at the centre of the festival, but other venues across the city are also pressed into service.

November

Ghent: Zesdaagse an Vlaanderen (The Six days of Flanders Cycling Event; six days in mid-Nov; ⓦwww.kuipke.be) This annual cycling extravaganza takes place in the vélodrome at the Citadelpark in Ghent. It attracts cyclists from all over Europe, who thrash around for dear life in six days of high-speed racing.

December

Le Marché de Noël (mid-Dec; ☏02 513 89 40) The capital's traditional Christmas market and fair, held on and around the Bourse and place Ste-Catherine for the weeks leading up to Christmas. Features food, drink and various wares from EU countries. The piped Christmas muzak is rather tacky, but the fair still gets even the most cynical humbugs in the Christmas spirit. Festivities include a skating rink installed in place Ste-Catherine.

Directory

Addresses In the French-speaking parts of Belgium, addresses are usually written to a standard format. The first line begins with the category of the street or thoroughfare (rue, boulevard, etc), followed by the name and then the number; the second line gives the area – or zip – code, followed by the town or area. Common abbrevations include *blvd* or *bd* for boulevard, *ave* or *av* for avenue, *ch* for chaussée and *pl* for place (square). An exception to the latter is the hyphenated Grand-Place (main square), written in full. In the Flemish-speaking areas, the first line gives the name of the street which is followed by (and joined to) its category – hence Krakeelplein is Krakeel square, Krakeelstraat is Krakeel street; the number comes next. The second line gives the area – or zip – code followed by the town or area. Consequently, Flemish abbreviations occur at the end of words: thus *Hofstr* for Hofstraat. An exception is *Grote Markt* (main square), which is not abbreviated. Common categories include *plein* for square, *plaats* for place, *laan* or *weg* for avenue, *kaai* for quay, and *straat* for street. In bilingual Brussels, all signs give both the French and Flemish versions. In many cases, this is fairly straightforward as they are either the same or similar, but sometimes it's extremely confusing, most notoriously in the name of one of the three principal train stations – in French, *Bruxelles-Midi*; in Flemish *Brussel-Zuid*.

Car rental A string of major operators have branches at both Brussels airport and at Gare du Midi train station. Two reliable options are Europcar (Gare du Midi ☎02 522 95 73, airport ☎02 721 05 92) and Hertz (Gare du Midi ☎02 524 31 00, airport ☎02 720 60 44).

Electricity The current is 220 volts AC, with standard European-style two-pin plugs. Brits will need an adaptor to connect their appliances, North Americans both an adaptor and a transformer.

Embassies Australia, rue Guimard 6 (☎02 286 05 00); Canada, ave de Tervuren 2 (☎02 741 06 11); Great Britain, rue d'Arlon 85 (☎02 287 62 11); Ireland, rue Wiertz 89–93 (☎02 235 66 76); New Zealand, 7th Floor, square de Meeus 1 (☎02 512 10 40); South Africa, rue de la Loi 26 (☎02 285 44 00); USA, blvd du Régent 27 (☎02 508 21 11).

Emergencies Call ☎100 for an ambulance or the fire brigade, ☎101 for the police.

Left luggage All three of the city's main train stations have both luggage offices (normally daily 6am–midnight) and coin-operated lockers.

Lost property For property lost on an aircraft, ring the airport on ☎02 723 60 11; if lost at the airport itself, call ☎02 753 68 20. The lost property office for the métro, trams and buses is at avenue de la Toison d'Or 15 (☎02 515 23 94).

Smoking Smoking is forbidden in many public places from theatres through to town halls. Trains are no-smoking too and so are the confined spaces of train stations, but you can light up on open-air platforms. No-smoking hotel rooms are commonplace, but as yet surprisingly few restaurants have (decent–sized) no-smoking areas.

Time One hour ahead of Britain; normally six hours ahead of Eastern Standard Time, nine hours ahead of Pacific Standard Time.

Tipping There's no need to tip when there's a service charge – as there often is – but when there isn't, restaurant waiters will anticipate a ten to fifteen percent tip, as will taxi drivers too.

Toilets Public toilets remain comparatively rare, but many cafés and bars in Brussels operate what amounts to an ablutionary side-line with a €0.20 fee to use the toilets; you'll spot the plate for the money as you enter.

Contexts

Contexts

A history of Brussels

Early settlement to the sixteenth century

Brussels takes its name from "Broekzele", or "village of the marsh", referring to the community which grew up beside the wide and shallow River Senne in the sixth century, reputedly around a chapel built here by St Géry, a French bishop sent to convert the pagans. A tiny and insignificant part of Charlemagne's empire at the end of the eighth century, it was subsequently inherited by the **dukes of Lower Lorraine** (or Lotharingia – roughly Wallonia and northeast France), who constructed a fortress here in 979; the first city walls were added a few decades later. Its inhabitants protected, the village began to benefit from its position on the trade route between Cologne and the burgeoning cloth towns of Bruges and Ghent, and soon became a significant trading centre in its own right. The surrounding marshes were drained to allow for further expansion, and by the end of the twelfth century Brussels had a population of around thirty thousand.

In 1229 the city was granted its first charter by the **dukes of Brabant**, the new feudal overlords who controlled things here, on and off, for around two hundred years, governing through seven *échevins*, or **aldermen**, each of whom represented one of the patrician families that monopolised the administration. This self-regarding oligarchy was deeply unpopular with the skilled workers who made up the **guilds**, the only real counterweight to the aristocrats. The guildsmen rose in rebellion in 1302 and again in 1356, when the Count of Flanders, Louis de Maele, occupied Brussels during his dispute with Jeanne, the Duchess of Brabant. The guildsmen rallied to the Brabantine cause under the leadership of **Everard 't Serclaes** and, after ejecting the count's garrison, exacted terms from the returning duchess. Jeanne was obliged to swear an oath – the *Joyeuse Entrée* – which stipulated the rights and responsibilities of the ruler and the ruled, effectively a charter of liberties, which also recognized the guilds and gave them more political power. This deal between the duchess and her craftsmen led to a period of rapid expansion and it was at this time that a second town wall was constructed, an eight-kilometre pentagon whose lines are followed by the boulevards of today's **petit ring**.

The early decades of the fifteenth century proved difficult: the cloth industry began its long decline and there was more trouble between the guildsmen and the patricians. Temporary solutions were, however, found to both these problems. The craftsmen started making luxury goods for the royal courts of Europe, while the city's governing council was modified to contain seven aristocrats, six guildsmen and two aldermen – a municipal compromise that was to last until the late eighteenth century. There was a change of overlord too, when, in 1430, marriage merged the territories of the duchy of Brabant with those of Burgundy. Initially, this worked against the interests of the city as the first Burgundian rulers – Philip the Good and his son Charles the Bold – paid little regard to Brussels, and indeed Charles' ceaseless warmongering resulted in a steep increase in taxation. But when Charles' daughter, Mary of Burgundy, established her court in Brussels, the city gained political stature and its guildsmen found a ready market for the luxury goods they were already making – everything from gold jewellery and silverware through to tapestries and illuminated books. Painters were drawn to Mary's court, too, and Rogier van der Weyden was appointed the city's first official artist.

Mary married **Maximilian**, a **Habsburg** prince and future Holy Roman Emperor in 1477. She died in a riding accident five years later and her territories passed to her husband, who ruled until 1519. Thus Brussels – along with the whole of present-day Belgium and Holland – was incorporated into the Habsburg Empire. A sharp operator, Maximilian whittled away at the power of the Brabantine and Flemish cities and despite the odd miscalculation – he was imprisoned by the burghers of Bruges in 1488 – had to all intents and purposes brought them to heel by the end of the century. Maximilian was succeeded by his grandson **Charles V**, whose vast kingdom included Spain, the Low Countries and large parts of Germany and Italy. By necessity, Charles was something of a peripatetic monarch, but he favoured Brussels, his home town, more than any other residence, running his empire from here for a little over twelve years, which made the city wealthy and politically important in equal measure. Just like his grandfather, Charles kept the city's guilds firmly under control.

The Reformation and the revolt against Spain

The **Reformation** was a religious revolt that stood sixteenth-century Europe on its head. The first stirrings were in the welter of debate that spread across much of western Europe under the auspices of theologians like **Erasmus** (see p.124), who wished to cleanse the Catholic church of its corruptions and extravagant ceremony; only later did some of these same thinkers – principally Martin Luther – decide to support a breakaway church. The seeds of this **Protestantism** fell on fertile ground among the merchants of Brussels, whose wealth and independence had never been easy to accommodate within a rigid caste society. Similarly, their employees, the guildsmen and their apprentices, who had a long history of opposing arbitrary authority, were easily convinced of the need for reform. In 1555, **Charles V abdicated**, transferring his German lands to his brother Ferdinand, and his Italian, Spanish and Low Countries territories to his son, the fervently Catholic **Philip II**. In the short term, the scene was set for a bitter confrontation between Catholics and Protestants, while the dynastic ramifications of the division of the Habsburg Empire were to complicate European affairs for centuries.

After his father's abdication, Philip II decided to teach his heretical subjects a lesson. He garrisoned Brussels and the other towns of the Low Countries with Spanish mercenaries, imported the Inquisition and passed a series of anti-Protestant edicts. However, other pressures on the Habsburg Empire forced him into a tactical withdrawal and he transferred control to his sister, **Margaret of Parma**, in 1559. Based in Brussels, the equally resolute Margaret implemented the policies of her brother with gusto. Initially, the repression worked, but in 1565 the Protestant workers struck back. In Brussels and most of the other big cities hereabouts they ran amok, sacking the churches and destroying their rich decoration in the **Iconoclastic Fury**.

Protestantism had infiltrated the nobility, but the ferocity of the rioting shocked the upper classes into renewed support for Spain. Philip was keen to capitalize on the increase in support and, in 1567, he dispatched the **Duke of Albe**, with an army of ten thousand men, to the Low Countries to suppress his religious opponents absolutely. Margaret was not at all pleased by Philip's decision and, when Albe arrived in Brussels, she resigned in a huff, initiating a long period of what was, in effect, military rule. One of Albe's first acts in the capital was to set up the Commission of Civil Unrest, which was soon nicknamed the "**Council of Blood**" after its habit of executing those it examined. No fewer than 12,000 citizens went to the block, most famously the counts of **Egmont** and **Hoorn** (see p.51), who were beheaded on the Grand-Place in June 1568.

Once again, the repression soon backfired. The region's greatest landowner, Prince William of Orange-Nassau, known as **William the Silent** (1533–84), raised the Low Countries against the Habsburgs and swept all before him, making a triumphant entrance into Brussels, where he installed a Calvinist administration. Momentarily, it seemed possible for the whole of the Low Countries to unite behind William and all signed the **Union of Brussels**, which demanded the departure of foreign troops as a condition for accepting a diluted Habsburg sovereignty. But Philip was not inclined to compromise. In 1578, he gathered together another army which he dispatched to the Low Countries under the command of Alessandro Farnese, the **Duke of Parma**. Parma was successful, recapturing most of modern Belgium including Brussels and finally Antwerp in 1585. He was, however, unable to advance any further north and the Low Countries were divided into two – the **Spanish Netherlands** and the **United Provinces** – beginning a separation that would lead, after many changes, to the creation of Belgium and the Netherlands.

The Spanish Netherlands

Parma was surprisingly generous in victory, but the city's weavers, apprentices and skilled workers – the bedrock of Calvinism – still fled north to escape the new Catholic regime, fuelling an economic boom in the province of Holland. The migration badly dented the economy of the **Spanish Netherlands** as a whole, but Brussels – the capital – was relatively immune, its economy buoyed by the Habsburg elite, whose conspicuous consumption fostered luxury industries like silk weaving, diamond processing and lace making. The city's industries also benefited from the digging of the Willebroek canal, which linked Brussels to the sea for the first time. This commercial restructuring underpinned a brief flourishing of artistic life both here and, in comparable circumstances, in Antwerp, where it was centred on **Rubens** (see p.256) and his circle, including Anthony van Dyck and Jacob Jordaens.

Meanwhile, months before his death in 1598, Philip II had granted control of the Spanish Netherlands to his daughter and her husband, appointing them the **Archdukes Isabella** and **Albert**. Failing to learn from experience, the ducal couple continued to prosecute the war against the Protestant north, but with so little success that they were obliged to make peace – the **Twelve Year Truce** – in 1609. When the truce ended, the new Spanish king, Philip IV, stubbornly resumed the campaign against the Protestants, this time as part of a general and even more devastating conflict, the **Thirty Years' War** (1618–48), a largely religious-based conflict between Catholic and Protestant countries that involved most of western Europe. Finally, the Habsburgs were compelled to accept the humiliating terms of the **Peace of Westphalia**, a general treaty whose terms formally recognized the independence of the United Provinces and closed the Scheldt estuary, thereby crippling Antwerp. By these means, the commercial pre-eminence of Amsterdam was assured and its Golden Age began.

The Thirty Years' War had devastated the Spanish Netherlands, but the peace was perhaps as bad. Politically dependent on a decaying Spain, economically ruined and deprived of most of its more independent-minded citizens, the country turned in on itself, sustained by the fanatical Catholicism of the **Counter-Reformation**. Literature disappeared, the sciences vegetated and religious orders multiplied to an extraordinary degree. In **painting**, artists – such as Rubens – were used to confirm the ecclesiastical orthodoxies, their canvases full of muscular saints and angels, reflecting a religious faith of mystery and hierarchy; others, such as David Teniers, retreated into minutely observed realism.

The Peace of Westphalia had also freed the king of France from fear of Germany, and the political and military history of the Spanish Netherlands after 1648 was dominated by the efforts of **Louis XIV** to add the country to his territories. Fearful of an over-powerful France, the United Provinces and England, among others, determinedly resisted French designs and, to preserve the balance of power, fought a long series of campaigns beginning in the 1660s. It was during one of these wars, the **War of the Grand Alliance**, that Louis XIV's artillery destroyed much of medieval Brussels, a disaster that led to the construction of the lavish Grand-Place that survives today.

The **War of the Spanish Succession** – the final conflict of the series – was sparked by the death in 1700 of **Charles II**, the last of the Spanish Habsburgs, who had willed his territories to the grandson of Louis XIV. An anti-French coalition refused to accept the settlement and there ensued a haphazard series of campaigns that dragged on for eleven years. Eventually, with the **Treaty of Utrecht** of 1713, the French abandoned their attempt to conquer the Spanish Netherlands, which now passed under the control of the Austrian Habsburgs in the figure of the Emperor Charles VI.

The Austrian Netherlands

The transfer of the country from Spanish to **Austrian control** made little appreciable difference: a remote imperial authority continued to oper-ate through an appointed governor in Brussels and the country as a whole remained poor and backward. This sorry state of affairs began to change in the middle of the eighteenth century when the Austrian oligarchy came under the influence of the **Enlightenment**, that belief in reason and progress – as against authority and tradition – that had first been proselytized by French philosophers. In 1753, the arrival of a progressive governor, the **Count of Cobenzl**, signified a transformation of Habsburg policy. Cobenzl initiated an ambitious programme of public works and set about changing the face of Brussels – which had become an urbanized eyesore – by pushing through the grand Neoclassical boulevards and avenues which still characterize the Upper Town.

In 1780, the **Emperor Joseph II** came to the throne, determined to "root out silly old prejudices", as he put it – but his reforms were opposed on all sides. The liberal-minded **Vonckists** demanded a radical, republican constitution, while their enemies, the conservative **Statists**, insisted on the Catholic status quo. There was pandemonium and, in 1789, the Habsburgs dispatched an army to restore order. Against all expectations, the two political groups combined and defeated the Austrians near Antwerp in what became known as the **Brabant Revolution**. In January 1790, the rebels announced the formation of the United States of Belgium, but the country remained in turmoil and when Emperor Joseph died in 1790, his successor, **Léopold**, quickly withdrew the reforming acts and sent in his troops to restore imperial authority.

French occupation and the Kingdom of the Netherlands

The new and repressive Habsburg regime was short-lived. French Republican armies brushed the imperial forces aside in 1794, and the Austrian Netherlands were annexed the following year, an annexation that was to last until 1814. The **French** imposed radical reforms: the Catholic Church was stripped of much of its worldly wealth, feudal privileges were abolished, and, most unpopular of all, conscription was introduced. The invaders were deeply resented and French authority had largely evaporated long before **Napoleon**'s final defeat just outside Brussels at the battle of **Waterloo** (see pp.134–139) in 1815.

At the **Congress of Vienna**, called to settle Europe at the end of the Napoleonic Wars, the main concern of the great powers – including Great Britain and Prussia – was to bolster the Low Countries against France. With scant regard to the feelings of those affected, they therefore decided to establish the **Kingdom of the Netherlands**, which incorporated both the old United Provinces and the Austrian Netherlands, and on the throne they placed Frederick William of Orange, appointed **King William I**. From the very beginning, the union proved problematic – there were even two capital cities, Brussels and The Hague – and William simply wasn't wily enough to hold things together. Nonetheless, the union struggled on until August 25, 1830, when the singing of a duet, *Amour sacré de la Patrie*, in the Brussels opera house hit a nationalist nerve. The audience poured out onto the streets to raise the flag of Brabant in defiance of King William, thereby initiating a countrywide **revolution**. William sent in his troops, but Great Britain and France quickly intervened to stop hostilities. In January of the following year, at the **Conference of London**, the great powers recognized Belgium's independence, with the caveat that the country be classified a "neutral" state – that is one outside any other's sphere of influence. To bolster this new nation, they dug out the uncle of Queen Victoria, Prince Léopold of Saxe-Coburg, to present with the crown.

Independent Belgium

Léopold I (1830–65) was careful to maintain his country's neutrality and encouraged an industrial boom that saw coalmines developed, iron foundries established and the rapid expansion of the railway system. His successor,

Léopold II (1865–1909), further boosted industry and supervised the emergence of Belgium as a major industrial power. The king and the reforming Brussels burgomaster (mayor) Anspach also set about modernizing the capital. New boulevards were built; the free university was founded; the Senne – which by then had become an open sewer – was covered over in the city centre; many slum areas were cleared; and a series of grandiose buildings was erected, the most unpopular of which was the Palais de Justice (see p.93), whose construction involved the forced eviction of hundreds of workers. To round the whole thing off – and turn Brussels into a city deserving of its king – Léopold held the golden jubilee exhibition celebrating the founding of the Belgian state in the newly inaugurated Le Cinquantenaire (see pp.117–120), a mammoth edifice he had built just to the east of the old city centre. The flip side of all this royal posturing was a good deal less pleasant. Determined to cut an international figure, Léopold II had decided to build up a colonial empire. The unfortunate recipients of his ambition were the Africans of the Congo River basin, who were effectively given to him by a conference of European powers in 1885. Ruling the Congo as a personal fiefdom, Léopold established an extraordinarily cruel colonial regime – so cruel in fact that even the other colonial powers were appalled and the Belgian state was obliged to end the embarrassment by taking over the region – as the Belgian Congo – in 1908.

The Belgian language divide

The Belgians are divided between two main groups, the **Walloons**, French-speakers concentrated in the south of the country who account for around forty percent of the population, and to the north the **Flemings**, Dutch- or Flemish- speakers, who form about sixty percent out of a total population of some ten million. There are also, in the far east of the country, a few pockets of German-speakers around the towns of Eupen and Malmédy.

The Flemish-French **language divide** has troubled the country for decades, its significance rooted in deep class and economic divisions. When the Belgian state was founded in 1830, its ruling and middle classes were predominantly French-speaking and they created the new state in their linguistic image: French was the official language and Flemish was banned in schools. This Francophone domination was subsequently reinforced by the way the economy developed, with Wallonia becoming a major coal mining and steel-producing area, while Flanders remained a predominantly agricultural, rural backwater. There were nationalist stirrings amongst the Flemings from the 1880s onwards, but it was only after World War II – when Flanders became the country's industrial powerhouse as Wallonia declined – that the demand for linguistic and cultural parity became irresistible. In the way of such things, the Walloons read Flemish "parity" as "domination", setting the scene for all sorts of inter-communal hassle.

As a response to this burgeoning animosity, a **Language Frontier** was formally drawn across the country in 1962, cutting the country in half, from west to east. The aim was to distinguish between the French- and Flemish-speaking communities and thereby defuse tensions, but it didn't work. In 1980, this failure prompted another attempt to rectify matters with the redrafting of the constitution and the creation of a federal system, with three separate **communities** – the Flemish North, the Walloon South and the German-speaking east – responsible for their own cultural and social affairs and education. At the same time, Belgium was divided into three **regions** — the Flemish North, the Walloon South and bilingual Brussels, with each regional authority dealing with matters like economic development, the environment and employment.

The first fly in the royal ointment came in the 1860s and 1870s with the first significant stirrings of a type of **Flemish nationalism** which felt little enthusiasm for the unitary status of Belgium, divided as it was between the French-speakers in the south of the country – the Walloons – and the Dutch-speakers in the north – the Flemings. The Catholic party ensured that, under the Equality Law of 1898, Dutch was ratified as an official language, equal in status to French – the forerunner of many long and difficult debates.

The twentieth century to the end of World War II

At the beginning of the twentieth century, Brussels was a thriving metropolis, which took a progressive lead in a country that was determined to keep on good terms with all the great powers. Nonetheless, Belgium could not prevent getting caught up in **World War I**. Indifferent to Belgium's proclaimed neutrality, the Germans had decided as early as 1908 that the best way to attack France was via Belgium, and this is precisely what they did in 1914. They captured

Although the niceties of this partition have undoubtedly calmed troubled waters, in **bilingual Brussels** and at national government level the division between Flemish- and French-speakers still influences many aspects of working and social life. Schools, political parties, literature and culture are all segregated along linguistic lines, leading to a set of complex regulations which can verge on the absurd. Government press conferences, for example, must have questions and answers repeated in both languages. Across Belgium as a whole, bitterness about the economy, unemployment and the government smoulders within (or seeks an outlet through) the framework of this linguistic division, and individual neighbourhoods can be paralyzed by language disputes. The communities of Fourons/Voeren, for instance, a largely French-speaking collection of villages in Flemish Limburg, almost brought down the government in the mid-Eighties when the Francophone mayor, Jose Happart, refused to take the Flemish language exam required of all Limburg officials. Dismissed, he stood again and was re-elected, prompting the prime minister at the time, Wilfred Martens, to offer his own resignation. The Fourons affair was symptomatic of the obstinacy that besets the country to this day. Jose Happart could probably have passed the exam easily – indeed rumour has it that he is fluent in Flemish – but he simply chose not to submit, giving succour to the political extremists on both sides – namely the Vlaams Blok – now Vlaams Belang – on the Flemish side, and, for the French-speakers, the Front des Francophones (FDF).

All this said, it would be wrong to assume that Belgium's language differences have gone beyond the level of personal animosity and institutionalized mutual suspicion. Belgian **language extremists** have been imprisoned over the years, but very few, if any, have died in the fight for supremacy. Indeed, some might see a bilingual nation as a positive thing in a Europe where trading – and national – barriers are being increasingly broken down. Suggesting this to a Belgian, however, is normally useless, but there again the casual visitor will rarely get a sniff of these tensions. It's probably better to speak English rather than Flemish or French in the "wrong" part of Belgium, but if you make a mistake, the worst you'll get is a look of glazed indifference.

almost all of the country, the exception being a narrow strip of territory in the west around De Panne. Undaunted, the new king **Albert I** (1909–34) and the Belgian army bravely manned the northern part of the Allied line. It made Albert a national hero.

The Germans returned in May 1940, launching a blitzkrieg that overwhelmed both Belgium and the Netherlands. This time there was no heroic resistance by the Belgian king, now **Léopold III** (1934–51), who ignored the advice of his government and surrendered unconditionally and in great haste. It is true that the Belgian army had been badly mauled and that a German victory seemed inevitable, but the manner of the surrender infuriated many Belgians, as did the king's refusal to form a government in exile. It took time for the Belgians to adjust to the new situation, but by 1941 a Resistance movement was mounting acts of sabotage against the occupying forces – and **liberation** by the Allies came three years later.

Post-World War II to the present

After World War II, the Belgians set about the task of **economic reconstruction**, helped by aid from the United States, but hindered by a divisive controversy over the wartime activities of King Léopold. Many felt his surrender to the Germans was cowardly and his subsequent willingness to work with them treacherous; others pointed out his efforts to increase the country's food rations and his negotiations to secure the release of Belgian prisoners. Inevitably, the complex shadings of collaboration and forced co-operation were hard to disentangle, and the debate continued until 1950 when a referendum narrowly recommended his return from exile. Léopold's return was, however, marked by rioting in Brussels and across Wallonia, where the king's opponents were concentrated, and Léopold abdicated in favour of his son, **Baudouin** (1951–93).

The development of the postwar Belgian economy follows the pattern of most of Western Europe – reconstruction in the 1950s; boom in the 1960s; recession in the 1970s; and retrenchment in the 1980s and 1990s. Significant events included the belated extension of the franchise to women in 1948; an ugly, disorganized and hasty evacuation of the Belgian Congo in 1960 and of Rwanda and Burundi in 1962; and the transformation of Brussels from one of the lesser European capitals into a major player when it became the home of the **EU** and **NATO** – the latter organization was ejected from France on the orders of de Gaulle in 1967. But, above all, the postwar period has been dominated by the increasing **tension between the Walloon and Flemish communities**. Every national institution is now dogged by the prerequisites of bilingualism – speeches in parliament, for example, have to be delivered in both languages – and in Brussels, the country's one and only **bilingual region**, every instance of the written word, from road signs to the yellow pages, has to be bilingual as well. Brussels has also been subtly affected by the **Linguistic Divide** (or Language Frontier), which was formally delineated in 1962. Bilingual Brussels is now encircled by Flemish-speaking regions and, partly as a result, many Francophones living in the city have developed something of a siege mentality; the Flemish, on the other hand, can't help but notice the prevalence of the French language in what is supposed to be their capital city.

Bogged down by these linguistic preoccupations, the federal government often appears extraordinarily cumbersome, but there again much of the political class is at least partly reliant on the linguistic divide for their jobs and, institutionally speaking, has little incentive to see the antagonisms resolved. A rare moment of national unity came in 1996 when communities from both sides of the linguistic divide rose up in protest at the Belgian police, which proved itself at best hopelessly inefficient, at worst complicit in the gruesome activities of the child murderer and pornographer **Marc Dutroux.** Over 350,000 people took to the capital's streets, demanding the police and justice system be overhauled. This outburst of public protest peaked again two years later when, amazingly enough, Dutroux escaped his police guards, stole a car and headed out of the city. Although he was subsequently recaptured, most Belgians were simply appalled, though there was some relief when Dutroux was finally sentenced to life imprisonment in June 2004.

The Dutroux affair dented the national psyche, and – conviction or not – few Belgians believe that the reforms imposed on the police have made much difference. Into this psychological breach rode the **royal family**, one of the few institutions to bind the country together. In 1999, the heir to the throne, Prince Philippe, broke with tradition and married Mathilde d'Udekem d'Acoz – a Belgian of non-royal descent, with family on both sides of the linguistic divide. The marriage may well have healed a few wounds, but its effects should not be over-estimated. Over 400,000 people snapped up the free travel tickets offered by the Belgian railways, but only around twenty percent were used to come to Brussels, and out of them one can only speculate as to how many loyal subjects chose to wave the flag on a cold December day rather than head for the nearest bar. More far-reaching were the changes to the appearance of the city in 2000, when, as a chosen European Capital of Culture, many of its old buildings were given a good spring clean, and there was some political spring cleaning when the liberals were voted out of power in the local election and replaced by a red-green coalition. In 2004, the next **election** to the Brussels Regional Parliament was marked by lurid threats from the Flemish nationalists as personified by the right-wing **Vlaams Belang** party. They rumbled on about taking control of Brussels as a first step in their avowed ambition of breaking up Belgium into its component French- and Flemish-speaking parts, but in the event they only got a handful of seats and the socialists remained the largest party, though the political atmosphere remains markedly sour.

An introduction to Belgian art

The following **outline** is the very briefest of introductions to a subject that has rightly filled volumes, and is designed to serve only as a quick reference. Inevitably, it covers artists that lived and worked in both the Netherlands and Belgium as these two countries have both been, for most of their history, bound together as the so-called Low Countries. For more in-depth and academic studies, see the recommendations in the "Books" section on p.260.

The early Flemish Masters

Throughout the medieval period, Flanders was one of the most artistically productive parts of Europe with each of the cloth towns, but especially Bruges and Ghent, trying to out-do its rivals with the quality of its religious art. Today, the works of these early Flemish painters, known as the **Flemish Primitives**, are highly prized and an excellent sample is displayed in both Ghent and Bruges as well as in Brussels. **Jan van Eyck** (1385–1441) is generally regarded as the first of the Flemish Primitives, and has even been credited with the invention of oil painting itself – though it seems more likely that he simply perfected a new technique by thinning his paint with (the newly discovered) turpentine, thus making it more flexible. His fame partially stems from the fact that he was one of the first artists to sign his work – an indication of how highly his talent was regarded by his contemporaries. Van Eyck's most celebrated work is the *Adoration of the Mystic Lamb*, a stunningly beautiful altarpiece displayed in St Baafskathedraal in Ghent (see p.161). The painting was revolutionary in its realism, for the first time using elements of native landscape in depicting Biblical themes, and was underpinned by a complex symbolism which has generated analysis and discussion ever since. Van Eyck's style and technique were to influence several generations of the Low Countries' artists.

Firmly in the Eyckian tradition was **Rogier van der Weyden** (1400–64), one-time official painter to the city of Brussels. Weyden's paintings do, however, show a greater degree of emotional and religious intensity than those of van Eyck, whilst his serene portraits of the bigwigs of his day were much admired across a large swathe of western Europe. Among the many painters influenced by Van der Weyden, one of the most talented was **Dieric Bouts** (1415–75). Born in Haarlem but active in Leuven (see p.155), Bouts is recognizable by his stiff, rather elongated figures and horrific subject matter, all set against carefully drawn landscapes. **Hugo van der Goes** (d.1482) was the next Ghent master after van Eyck, most famous for the Portinari Altarpiece in Florence's Uffizi. After a short painting career, he died insane, and his late works have strong hints of his impending madness in their subversive use of space and implicit acceptance of the viewer's presence. Few doubt that **Hans Memling** (1440–94) was a pupil of van der Weyden. Active in Bruges throughout his life, he is best remembered for the pastoral charm of his landscapes and the quality of his portraiture, much of which survives on the rescued side panels of triptychs. The Memling Museum in Bruges (see p.171) has a wonderful sample of his work. Both **Gerard David** (1460–1523) and **Jan Provoost** (1465–1529) moved to Bruges at the back end of the fifteenth century. They mostly painted religious scenes, but their secular works are much more memorable, especially David's *Judgement of Cambyses*, exhibited in the Groeninge in Bruges (see p.170). David's best-known apprentice was **Adriaen Isenbrant** (d.1551), whose speciality was small, precisely executed panels – his *Madonna of the Seven Sorrows* in Bruges' Onze Lieve Vrouwekerk (see p.170) is quite superb. Isenbrant was the last of the great painters to work in that city before it was superseded by Antwerp – which itself became the focus of a more Italianate school of art in the sixteenth century.

Hieronymus Bosch (1450–1516) lived for most of his life in Holland, though his style is linked to that of his Flemish contemporaries. His frequently reprinted religious allegories are filled with macabre visions of tortured people and grotesque beasts, and appear at first faintly unhinged, though it's now thought that these are visual representations of contemporary sayings, idioms and parables. While their interpretation is far from resolved, Bosch's paintings draw strongly on subconscious fears and archetypes, giving them a lasting, haunting fascination.

The sixteenth century

By the end of the fifteenth century, the Flemish cloth towns were in decline and the leading artists of the day were drawn instead to the booming port of Antwerp. The artists who worked here soon began to integrate the finely observed detail that characterized the Flemish tradition with the style of the Italian painters of the Renaissance. **Quentin Matsys** (1464–1530) introduced florid classical architectural details and intricate landscapes to his works, influenced perhaps by the work of Leonardo da Vinci. As well as religious works, he painted portraits and genre scenes, all of which have recognizably Italian facets, and paved the way for the Dutch genre painters of later years. **Jan Gossart** (1478–1532) made the pilgrimage to Italy too, and his dynamic works are packed with detail, especially finely drawn classical architectural backdrops. He was the first Low Countries artist to introduce the subjects of classical mythology into his works, part of a steady trend through the period towards secular subject matter, which can also be seen in the work of **Joachim Patenier** (d.1524), who painted small landscapes of fantastical scenery.

The latter part of the sixteenth century was dominated by the work of **Pieter Bruegel the Elder** (c.1525–69), whose gruesome allegories and innovative interpretations of religious subjects are firmly placed in Low Countries settings. Pieter also painted finely observed peasant scenes, though he himself was well connected in court circles in Antwerp and, later, Brussels. **Pieter Aertsen** (1508–75) also worked in the peasant genre, adding aspects of still life: his paintings often show a detailed kitchen scene in the foreground, with a religious episode going on behind. Bruegel's two sons, **Pieter Bruegel the Younger** (1564–1638) and **Jan Bruegel** (1568–1625), were lesser painters: the former produced fairly insipid copies of his father's work, while Jan developed a style of his own – delicately rendered flower paintings and genre pieces that earned him the nickname "Velvet". Towards the latter half of the sixteenth century highly stylized Italianate portraits became the dominant fashion, with **Frans Pourbus the Younger** (1569–1622) the leading practitioner. Frans hobnobbed across Europe, working for the likes of the Habsburgs and the Médicis, his itinerant life in contrast to that of his grandfather, the Bruges-based **Pieter Pourbus** (1523–84), the founder of this artistic dynasty.

The seventeenth century – Rubens and his followers

Belgian painting of the early seventeenth century was dominated by **Pieter Paul Rubens** (1577–1640), the most important exponent of the Baroque in northern Europe. Born in Siegen, Westphalia, he was raised in Antwerp, where he entered the Painters' Guild in 1598. He became court painter to the Duke of Mantua in 1600, and until 1608 travelled extensively in Italy, absorbing the art of the High Renaissance and classical architecture. By the time of his return to Antwerp in 1608 he had acquired an enormous artistic vocabulary: the paintings of Caravaggio in particular were to influence his work strongly. His first major success was *The Raising of the Cross*, painted in 1610 and displayed today in Antwerp cathedral (see p.150). A large, dynamic work, it caused a sensation at the time, establishing Rubens' reputation and leading to a string of commissions that enabled him to set up his own studio. *The Descent from the Cross*, his next major work (also in the cathedral), consolidated this success: equally Baroque, it is nevertheless quieter and more restrained.

The division of labour in Rubens' studio, and the talent of the artists working there (who included Antony van Dyck and Jacob Jordaens – see below) ensured a substantial output of outstanding work. The degree to which Rubens personally worked on a canvas would vary – and would determine its price. From the early 1620s onwards he turned his hand to a plethora of themes and subjects – religious works, portraits, tapestry designs, landscapes, mythological scenes, ceiling paintings – each of which was handled with supreme vitality and virtuosity. From his Flemish antecedents he inherited an acute sense of light, and used it not to dramatize his subjects (a technique favoured by Caravaggio and other Italian artists), but in association with colour and form. The drama in his works comes from the vigorous animation of his characters. His large-scale allegorical works, especially, are packed with heaving, writhing figures that appear to tumble out from the canvas.

The energy of Rubens' paintings was reflected in his private life. In addition to his career as an artist, he also undertook diplomatic missions to Spain and England, and used these opportunities to study the works of other artists and – as in the case of Velázquez – to meet them personally. In the 1630s, gout began to hamper his activities, and from this time his painting became more domestic and meditative. Hélène Fourment, his second wife, was the subject of many portraits and served as a model for characters in his allegorical paintings, her figure epitomizing the buxom, well-rounded women found throughout his work.

Rubens' influence on the artists of the period was enormous. The huge output of his studio meant that his works were universally seen, and widely disseminated by the engravers he employed to copy his work. Chief among his followers was the portraitist **Antony van Dyck** (1599–1641), who worked in Rubens' studio from 1618, often taking on the depiction of religious figures in his master's works that required particular sensitivity and pathos. Like Rubens, van Dyck was born in Antwerp and travelled widely in Italy, though his initial work was influenced less by the Italian artists than by Rubens himself. Eventually van Dyck developed his own distinct style and technique, establishing himself as court painter to Charles I in England, and creating portraits of a nervous elegance that would influence portraiture there for the next hundred and fifty years. Most of his great portrait paintings remain in England, but his best religious works – such as the *Crucifixion* in Mechelen's cathedral – can be found in Belgium. **Jacob Jordaens** (1593–1678) was also an Antwerp native who studied under Rubens. Although he was commissioned to complete several works left unfinished by Rubens at the time of his death, his robustly naturalistic works have an earthy – and sensuous – realism that is quite distinct in style and technique.

As well as the Baroque creations of Rubens and his acolytes, another style emerged in the seventeenth century, that of **genre painting**. Often misunderstood, the term was initially applied to everything from animal paintings and still lifes through to historical works and landscapes, but later came to be applied only to scenes of everyday life. One of its early practitioners was **Frans Snijders** (1579–1657), who took up still-life painting where Aertsen left off, amplifying his subject – food and drink – to even larger, more sumptuous canvases, while doubling up as a member of the Rubens art machine, painting animals and still-life sections for the master's works. In the Spanish Netherlands (roughly today's Belgium), the most skilful practitioner was **Adriaen Brouwer** (1605–38), whose peasant figures rivalled those of the painters Jan Steen and Adriaen van Ostade in the United Provinces (now the Netherlands) to the north. Brouwer's output was unsurprisingly small given his short life, but his riotous tavern scenes and tableaux of everyday life are deftly done, and were well received in their day, collected by, among others, Rubens and Rembrandt. Brouwer studied in Haarlem for a while under Frans Hals (and may have picked up much of his painterly technique from him), before returning to his native Flanders to influence **David Teniers the Younger** (1610–90), who worked in Antwerp, and later in Brussels. Teniers' early paintings are Brouwer-like peasant scenes, although his later work is more delicate and diverse, including *kortegaardje* – guardroom scenes that show soldiers carousing.

The eighteenth century

By the end of the seventeenth century, French influences had overwhelmed Belgium's native artistic tradition with painters like **Jan Joseph Horemans I** and **Balthasar van den Bossche** modifying the Flemish genre painting of the previous century to suit Parisian tastes. Towards the end of the century Neoclassicism came into vogue, a French-led movement whose leading light was **Jacques Louis David** (1748–1825), the creator of the *Death of Marat*, an iconic work displayed in Brussels' Musées Royaux des Beaux Arts (see p.80). **Laurent Delvaux** (1696–1778) was also an important figure during this period, a Flemish sculptor who produced a large number of works for Belgian churches, including the pulpit of Ghent's cathedral.

The nineteenth century

French artistic fashions ruled the Belgian roost well into the nineteenth century, and amongst them Neoclassicism remained the most popular. Of the followers of Jacques Louis David, **François Joseph Navez** (1787–1869) was the most important to work in Belgium, furthering the influence of the movement via his position as director of the Brussels academy. With Belgian independence (from the Netherlands) in 1830, came, as might be expected, a new interest in nationalism, and artists such as **Louis Galliat** (1810–87) and **Henri Dobbelaere** (1829–85) spearheaded a romantic interpretation of historical events, idealizing Belgium's recent and medieval history.

Antoine Wiertz (1806–65) – who has his own museum in Brussels (see p.114) – was celebrated for his grandiose amalgamation of romantic and Neoclassical themes in his sculptures and paintings, while **Henri de Braekeleer** (1840–88) was highly regarded for his Dutch-inspired interiors and landscapes. Indeed, landscape painting underwent a resurgence of popularity in France in the mid-nineteenth century, and once again Belgian artists flocked to reflect that country's tastes. More positively, **Emile Claus** (1849–1924) adapted French Impressionist ideas to create an individual style known as Luminism, and **Théo Rysselberghe** (1862–1926) followed suit. The talented **Fernand Khnopff** (1858–1921) developed his own style too, in his case inspired by the English Pre-Raphaelites.

One artist who stands out during this period is **Constantin Meunier** (1831–1905), a painter and sculptor whose naturalistic work depicting brawny workers and mining scenes was the perfect mirror of a fast-industrializing Belgium; Meunier is another artist to have his own museum in the capital – see p.102. However, the most original Belgian artist of the late nineteenth century was **James Ensor** (1860–1949). Ensor, who lived in Ostend for most of his life, painted macabre, disturbing works, whose haunted style can be traced back to Bosch and Bruegel and which was itself a precursor of Expressionism. He was active in a group known as **Les XX** (*Les Vingt*; see box on p.107), which organized exhibitions of new styles of art from abroad, and greatly influenced contemporary Belgian painters.

The twentieth century

Each of the major modern art movements had its followers in Belgium, and each was diluted or altered according to local taste. **Expressionism** was manifest in a local group of artists established in a village near Ghent, with the most eye-catching paintings produced by **Constant Permeke** (1886–1952), whose bold, deeply coloured canvases can be found in many Belgian galleries. There was also **Jean Delville** (1867–1953), not as talented as Permeke perhaps, but an artist who certainly set about his religious preoccupations with gigantic gusto. **Surrealism** also caught on in a big way, perhaps because of the Belgian penchant for the bizarre and grotesque. **René Magritte** (1898–1967), one of the leading lights of the movement, was born and trained in Belgium and returned there after being involved in the movement's birth in 1927. His Surrealism is gentle compared to the work of Dalí or de Chirico: ordinary images are used in a dreamlike way, often playing on the distinction between a word and its meaning. His most famous motif was the man in the bowler hat, whose face was always hidden from view. **Paul Delvaux** (1897–1994) adopted his own rather salacious interpretation of the movement – a sort of "what-the-butler-saw" Surrealism.

Most of Belgium's interwar artists were influenced by van Doesburg and de Stijl in the Netherlands, though none figured highly in the movement. The abstract geometrical works of **Victor Severanckx** (1897–1965) owed much to de Stijl, and he in turn inspired the postwar group known as **La Jeune Peinture**, which gathered together some of the most notable artists working in Belgium, the antecedents of the Abstract Expressionists of the 1950s. A similar collective function was served by **CoBrA**, founded in 1948 and taking its name from the first letters of Copenhagen, Brussels and Amsterdam. While none of the Belgian participants in CoBrA achieved the fame of one of its Dutch members, Karel Appel, the name of **Pierre Alechinsky** (1927–) is certainly well known in his hometown, Brussels. Probably the most famous recent Belgian artist is **Marcel Broodthaers** (1924–1976). He initially worked in the Surrealist manner, but soon branched out, quickly graduating from cut-paper geometric shapes into both the plastic arts and most famously, sharp and brightly coloured paintings of everyday artefacts, especially casseroles brimming with mussels.

Books

Most of the following books should be readily available in the UK, US, Australasia and Canada, though you may have a little more difficulty tracking down those few titles we mention which are currently out of print, signified by "o/p". Titles with the ★ symbol are especially recommended.

Art and architecture

Kristin Lohse Belkin *Rubens*. Too long for its own good, this book details Rubens' spectacularly successful career both as artist and diplomat. Belkin is particularly thorough in her discussions of technique and the workings of his workshop. Extensive reference is made to Rubens' letters. Excellent illustrations.

Robin Blake *Anthony van Dyck*. Whether or not van Dyck justifies 448 pages is a moot point, but he did have an interesting life and certainly thumped out a fair few paintings. This volume explores every artistic nook and cranny.

Aurora Cuito (ed) *Victor Horta*. Concise and readily digestible guide to the work of Belgium's leading exponent of Art Nouveau (see p.98).

★ **R. H. Fuchs** *Dutch Painting*. Thoughtful and well-researched title in the outstanding Thames & Hudson art series which tracks through the history of its subject from the fifteenth century onwards. Highly recommended.

R. H. Fuchs et al *Flemish and Dutch Painting (from Van Gogh, Ensor, Magritte and Mondrian to Contemporary)*. Excellent, lucid account giving an overview of the development of Flemish and Dutch painting.

Suzi Gablik *Magritte*. Suzi Gablik lived in Magritte's house for six months in the 1960s and this personal contact informs the text, which is lucid, perceptive and thoughtful. Most of the illustrations are, however, black and white. At 208 pages, much longer than the Hammacher version (see below).

★ **Walter S. Gibson** *Hieronymus Bosch*. Everything you wanted to know about Bosch, his paintings and his late fifteenth-century milieu. Superbly illustrated; one of the Thames & Hudson art series. Also, try the beautifully illustrated *Bruegel* (Thames & Hudson again), which takes a detailed look at the artist with nine well-argued chapters investigating the components of Pieter Bruegel the Elder's art.

A M Hammacher *René Magritte*. Thames & Hudson produce some of the finest art books in the world and this is an excellent sample, beautifully illustrated and featuring a detailed examination of Magritte's life, times and artistic output. One of the "Masters of Art" series. Very competitively priced too.

Craig Harbison *Jan van Eyck: the Play of Realism*. Not much is known about van Eyck, but Harbison has done his best to root out every detail. The text is accompanied by illustrations of all of Eyck's major paintings.

Philippe Roberts-Jones *Brussels: Fin de Siècle*. Specialist text describing – and illustrating – the fizz of architectural and artistic endeavour that swept Brussels at the turn of the twentieth century. Art Nouveau and Symbolism are the two leading protagonists.

Peter Weiermair *Eros & Death: Belgian Symbolism* (o/p). Great title for an original book exploring the nature of Belgian symbolism, with reference to drawings, prints, paintings and sculptures. Artists featured include James Ensor and Felician Rops.

Christopher White *Peter Paul Rubens: Man and Artist* (o/p). A beautifully illustrated introduction to both Rubens' work and social milieu.

History and politics

Neal Ascherson *The King Incorporated: Leopold the Second and the Congo*. You'd never guess from Brussels' Musée de la Dynastie (see p.87), but King Léopold II was responsible for one of the cruelest of colonial regimes, a savage system of repression and exploitation that devastated the Belgian Congo. Ascherson details it all.

Ulrike Becks-Malorny *Ensor*. Eminently readable and extensively illustrated account of the often-neglected life and art of the brilliant Ostend-born painter, James Ensor. Inexpensive, too.

★ J. C. H. Blom (ed.) *History of the Low Countries*. Belgian history books are thin on the ground, so this incisive, well-balanced volume is very welcome. A series of historians weigh in with their specialities to build a comprehensive picture of the region from the Celts and Romans through to the 1980s. Highly recommended, though hardly sun-lounge reading.

Paul van Buitenen *Blowing the Whistle* (Politico's Publishing, UK). All your worst fears about the EU confirmed. Buitenen was an assistant auditor in the EU's Financial Control Directorate in Brussels and this book, published in 1998, exposed the fraud and corruption. Needless to say, the EU was far from grateful for his revelations and forced him to resign, but even so the scandal stories became so widespread that the entire Commission was obliged to resign en bloc. Since then, there have been earnest declarations that things would be much better (ho, ho).

Martin Conway *Collaboration in Belgium*. Detailed analysis of wartime collaboration and the development of Fascism in Belgium in the 1930s and 1940s. Authoritative and well written, but something of a special interest text.

Nicholas Crane *Mercator*. Arguably the most important map-maker of all time, Gerard Mercator was born in Rupelmonde near Antwerp in 1512. This book details every twist and turn of his life and provides oodles – perhaps too many oodles – of background material on the Flanders of his time.

Michael Farr *Tintin: The Complete Companion*. A Tintinologists' treat, this immaculately illustrated book – written by the world's leading Tintinologist – explores every aspect of Hergé's remarkably popular creation. Particularly strong on the real-life stories that inspired Hergé, but you do have to be seriously interested in Tintin to really enjoy this book.

Pieter Geyl *The Revolt of The Netherlands 1555–1609*. Geyl presents a detailed account of the Netherlands during its formative years, chronicling the uprising against the Spanish and both the formation of the United Provinces and the creation of the Spanish Netherlands (the Belgium of today). First published in 1932, it has long been regarded as the classic text on the subject, though it's a hard and often ponderous read.

Christopher Hibbert *Waterloo*. Hibbert is one of Britain's leading historians, an astute commentator who writes in a fluent, easily accessible style. This book is divided into three parts. The first examines Napoleon's rise to power, the second looks at Wellington and his allies, the third deals with the battle. Hibbert is also responsible for editing *The Wheatley Diary*, the journal and sketchbook of a young English officer who fought his way across Europe during the Napoleonic Wars.

★ **Adam Hochschild** *King Leopold's Ghost*. Harrowing and detailed account – a little on the long side – of King Leopold's savage colonial regime in the Congo. Particularly good on Roger Casement, the one-time British consul to the Congo, who publicized the cruelty and helped bring it to an end. Hochschild's last chapter – "The Great Forgetting" – is a stern criticism of the Belgians for their failure to acknowledge their dreadful colonial history.

B. H. Liddell Hart (ed.) *The Letters of Private Wheeler* (o/p). A veteran of World War I, Liddell Hart writes with panache and clarity, marshalling the letters penned by the eponymous private as he fought Napoleon and the French across a fair slice of Europe. Wheeler fought at Waterloo, but the section on the battle is surprisingly brief. As a whole, the letters are a delight, a

witty insight into the living conditions and attitudes of Wellington's infantry. In a similar vein, Hart's *History of the Second World War* (o/p) is an excellent introduction to military strategy and tactics. The author always claimed (with some justification) that he foresaw the potential importance of tanks – a voice crying in the British military wilderness before Hitler unveiled his blitzkreig.

Geoffrey Parker *The Dutch Revolt* ⊡ . Compelling account of the struggle between the Netherlands and Spain. Quite the best thing you can read on the period. Also *The Army of Flanders and the Spanish Road 1567–1659* ⊡ . The title may sound academic, but this book gives a fascinating insight into the Habsburg army, which occupied the Low Countries for well over a hundred years – how it functioned, was fed and moved from Spain to the Low Countries along the so-called Spanish Road.

Andrew Wheatcroft *The Habsburgs*. Excellent and well-researched trawl through the dynasty's history, from its eleventh-century beginnings to its eclipse at the end of World War I. Enjoyable background reading.

Geoffrey Wootten *Waterloo 1815*. About one-third of the length of Hibbert's *Waterloo* (see above), this 96-page book focuses on the battle, providing a clear, thorough and interesting account.

Travel and specialist guides

★ **Patrick Bentin** (ed) *Guide Delta Bruxelles 2005*. Over four hundred pages of detailed and perceptive hotel and restaurant reviews – ideal if you're moving to Brussels. Only in French; available at leading bookshops in Brussels.

Charlotte and Emily Brontë (ed. Sue Lonoff) *The Belgian Essays*.

The Brontë sisters left their native Yorkshire for the first time in 1842 to make a trip to Brussels. Charlotte returned to Brussels the following year. This handsome volume reproduces the 28 essays they penned (in French) during their journey and provides the English translation opposite. It makes a delightful read with particular highlights being "The Butterfly", "The Caterpillar" and "The Death of Napoleon".

Ernest Gilliat-Smith *The Story of Brussels* (o/p). Quirky, good-humoured account of Brussels written in 1906. In the UK, pick it up at the library or a secondhand bookshop.

Hergé *The Calculus Affair* and *The Making of Tintin: Cigars of the Pharaoh & the Blue Lotus.* Tintin comic strips come in and out of print at a rapid rate, usually in anthologies; there's a wide selection of audio cassettes too. The two anthologies listed here are as good a place as any to start.

Michael Jackson *The Great Beers of Belgium.* Belgium produces the best beers in the world. Michael Jackson is one of the best beer writers in the world. The result is cheeky, palatable and sinewy with just a hint of fruiti-ness. Most recently updated edition dates from 2001.

Bruce McCall *Sit!: The Dog Portraits of Thierry Poncelet.* This weird and wonderful book features the work of the Belgian Thierry Poncelet, who raids flea markets and antique shops for ancestral portraits, then restores them and paints dogs' heads over the original faces. Uuummmm.

Harry Pearson *A Tall Man in a Low Land.* The product of an extended visit to the lesser-known parts of Belgium, this racy book is in the style of (but not as perceptive as) Bill Bryson. Pearson has oodles of comments to make on Belgium and the Belgians – on everything from

DIY to architecture – and although he sometimes tries too hard, this is a very enjoyable read.

Benoit Peeters *Tintin and the World of Hergé: an Illustrated History.* Exam-ines the life and career of Hergé, particularly the development of Tintin, and the influences on his work. No fewer than three hundred illustrations.

⭐ **Luc Sante** *The Factory of Facts.* Born in Belgium but raised in the US, Sante returned to his native land for an extended visit in 1989 – at the age of 35. His book is primarily a personal reflection, but he also uses this as a base for a thought-ful exploration of Belgium and the Belgians – from their art to their food and beyond. Highly recommended.

Marianne Thys *Filmography of Belgian Movies, 1896–1996.* This authoritative hardback volume has reviews of every Belgian film ever made. Published in 2000, it's 992 pages long, as is reflected in the cost.

San van de Veire *Belgian Fashion Design.* The staggering success of Flemish fashion designers is chroni-cled in this well-illustrated book. The centre of the action is Antwerp, but Brussels also gets a look-in.

⭐ **Tim Webb** *Good Beer Guide to Belgium.* Detailed and enthusiastic guide to the best bars, beers and brew-eries. A good read, and extremely well informed to boot. Undoubtedly, the best book on its subject on the market. Published in 2005 by CAMRA (Campaign For Real Ale books).

Literature

Mark Bles *A Child at War.* This powerful book describes the tribula-tions of Hortense Daman, a Belgian girl who joined the Resistance at the tender age of fifteen. Betrayed to the Gestapo, Daman was sent

to the Ravensbruck concentration camp, where she was used in medi-cal experiments, but remarkably survived. This is her story, though the book would have benefited from some editorial pruning.

Hugo Claus *The Sorrow of Belgium.* Born in Bruges in 1929, Claus is generally regarded as Belgium's foremost Flemish-language novelist, and this is generally regarded as his best novel. It charts the growing maturity of a young boy living in Flanders under the Nazi occupation. Claus' style is somewhat dense to say the least, but the book gets to grips with the guilt, bigotry and mistrust of the period, and caused a minor uproar when it was first published in the early 1980s. His *Swordfish* is a story of an isolated village rife with ethnic and religious tensions. The effects of this prove too much for a boy, precipitating his descent into madness. Also *Desire*, the strange and disconcerting tale of two drinking buddies, who, on an impulse, abandon small-town Belgium for Las Vegas, where both of them start to unravel.

Amelie Nothomb *Loving Sabotage.* English-language translations of modern Belgian writers (in both French and Dutch) are a rarity, but Nothomb, one of Belgium's most popular writers, has made the linguistic leap. This particular novel deals with the daughter of a diplomat stationed in Peking in the 1970s, a rites-of-passage story with a Maoist backdrop. *The Stranger Next Door*, perhaps Nothomb's most successful translated work, deals with weird and disconcerting happenings in the Belgian countryside, while *Fear and Trembling* is a sharply observed tale of the shoddy treatment meted out to a young Western businesswoman in a big corporation in Tokyo.

Jean Ray *Malpertuis.* This spine-chilling Gothic novel was written by a Belgian in 1943. It's set in Belgium, too, where the suffocating Catholicism of the Inquisition provides a perfect backcloth.

Georges Rodenbach *Bruges la Morte.* First published in 1892, this slim and subtly evocative novel is all about love and obsession – or rather a highly stylized, decadent view of it. It's credited with starting the craze for visiting Bruges, the "dead city" where the action unfolds.

Georges Simenon *Maigret loses his Temper* and *Maigret and the Killer.* There can be no dispute that Simenon was Belgium's most famous crime writer, his main creation being the Parisian detective Maigret. There are dozens of books: these two can get you started. Ripping yarns.

Emile Zola *Germinal.* First published in 1885, *Germinal* exposed the harsh conditions of the coalmines of northeast France. It was also a rallying call to action with the protagonist, Etienne Lantier, organizing a strike. A vivid, powerful work, Zola had a detailed knowledge of the mines – how they were run and worked – and makes passing reference to the coal fields of southern Belgium, where conditions and working practices were identical. This novel inspired a whole generation of Belgian radicals.

Language

Language

Language

I n Brussels, the majority of Belgians speak a dialect of French known as Walloon, as they do in the country's southern provinces, known logically enough as Wallonia. Walloon is almost identical to French, and if you've any knowledge of the language, you'll be readily understood. One peculiarity of the city is that French has linguistic parity with Dutch, which is spoken both here and across the northern part of Belgium in a variety of distinctive dialects commonly lumped together as Flemish. In Brussels, all manifestations of the written word have to be in both languages, though in this guidebook we have opted just for French – the language of the majority of city folk. Most Belgians working in the capital's business and tourist industries have at least some knowledge of English, but perhaps surprisingly you're likely to need a modicum of French in many restaurants and cafés.

French isn't a particularly easy language, despite the number of words shared with English, but learning the bare essentials is not difficult and makes all the difference. Even just saying "Bonjour, Madame/Monsieur" when you go into a shop and then pointing will usually get you a smile and helpful service.

Differentiating words is the initial problem in understanding spoken French – it's very hard to get people to slow down. If, as a last resort, you get them to write it down, you'll probably find you know half the words anyway. Of the available **phrasebooks**, Rough Guide's own *French Dictionary Phrasebook* should sort you out better than most.

French consonants

Consonants are pronounced much as in English, except:

c is softened to the "s" sound when followed by an "e" or "i", or when it has a cedilla (ç) below it
ch is always **sh**
g is softened to a French "j" sound when followed by e or i (eg, Gérard)
h is silent
j is like the "s" sound in "measure" or

"treasure"
ll is like the "y" in yes
qu is normally pronounced like a "k" (eg, quatre)
r is growled (or rolled)
th is the same as t
w is pronounced "v"

Vowels

These are the hardest sounds to get right. Roughly:

a as in hat
e as in get
é between get and gate
è between get and gut
eu like the u in hurt

i as in machine
o as in hot
o, au as in over
ou as in food
u as in a pursed-lip version of use

More awkward are the combinations below when they occur at the ends of words, or are followed by consonants other than n or m:

in/im like the an in anxious

an/am, en/em as in don when said with a nasal accent

on/om like the don in Doncaster said by someone with a heavy cold

un/um like the u in understand

Useful words and phrases

Greetings and civilities

s'il vous plaît	please	bonsoir	good evening
(non) merci	(no) thank you	bonne nuit	good night
bonjour	hello	au revoir	goodbye
comment allez-vous?/ça va?	how are you?	à bientôt	see you later
bonjour	good morning	pardon, Madame, Monsieur/ je m'excuse	sorry
bonjour	good afternoon		

Basic terms and phrases

oui	yes	grand	big
non	no	petit	small
parlez-vous anglais?	do you speak English?	ouvert	open
je (ne) comprends (pas)	I (don't) understand	fermé	closed
femmes	women	pousser	push
hommes	men	tirer	pull
les enfants	children	nouveu	new
quand?	when?	vieux	old
je veux . . .	I want . . .	chaud	hot
je ne veux pas	I don't want	froid	cold
d'accord	OK/agreed	avec	with
bon	good	sans	without
mauvais	bad	beaucoup	a lot
		un peu	a little

Money

c'est combien . . . ?	how much is . . . ?	timbre(s)	stamp(s)
bon marché	cheap	bureau de change	money exchange
cher	expensive	la caisse	cashier
la poste	post office	le guichet	ticket office

Getting around

comment est-ce que je peux arriver à . . . ?	how do I get to . . . ?	à gauche	left
		à droite	right
		tout droit	straight ahead
où est . . . ?	where is . . . ?	derrière	behind
combien y a-t-il jusqu'à . . . ?	how far is it to . . . ?	ici	here
		là	there
loin	far	quai	platform
près	near	voie de traversée	through traffic only

Days, times and months

lundi	Monday	semaine	week
mardi	Tuesday	mois	month
mercredi	Wednesday	année	year
jeudi	Thursday	maintenant	now
vendredi	Friday	plus tard	later
samedi	Saturday	janvier	January
dimanche	Sunday	février	February
le matin	morning	mars	March
l'après-midi	afternoon	avril	April
le soir	evening	mai	May
la nuit	night	juin	June
hier	yesterday	juillet	July
aujourd'hui	today	août	August
demain	tomorrow	septembre	September
demain matin	tomorrow morning	octobre	October
minute	minute	novembre	November
heure	hour	décembre	December
jour	day		

Numbers

zéro	0	treize	13
un	1	quatorze	14
deux	2	quinze	15
trois	3	seize	16
quatre	4	dix-sept	17
cinq	5	dix-huit	18
six	6	dix-neuf	19
sept	7	vingt	20
huit	8	vingt-et-un	21
neuf	9	trente	30
dix	10	quarante	40
onze	11	cinquante	50
douze	12	soixante	60

soixante-dix (local usage is septante)	70	cent	100
		cent-et-un	101
		deux cents	200
quatre-vingts	80	cinq cents	500
quatre-vingt-dix (local usage is nonante)	90	mille	1000

A French food and drink glossary

Basic terms and ingredients

à point	medium	légumes	vegetables
beurre	butter	oeufs	eggs
bien cuit	well done	pain	bread
chaud	hot	poisson	fish
crème fraîche	sour cream	poivre	pepper
dessert	dessert	saignant	rare
escargots	snails	salade	salad
frappé	iced	sel	salt
fromage	cheese	sucre	sugar/sweet (taste)
froid	cold	tourte	tart or pie
gibiers	game	tranche	slice
hors d'oeuvre	starters	viande	meat

Cooking methods

au four	baked	mijoté	stewed
bouilli	boiled	pané	breaded
frit/friture	fried/deep fried	rôti	roast
fumé	smoked	sauté	lightly cooked in butter
grillé	grilled		

Meat and poultry

agneau	lamb	foie	liver
bifteck	steak	gigot	leg of venison
boeuf	beef	jambon	ham
canard	duck	lard	bacon
cheval	horsemeat	porc	pork
cuisson	leg of lamb	poulet	chicken
côtelettes	cutlets	saucisse	sausage
dindon	turkey	veau	veal

Fish and seafood

anchois	anchovies	maquereau	mackerel
anguilles	eels	morue	cod
carrelet	plaice	moules	mussels
crevettes roses	prawns	saumon	salmon
hareng	herring	sole	sole
lotte de mer	monkfish	truite	trout

Vegetables and grains

ail	garlic	laitue	lettuce
asperges	asparagus	oignons	onions
carottes	carrots	petits pois	peas
champignon	mushrooms	poireau	leek
choufleur	cauliflower	pommes (de terre)	potatoes
concombre	cucumber	riz	rice
genièvre	juniper	tomate	tomato

Fruit and nuts

amandes	almonds	marrons	chestnuts
ananas	pineapple	noisette	hazelnut
cacahouète	peanut	pamplemousse	grapefruit
cérises	cherries	poire	pear
citron	lemon	pomme	apple
fraises	strawberries	prune	plum
framboises	raspberries	pruneau	prune
		raisins	grapes

Snacks

un sandwich	a sandwich . . .	omelette . . .	omelette . . .
/une baguette . . .		nature	plain
de jambon	with ham	au fromage	with cheese
de fromage	with cheese	salade de . . .	salad of . . .
de saucisson	with sausage	tomates	tomatoes
à l'ail	with garlic	concombres	cucumbers
au poivre	with pepper	crêpes . . .	pancakes . . .
croque monsieur	grilled cheese and ham sandwich	au sucre	with sugar
		au citron	with lemon
oeufs . . .	eggs . . .	au miel	with honey
au plat	fried eggs	à la confiture	with jam
à la coque	boiled eggs		
dur	hard-boiled eggs		
brouillés	scrambled eggs		

Soups and starters

assiette anglaise	plate of cold meats	**consommé**	clear soup
bisque	shellfish soup	**crudités**	raw vegetables with dressing
bouillabaisse	fish soup from Marseilles	**potage**	thick soup, usually vegetable
bouillon	broth or stock		

Sweets and desserts

crêpes	pancakes	**parfait**	frozen mousse, sometimes ice cream
crêpes suzettes	thin pancakes with orange juice and liqueur	**petits fours**	bite-sized cakes or pastries
glace	ice cream		
madeleine	small, shell-shaped sponge cake		

Drinks

bière	beer	**thé**	tea
café	coffee	**vin . . .**	wine . . .
eaux de vie	spirits distilled from various fruits	**rouge**	red
		blanc	white
jenever	Dutch/Flemish gin	**brut**	very dry
lait	milk	**sec**	dry
orange/citron pressé	fresh orange/ lemon juice	**demi-sec**	sweet
		doux	very sweet

Glossaries

French terms

Abbaye Abbey or group of monastic buildings

Aéroport Airport

Auberge de la Jeunesse Youth hostel

Beaux Arts Fine arts

Beffroi Belfry

Béguinage Convent occupied by *béguines*, ie members of a sisterhood living as nuns but without vows and with the right of return to the secular world

Bicyclette Bicycle

Bourse Stock exchange

Chapelle Chapel

Château Mansion, country house, or castle

Cour Court(yard)

Couvent Convent, monastery

Dégustation Tasting (wine or food)

Donjon Castle keep

Eglise Church

Entrée Entrance

Etage Floor (of a museum, etc)

Fermeture Closing period

Fouilles Archeological excavations

Gare Train station

Gîte d'Etape Dormitory-style lodgings situated in relatively remote parts of the country which can house anywhere between ten and one hundred people per establishment

Grand-Place Central town square and the heart of most Belgian communities

Halle aux Draps Cloth hall – the building in medieval weaving towns where cloth would be weighed, graded, stored and sold

Halle aux Viandes Meat market

Halles Covered, central food market

Hôpital Hospital

Hôtel Either hotel, or – in its earlier sense – (private) town house

Hôtel de Ville Town hall

Jardin Garden

Jours Feriés Public holidays

Maison House

Marché Market

Moulin Windmill

Municipal Civic, municipal

Musée Museum

Nôtre-Dame Our Lady

Palais Palace

Place Square, market place

Pont Bridge

Porte Gateway

Quai Quay, or station platform

Quartier District or neighbourhood of a town

Rue Street

Sortie Exit

Syndicat d'initiative Tourist office

Tour Tower

Trésor Treasury

Flemish terms

Abdij Abbey or group of monastic buildings

Begijnhof Convent occupied by *béguines (begijns)*, i.e. members of a sisterhood living as nuns but without vows and with the right of return to the secular world

Beiaard Carillon (a set of tuned church bells, either operated by an automatic mechanism or played by a keyboard)

Belfort Belfry

Beurs Stock exchange

Botermarkt Butter market

Brug Bridge

Burgher Member of the upper or mercantile classes of a town, usually with civic powers

Fiets Bicycle

Fietspad Bicycle path

Gasthof Inn

Gasthuis Hospital

Gerechtshof Law Courts

Gilde Guild

Gracht Urban canal

Groentenmarkt Vegetable market

Grote Markt Central town square and the heart of most Belgian communities

Hal Hall

Hof Court(yard)

Huis House

Ingang Entrance

Jeugdherberg Youth hostel

Kaai Quay

Kapel Chapel

Kasteel Castle

Kerk Church, eg, Grote Kerk: the principal church of the town; Onze Lieve Vrouwekerk: church dedicated to the Virgin Mary

Koning King

Koningin Queen

Koninklijk Royal

Korenmarkt Corn market

Kunst Art

Kursaal Casino

Lakenhalle Cloth hall – the building in medieval weaving towns where cloth would be weighed, graded and sold

Luchthaven Airport

Markt Marketplace

Molen Windmill

Ommegang Procession

Paleis Palace

Plaats A square or open space

Plein A square or open space

Poort Gate

Rijk State

Schatkamer Treasury

Schepenzaal Alderman's Hall

Schouwburg Theatre

Sierkunst Decorative arts

Schone Kunsten Fine arts

Spoor Track (as in railway) – trains arrive and depart on track (as distinct from platform) numbers

Stadhuis Town hall

Station (Train or bus) station

Stedelijk Civic, municipal

Steen Fortress

Toren Tower

Tuin Garden

Uitgang Exit

Vleeshuis Meat market

Volkskunde Folklore

Art and architectural terms

Ambulatory Interior covered passage around the outer edge of thze choir of a church

Apse Semicircular protrusion at (usually) the east end of a church

Art Deco Geometrical style of art and architecture especially popular in the 1930s

Art Nouveau Style of art, architecture and design based on highly stylized vegetal forms. Particularly popular in the early part of the twentieth century

Balustrade An ornamental rail, running, almost invariably, along the top of a building

Basilica Roman Catholic church with honorific privileges

Baroque The art and architecture of the Counter-Reformation, dating from around 1600; distinguished by its extreme ornateness, exuberance and by the complex but harmonious spatial arrangement of interiors

Carillon A set of tuned church bells, either operated by an automatic mechanism or played by a keyboard

Caryatid A sculptured female figure used as a column

Chancel The eastern part of a church, often separated from the nave by a screen (see "rood screen" below); contains the choir and ambulatory

Classical Architectural style incorporating Greek and Roman elements – pillars, domes, colonnades, etc – at its height in the seventeenth century and revived, as Neoclassical, in the nineteenth century

Clerestory Upper storey of a church, incorporating the windows

Diptych Carved or painted work on two panels, often used as an altarpiece

Expressionism Artistic style popular at the beginning of the twentieth century, characterized by the exaggeration of shape or colour; often accompanied by the extensive use of symbolism

Flamboyant Florid form of Gothic (see below)

Fresco Wall painting – durable through application to wet plaster

Gable The triangular upper portion of a wall – decorative or supporting a roof

Genre painting In the seventeenth century the term "genre painting" applied to everything from animal paintings and still lifes through to historical works and landscapes, while in the eighteenth century, the term came only to be applied to scenes of everyday life

Gobelins A rich French tapestry, named after the most famous of all tapestry manufacturers, based in Paris, whose most renowned period was in the reign of Louis XIV; also loosely applied to tapestries of similar style

Gothic Architectural style of the thirteenth to sixteenth century, characterized by pointed arches, rib vaulting, flying buttresses and a general emphasis on verticality

Misericord Bracket on the underside of a hinged choir stall seat, which, when the seat was upright, could help a worshipper keep on his feet; they were often carved with secular subjects as bottoms were not thought worthy of religious carvings

Nave Main body of a church

Neoclassical Architectural style derived from Greek and Roman elements – pillars, domes, colonnades, etc – popular in the Low Countries during French rule in the early nineteenth century

Rococo Highly florid, light and graceful eighteenth-century style of architecture, painting and interior design, forming the last phase of Baroque

Renaissance The period of European history – beginning in Italy in the forteenth century – marking the end of the medieval period and the rise of the modern world, defined, amongst many criteria, by an increase in classical scholarship, geographical discovery, the rise of secular values and the growth of individualism (the term is also applied to the art and architecture of the period)

Retable Altarpiece

Romanesque Early medieval architecture distinguished by squat forms, rounded arches and naive sculpture

Rood screen Decorative screen separating the nave from the chancel; a rood loft is the gallery (or space) on top of it

Stucco Marble-based plaster used to embellish ceilings, etc

Transept Arms of a cross-shaped church, placed at ninety degrees to nave and chancel

Triptych Carved or painted work on three panels. Often used as an altarpiece

Tympanum Sculpted, usually recessed, panel above a door

Vault An arched ceiling or roof

A Rough Guide to Rough Guides

In the summer of 1981, Mark Ellingham, a recent graduate from Bristol University, was travelling round Greece and couldn't find a guidebook that really met his needs. On the one hand there were the student guides, insistent on saving every last cent, and on the other the heavyweight cultural tomes whose authors seemed to have spent more time in a research library than lounging away the afternoon at a taverna or on the beach.

In a bid to avoid getting a job, Mark and a small group of writers set about creating their own guidebook. It was a guide to Greece that aimed to combine a journalistic approach to description with a thoroughly practical approach to travellers' needs – a guide that would incorporate culture, history and contemporary insights with a critical edge, together with up-to-date, value-for-money listings. Back in London, Mark and the team finished their Rough Guide, as they called it, and talked Routledge into publishing the book.

That first *Rough Guide to Greece*, published in 1982, was a student scheme that became a publishing phenomenon. The immediate success of the book – with numerous reprints and a Thomas Cook prize shortlisting – spawned a series that rapidly covered dozens of destinations. Rough Guides had a ready market among low-budget backpackers, but soon also acquired a much broader and older readership that relished Rough Guides' wit and inquisitiveness as much as their enthusiastic, critical approach. Everyone wants value for money, but not at any price.

Rough Guides soon began supplementing the "rougher" information about hostels and low-budget listings with the kind of detail on restaurants and quality hotels that independent-minded visitors on any budget might expect, whether on business in New York or trekking in Thailand.

These days the guides – distributed worldwide by the Penguin Group – offer recommendations from shoestring to luxury and cover more than 200 destinations around the globe, including almost every country in the Americas and Europe, more than half of Africa and most of Asia and Australasia. Our ever-growing team of authors and photographers is spread all over the world, particularly in Europe, the USA and Australia.

In 1994, we published the *Rough Guide to World Music* and *Rough Guide to Classical Music*; and a year later the *Rough Guide to the Internet*. All three books have become benchmark titles in their fields – which encouraged us to expand into other areas of publishing, mainly around popular culture. Rough Guides now publish:

- Travel guides to more than 200 worldwide destinations
- Dictionary phrasebooks to 22 major languages
- History guides ranging from Ireland to Islam
- Maps printed on rip-proof and waterproof Polyart™ paper
- Music guides running the gamut from Opera to Elvis
- Restaurant guides to London, New York and San Francisco
- Reference books on topics as diverse as the weather and Shakespeare
- Sports guides from Formula 1 to Man Utd
- Pop culture books from *Lord of the Rings* to Cult TV
- World Music CDs in association with World Music Network

Visit **www.roughguides.com** to see our latest publications.

Rough Guide credits

Text editor: Melissa Graham
Layout: Ankur Guha
Cartography: Manish Chandra and Katie Lloyd-Jones
Picture editor: Sarah Cummins
Production: Julia Bovis
Proofreaders: Jitendra Pant and Madhulita Mohapatra
Cover design: Chloë Roberts
Photographer: Roger Mapp
Editorial: London Kate Berens, Claire Saunders, Geoff Howard, Ruth Blackmore, Polly Thomas, Richard Lim, Clifton Wilkinson, Alison Murchie, Karoline Densley, Andy Turner, Ella O'Donnell, Keith Drew, Edward Aves, Nikki Birrell, Helen Marsden, Alice Park, Sarah Eno, Joe Staines, Duncan Clark, Peter Buckley, Matthew Milton, Tracy Hopkins; **New York** Andrew Rosenberg, Richard Koss, Steven Horak, AnneLise Sorensen, Amy Hegarty, Hunter Slaton, April Isaacs
Design & Pictures: London Simon Bracken, Dan May, Diana Jarvis, Mark Thomas, Jj Luck, Harriet Mills, Chloë Roberts; **Delhi** Madhulita Mohapatra, Umesh Aggarwal,

Ajay Verma, Jessica Subramanian, Amit Verma
Production: Sophie Hewat, Katherine Owers
Cartography: London Maxine Repath, Ed Wright; **Delhi** Rajesh Chhibber, Jai Prakash Mishra, Ashutosh Bharti, Rajesh Mishra, Animesh Pathak, Jasbir Sandhu, Karobi Gogoi
Online: New York Jennifer Gold, Kristin Mingrone; **Delhi** Manik Chauhan, Narender Kumar, Shekhar Jha, Rakesh Kumar, Lalit K. Sharma, Chhandita Chakravarty
Marketing & Publicity: London Richard Trillo, Niki Hanmer, David Wearn, Demelza Dallow, Louise Maher; **New York** Geoff Colquitt, Megan Kennedy, Katy Ball; **Delhi** Reem Khokhar
Custom publishing and foreign rights: Philippa Hopkins
Manager India: Punita Singh
Series editor: Mark Ellingham
Reference Director: Andrew Lockett
PA to Managing and Publishing Directors: Megan McIntyre
Publishing Director: Martin Dunford
Managing Director: Kevin Fitzgerald

Publishing information

This third edition published February 2006 by **Rough Guides Ltd,**
80 Strand, London WC2R 0RL
345 Hudson St, 4th Floor,
New York, NY 10014, USA
14 Local Shopping Centre, Panchsheel Park,
New Delhi 110017, India
Distributed by the Penguin Group
Penguin Books Ltd,
80 Strand, London WC2R 0RL
Penguin Putnam, Inc.
375 Hudson Street, NY 10014, USA
Penguin Group (Australia)
250 Camberwell Road, Camberwell
Victoria 3124, Australia
Penguin Books Canada Ltd,
10 Alcorn Avenue, Toronto, Ontario,
Canada M4V 1E4
Penguin Group (New Zealand)
Cnr Rosedale and Airborne Roads
Albany, Auckland, New Zealand

Typeset in Bembo and Helvetica to an original design by Henry Iles.

Printed and bound in China

© Martin Dunford and Phil Lee 2006

288pp includes index

A catalogue record for this book is available from the British Library

ISBN-13: 978-1-84353-574-4
ISBN-10: 1-84353-574-2

1 3 5 7 9 8 6 4 2

Help us update

We've gone to a lot of effort to ensure that the third edition of **The Rough Guide to Brussels** is accurate and up to date. However, things change – places get "discovered", opening hours are notoriously fickle, restaurants and rooms raise prices or lower standards. If you feel we've got it wrong or left something out, we'd like to know, and if you can remember the address, the price, the time, the phone number, so much the better.

We'll credit all contributions, and send a copy of the next edition (or any other Rough

Guide if you prefer) for the best letters. Everyone who writes to us and isn't already a subscriber will receive a copy of our full-colour thrice-yearly newsletter. Please mark letters: "**Rough Guide Brussels Update**" and send to: Rough Guides, 80 Strand, London WC2R 0RL, or Rough Guides, 4th Floor, 345 Hudson St, New York, NY 10014. Or send an email to **mail@roughguides.com**

Have your questions answered and tell others about your trip at
www.roughguides.atinfopop.com

Acknowledgements

Phil Lee and Martin Dunford would like to extend a special word of thanks to Karin Sinnaeve of OPT in Brussels; Dawn Page of Tourism Flanders–Brussels in London; and Sophie Bouallegue of the Belgian Tourist Office Brussels and Wallonia, also in London.

Thanks also to Suzy Sumner and Loïk Dal Molin for filling in all the gaps and writing so fluently and knowledgeably and to Karoline Densley for her help and enthusiasm. Finally, last but not least, thanks to our diligent and enthusiastic editor, Melissa Graham.

Readers' letters

Thanks to all those readers of the second edition who took the trouble to write in with their amendments and additions, including Eric Van Geertruyden, Tony Hallas and B.E. Neale. Apologies for any misspellings or omissions.

Photo credits

All photos © Rough Guides except the following:

Cover
Main front picture: Café on the Grand-Place © Alamy
Small front top picture: Bakery window © Corbis
Small front lower picture: Glass City Fountain © Alamy
Back top picture: Statues in place du Petit Sablon © Getty
Back lower picture: Grand-Place by night © Alamy

Introduction
p.5 European Parliament © Lourens Smak/Alamy
p.6 Hôtel Solvay © Amar Grover

Things not to miss
01 Grand-Place © Mark Henley/Impact
11 Frites © Alan Copson/Alamy
18 Musée des Instruments de Musique © Emma Lee/Life File Photos Ltd/Alamy
21 Ommegang © Patrick Ward/Alamy

Black and whites
p.99 Musée Victor Horta © All Over Photography/ Alamy

Index

Map entries are in colour.

O

Map symbols

maps are listed in the full index using coloured text

▬▬▬·	International boundary	▲	Peak
▬▬··	Provincial boundary	♦	Point of interest
▬ ▬ ▬	Chapter boundary	⚚	Fountain
▬▬▬	Motorway	⊙	Statue
═══	Major road	@	Internet
═══	Minor road	ⓘ	Tourist office
▬▬▬	Pedestrianised street	◼	Restaurant
··········	Tunnel	★	Bus stop
- - - -	Tracks	Ⓟ	Premetro
▬■▬	Railway line	⊠	Post office
─Ⓜ─	Metro line and station	✛	Church
───	River	▬	Building
‿	Bridge	▨	Park

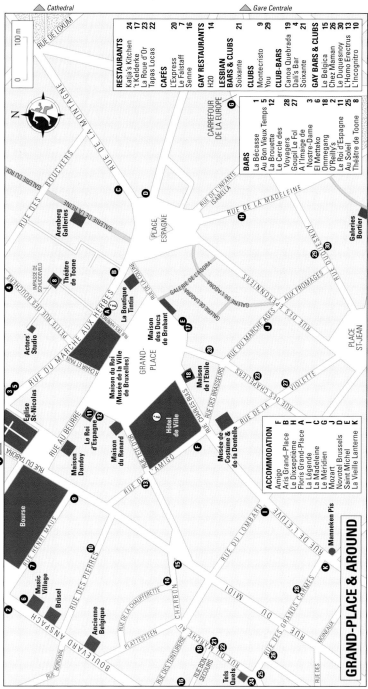

GRAND-PLACE & AROUND

△ Cathedral

△ Gare Centrale

0   100 m

N

RESTAURANTS
Katja's Kitchen   24
't Kelderke   17
La Roue d'Or   23
Tapas Locas   22

CAFÉS
L'Express   20
Le Falstaff   7
Senne   16

GAY RESTAURANTS
H2O   14

LESBIAN BARS & CLUBS
Soixante   21

CLUBS
Montecristo   9
You   29

CLUB-BARS
Canoa Quebrada   19
Dali's Bar   4
Soixante   21

GAY BARS & CLUBS
Le Belgica   15
Chez Maman   26
Le Duquesnoy   11
L'Homo Erectus   30
L'Incognitro   10

BARS
La Bécasse   1
Au Bon Vieux Temps   5
La Brouette   12
Le Cercle des
  Voyagers   28
Goupil Le Fol   27
A l'Imaige de
  Nostre-Dame   3
El Metteko   6
Ommegang   18
O'Reilly's   2
Le Roi d'Espagne   11
Au Soleil   25
Théâtre de Toone   8

ACCOMMODATION
Amigo   F
Aris Grand-Place   B
Le Dixseptième   H
Floris Grand-Place   A
La Légende   I
La Madeleine   C
Le Méridien   G
Mozart   J
Novotel Brussels   D
Saint Michel   E
La Vieille Lanterne   K

CARREFOUR
DE LA EUROPE

G

RUE DE LOXUM

RUE DE LA MONTAGNE

GALERIE DU ROI

RUE DES BOUCHERS

GALERIE DE LA REINE

Arenberg
Galleries

PETITE RUE DES BOUCHERS

IMPASSE DE
SCHUDDEVELD

Théâtre
de Toone

8

4

RUE DES HARENGS

La Boutique
Tintin

RUE DE LA COLLINE

PLACE
ESPAGNE

RUE DE L'INFANTE
ISABELLA

RUE DE LA MADELEINE

H

Actors'
Studio

RUE DU MARCHÉ AUX HERBES

RUE CHAIR ET PAIN

Maison des Ducs
de Brabant

B

GRAND-
PLACE

Maison du Roi
(Musée de la Ville
de Bruxelles)

GALERIE DE L'AGORA

GALERIE DE L'AGORA

Maison
des Ducs
de Brabant

E

17

C

D

RUE DES FRIPONS

RUE AUX FROMAGES

RUE DU MARCHÉ AUX CHARBONS

I

RUE DU MARCHÉ AUX HERBES

20

Maison
de l'Étoile

18

23

Église
St-Nicolas

3   5

Maison
Dandoy

RUE AU BEURRE

Le Roi
d'Espagne

11

12

Maison
du Renard

RUE DE LA TÊTE D'OR

Hôtel
de Ville

RUE DES CHAPELIERS

27

RUE DE LA
VIOLETTE

RUE DU MARCHÉ AGES

J

Galeries
Bortier

29

30

RUE DU NISON

PLACE
ST-JEAN

Bourse

RUE HENRI MAUS

9

Music
Village

Brüsel

10

RUE DES PIERRES

F

RUE DE L'AMIGO

RUE DES BRASSEURS

13

Musée de
Costume &
de la Dentelle

RUE CHARLES BULS

Ancienne
Belgique

BOULEVARD ANSPACH

6

2

RUE DE LA CHAUFFERETTE

PLATTESTEEN

CHARBON

15

14

RUE DU MIDI

RUE DU LOMBARD

Manneken Pis

L

RUE DE L'ÉTUVE

BORGVAL

RUE DES
TEINTURIERS

16

Tels
Quels

24

25

RUE DES
SECOURS

19

RUE DU MARCHÉ AU

21

22

26

RUE DES GRANDS CARMES

20

RUE DES
MONBEAUX

△ Jacques Brel Fondation

LOWER & UPPER TOWN

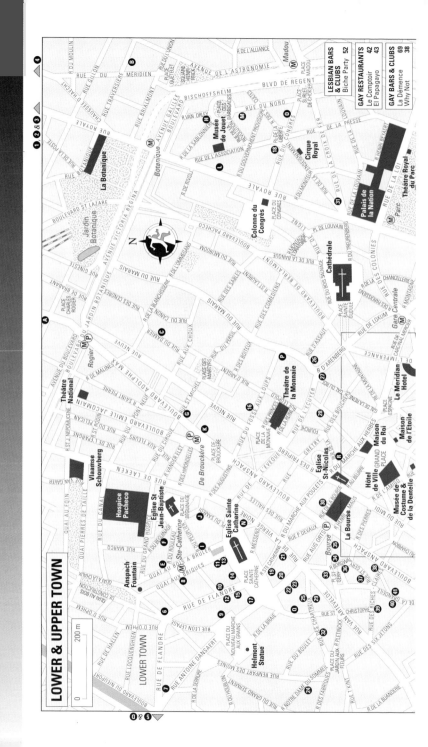

| 0 | 200 m |

LOWER TOWN

LESBIAN BARS & CLUBS
Biche Party   52

GAY RESTAURANTS
Le Comptoir   42
El Papagayo   43

GAY BARS & CLUBS
La Démence   69
Why Not   38

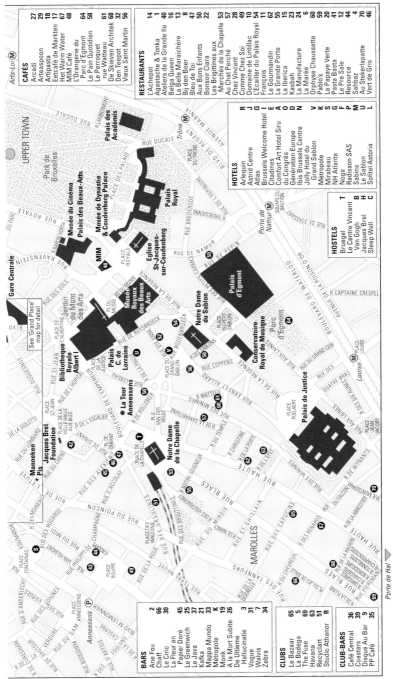

Arts-Loi Ⓜ

CAFÉS

Arcadi	27
Arteaspoon	29
Aripasta	18
Eetcafé de Markten	17
Het Warm Water	67
MIM Café	48
L'Orangerie du Parc d'Egmont	64
Le Pain Quotidien	58
Le Perroquet rue Watteau	61
De Skieven Architek	68
Den Teepot	32
Vieux Saint Martin	56

RESTAURANTS

L'Achepot	14
Agastache & Tonka	1
Ateliers de la Grande Ile	40
Belga Queen	16
La Belle Maraichère	13
Bij den Boer	8
Bleu de Toi	47
Aux Bons Enfants	50
Bonsoir Clara	22
Les Brigittines aux Marchés de la Chapelle	53
Au Chat Perché	57
Chez Vincent	28
Comme Chez Soi	49
Domaine de Lintillac	10
L'Écailler du Palais Royal	54
François	11
Le Gourmandin	62
La Grande Porte	55
La Iberica	15
Kasbah	23
La Manufacture	24
La Marée	6
Orphyse Chaussette	60
Pablo's	59
La Papaye Verte	20
Pasta Basta	41
Le Pre Sale	12
Resource	44
Sahbaz	4
Au Stekerlapatte	70
Vert de Gris	46

HOTELS

Arlequin	R
Astrid Centre	J
Atlas	I
Brussels Welcome Hotel	E
Citadines	A
Comfort Art Hotel Siru	Q
Génération Europe	O
Ibis Brussels Centre	D
Jolly Hotel du Grand Sablon	N
Métropole	V
Mirabeau	K
NH Atlanta	S
Noga	G
Radisson SAS	F
Sabina	U
Le Sablon	P
Sofitel Astoria	M

HOSTELS

Bruegel	T
Le Centre Vincent Van Gogh	B
Jacques Brel	H
Sleep Well	C

BARS

Ane Fou	2
Chaff	66
Le Crio	30
La Fleur en Papier Doré	45
Le Greenwich	25
Le Java	37
Kafka	21
Mappa Mundo	33
Métropole	K
Monk	19
A la Mort Subite	26
De Ultieme Hallucinatie	3
Vogue	31
Walvis	7
Zebra	34

CLUBS

Le Bazaar	65
La Bodega	5
The Fuse	69
Havana	63
Recyclart	51
Studio Athanor	R

CLUB-BARS

Café Central	36
Coasters	39
Disque Au Bar	9
PP Café	35

UPPER TOWN

Porte de Hal

Gare du Midi

Annessens Ⓟ

See 'Grand Place' map for detail

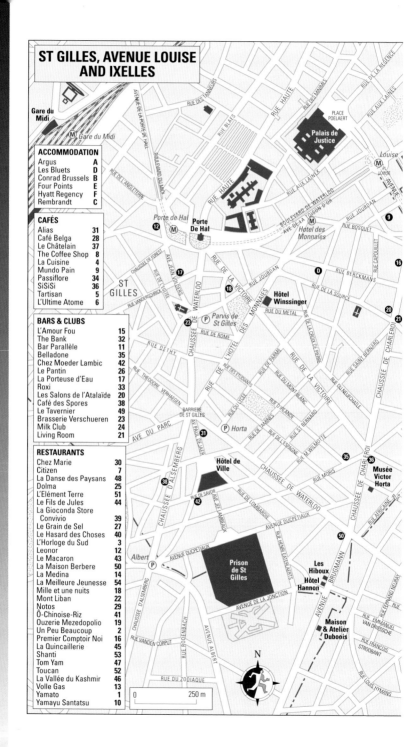

ST GILLES, AVENUE LOUISE AND IXELLES

Gare du Midi

M Gare du Midi

ACCOMMODATION

Argus	**A**
Les Bluets	**D**
Conrad Brussels	**B**
Four Points	**E**
Hyatt Regency	**F**
Rembrandt	**C**

CAFÉS

Alias	31
Café Belga	28
Le Châtelain	37
The Coffee Shop	8
La Cuisine	4
Mundo Pain	9
Passiflore	34
SiSiSi	36
Tartisan	5
L'Ultime Atome	6

BARS & CLUBS

L'Amour Fou	15
The Bank	32
Bar Parallèle	11
Belladone	35
Chez Moeder Lambic	42
Le Pantin	26
La Porteuse d'Eau	17
Roxi	33
Les Salons de l'Atalaïde	20
Café des Spores	38
Le Tavernier	49
Brasserie Verschueren	23
Milk Club	24
Living Room	21

RESTAURANTS

Chez Marie	30
Citizen	7
La Danse des Paysans	48
Dolma	25
L'Elément Terre	51
Le Fils de Jules	44
La Gioconda Store Convivio	39
Le Grain de Sel	27
Le Hasard des Choses	40
L'Horloge du Sud	3
Leonor	12
Le Macaron	43
La Maison Berbere	50
La Medina	14
La Meilleure Jeunesse	54
Mille et une nuits	18
Mont Liban	22
Notos	29
Ô-Chinoise-Riz	41
Ouzerie Mezedopolio	19
Un Peu Beaucoup	2
Premier Comptoir Noi	16
La Quincaillerie	45
Shanti	53
Tom Yam	47
Toucan	52
La Vallée du Kashmir	46
Volle Gas	13
Yamato	1
Yamayu Santatsu	10

Gare du Midi

Palais de Justice

PLACE POELAERT

Louise

M PL. LOUISE

Porte de Hal
Porte De Hal

Hôtel des Monnaies

ST GILLES

Hôtel Winssinger

Parvis de St Gilles

P Horta

Hôtel de Ville

Musée Victor Horta

Albert

P

Prison de St Gilles

Les Hiboux
Hôtel Hannon

Maison & Atelier Dubois

N

0   250 m

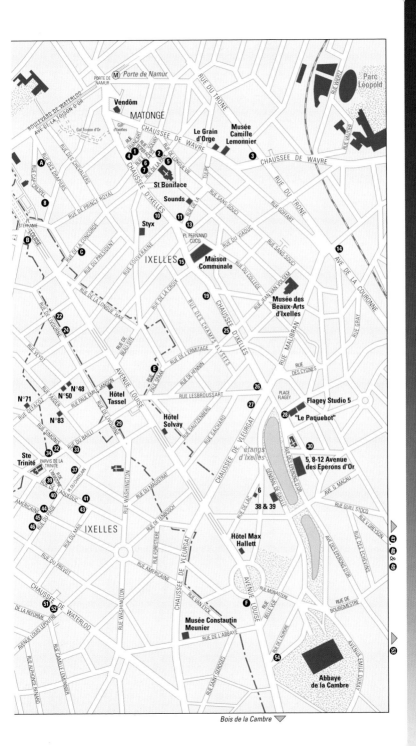

Bois de la Cambre ▽

RUE DE LA TRIBUNE
RUE DE LA CROIX DE FER
RUE DE LA PRESSE
CHARITÉ
RUE DE LA BIGORNE
RUE HYDRAULIQUE
RUE DE LA ARTICHAUT
RUE DE VERVIERS
RUE DES GILDES
RUE DES EBURONS
RUE DES GRAVELINES
RUE DU PARLEMENT
RUE DE LA LOUVAIN
RUE HENRI BEYAERT
RUE DE LA LOI
RUE MARIE DU THÉRÈSE
RUE DES DEUX ÉGLISES
MARTEAU
RUE DU BERCEAU
RUE PHILIPPE LE BON
RUE ORTELIUS
PACIFICATION
Hôtel van Eetvelde
SQUARE MARIE LOUISE
Villa Germaine
AVENUE PALMERSTON

Parc de Bruxelles

BOULEVARD DU RÉGENT
AVENUE DES ARTS
RUE ZINNER
RUE DUCALE
RUE LAMBERMONT
RUE DE COMMERCE
RUE JOSEPH II
RUE JOSEPH II
RUE DE SPA
RUE STEVIN
RUE LIVINGSTONE
AVE LIVINGSTONE
CHAUSSÉE JOSEPH II
RUE DU TACITURNE 34
RUE ST QUENTIN
RUE CHARLES MARTEL
BOULEVARD CHARLEMAGNE
RUE BODEGHEM
RUE DE LA LOI

RUE DE LA LOI
RUE JACQUES
GUIMARD
RUE DE L'INDUSTRIE
SQUARE FRÈRE ORBAN
RUE DE LA SCIENCE
RUE JACQUES
9
DE
LALAING
Charlemagne
RUE DE LA LOI
4
7

RUE DUCALE
BOULEVARD DU RÉGENT
AVENUE DES ARTS
RUE DE COMMERCE
RUE DE L'INDUSTRIE
RUE DE LA SCIENCE
RUE D'ARLON
BELLIARD
RUE DE TRÈVES
RUE DE TOULOUSE
Gare Schuman
Résidence Palace
CHAUSSÉE D'ETTERBEEK
RUE

RUE MONTOYER
RUE MARIE DE BOURGOGNE
RUE DE PASCALE
RUE D'ARDENNE

AVENUE DU LUXEMBOURG
SQUARE DE MEEUS
A
RUE DU LUXEMBOURG
Gare du Quartier Leopold
RUE REMORQUER
Bibliothèque Solvay
CHAUSSÉE D'ETTERBEEK

RUE DU CHAMP DE MARS
RUE DU TRÔNE
RUE DE PARIS
RUE DE FLEURUS
RUE CAROLY
PLACE DU LUXEMBOURG
European Parliament
Parc Léopold

RUE DE NAPLES
RUE DE LONDRES
RUE DU MAJOR RENÉ DUBREUCQ
RUE DU PARNASSE
RUE DE TRÈVES
13
14
Musée des Sciences Naturelles
15
AVENUE DE MAELBEEK
PLACE JOURDAN
16 **17**

CHAUSSÉE DE
RUE ERNEST SOLVAY
RUE DE LA PAIX
RUE ANOUL
RUE D'IDALIE
RUE GODECHARLE
Musée Camille Lemonnier
WAVRE
Musée Wiertz
RUE WIERTZ
RUE VAUTIER
CHAUSSÉE DE GRAY
RUE DE GRAY
RUE DE

RUE DE LONGUE VIE
RUE DE LA TULIPE
RUE GEORGES LORAND
CHAUSSÉE DE WAVRE
RUE

RUE JULES BOUILLON
RUE DE LA CRÈCHE
CONSEIL
RUE GOFFART
RUE DU VIADUCT
RUE VANDENBROECK
RUE LIMALGE
RUE WEYENBERG
RUE DE
RUE DU BROCHET

RUE SOUVERAINE
CHAUSSÉE D'IXELLES
RUE MERCELIS
RUE DES CHAMPS
RUE CANS
RUE VAN AA
RUE DE LA CITÉ
SANS SOUCI
RUE DE VENISE
RUE COLLÈGE
VAN VOLSEM
RUE MAES
RUE DU TRÔNE AVENUE
RUE DU SCEPTRE
RUE CLÉMENTINE
RUE WERY
RUE KERCKX
RUE DU VIVIER
RUE GRAY
RUE DU

THE EU QUARTER & AROUND

0   300 m

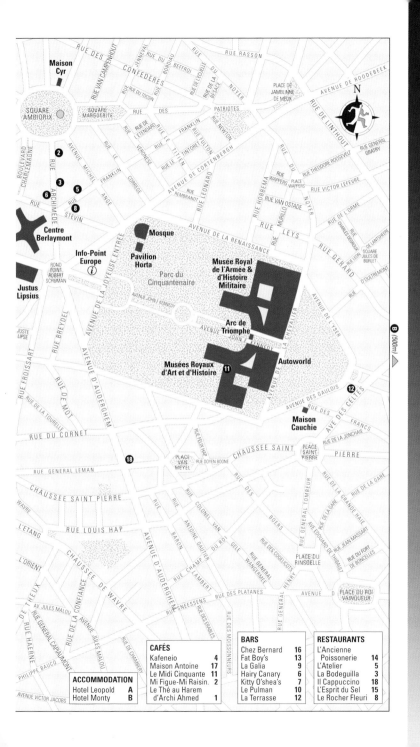

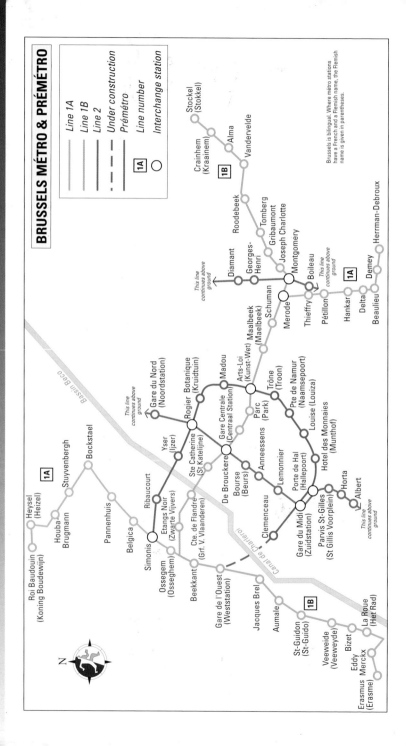

BRUSSELS MÉTRO & PRÉMÉTRO

Line 1A
Line 1B
Line 2
Under construction
Prémétro
Line number — 1A
Interchange station — ○

Brussels is bilingual. Where métro stations have a French and a Flemish name, the Flemish name is given in parentheses.